SYM

C000134163

AND

In Popular Beliefs

An Outline of the
Origins of Moon and Sun Worship, Astrol-
ogy, Sex Symbolism, Mystic Meaning of
Numbers, the Cabala, and Many Popular
Customs, Myths, Superstitions and Religious
Beliefs.

by

ERNEST BUSENBARK

88 Plates, Containing Over 300
Illustrations and Diagrams

The Book Tree
San Diego, California

Published by
The Book Tree
P.O. Box 16476
San Diego, CA 92176
www.thebooktree.com

We provide fascinating and educational products to help awaken the public to new ideas and
information that would not be available otherwise.
Call 1 (800) 700-8733 for our *FREE BOOK TREE CATALOG*.

PREFACE

By Jordan Maxwell

The World Condition

In today's world we are beset by uncertainties. Those of most concern involve the potential of sudden violence based on religious beliefs and fanaticism. This world spends much of its time fighting over God, and has done so for centuries. While we fight over God, we also seek Him.

After centuries of pursuing God we appear no closer to reaching Him than when we first started, in ancient times. In fact, the complexities created by numerous religions and their factions seem to remove us further from God than when we were living closely with nature in our primitive past. As soon as mankind created a conception of God, certain rules of observance followed. And as various groups and conceptions appeared, rules of observance clashed. Wars began. Of course we fight over territory as much as theology, but religion somehow seems to create more viscous and fanatical fighters.

It was believed that God would protect those who observed their sacred rules more rigorously. So the rules became more demanding—to the point of murdering others in the very name of God. But it is my belief that an all-loving God would never pit us against each other, at each other's throats. If we could understand where religion *really* came from, maybe then we could change, or start to change, our conceptions and rules of observance. Maybe then will we succeed, or start to succeed, in finding out who and what the true God is.

The philosopher George Santaya once said, "Those who cannot remember the past are condemned to repeat it." This has always been the case, but why is it so difficult to learn from our past? Why must we keep making the same mistakes over and over again? The answer is simple—human ignorance based on laziness and pride, together with an ever-present DENIAL. Ignorance and its denial will, sad to say, lead us down the same road as it did in all past history. If enough people are to read a book like this one and truly glean its information, then we at least have a chance at overcoming this ignorance.

Lies, Lies, Lies

The reason we are in the current evil situation is because we have been told LIES by our surrogate parents, the leaders of the world. They are the ones we look to whenever anything goes wrong ("Somebody ought to do something about [...]"). They tell us what they want us to hear. What they want us to hear, what they tell us, are LIES.

Today and every day we are faced with mounting lies, half-truths and corruption in every field of endeavor the world over. Mankind has pretty much lost its way. The three great powers of human corruption is the same today as it has always been, namely POLITICS—MONEY—RELIGION, the triune God! In the world of politics and banking, we can accept the obvious with a little research—that our so-called leaders are, in point of fact, MIS-LEADERS. Of this there is ample proof.

The Church

There is even a bigger story yet to be told when we turn to the third part of this triad, the church. Nowhere is a story of lies, half-truths, misunderstandings and cover-ups more blatant and dangerously misleading. Millions of lives have been wasted and squandered because of a basic misunderstanding of ancient theologies and modern religions. Outrageously, people have been led to devote time, money, energy and, for some, their whole lives in the pursuit of a religious ideal that is, in fact, nothing more than a misunderstanding (a MYTHOLOGY).

To this very day "the blind are still leading the blind." How many people today know, for instance, that the English word "CHURCH" comes directly from the Scottish word "KIRK." "Kirk" comes to us from "Circe," the ancient female Greek goddess. Circe was an enchantress who tricked and deceived men when they came in to her—and changed them into swine!

Female Goddess (CIRCE) = Mother (CHURCH)

The Mechanism of Lies

Symbols have their exoteric or open meanings for the masses, but they also have their esoteric or closed meanings for the "elect," the "chosen," the "cognoscenti," or the "Illuminati."

The symbols of the CHURCH also have their esoteric meanings as well. The symbols of the church are "open secrets." The meaning of the symbols is not hidden, but are only understood if you have the KEYS. The keys are secret. One of the keys is the symbolism of the stars. Another key is sexual symbolism. Both keys needed to unlock the symbols are presented in this important volume.

From early childhood days, to the earnest beginning of my studies in 1959, and up to the present day, I never cease to be amazed to what extent people fail to understand the symbols and stories of ancient religions. Very few understand how vitally important this is. I have been saddened by how that ignorance has harmed us as a race.

Therefore, it is with great pleasure that I highly recommend this Book Tree reissue of Ernest Busenbark's landmark book. Its full title is explanatory: *Symbols, Sex and the Stars in Popular Beliefs: An Outline of the Origins of Moon and Sun Worship, Astrology, Sex Symbolism, Mystic Meaning of Numbers, the Cabala, and Many Popular Customs, Myths, Superstitions and Religious Beliefs*. While subtle points of difference from current knowledge may be debated with author Busenbark, they are differences of opinion as to causation, not differences of fact. Where he gives evidence, the evidence is compelling.

I have been so impressed with this book that, since its earlier printing in 1997, I did three separate videos based on its teachings. From all my years of study, I've found no better book one can use to unravel man's true religious past.

This book is not for everyone. But it is a **must read** for those who are tired of being played for fools and led to believe the lies. This work is valuable only to those whom the spirit calls to freedom. It is for those who are not afraid to face hard facts about life and who want to know the truth about religion and its origins.

Jordan Maxwell

By JACK BENJAMIN

Member of History of Science Society

The use of symbols to convey knowledge to the initiated and to conceal it from the unitiated is as old as civilization. A clear understanding of the symbolic way of thinking is necessary if we would unveil and comprehend the "esoteric" (hidden or secret) meaning of the symbols of ancient and modern faiths.

Every object is connected with its origins through progressive change. The complex was evolved from the simple. In the realm of popular beliefs, however, especially of the theological type, the tendency has been to conceal from the common people the sources and nature of archaic symbols and practices.

So long as men express thought by the use of symbols, the explanation of the origin and nature of their use is worthy of the best efforts of scholars. Genuine culture cannot be based upon the undeciphered paleography of primitive ages.

The ancient faiths had their "mysteries", forms of initiation, secret signs of recognition, and a body of symbolic lore generally kept from the public. Supernatural belief evolved through many stages. The initial stages are of chief interest to the scholar and serious student. In the early form of such belief we find the core from which present ideas and practices have evolved. As a belief is a composite of previous ideas and experiences, the primitive mentality revealed in early symbolism appears also in modern emblematic representations.

In his "Ancient Pagan and Modern Christian Symbolism", Inman pertinently observes:

> "When there exist two distinct explanations, or statements, about the significance of an emblem, the one 'esoteric', true, and known only to the few, the other 'exoteric', incorrect, and known to the many, it is clear that a time may come when the first may be lost, and the last alone remain". (P. xii)

Inman illustrates the thought by showing that the correct pronunciation of "Jehovah" was supposed originally to be known only to a select few, and later was lost, while the admittedly incorrect pronunciation survived.

Every state of society continues from the point of development at which its predecessor left off. Every statement of beliefs takes on in the course of time different values or interpretations. The god of the ancient Hebrews or Christians is certainly not the god of modern believers, and present day religious worship embodies many departures from that which the ancients accepted as the ultimate standard. To understand the nature of this cultural change requires study of the development and migration of symbols and their utilization to express supernatural concepts. The social environment usually makes such study seem inadvisable.

As all culture is inter-related, the accumulation of symbols throughout the ages has resulted in a kind of condensed version, which is offered to the worshipers of the various faiths. The secret of the origin of the symbols, however, has been zealously guarded from the public. Doubtless it is feared that such knowledge may weaken confidence in theological dogmas. Be that as it may, the fact remains that at the heart of religious belief we find the ever-present symbol. Only a few persons go beyond its exoteric meaning in order to ascertain its esoteric significance. While many individuals are interested in tracing back their family "tree", few have sufficient curiosity to make an effort to learn the origin of their religious faith. The study of comparative religion has proved the common background or source of all supernatural and kindred beliefs. The hidden knowledge which in far off times was conveyed by symbols is almost unknown to most believers. It is retained by a mere handful of objective scholars, and the heads of the various faiths are not encouraging its study.

Of the few brave and indefatigable scholars who have written on the subject, the more outstanding are Forlong, Inman, Massey, Higgins, Dupuis, O'Neill, Faber, Oman, Ferguson, Hannay, and a handful of others. Their books are now scarce and expensive. These men did the spadework. They have shown that it was not alone in sex that the symbol became dominant; that it took on importance in astral, lunar, animal, plant, and other worships. Symbolism thus became the language of supernatural belief and practice. John Newton, in his able appendix to Inman's "Ancient Pagan and Modern Christian Symbolism", comments:

"As civilization advanced, the gross symbols of creative power were cast aside, and priestly ingenuity was taxed to the utmost in inventing a crowd of less obvious emblems, which should represent the ancient ideas in a decorous manner".

Life is based upon reproductive forces and despite whatever prudery or refinement of emotion we have attained we cannot ignore their influence. Many investigators of the subject have noted the relation between sex and religion. The distinguished sexologist, Iwan Bloch, wrote:

"Anthropological science has hitherto been occupied more with the fact than with the explanation of the remarkable relation between religion and sexuality. There can, however, be no doubt that these relations arise out of the very nature of mankind. The various anthropologists and physicians who have occupied themselves with these problems are in agreement upon this point: that the connection between religion and the sexual life can be explained only on anthropomorphic-animistic grounds—that is, by the same kind of ideas which Tylor had proved to be the foundation of the primitive mental life". (*Sexual Life of Our Time*, p.98.)

The question of origin is of prime importance in understanding either a species or a belief. Whatever changes the interpretation of symbols has undergone has been quantitative rather than qualitative. Why must a priest wear certain vestments at religious services? Why is there a cross on a church? Why does a synagogue have a *Mogen Duvid* (star of David)? All faiths conduct their services in accordance with a strict ritual. It takes but little power of observation to note that supernatural worship is replete with a variety of symbols, the nature and origin of which are not made known to the laity.

Many persons today follow phallic rites and rituals of antiquity, not knowing that they do so. To the student of the subject this is a significant fact, as likewise is the persistence of the symbol throughout many thousands of years.

The study of symbology, sex rites, and the worship of various animals, objects and astral bodies has been limited to a few. The findings of these men have been known to only those who delved into out-of-the-way source books. As there has not been hitherto a large buying public for such works and as the writing of them requires most of a lifetime, it is not difficult to understand why the general public has remained unaware of the source of current beliefs and practices.

The scholars who in the past have treated this subject chose a special section for investigation. It remained for someone to compose a work comprising not alone the conclusions arrived at by former students but to add the results of modern exploration in this wide field. The debt we owe to those who wrote the pioneering studies is obvious. Most of our current writers, because of social pressures and for other reasons, shy away from this field. In "Symbolism, Sex, and the Stars", Mr. Ernest Busenbark brings forth the results of many years of study.

This treatise may truly be called encyclopaedic. The author has not only carefully covered the ground explored by past researchers; he has collated their findings and enriched the whole study with much new material. This work goes back to the "origins" of much modern thinking in a thoroughgoing way.

It is to be regretted that past studies in this comprehensive field are not readily available to the public. Most of them, as we have observed, have long been out of print; others, expensive because rare, are far beyond the purse of most of those who are interested in the background of religious beliefs. These students may now profit from this work, the fruit of many years of painstaking scholarship and a dominating interest in historical accuracy.

The trend of the times is to seek explanations and means of understanding phenomena. Mr. Busenbark's labors in this direction have been truly herculean. His book is an outline of the principal religious beliefs and customs. Through his unwearied efforts to discover and make known the truth, we now have available in one volume a "key" to the popular beliefs and occult writings treasured by mankind. This work enables the student of religious history to follow the stages through which religion has evolved. Its many illustrations present to the eye something of the wealth of symbols used in popular beliefs throughout the ages, with interpretations of their secret meaning, and thus increase greatly the comprehensiveness and value of the volume.

"Symbolism, Sex, and the Stars" is a mariner's compass on the vast sea of symbolic mythology.

The world is finally coming of age. There is a large and rapidly increasing number of persons who, like the author, are unable to accept a belief or a set of beliefs merely because they are very old and widely accepted. Rather than adopt a ready-made philosophy of life based upon beliefs which have come down from the Stone Age, they prefer to weigh the evidence, do their own thinking and draw their own conclusions. This is particularly true in regard to beliefs which cannot be proved by daily experience, such as those based upon the miraculous or the supernatural.

The author can truly testify that problems confronting one who embarks upon thinking for himself are difficult indeed. The independent investigator soon learns that tracing popular beliefs and superstitions to their origin leads to an almost endless amount of research. He learns, for instance, that stories about the creation of the universe, the creation and the "fall" of the first man and woman, the deluge, heaven, hell, the coming of a savior and the end of the world are not confined to the Bible but may be found in the literature of ancient peoples in almost every part of the world. Many of these stories were developed from moon and sun worship, or from customs, myths, astrology, astronomy, symbolism, and numerous other beliefs and practices, some of which were in existence long before the Bible was written and even before the Jews existed as a distinct branch of the Semitic peoples.

Scholars who have written on these subjects have been more or less specialists. Some of them have emphasized the influence of astrology and astronomy upon ancient culture: others have been inclined to emphasize the influence of mythology, symbology or some other subject. To acquire even a moderate knowledge of the various beliefs which shaped ancient culture therefore entails the reading of literally hundreds of volumes.

Many of these works are quite rare and, in the United States, can be found in only a few great libraries. Moreover, they were written by scholars for scholars and are so technical and dry that even if the general reader had access to them, he would probably not have the patience to struggle through them.

The author believes, therefore, there is urgent need for a work, written not for the scholar, but for the general reader, a condensed, non-technical work, which will give the reader a broad, panoramic picture of the ancient customs and beliefs from which our principal beliefs, religious and otherwise, were developed. This is what I have tried to accomplish. The contents of this book were assembled from notes gathered from a wide variety of sources over many years.

In instances where statements are made which may be deemed controversial, I have provided footnotes giving the sources from which the statements were derived.

In conclusion, I wish to express my deep appreciation for the helpful criticism and advice given me by my friends Charles Smith, Woolsey Teller, Marshall Gauvin, and Arvin Schmid, and particularly for the assistance and encouragement given me by my friend Jack Benjamin.

E. B.

CONTENTS

APPENDICES

ILLUSTRATIONS

BEGINNING OF MOON AND SUN WORSHIP

All that we do not know is miraculous.

—TACITUS.

In MAN'S EARLY EFFORTS to comprehend the workings of the world about him, probably no phenomenon stirred his interest and imagination so greatly as did the magnificent and mysterious spectacle of the heavens. A picture easily comes to mind of the shepherd tribesmen scanning the heavens questioningly, trying to form theories which would explain the scene spread out above them in the sky. In seeking the reason for things beyond their comprehension, they were inclined to seek analogies, to draw comparisons, and to look for relationships between the events which they observed in the sky, and those which they saw around them on earth, for it was characteristic of primitive people that they conceived the earth and the heavens to be alike in character, one being made in the image of the other. To them the part was always similar to the whole.

Whenever knowledge has been insufficient to provide man with a true explanation of the mechanics of the universe, his imagination has invented one. In the effects of the sun and moon upon vegetable and animal life, in the varying length of the days, the changes of the seasons, and the influence of these changes upon plant and animal life, man inevitably looked upon the heavenly bodies as the powers which governed his destiny.

In his search for explanations of how these deities or demons could accomplish tasks which were beyond his own ability to perform, ancient man developed a belief in the supernatural. In every part of the world and in practically every tribe or nation there were local gods who were believed to possess the ability to render themselves invisible, to violate the laws of gravity, to fly through the air, to walk upon water, to come down to the earth in the form of birds and animals, to become the parents of human offspring by "overshadowing" young maidens or by impregnating them with a gentle gust or ghost. By virtue of their supernatural powers, the deities which man's imagination created, were believed to be able to turn the tides of battle and determine the outcome of wars, to produce good crops, fair weather, good health, and prosperity, or to produce fire, famine, floods, lightning, storms, disease, and desolation at will. In short, the powers of the gods were limited only by man's ability to invent or imagine newer or greater feats for them to perform.

Every event in the lives of men from birth to death was ruled by a deity or spirit; all the mysterious activities of nature were attributed to the benevolence of a friendly power or to the malevolence of an evil one. Events did not take place by virtue of an orderly process of natural law but by mere whim or caprice of the gods. Every great religion, past or present, has had for its basis this belief in a supreme deity or deities who were not subject to natural laws.

By means of prayers, ceremonies, gifts, and sacrifices, the ancient people sought to insure the good will of the friendly powers and to cause the evil ones to discontinue or withhold their harmful activities. The mighty deeds of supernatural deities became the subject of myths, legends, and fables which constituted the literature of all ancient peoples. The highest and most widespread expression of these ancient beliefs was embodied in worship of the sun and the moon.

The Chinese were sun worshipers and the most solemn period of the year in China was December 21st, when ceremonies were held at the temples of the sun on the sacred mountain at Pekin to commemorate the sun's passage of the winter solstice point. Formerly these ceremonies were conducted by the emperor and his highest functionaries.

Although the Japanese were originally moon worshipers, they later became sun worshipers and a shrine of the sun goddess stood in the Mikado's palace. A copper mirror serving as her emblem is considered one of the sacred treasures of the Japanese sovereign to the present day. A symbol of the sun in the form of a golden disk appears on the Japanese national emblem to signify the Emperor's descent from the sun.

In the folklore of northern Europe and Britain, traditions existed from very early times in which the sun and moon were personified in human form, either as the heroes of simple fables or as mighty deities who were able to bring either good or evil upon the inhabitants of the earth. If the early Druids in England were not actually sun worshipers, the huge stone ruins at Stonehenge and elsewhere remain as evidence that they at least observed the critical periods of the sun's annual cycle with important ceremonies.

In ancient Mexico, the sun, the moon, and the planet Venus were honored as gods. The Mexicans shared their meat and drink with them, believing themselves to be their descendants. Many Mexican peasants still practice the old custom of throwing a kiss to the sun on entering a church.

The Incas of Peru regarded the moon as female and as being both sister and wife of the male sun. The Incas called themselves "children of the sun" and the solar orb was honored by them with human sacrifices in the most lavishly ornamented temple in the world.

Early inhabitants of the Malay Peninsula regarded both the sun and moon as female. The Eskimos believed the moon was the younger brother of the female sun. In North America many Indian tribes were worshipers of the sun and moon, evidence of which fact remains in their tribal ceremonies to this day.

Sun worship existed at various times in Rome and the annual festival celebrated on December 25th in honor of the "Birthday of the Unconquerable Sun" was not terminated there until the death of Emperor Julian, in the 4th century A.D. In the 5th century, about one hundred years after the Christianization of Rome, it was still the custom of the Romans to bow to the sun before entering a church and to salute the rising sun from the summit of a hill.

Worship of the sun and moon gods formed the basis for the religions of Egypt, Persia, and India. From Babylonia, where they perhaps reached their highest, or at least most widespread development, the sun and moon cults spread throughout southwest Asia and extended as far as Greece, Rome, and Gaul. The science of astronomy, in fact, had its origin in the efforts of the Babylonian astrologer-priests to foretell the moods and actions of the gods of the sun and the moon by studying their movements from the summit of their seven-storied ziggurats. The Biblical Tower of Babylon was such an observation tower.

The many references in the Bible to the heathen cults give ample evidence that both sun and moon worships were practiced widely by the Hebrews in ancient Palestine. Prior to the promulgation of the Mosaic Code, the Jews employed lunar time, and it still remains the basis of their religious calendar.

The changes in the moon's appearance were made the subject of fables by ancient people long before they knew that the light of the moon was merely reflected from the sun, or before they realized that the moon which dwindled and died was the same one that reappeared each month.

Many of the figures in Greek mythology are purely solar or lunar in character and it is believed by some scholars that all the great bodies of mythical lore originated in ancient astral worship.

If the ceremonies and sacrifices which were part of sun worship are much better known to us than those which accompanied moon worship, it may be attributed to the fact that moon worship was already being over-shadowed by the spreading worship of the sun at the beginning of written history. The very earliest records of the ancient nations best known to us date from 3000 to 4000 B.C. to a time when the sun cults were already gaining the ascendency. Consequently, such knowledge as we have of the moon cults is derived from myths and legends which have continued to live in literature and customs many centuries after the forms of worship to which they related had dissolved in the mists of the ages. (We know practically nothing of the Trojan Wars except from the bits gathered from Homer's Iliad.)

The myths, legends, and fables which in time were woven about the feats of the mythical gods had their origin in the simple fact that it is in the nature of people to create rumors, gossip, and fables about the great and the near-great in all ages. We invent stories about Washington and Lincoln, and the ancients did likewise with their gods.

If read superficially, many legends derived from ancient beliefs may seem ridiculously childish or preposterous to modern readers. It was not long ago that nearly every one believed in witches, devils, miracles, and fairies, and many persons still believe in their existence.

The ancient myths, however, were not the product of imagination alone. In every instance they were based upon observable natural phenomena, there being some fundamental relationship between the portrayal and the portrayed. The high reverence which the Egyptians held for the sacred scarab is an example which well illustrates this point. The scarab or beetle reputedly rolled itself into a ball and then, like the moon, emerged in 28 days with renewed life. We now know that the Egyptians were in error, both as to facts and conclusions for, although the tumblebug does roll a ball of dung, the ball contains its eggs instead of the bug itself. When we consider that they believed in reincarnation, it is not difficult to understand why the Egyptians honored this lowly bug as a symbol of reincarnation and immortality.

In our own day, the importance of the sun to life on earth is known to be so overwhelmingly greater than that of the moon that, at first thought, it seems strange that moon worship should have been widely practiced long before the development of sun worship. Nevertheless, the findings of modern scientists leave no room to doubt this fact. In Babylonia, for instance, the principal gods were identified by numbers according to their rank. The first triad of gods is composed of Anu 60, Bel 50, Ea 40. The second triad is the Moon 30, Sun 20, and Mylitta or Beltis (Venus) 15. The third triad is Air 10, Nergal or Mars 12, and Nur or Saturn 10. Wherever the sun and the moon are mentioned, the sun is spoken of as "the son of the moon" and not "the father," as might be expected. One of the ancient gods of Ur in Sumeria was called Shamash (the sun), the offspring of Nannar, which is one of the names of the moon god. Nabonides, the last native king of Babylonia, assigned the same father to Shamash, so that from first to last, the sun god ranked below the moon god in dignity.

Many theories have been advanced to account for this anomaly, one of them being that as the great early civilizations originated in regions whose climate varied from warm to hot, the sun was considered more of an enemy than friend to man, because its intense heat scorched vegetation and destroyed crops and pasturage.

A more probable solution would seem to be provided by the fact that in warm countries in which early civilization first reached a high state of development, the heat and altitude of the sun vary but little from season to season. There the sun rises and sets rapidly, the periods of dawn and twilight being very short, with the hours of day and night being sharply defined. Also, in regions close to the equator the length of the day varies but little throughout the year; there the moon and stars shine with special brilliance and in some tropical countries the planets Venus and Jupiter are often bright enough to cast shadows. Moreover, the sun is too remote, too brilliant, too slow in its apparent movements to permit of easy observation, whereas the moon changes from night to night, passing from a wholly dark to a wholly light phase in such a short period that man can not forget it.

Time was first reckoned as so many "sleeps" or as so many "nights".[1] Then, when it was learned that the changes from full moon to full moon were repeated in a cycle of 28 days (actually 29.53), time was reckoned by moons or months. Eclipses of the moon marked the years. The moon was therefore known as the "Measurer" or "Reckoner".

Even today Mohammedans reckon time by the moon, and our Easter is reckoned by lunar time instead of solar time. Arabs greet the new moon with shouts of joy and the Jewish ritual prescribes a special service for the occasion, which includes the recital of "psalms of joy".

It is not strange, therefore, that sun worship preceded moon worship only in countries far from the equator, where the length of the day varies considerably in the course of the year. During the winter in these latitudes, the low, slanting rays of the sun give but little heat to the earth; vegetation dies and the long warm days of summer are succeeded by equally long nights and the biting cold of winter. Here, where the beneficial light and warmth of the sun were most welcome, the priority of sun worship to moon worship was but natural.

1—The reckoning of time by nights is common among all nomads and especially those who travel by night because of daytime heat. With the Hebrews the day began with sunset; with the Egyptians and Babylonians it began with sunrise, and with the Romans the day began with midnight.

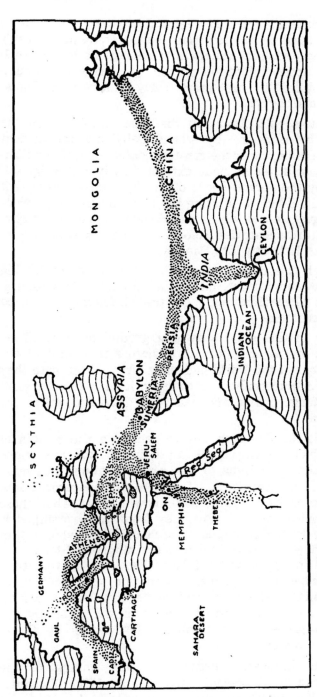

1. Map showing the belt in which civilization first reached a high state of development.

The temperate or cold regions, however, were either thinly populated or isolated from the main stream of man's development, and local beliefs in those regions left no such impression upon civilization as did the forms of worship which prevailed in the great early cultures of India, Babylonia, and Egypt.

In contact with Egypt on the west and India on the east, both by land and by water, Babylonia (or ancient Sumeria) became one of the greatest centers of early civilization. Here, in a region made extraordinarily fertile by soil deposited by the annual floods of the Euphrates where that river spread out before entering the Persian Gulf, there were numerous great cities which had developed old and highly mature cultures centuries before Abraham is supposed to have led the Hebrews into Canaan.

Through this region passed the caravan routes linking Egypt, Asia, and Europe, making southwest Asia a natural melting pot where East met West, traded, fought, exchanged ideas and customs.

It was in this great spawning ground of Oriental religions and myths of supernatural heroes that most of the great religions of the world had their birth. From here they were carried from country to country, leaving their imprint on the customs, habits, and beliefs of nations down to the present time.

Perhaps the first step toward removing the curtain of mystery which enveloped the mysticism of the East came with the opening of India to western civilization, thus making possible the translation of ancient Indian records into modern languages. Present day knowledge of what those ancient peoples believed, how they lived and worshiped is largely due to the triumphs of archaeologists who, within the past 150 years, have dug into the mounds of long vanished cities in Egypt and the Near East. Up to that time our knowledge of Babylonian civilization was confined to a few Biblical references and some astrological works, compiled at the command of Alexander the Great by the Babylonian priest Berossus, plus a few works by Greek and Roman writers.

Modern discoveries began with the finding of the Rosetta stone by Napoleon's engineers in 1799. This provided the key which enabled us to unlock the mysteries concealed in the ancient Egyptian inscriptions. (The Rosetta stone contained trilingual inscriptions in hieroglyphics, demotic characters, and Greek, thus making it possible to translate the inscriptions into modern languages.)

One of the most thrilling achievements of modern archaeology came in 1853 with the discovery of the great library of King Assurbanipal (called Sardanapalus by the Greeks), at Kouyunjik, the site of Nineveh in ancient Assyria. In 648 B.C., Assurbanipal deposed his brother as

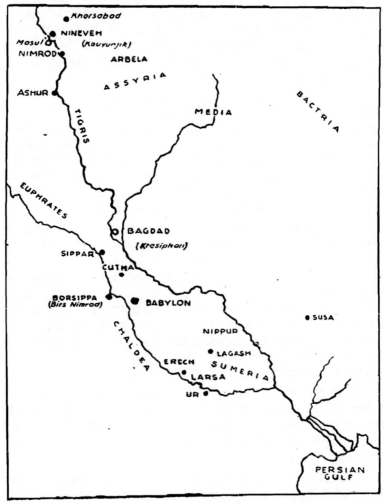

2. Region of the Euphrates and Tigris Rivers, showing the location of Sumeria, Chaldea and Babylon.

king of Babylonia and made that country a mere province of Assyria. Assurbanipal was an unusually far-sighted ruler, who not only assembled a library containing a complete record of his own period, but tried as well as he could to compile a record of all the preceding ages.

Much of our present-day knowledge of Babylonian culture has been derived from the official archives, pottery, omens, prayers, psalms, and historical, astrological, and scientific works inscribed on the clay bricks found in this library. In 1872 George Smith, an English archaeologist, discovered parts of a Babylonian version of the Deluge on bricks in the British Museum, and in the following year he discovered more fragments of the story in the library at Kouyunjik. Nearly 20,000 bricks or fragments from this library are now in the British Museum.

The scientific world was again thrilled by a discovery made by J. De Morgan, a French scientist, at Susa, in Assyria, in December 1901. He found a black diorite pillar about eight feet high which contained a code of laws promulgated about 2050 B.C. by King Hammurabi. Later the pillar was removed to the Louvre, in Paris. Engraved on top of the stone is a striking picture showing Hammurabi receiving the laws from the sun god Shamash.

Although five columns of the inscriptions had been effaced, there still remained forty-four columns containing 3600 lines of the laws, engraved in cuneiform characters. The laws are judged to have been compiled from several older codes, some of which are thought to date from 3000 to 4000 B.C. The Hammurabic laws so closely parallel Old Testament Mosaic Laws that competent authorities concede that many of the Laws which the Lord is supposed to have given Moses on Mount Sinai were really in effect in Babylonia centuries before the Mosaic period.

Even the story of Moses' life bears a marked similarity to the life of King Sargon of Babylonia, and the Biblical account of Moses now appears to have been adapted in part from legends dating from 3000 B.C. or earlier, concerning the great Babylonian king.

Like Moses, Sargon was a popular leader and law-giver who secured the independence of his people. Also like Moses, Sargon was said to have been born from a goddess by an unknown father. She hid him in a basket made of

*3. Babylonian sun god Shamash giving King
Hammurabi the scroll of Laws. From carving
on the Tablet of Hammurabi.*

rushes, daubed with bitumen, and set him adrift in the
Euphrates where he was found by Akki, "the irrigator", who
raised him as his own. Although brought up in squalid
surroundings, Sargon became the much-beloved "Law-
giver". To him was attributed the compilation of the Chaldean
works on astrology and augury.[2]

In addition to these discoveries, quantities of Hittite
tablets were found in 1906 at Baghoz-Keui, in Anatolia, and
more recently there has come to light a Hittite version of
an Egyptian-Hittite treaty of 1272 B.C. At Tell-el-Amarna,
about 170 miles south of Cairo, in Egypt, a peasant woman
found a large quantity of tablets which proved to be letters
written to the Egyptian Kings Amenhotep III and IV by
kings of various Asiatic countries and by Egyptian vassals

2—*Origin and Growth of Religion*, A. B. Sayce, p.26.

in Phoenicia, Syria, and Palestine. These tablets have been the greatest source of information regarding events in Canaan in the 14th and 15th centuries B.C. One of the most remarkable facts established by this discovery is that the natives of this region used the Babylonian cuneiform style of writing even when addressing diplomatic correspondence to the kings of Egypt.

Personal archives have also been found of Kings Sargon, Sennacherib, Nebuchadnezzar, and other Assyrian rulers. These archives contain records of their relations with the Israelite kings.

Thousands of tablets, steles, and clay bricks have been recovered on which are recorded the laws, contracts, prayers, psalms, incantations, poems, myths, and historical, astronomical, astrological, and religious texts of long vanished cities. This flood of new light on the ancient civilization of southwestern Asia and Egypt has made it necessary to revise many theories which had been unchanged for centuries regarding the historical, cultural, and religious origins of the people in these regions.

The contents of many of these tablets were known only to the priests and others who were initiated into the holy "Mysteries". We are, therefore, today able to learn much about that ancient culture that was not known by the common people of those countries. The following pages are devoted to an examination of many of the beliefs and practices described in those ancient records, with a view to tracing the origin of many of the customs, beliefs, and superstitions which are still held by a large portion of the civilized world.

II

THE MOON AS THE REGULATOR OF TIME AND FATE

Inasmuch as the myths, customs, and religious rites which were woven about the moon gods and goddesses had their origin in the various aspects of the lunar orb, their significance and origin will be made clearer if we first recall the moon's varying phases, movements, and changes in appearance.

The new moon first appears in the early evening as a thin crescent, with its horns pointing eastward, and can be seen in the western sky shortly before or after the first of the month. It increases in size and luminosity each day, and as its waxing phase increases, the horns disappear, and early in the evening of the 14th, 15th, or 16th day, it shines brilliantly in the eastern sky as the glorious full moon.

For about three days, including the day before and the day after the full phase, it seems to change but little; then it gradually begins to decrease in size and brilliance. As it becomes thinner and wanner with the passing days, its horns reappear, this time facing westward (as the ancients expressed it, "the moon is now looking over its shoulder"), and on about the 28th day the end of the cycle is reached.

Moonrise occurs about 50 minutes later each day, so that in the last (dark) phase, the moon does not appear above the horizon until early morning. In this phase it passes between the earth and the sun, and as its passage occurs in the daytime, it is rendered invisible during most of the dark phase by the light of the sun. After a short period of dark moon, a thin crescent again appears in the western sky, marking the beginning of a new cycle.

As "Regulator" or "Measurer" of Time

The fact that the lunar cycle is divided into four phases of equal length, made this period a convenient means for computing time in periods of weeks and months. For this purpose the movements of the moon through the heavens may be calculated in several ways: a sidereal month of 27 days, 7 hrs., 43 min., 11:5 sec. (27.32 days); a synodic or ordinary month of 29 days, 12 hrs., 3 min. (29.53) from new moon to new moon; and a dragon month of 27 days, 5 hrs., 5 min: A tropical month is the time required for the moon to pass through 360 degrees of longitude, as from one vernal equinox to the next. A solar month is 30 days, 10 hrs. 29 min., 3. sec.

The moon actually revolves around the earth in 27.32 days, but the interval between two new moons or full moons is 29.53 days. The reason for this discrepancy is that while the moon is revolving around the earth in 27.32 days, the earth is also advancing in its path around the sun. The moon must therefore make more than a full revolution before it returns to a point of alignment with the sun. In other words, it takes the moon two days to catch up with the advance of the earth. This is explained in the illustration which depicts the distance the moon must travel after completing one revolution before returning to its same position relative to the earth and sun.

It is apparent that a lunar month may be approximately calculated as 27, 28, or 29.5 days. All of these periods were familiar to man before the 30-day month came into use. In China, India, Persia, Arabia, and Ceylon, there were lunar zodiacs containing 27 houses which were later increased to 28. One of the Babylonian lunar calendars used a year of 324 days, whose month consisted of 27 days. The month was divided into 3 weeks of 9 days each, or 60 uddu, the uddu being reckoned as 216 minutes.[1]

In Genesis 7:11 and 8:14, the Flood is said to have lasted from the 17th of the 2nd month in one year to the 27th day of the second month of the following year, or 1 year, 11 days. Since one 354-day lunar year, plus 11 equals 1 solar year of 365 days, the historian seems to have translated a solar year into its equivalent of lunar time. The period seems to be symbolical rather than historical.

A dragon month is measured from the time the moon crosses the sun's orbit and reaches a node until it again

---

1—In Babylon and Athens the moon year was reckoned at 12-3/8 (12.375) mean months. Modern astronomy gives 12.368746 mean lunar months to the sidereal year. The Greek astronomer Meton arrived at almost the identical figure in 432 B.C.

In the 2nd century B.C., Hipparchus and his Babylonian contemporaries adopted 29 d., 12 h., 44 min., 3.3 s. as the true length of the mean lunar month, a value as exact as any that modern astronomy can give. Callippus, in 330 B.C., proposed 29 d., 12 h., 44 m. 25.52 s. The true length of the mean lunar month is 29 d., 12 h., 44 m., 2.81 s. for the present day, or 29 d., 12 h., 44 m., 3.30 s. for the time of Hipparchus.

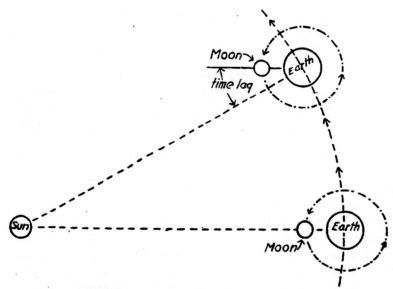

4. *Diagram showing why the moon has to make more than a complete revolution before returning to the same position relative to the sun and earth.*

crosses the sun's orbit (which meanwhile has retrogressed toward the west 2 hrs., 38 min.). Because of this retrogression of the nodes, eclipses are repeated in the same order in 18 years, 10 or 11 days.

This 18-year period, called a Saros, was anciently reckoned as 6585-½ days, and is equal to 19 ecliptic years of 346.6 days. The correct length is 6585.23 days, therefore, the error was not more than 1 day in 1800 years. This period was familiar to the early Chinese, Hindus, and Babylonians, who also reckoned it as equivalent to 223 synodic months, or 242 dragon months. Another ecliptic period which came into use in the west about 300 B.C., consisted of 235 synodic months, or approximately 19 solar years. In the Chinese record called the Ssu Ki of Ssu Ma Chien mention is made of the 19-year lunar period being put into use in China by Hwang Ti, the yellow emperor, 2698 B.C., or more than 2000 years before Meton introduced it to the Greeks.

It is only once in 8 years, or more correctly 99 months, that full moon coincides with the longest or shortest day of the year. This octennial period is the shortest cycle at the end of which the sun and moon really mark time together, after having overlapped throughout the whole eight years. It furnishes the basis for a calendar which brings lunar and solar time into reasonable, although not exact, harmony.

As Regulator of Fate

Very few books are available from which a reader may form a fairly clear picture of the beliefs which were based upon the moon's movements and phases; yet moon worship was the basis of one of the very oldest and most widespread cults the world has known. Before it was superseded by the so-called "ethic" religions, moon worship had left a lasting impression on the customs, legends, religions, literature, and governments of people in all parts of the world.

Doubtless the principal reason for the lack of information about this ancient religion is that by the time man had learned to write and to leave written records, the sun was already replacing the moon as an object of adoration.

One of the oldest clay tablets in existence records a reformation of the calendar by King Sargon of Babylonia, about 3000 B.C., to make the year begin with the entry of the sun into the zodiacal sign of Taurus, at the spring equinox. It is evident, therefore, that as early as that time the cult of the sun was challenging the older cult of the moon for supremacy.

Although the moon cults declined in importance with the rise of the newer beliefs, moon worshipers continued to build temples in her honor. Long after many places had adopted the sun as the central figure of their religious system, others continued to worship the moon, while, in some cities, followers of both cults were to be found worshiping harmoniously side by side. In fact, sun worship does not appear to have existed as a distinct and wholly separate system, but was simply grafted on the older cult; and after the two became fused, the sun eventually became the dominant figure. For this reason, both sun and moon motifs are usually found even in the earliest recorded myths.

It is not clear whether sun worship and its many myths began to develop before the beginning of astronomy and astrology, or whether they developed simultaneously, but it is evident that as the new cult took root, new deities were created, and the scope of the religion was greatly enlarged, making it more complex and giving it a new orientation.

The profoundly religious character of this early period was a dominant social factor and every phase of life had a religious background or origin. The literature, architecture, crafts, dress, customs, myths, legends, festivals, and the sciences, or pseudo-sciences, of astronomy, astrology, symbology, philology, numerology, and the more recent outgrowth of oriental mysticism expressed in the Cabala, were all influenced by or derived from the astral character of the primitive religious systems.

The evidence seems to indicate that a nation's myths and superstitions are more resistant to social upheavals and die more slowly than any other elements which determine the national character. Although a nation may be destroyed, its myths and superstitions may survive for centuries after their origin and significance are forgotten.

In the folklore of the most enlightened nations, remnants of these ancient beliefs are still to be found in a great mass of myths, fables, legends, traditions, and superstitions which are firmly believed by persons who little suspect their origin or extreme antiquity. By gathering from here and there, these bits of debris from former civilizations and placing them together, we can form a link between past and present more revealing than is to be found in the dry pages of standard histories.

From the earliest periods of which we have record, the moon was thought to exercise a strong influence on, if not actual control of, all organic life, both animal and vegetable. In what were regarded as favorable aspects, she was believed to exert an influence on the raising of crops and animals; on fecundity and childbirth, weather, commerce, etc. In her unfavorable aspects, she was thought to be a cause of sterility, lunacy (from Luna, the moon), fevers, diseases (especially of women), and in many ways adversely affect man's health and well being.

Having first seen or imagined a connection between phases of the moon and vital phenomena on earth, primitive man naturally believed that the moon regulated or brought them about. Furthermore, when primitive people lacked a true or scientific explanation of any event, they were inclined to attribute it to a supernatural power which they personified and called a deity. The very name of this planet indicates the extreme antiquity of the belief that the moon is the Great Regulator or Measurer, not only of time but of the fates of men. The Latin derivative is the word Mensis, from which is derived our word Mensuration. In India it is Meen or Manu, Sanscrit Mas, Persian Mah,[2] German Mond, Dutch Maan, Mexican Metzle, Greek Minos, Egyptian Min.[3]

At an extremely early date, a connection had doubtless been observed between the 28-day cycle of the moon and the menstrual cycle of women and between changes of the moon and ocean tides. To people of the East, marriage and childbirth have always been the supreme duty and goal of women, and the moon, who they believed controlled or regulated fecundity and the generation of life, became known as the Great Regulator.

Some significance may also have been seen in the fact that the human foetus is fully developed in 7 months, or that gestation of both women and cows takes place in 280 days, or ten 28-day months. This period also represents 40 weeks, which may explain why, among ancient people, the number 40 is habitually associated with periods of temptation, trial, hardship, and pain for 40 days, weeks, months, or years. For example, we have the 40 days and nights of the Deluge, 40 years of wandering in the Wilderness by the Israelites, 40 days and nights of fasting by Moses on Mt. Sinai,[4] 40 days and nights of Christ in the Wilderness,[5] 40 days between the resurrection of Christ and his final disappearance from the earth,[6] 40 days mourning for the death of Jacob, 40 days fasting by Elijah on Mt. Horeb, 40 days in which Ezekiel bore the iniquity of the house of Judah, 40 days of sacrifice in the old Persian *Salutation of Mithra,* 40 nights of mourning in the "Mysteries of Per-

---

2—In Persian books of the Avesta the word for moon is Maongh, Pahlavi Mah and Persian Mah. The Avesta word for wealth also is Maya, Persian Mayeh. The same Pahlavi word Mah signifies moon as well as sexual intercourse. The Persian word which denotes wealth also signifies *semen virile,* as well as female or woman. *The Ancient Iranian Belief and Folklore of the Moon* by Jivanji Jamashedji Modi, Anthropological Society of Bombay, Journal, 1917, v. 11, pp. 14-39.

3—In English, French, Italian, Latin and Greek the moon is spoken of as feminine, but in Sanscrit and all Teutonic languages it is considered masculine.

4—Gen. 7:4,12.

5—Luke 4:2.

6—Matt. 4:2.

sephone," 40 days of mourning by the Babylonians before the celebration of the festival of the *Descent of Ishtar*, which corresponds to the Christian Lenten period of 40 days from Ash Wednesday to Easter. Forty is the number for the punishment of sinners, says Deuteronomy (25:3).

The number 40, by the way, is employed interchangeably with 42 in ancient numerical systems, thereby making an even multiple of weeks.

Mr. Grattan Guinness in *The Approaching End of the Age* (p. 258), observed that "the birth, growth, maturity of vital functions, health, revolution of each disease; decay and death of insects, reptiles, birds, mammals, and even of man, are more or less controlled by a law of computation (completion in weeks, or multiples of 7 days)."

Charles Darwin remarked in *The Descent of Man* that animals living at the mean high water, or at the mean low water, pass through complete cycle changes in about two weeks. People who live near the sea have always professed to see a close connection between the rise and fall in the fates of men and the ebb and flow of the ocean tides. It is very widely believed that all births occur at the time of an incoming tide and that all deaths occur during the ebb tide. The planting of clover seed, the milking of cows, the churning of milk, and many other activities must be properly timed with the tides if they are to be successful. Sir James Frazer[7] mentions many such odd beliefs.

Dr. Laycock concluded in *The Periodicity of Vital Phenomena*, that animal changes occur in every 3½, 7, 14, or 28 days, or at some definite number of weeks. For pigs the period of gestation is 17 weeks, for rabbits 6 weeks, pigeon eggs hatch in 2 weeks, chicken eggs in 3, duck and turkey eggs in 4, goose eggs in 5, and ostrich eggs in 7. Dr. Laycock also observed that the crucial periods in fevers occur in 7, 14, or 21 days. Pythagoras said that infants acquire teeth in 7 months, and lose them in 7 years.

Dr. Francis Balfour,[8] a physician employed by the East India Co., in Calcutta, wrote that he had observed that fevers invariably occur "on one of the 3 days which immediately precede the full of the moon, or on one of the 3 days

7—*The Golden Bough*, abdg. ed., Sir James Frazer, 1922, p. 35.
8—Dr. Francis Balfour, M.D., *A Treatise on the Influence of the Moon in Fevers*, Calcutta, 1784.

which immediately follow it; or on one of the 3 days which immediately precede and follow the change of moon." And further: "With regards to headaches, toothaches, inflammation of the eyes, asthma, pains and swellings of the liver and spleen, fluxes, spasms, obstructions in the bowels, complaints in the urinary passages, eruptions of various kinds, and a great many more which return periodically with the moon, whether contained with fever or not, the cure entirely depends on a constant attention of these (the moon's) revolutions." It is very doubtful whether any present day medical authority would concur in these observations, but they are, nevertheless, indicative of the influences which have been attributed to the moon in modern times.

From the beginning of history, changes of the moon were believed to have a decisive influence on all existence, and the number seven was deemed the most powerful of magic numbers. The day of the full moon, called "Shabbatu" in ancient Sumeria, was described as "the day of the heart, the day when the heart of the god is appeased". Work was laid aside, and old and young gathered in the street to celebrate. Later, Shabbatu came to mark the four quarters of the moon; and the seventh, fourteenth, twenty-first, and twenty-eighth days of the month were celebrated by religious services and the cessation of work. Although the Bible is not clear on this point, it appears that adoption of the seven-day week marked the change from lunar to solar time by the Hebrews.[9]

The entry of the sun into the zodiacal sign of the Ram (Aries), at the vernal equinox, was celebrated by the sacrifice of a lamb in both India and Egypt.[10] Moses Maimonides, the famous Jewish theologian, intimated that the paschal[11] lamb which Moses commanded the Israelites to sacrifice at the Passover, was for a similar purpose.

It would require a great many pages to catalog the multitude of instances in which the number 7 seems to have a mystical or astral significance. The Babylonians,

9—Exod. 31:16; Exod. 12:6,18.
10—Before the time of Moses, the Egyptians fixed the beginning of the year at the vernal equinox.
11—The Hebrew name was *Psh, pesach,* meaning "transit." The lamb itself is often called *pesech* or Passover. *Anacalypsis* Godfrey Higgins, v. 1, p. 261.

Hebrews,[12] and Egyptians were extremely partial to that number and in the Koran, the number 7 and 7 times 7 is employed repeatedly.

Many modern mythologists attribute the wide use of this number to its astrological significance, as it represents the number of planets in the heavens; but there is much evidence to indicate that it was particularly venerated long before the development of astrology.

Another theory, reported by Philo, is that Pythagoras called the number 7 the ever-virgin number "because it neither produces any of the numbers within the decad, i.e. from 1 to 10, nor is produced by them".

Ancient ideas relating to the generative powers of the moon are reflected in a multitude of old sayings, beliefs, and superstitions which still are to be found in parts of all the world. Ancient astrologers believed that conception was regulated by the moon, a belief which is still widely held. By the Greeks, Britons, and others, the full moon was considered as the most propitious time for the marriage ceremony. This belief still persists in Lithuania. Orkney Islanders object to marrying except with a growing moon, while some wish even for a flowing tide.[13]

A male child should be weaned when the horned moon is waxing, and a female, when it is waning, no doubt, to make the boys sturdy and the girls slim and delicate.

In the Austrian Tyrol, it is "believed that the moon influences nature, therefore nothing is done in either field, stall, house, or wood without first consulting the moon."[14] The hair is cut only at the change of the moon, in order

12—"The sacred number 7 dominates the cycle of religious observances. Every 7th day was a Sabbath and every 7th month was a sacred month. And every 7th year was a Sabbatical year. After 7 times 7 was the year of Jubilee. The feast of the Passover with the feast of unleavened bread began 14 days (2 x 7) after the beginning of the month and lasted 7 days. The feast of the Pentecost was 7 times 7 days, after the feast of the Passover. The feast of Tabernacles began 14 days (2 x 7) after the beginning of the month and lasted 7 days. The 7th month was marked by (1) Feast of Trumpets on the 1st day; (2) Feast of Atonement on the 10th; (3) Feast of Tabernacles from the 15th to 21st; the days of the Holy Convocation were 7 in number; 2 at the Passover; 1 at the day of Atonement; 1 at the Feast of Trumpets; 1 at the day of Atonement; 1 at the Feast of Tabernacles and 1 on the day following the 8th day." *Worship of the Old Testament*, Willis, pp. 19-191.

13—*Moon Lore*, by Rev. Timothy Harley, London, p. 195.

14—*Symbolism of the East and West*, by Mrs. M. J. M. Murray-Aynsley, p. 15.

that it may not grow again too quickly.[15] Some women in Fife (Scotland), do not comb their hair at certain stages of the moon.[16]

Corns should be cut during the wane of the moon, if you would have them disappear quickly. Weeds cut in the dark of the moon will not come up again. It is believed that medicines for worms should be given at the height of the moon. The worms are then believed to come out easily.[17]

In his book *Moon Lore,* the Rev. Timothy Harley assembled an immense number of superstitions from many sources, relating to various aspects of the moon. Some of them are cited here. Numerous examples are also given by Edward B. Tylor[18] and Sir James Frazer.[19]

According to Rev. Harley, the time of the full moon was chosen in both Mexico and Peru to celebrate festivals for water deities, patronesses of agriculture and, generally, the ceremonies connected with the crops were regulated by the moon's phases.[20]

On the day of the new moon, in Bombay, Parsee ladies, in their sarees of variegated colors, stroll along the shore, or sit on the small parapet wall, on the west of the Queens Road and, as sunset approaches, they give offerings of flowers and sugar, and sometimes of cocoanuts, to the sea, thus paying homage to Ardvicura Anahita, the female Yazata or angel, who presides over waters. This Yazata presides also over the divine powers who grant boons to maidens praying for wealthy husbands who can make them mothers of robust children.

With the appearance of the moon over the horizon, they make their curtsy, at times with simple and respectful bowing, with their hands at their foreheads, and, at times, with their usual curtsy known as *overna,* wherein they raise both their hands to the moon and, giving them a turn in two directions, apply the back of their hands to their temples. An ordinary homage is paid to the new moon, even by Parsee men with a bow of the head, and

15—*Symbolism of the East and West,* Mrs. M. J. M. Murray-Aynsley, p. 15.
16—*Lore of Fife,* J. E. Sempkins, p. 18.
17—*Ibid* p. 409.
18—*Primitive Culture,* by Edw. B. Tylor, 2 vols., London, 1891.
19—*The Golden Bough,* Abgd. Ed., by Sir James Frazer, London, 1922.
20—*Moon Lore,* p. 138.

a salaam with the hands raised to the forehead. Homage to the new moon, in this or some other form, is observed also by people in Bombay other than the Parsees.[21]

In East Lancashire, and other parts of England, superstitious people consider it disrespectful or sinful to point at the moon.[22] In Berkshire there is a tradition that a girl was stricken dead after so doing. This belief is held in many parts of the world. Many old men take off their hats to the moon, and devout girls curtsy to the new moon. "In Scotland generally, and particularly amongst the Highlanders, it is the custom of women to curtsy to the new moon."[23] "English women too, have a touch of this (custom), some of them sitting astride a gate or stile the first evening the new moon appears, and saying 'A fine moon, God bless her.' "[24] The Jews had a similar custom (see Jer. 8:1,2). The Persians believed leprosy to be an affliction of those who had committed some offense against the moon.

An English writer of the 17th century states that in Lancashire and parts of Northern England, "some country women doe worship of the moon on their bare knees, kneeling upon an earthfast stone, and the people of Athol, in the islands, doe worship the new moon." Camden wrote of the Irish "whether or not they worship the moon I know not, but when they first see her after a change, they commonly bow the knee and say the Lord's prayer and, near the wane, address themselves to her in a low voice after this manner: 'Leave us well as thou foundest us'."[25] In Lancashire there is still a custom of making cakes in her honor.[26]

From the *Penitential of Theodore*, Archbishop of York in the 7th century, and *Confessionals of Egbert*, Archbishop of York, in the early part of the 8th century, we may surmise that homage was then offered to the moon and sun.[27]

The Japanese sacred festivals are held at certain seasons of the year and at changes of the moon. According to Plutarch, carpenters in the first century rejected timber fallen

21—Jivanji Jamshedji Modi, *The Ancient Iranian Belief and Folklore of the Moon*, The Anthropological Society of Bombay, 1917, v. 11, pp. 14-39.
22—*Moon Lore*, p. 131.
23—*Moon Lore*, p. 214.
24—*Symbolism of the East and West*, p. 35.
25—*Moon Lore*, p. 121.
26—*Ibid*, p. 104.
27—*Ibid*, p. 120.

in the full·moon as being soft and tender, subject also to worms and quick putrefaction by reason of excessive moisture. Husbandmen should make haste to gather up their wheat and grain from the threshing floor in the wane of the moon and toward the end of the month.[28]

Prof. Lindley said "Columella, Cato, Vitruvius, and Pliny all had their notions of the advantages of cutting timber at certain ages of the moon, a phase of mummery which is still preserved in the royal ordonnances of France to the conservators of the forests who are directed to fell oaks only 'in the waning of the moon' and 'when the wind is at the north.' "[29]

Beef and pork killed in the wane of the moon is said to shrink badly when cooked.[30] People in Cornwall and many other parts of the world still gather their medical herbs when the moon is at a certain phase, a custom probably of Druidical origin. Cucumbers, radishes, leeks, lilies, horseradish, saffron, and other plants, are said to increase during the fullness of the moon, but onions, on the contrary, are much larger and better nourished during the decline.[31]

In Iceland, it is said "if a pregnant woman sits with her face toward the moon, her child will be a lunatic." In French Brittany, peasant girls never squat in the fields when facing the full moon, because they believe to do so would make them pregnant. They always turn their backs to the moon.[32] In Greenland, girls also avoid looking long at the moon, for fear of becoming pregnant.[33]

Brazilian mothers carefully shield their infants from the lunar rays, believing that exposure to them causes sickness. The hunting tribes of Mexico will not sleep in moonlight, nor leave their game exposed to its influence.

Emile Nourry, a French author, says that when the moon is angular and unaffected during a nativity, it is deemed an augury of great success and of continued good fortune.[34] Her usual diseases are rheumatism, consumption,

---

28—*Moon Lore*, p. 178.
29—*Ibid*, p. 180.
30—*Ibid*, p. 216.
31—*Ibid*, p. 178.
32—See *L'Astrologie populaire et influences de la luna*, by Emile Nourry, 1937.
33—*Ibid*, p. 173.
34—*L'Astrologie populaire*, p. 192.

palsy, cholic, apoplexy, vertigo, lunacy, scrofula, smallpox, dropsy, most diseases peculiar to young children, etc. Shortness of breath, grippe. influenza, dropsy, and glandular tumors, become worse when the moon is on the wane. Cutaneous sickness, eye troubles, blindness, intestinal ailments and other forms of illness increase during the full moon.[35]

In Scotland, it was formerly believed that if a child be taken from the breast during the waning of the moon, it will decay during the time the moon wanes.[36] Galen taught, in the 2nd century, that those who were born when the moon was falciform, or sickle-shaped, were weak and short lived, while those born during the full moon, were vigorous and of long life.[37]

"The new moon is considered preeminently auspicious for commencements for all kinds of building up and beginning, *de novo*. Houses are to be erected and moved into; marriages are to be concluded, money counted, hair and nails cut, healing herbs and pure dew gathered, all at the new moon. The full moon is the time for pulling down and thinking of the nature of things. It is the time to cut timber; to mow grass and to make hay, not while the sun shines, but while the moon wanes. It is also the time to stuff feather beds so as to kill the newly plucked feathers completely and bring them to rest."[38]

Linen should be washed in the waning moon so that the dirt may disappear with the dwindling light. According to an old notion, it was deemed unlucky to put on a new dress when the moon was in her decline.

"In an old Chap Book giving the meaning of different kinds of dreams and ways to make them come true, the following prayer is to be repeated:

" 'Luna, everywoman's friend,
To me thy gladness descend:
Let me this night visions see,
Emblems of my destiny.'-"[39]

35—*Ibid*, p. 173.
36—*Moon Lore*, p. 195.
37—*Ibid*, p. 198.
38—*Moon Lore*, p. 216.
39—*Ibid*, p. 213.

To see the moon for the first time through trees, through a veil or a window is an unlucky omen.[40] To see the new moon on the right hand or directly before you the first time after her change betokens good fortune that month, but to see her for the first time over your left shoulder is an unlucky sign.

In Scotland, Ireland, France, Italy, and Germany people believed that to have good fortune it was necessary to carry in one's pocket a piece of silver money when the last quarter of the moon began.[41] In India "when one's eyes catches the new moon first, he does not like to avert it from her but he quickly takes out of his purse a rupee or silver coin. This is held to be auspicious as presaging the acquisition of much wealth and happiness. The new moon of the Dewali is believed to be very auspicious among the Hindus. The women prepare on the occasion a lampblack known as the 'new moon lampblack' which serves as a charm against the evil eye."[42]

Emile Nourry informs us that in India, on the third day of the quarter of the third moon of the year after the birth of a child, the father takes the child in his arms and pledges it to worship of the moon. When bridal couples desire a male offspring, they repeat a magic sentence and put an arrow in a dish full of rice at the beginning of the third moon of the year.[43]

In the 16th and 17th centuries many physicians published almanacs and ephmerides indicating the favorable times to take baths, to shave, to purge and bleed. Health baths should be taken on the sign contrary to the sickness, that is, if the sickness were humid, baths were taken when the moon was in her dry period; and vice versa. The humid or water signs are Cancer, Scorpion, and Pisces.

Jean Fernel, 1508-1588, physician and astrologer of Henry II and Catherine de Medici, wrote that in his time, it was a custom in the Italian, French, English, and other courts, to swear only by the planets.[44]

In his *Secrets of the Moon*, Antoine Mizauld, 1510-1578, a pupil of Agrippa and Paracelsus, described the mysterious

---

40—*Ibid*, p. 216.
41—*Moon Lore*, p. 218.
42—*L'Astrologie populaire*, p. 127.
43—*Ancient Iranian Belief*, p. 33.
44—*L'Astrologie populaire*, p. 155 et seq.

influence of the moon and designated her "the Great Magician". He composed a hymn to glorify the marriage of the sun and moon.[45]

In all parts of the world, the moon has for ages been considered a feminine genetrix and protectress of mankind, ruling over women's breasts, matrix, and other sex organs. The moon rules all liquids; therefore, she rules over menstruation. The full moon is believed to be propitious for childbirth. If there is no moon in the sky, delivery will be very difficult. Primitive people called the moon "the Great Midwife".

The moon is thought to have an influence over shellfish,[46] and Horace commented upon the superiority of shellfish during the moon's increase. Pliny had similar beliefs. The poet Lucilius said that mussels, oysters, and other shellfish are fatter during the waxing of the moon than during the waning.

Sheep should be sheared in the first quarter. Castration of animals should be done in the third quarter. Medical herbs should be cut in the first quarter.[47]

Superstitious agriculturists still consult almanacs before planting crops. Root vegetables are generally planted in the dark of the moon and flowering plants and vegetables are planted in the light of the moon. There is a tradition, based upon the Resurrection, that potatoes planted on Good Friday are sure to come up.

A recent farmer's almanac giving the zodiacal aspects of the twelve months contains such items as this: "Sign of Taurus; Root crops of quick growth will be good when planted in this sign. These crops should be planted in the light or decreasing light of the moon to produce the best yield." And again, "Capricornus; This is a moist sign; produces rapid growth of pulp truck or roots but not much green", and so forth.

If the groundhog sees his shadow on February 2nd, six weeks more of winter weather will follow: if it rains on St. Swithins' Day it will rain on every day for forty days; the wearing of a St. Christopher's medal is protection against disaster at sea; it is unlucky to start new business

---

45—*Ibid*, p. 155 et. seq.
46—*Moon Lore*, p. 173.
47—*Ibid*, p. 173.

ventures on Friday; it is unlucky to light three cigarettes with one match. These and a multitude of other superstitions, are firmly accepted by people who think they are very realistic and who laugh at customs and taboos of as recent origin as the Victorian period.

In this work, it will be shown that many of the customs and superstitions of the present day had their origin in beliefs which prevailed several thousands of years ago. Although the subjects considered may appear, at first, to be unrelated, they will be found, on examination, to be products of the same mode of thought. In fact, practically all customs, myths, superstitions and religions of the ancient world stemmed, originally, from a few simple ideas. For reasons which will become clear as we go along, we will first consider some of the beliefs of the ancient Babylonians.

III

LUNAR MYTHS AND CULTS

W̲HEN MODERN ARCHAEOLOGISTS began digging into the ruins of long vanished cities to gain a wider knowledge of past civilization, it was with very excellent reason that they chose the plains of southern Mesopotamia as one of the major sites for their labors. No region is more heavily steeped in history, romance, and mystery than that lying in the valley of the Tigris and Euphrates rivers, ancient Babylonia.

So immense has been the quantity of evidence of the ancient world which scientists have unearthed with pick and shovel, that it has become increasingly rash to speak of any particular city or locality as the "cradle of civilization". The new light which these discoveries have thrown upon early Babylonian codes of civil and religious law, literature, mythology, astrology, and astronomy has made clear the tremendous influence which Babylonian culture has exerted upon the civilizations of Asia Minor, Egypt, Greece, Rome, and all of the western world.

The Babylonians devised a very practical and ingenious system of measures of weight, volume, and distance. They developed the science of metallurgy and processes were in use for smelting iron and the making of bronze from tin and copper. They knew how to make glass as early as 1500 B.C. and cobalt was being used as a substitute for the costly lapis lazuli in the manufacture of blue glass. Weaving, too, was a highly developed art and Babylonia was famous for its magnificent carpets and rugs.

The site of ancient Babylon ("Gate of the Gods") lies about fifty miles south of the fabled city of Bagdad, in one of the most fertile spots on earth. The land, called by the Babylonians Edin or Edinu, "the plain", is the same as the Eden mentioned in the Book of Genesis, Ch. 2.

Lowness of the land made necessary the construction of an elaborate system of drainage canals, dams, sluices, cisterns, etc. The Babylonians share with the Egyptians the honor of being the first hydraulic engineers.[1] Lack of

---

1—Drain pipes have been unearthed which are thought to date from about 4500 B.C.

timber and building stone made necessary the use of both baked and sun dried brick in the construction of their buildings. These were generally erected on mud platforms several feet high because of the low, swampy nature of the soil. Clay tablets also served as their writing material, the words being inscribed in the wet clay, which was then baked in the sun.

The oldest clay tablet in which Babylon is mentioned dates from about 3,000 B.C. To the south, between Babylon and the Persian Gulf, in the region known as Sumeria, lay the far older cities of Ur, Eridu, Erech, Lagash and Larsa. To the north, lay Accad, Sippar, Kish, and Nippur comprising the region roughly defined as Accadia. About 2700 B.C. the Semites of northern Sumer became masters of the region and founded a great empire at Accad, near Sippar. Babylonian culture developed out of the social structure of these ancient cities, and it is in their ruins that archaeologists have made many of their most important discoveries.

Before 4000 B.C. the Sumerians had attained a high degree of culture.[2] Their development of pictograph and cuneiform script has provided us with the oldest written records in existence.[3] Engravings of that period were of particularly high quality and the sculpture was, in some respects, equal to or superior to that of later centuries.

Architects of Nippur had learned how to construct arches of burned brick. Poetry and music were carefully cultivated and a 12-string harp was in use as early as 2900 B.C. With the rise of Babylon as a great political power, between 3000 and 2000 B.C., the old Sumerian city states came under the leadership of their northern neighbor, and soon dwindled in significance.

Seals and clay tablets so far discovered indicate that the Sumerians, from the earliest recorded period of civilization, paid homage to a great triad of gods called Anu, the supreme god of the heavens and ruler of the universe in general; Enlil, who governed the earth, and Ea or Enki, god of waters and the benefactor who brought the fruits of civilization to man. Their roles, however, are largely honorary and passive, as the principal activities on the

---

2—Moderate estimates place the date of cultural evidence from 5000 to 6000 B.C. Highest estimates place the date from 8000 to 10,000 B.C.

3—Writing had passed the pictograph stage before 4000 B.C.

earth were ruled by a secondary triad of gods representing the moon, sun, and earth.

The old city of Eridu was situated at the mouth of the Euphrates, on the shore of the Persian Gulf, which fact no doubt accounts for its association with Ea, the water god and his consort Davinka or Damkina.

Ur was originally on or near the Persian Gulf. The deposit of silt at the mouth of the Euphrates has pushed the shore line back about 130 miles. Ur paid traditional homage to Ea, but from the earliest historic time, was a center of moon worship. It was from here that, in a later day, Abraham the father of the Jews, began his journey to the Land of Canaan.

At Nippur there were temples to Enlil the earth god and his consort Ninlil or Nin, the mistress par excellence, a goddess of procreation and fertility, whose name is a feminine form of Enlil. Later, under Semitic influence, his name was changed to Bel.

5. *Fig. 1 is the Assyrian fish-god Ea-Oannes from a bas relief from Nimrud. Fig. 2 shows the resemblance between the fish-head mask and a modern bishop's mitre. Fig. 3 is a Persian design representing the sun and moon as male and female. (From Layard's,* SUR LE CULTE DE VENUS.)

At Larsa in southern Babylonia there was perhaps the earliest temple of Shamash the sun god.

In early Sumerian records, the name of the moon god is Nannar, who ruled with the goddess called Ningal or Nana. As the Sumerian cities became dominated by the Semitic culture of Babylon, the influence of Sin the moon god of Ur became greater and more widespread not only in Babylonia but in other parts of the ancient world. It was only in Babylon, however, where Semitic influence was strong, that Sin was particularly honored as the father of the gods.

Sin was represented as an old man with long beard, seated beneath a crescent moon. He was identified with the healing art and as governor of oracles and dreams: on the other hand, he had a sinister aspect as bringer of sickness and misfortune to mortals and could punish evildoers with leprosy. Texts exalt him as the governor of light and wisdom. His titles designate him as the "wanderer", "the living father", "uncle" or "the old one".

Importance of the goddess of fertility and fecundity in the ancient scheme is perhaps indicated by her identification under more than forty different titles which describe her numerous attributes in various localities and periods.

As Nintud, she is the virgin goddess of procreation and fecundity, sometimes called Makh, "the supreme goddess", and known to the Babylonians and Assyrians as Belit-itani, "queen of the gods". As Makh or Mah, spouse of Merodach or Marduk, the local god of Babylon, she is spoken of as the "mother of childbirth", the "mother who opens the loins", "the framer of the foetus" or as goddess of the foetus.

As Ninkhursag, she is "queen of the earth" and, in sculpture, is portrayed with the same horned headdress as the Egyptian cow-goddess Hathor. Sometimes she is referred to as Anu's heifer and, on boundary stones, her symbol is a cow. As Aruru, she appears as goddess of childbirth; as Ma or Mama, she is the goddess who created the first man from clay. She is sometimes represented as the consort of the earth god Enlil, but she is still called virgin. As Innini, the virgin goddess is a specialized aspect of the earth mother, particularly as the sister of Tammuz, god of the spring equinox, who brings vegetation to the earth.

She is mistress of magic and administration of law and order "who exalts judgments and decisions". Throughout history, she appears as a merciful, compassionate friend of man, the "Weeping Mother" who intercedes in his behalf with the wrathful gods. Paradoxically, she is also the bringer of hatred, strife and storm, the goddess who causes the heavens to tremble and the earth to shake.

The entry of the Semites into Babylonia occurred at such an early period that it is impossible to determine definitely whence they came, what deities they brought with them, or the exact character of the Sumerian religion at that time. But it appears that the south Arabic Athtar, goddess of the planet Venus, was identified with the Sumerian virgin goddess Venus Ninsianni or Innini, and subsequently became a female deity in Babylon and Assyria under the name of Ishtar. In later texts Ishtar sometimes appears as Zarpanit or Sarpanit.

In very early myths, Ishtar is represented as the daughter of Enlil or Bel, the earth god. She is sometimes portrayed as Davinka, the wife of Ea and therefore the mother and

6. *Illustration at left shows a primitive mother goddess from early Assyrian sculpture. The figure at right is from an early Babylonian sculpture of Ishtar.*

sister as well as consort of Tammuz, who was addressed in an ancient Accadian hymn as "Shepherd and Lord, the Husband of Ishtar, Queen of Heaven." She is often represented as the daughter of Anu. A myth speaks of Erech as "the dwelling of Anu and Ishtar, the city of harlots or joy maidens and hierodouloi". Elsewhere the moon god Sin is represented as having been the father of both Ishtar and Shamash the sun god. In astrology the character of Ishtar as ruler over the forces of generation was assigned to the planet Venus, but this usage does not seem to have passed into the popular religion.

In a hymn she is called "the glad-eyed goddess of desire". Sometimes she calls herself "a loving courtesan" or a "temple harlot". In this respect she is portrayed in art as a nude woman with prominent pudendum or as lifting her robe to disclose her charms. In another hymn she says "I turn the male to the female: I turn the female to the male". "She is the harlot who leans from the windows to flirt with men and seduce them; a temptress who 'causes maidens to depart from their couches'. One of her titles is 'she who leans out (of the windows)' or 'queen of the windows.' "[4] In a prayer, a woman begs Ishtar to cause her husband or lover to return safely, that he may continue to love her and that she may bear children. As a regulator of childbirth, she is the goddess of Fate.

Very early in Babylonian history she appears as the great central figure who dominates the whole scene, just as in later centuries the central figure is the sun. The pages of mythology do not contain the name of any god or goddess whose popularity continued as long through the centuries as hers; there was none other to whom the changes made by political upheavals and the natural evolutionary process brought such great confusion and contradictions in their character and attributes.

Under many forms and titles she is the goddess associated with the earth, the Great Mother Goddess who gives birth to everything. The earth was esteemed as the womb from which all life came and the moon was honored as the generator of the life-giving forces by which birth, growth, decay and death of all plant and animal life was regulated. Undoubtedly one of the reasons for the moon's being asso-

---

4—*Mythology of All Races*, Stephen H. Langdon, v. 5, p. 33.

ciated with growth is that the lowering of the temperature during the night causes moisture in the air to condense and settle in the form of dew which nourishes vegetation and causes growth. In both mythology and astrology the moon is associated with humidity, moisture, water, and femininity, whereas the sun is considered dry, hot, and masculine.

Although she has characteristics of both earth and moon, Ishtar is not strictly an earth goddess, nor is she specifically a moon goddess. She is the Great Mother principle in its widest and most inclusive sense.

In the great Gilgamesh Epic an effort seems to have been made to account for the earth-moon character of the goddess, for in that Babylonian epic she is transferred from earth to heaven by the supreme god Anu and made the consort of the moon god Sin. But whether she is spoken of as earth, vegetation or moon goddess, her true role in all ages was that of ruler of the generative powers of nature.

After the conquest of Babylon by Assyria, Ishtar acquired a more sinister aspect as goddess of war and destruction as well as goddess of creation. She was given masculine attributes, sometimes portrayed with a beard and spoken of as an androgyne. By this time she had absorbed the attributes of so many other goddesses and exercised such a variety of functions that she came near to becoming the supreme deity. But to the very end, the maid planning marriage and the wife approaching motherhood continued to offer prayers and gifts, not to the sun god, not to Sin the moon god, nor to Ishtar as earth goddess, but to Ishtar the moon goddess, the Queen of Heaven. She was an incarnation of the mystery of conception, the goddess of love and elemental desire, patron of fecundity and childbirth, beneficent deity of motherhood in all ages.

Childless women prayed that she intercede for them, pregnant women prayed that she give them an easy delivery: she was asked to provide abundant harvests and so forth. The great mass of lunar folklore to be found throughout the world shows that many people still believe much the same superstitions about the moon that the Babylonians believed 5000 or more years ago.

Her lunar characteristics are continually revealed in Babylonian mythology and sculpture, where she is often portrayed seated or standing, with her bosom bared, and a

suckling infant at her breast. At her feet, or overhead, is
a crescent moon with seven bright stars, thought to represent the sun, moon and five planets Venus, Jupiter, Mercury,
Mars, and Saturn. The Indian Devaki, Egyptian Isis, and
Virgin Mary were similarly portrayed. Like Isis, Aphrodite,
Semiramis, and Virgin Mary, Ishtar was also often accompanied by a dove. Sometimes she appears surrounded
by maidens, each representing some phase of the female
principle, and forming a Court of Love.

In a figure in the Merrill Collection, in the Semitic
Museum of Harvard University, she appears naked, with
rays around her head and a crescent moon under her feet,
with one foot like the tail of a fish and the other like the
hoof of a cow. Beneath the figure is the inscription "divine
producer of all".

Hundreds of inscriptions of the kings, mythological
texts, boundary stones and artistic representations in statues,
reliefs and seals, as well as incantations, prayers and psalms
addressed to Ishtar have been found by archaeologists in
Babylonian ruins. But her name is perhaps best known to
mythologists by two poems, the Gilgamesh Epic and the
Descent of Ishtar. The latter poem consists of but 137 lines
and dates from perhaps 4000 B.C., or earlier, and narrates
her descent into the Land of No-Return.

The reason for her descent into hell is not given but
mythologists have generally interpreted the poem as an
astronomical allegory in which Ishtar is represented as an
earth goddess seeking the return of Tammuz, the young
sun god. Her loss of clothing as she passes through the
gates of the Underworld has been thought to represent the
loss of verdure in the earth's vegetation at the end of summer, when the sun appears to move southward. But the
story contains both solar and lunar motifs and it might
well have been intended to describe the period in the
dark phase when the moon can no longer be seen and,
therefore is represented allegorically as having gone to the
Underworld in search of her lover, the sun god.

Ishtar is portrayed in the poem as the lover as well
as the sister of Tammuz. The gods and kings of ancient
nations were not judged by ordinary standards. Legends
of many countries make all people descend from the incestous marriage of the first man and woman who are
represented as brother and sister or father and daughter.

7. *Goddess Allat passing through the Underworld in her sacred bark.
From a bronze plaque.*

In Egypt it was customary for the king to marry his sister and a similar custom prevailed among the Incas of Peru.

After describing the Underworld[5] as a region of darkness, "the region whence the wayfarer never returns," the poem narrates Ishtar's arrival at the entrance of the Underworld where she demands admittance and threatens to break down the door. Ereshkigal, the sister of Ishtar and

5—Allatu, the Underworld, is described as the region of darkness, the dwelling of Eresh-kigal, the inhabitants of whose house see no light; the region where dust is their bread and mud is their food; the region whence the wayfarer never returns; whose inhabitants are clothed, like birds, in a garment of feathers. On the door is a bolt covered with dust.

mistress of the Underworld, receives the news of her arrival with anger but bids the gatekeeper let her enter.

The fading beauty of the moon in its last quarter may then be imagined in the succeeding lines which describe Ishtar's passage through seven gates, at each of which she loses one article of dress or ornament until finally she stands naked before Eresh-kigal, who greets her with scorn and bids a black demon smite her with disease.

During Ishtar's sojourn in the Underworld a messenger reports to Shamash, the sun god, that all life on earth is at a standstill; animals no longer mate and vegetation is withered and dying. The lines are as follows:

> Ishtar has descended into the earth
> and has not come up.
> Since Ishtar is gone to the Land
> of No-Return
> The bull cares not for the cow; the
> ass not for the jenny;
> The man cares not for the maid in
> the market
> The man sleeps in his place
> The wife sleeps alone.[6]

Shamash weeps but confesses he can do nothing about the situation. He tells Sin and Ea, the god of subterranean waters about it and Ea, who exercises a paternal interest in the welfare of man, sends a messenger to Allatu to demand Ishtar's release. Eresh-kigal receives the messenger with curses and abuse but is unable to withstand the power of Ea, and Ishtar is ordered released. After being sprinkled with the waters of life she is again conducted through the seven gates and her clothing and jewelry are restored. Finally she emerges into the upper world and all life on earth resumes its normal course. At the end there are a few lines in which mention is made of "wailing men and wailing women" mourning Ishtar's disappearance.

The death of Tammuz was mourned in the fourth month of each year in Sumerian cities; and effigies of the dead god, anointed with oil and clad in a red robe, were borne in processions of men and women chanting sad dirges

6—*Aspects of Religious Beliefs & Practices in Babylonia & Assyria*, Morris Jastrow, 1911, p. 3707.

8. *Left: Terra cotta bas relief of Ishtar from temple at
Hursagkalami, in Kish.
Right: Ishtar in a war chariot. From Kish.*

to the music of wailing flutes. This month, corresponding
to our June, was called Tammuz in honor of the young
god, a name which it carries in the Hebrew calendar to the
present time.

The month Ab (July) was the time of funeral offerings, while Elul (August) was the month of Ishtar's descent
to hell in search of her lover, the three months forming a
cycle of the dying god.[7] In later times, however, the popularity of Tammuz became so completely overshadowed by
that of the virgin goddess that the festival originally named
in his honor came to be known as the festival of the
Descent of Ishtar.

According to Langdon,[8] the worship of Tammuz was
maintained as late as the 10th century A.D. at Harran in
Syria by the Arabian sect known as the Sabeans. Here the
name was pronounced Tammuz or Ta-uz. The festival of
Tammuz was also known as the Festival of the Weeping
Women and occurred on the first of the month Ta-uz. The

7—*Menologies & Almanacs of the Sumerian Calendar*, Stephen H.
Langdon, p. 19.
8—*The Mythology of All Races*, Stephen H. Langdon, v. 5, p. 336.

Harranian sect is said to have existed at Babylon as late as the 10th century A.D.[9]

The discovery of tablets relating this and other mythical adventures of Babylonian gods and goddesses has proved of absorbing interest to mythologists because of the light these myths have thrown upon the possible origin of numerous characters in classical mythology.

Although there is an obvious similarity between the myths of Babylonia and those of the nations lying westward, it has not been possible to trace, step by step, the migration of Ishtar, nor is it possible to say definitely whether she was the prototype for the virgin goddesses of the Mediterranean countries or all of them developed from some other Semitic source. All available evidence indicates, however, that the western myths originated much later.

Between 1700 and 1100 B.C. the cult of Isis became prominent in Egypt and Ishtar's search for Tammuz was paralleled by the wandering of Isis in search of her dead lover, Osiris. Like Ishtar, Isis was the ever-virgin mother and in her temple at Sais was the famous inscription: "I am whatsoever is and shall be. No mortal hath yet drawn my peplum (veil) and the fruit which I brought forth was the sun". In sculpture she is portrayed seated with an infant in her left arm and in her right hand there is an ear of wheat.

By the 7th century B.C., or earlier, Ishtar was known in Phoenicia as Astarte (Ashtoreth) where she was identified with the god Adonis in a myth which clearly echoes the Babylonian myth of Ishtar and Tammuz. In Greece she was known as Aphrodite and, in Rome, her name was Venus.

The word Adonis (my lord) is a Semitic title which the Phoenicians bestowed upon the sun. Adonis was born of an incestous union between a Syrian king and his daughter, Smyrna (Myrrha), a relationship which recalls that of Ishtar and Tammuz.

9—On the 17th of Sivan, the month of the moon goddess, the Akitu festival was held in Harran, the ancient lunar city of Mesopotamia. In Arbela, however, it fell on the 17th of Elul the month of the goddess Ishtar who was greatly venerated in that city. A festival of the "Mysteries of Babylon" was held there on the 25th day of Sivan. *Enc. of Rel. & Eth.* v. 3, p. 77.
In Jewish tradition the 17th day of Tammuz is associated with the capture of Jerusalem, but was probably derived from a much older festival.

9. *Left: Crisna being nursed by Devaki, a Hindu version of the
virgin mother.
Right: Ishtar with child; an Assyrian representation of the
virgin mother.*

Aphrodite fell deeply in love with the handsome young
god and placed him in care of Proserpine, queen of the
Underworld, who became so enamoured of him that she
refused to give him up. Aphrodite herself descended to the
Underworld to recover her lover but without success. Then
she appealed to Zeus who decreed that Adonis should spend
six months of each year with Aphrodite in the upper world
and a similar period with Proserpine in the Underworld.
He was afterward slain by a boar through the malevolence
of Artemis who, in turn, is also a reflection of Ishtar.

In keeping with the changes in most of the fertility
myths which developed in the west, the character of Aphrodite as an earth or vegetation goddess is emphasized, and
her lunar attributes recede in to the background. Also, the
character of Adonis as a sun god is more clearly revealed
than was that of the earlier Tammuz. The earth is visualized
as the womb in which the seed of all life is germinated by
the warm rays of the sun which thus becomes the great
father as the earth is the great mother. In India this
ancient conception of the sun and earth is still reflected in

the Brahmanic marriage vows wherein the man says to the woman: "I am the sun, thou art the earth, let's wed."

The six months which Adonis spends with Aphrodite represent the six vernal months and festivals were held annually in honor of the lusty young spring sun whose return brought a quickening and renewing of life and energy to the earth.

The time which Adonis spends with Proserpine represents the infertile winter months when the sun dies or drops into the lower or unfavorable signs of the zodiac which typify the Underworld. The killing of the sun god by a boar has been interpreted as an allusion to the fact that the Syrian month Haziran[10] in which the event occurred is derived from the Chaldean word Hazir or Hazira signifying sus, procus, hog. This was the month in which the sun completed its annual course, thus accounting for the story of the young and beautiful Adonis being killed by a boar.

In another sense Adonis is sometimes depicted as a corn spirit, his journey to the Underworld representing the period in which seed lies dormant in the earth before bursting into new life and growth.

At the festivals which were held in Greece and Asia Minor in honor of the death and resurrection of the god, his image was carried in processions, followed by wailing women. At the end of the festival his effigy was generally thrown into the sea or into a spring, and his resurrection was celebrated on the following day. But details of the ceremonies as well as their meaning varied in different localities.

Sir James Frazer states that: "At Alexandria, images of Aphrodite and Adonis were displayed on two couches; beside them were set ripe fruits of all kinds, cakes, plants growing in flower pots and green bowers, twined with anise. The marriage of the lovers was celebrated one day and on the morrow women attired as mourners, with streaming hair and bared breasts, bore the image of the dead Adonis to the seashore and committed it to the waves. Yet they sorrowed not without hope, for they sang that the lost one would come back again. In Sardinia, Sicily, Ca-

---

10—*History of Hindustan,* Thos. Maurice, 1795, v. 1, p. 563.

*10. Left: An Aztec conception of the virgin mother.
From a temple in Yucatan.
Right: The Egyptian conception of the virgin mother:
Isis nursing the infant Horus.*

tania, and other parts of southern Italy, St. John's Day is still celebrated in very much the same way."[11]

"In Sicily, gardens of Adonis are still sown in spring and in summer, from which we may perhaps infer that Sicily, as well as Syria, celebrated of old a vernal festival of the dead and risen god. At the approach of Easter, Sicilian women sow white lentils and canary seed in plates which they keep in the dark and water every two days. The plants soon shoot up; the stalks are tied together with red ribbons and the plates containing them are placed in the sepulchre which, with effigies of the dead Christ, are made up in Catholic and Greek churches on Good Friday, just as the gardens of Adonis were placed on the graves of the dead Adonis. This practice is not confined to Sicily, for it is observed also at Casenza in Calabria and perhaps in other places."

The story of Ishtar and Tammuz also serves as the motif of a Greek myth in which Persephone (Proserpine), the daughter of Ceres, a vegetation goddess, is carried away

11—*The Golden Bough*, Abgd. Ed., Sir James Frazer, p. 344.

by Pluto, god of the Underworld. The enraged mother will not permit vegetation to grow until her daughter is restored to her. Ceres seeks her child with weeping and lamentations, as Ishtar sought Tammuz. By the aid of a pomegranate, Persephone is finally permitted to live part of each year on earth (during the growing season) and to pass the remaining months underground as the consort of her dark captor Pluto.

Closely related to the Adonis-Aphrodite myth was that of Attis or Atys and Cybele, in Phrygia. In some accounts Attis is represented as the son of Cybele, an Asiatic goddess of fertility; in others, he is the son of Nana, a virgin who conceives him by placing an almond or pomegranate in her bosom. The death and re-birth of Attis each year and his connection with the growth of vegetation stamps him as a solar god similar to Adonis.

Again, according to one account he was killed, like Adonis, by a boar; and according to another version, he emasculated himself under a pine tree and bled to death, a circumstance which is thought to account for the custom of priests of Attis mutilating themselves on entering the service of the cult.

In 204 B.C., toward the close of the war with Hannibal, Cybele was adopted in Rome and the orgies of her army of priests shocked the citizens of that sophisticated metropolis.

Cybele is equated with Da-mater, the great mother and Selene, the moon goddess. She was also called (by the Greeks) the Idean mother, or mother Ida. This is the title of the mother of Meru, called in India Idavratta, or the circle, an apparent allusion to the path followed by the sun on its annual journey.

In Ephesus, where the nature cult existed in a most exaggerated form, the goddess Diana or Artemis was honored as the Multimammia "the many breasted mother of all." In sculpture she is often depicted with many breasts covering the front of her body, with animals and plants springing from her head, limbs, and breasts. Sometimes she wears around her waist a girdle of lions, elephants and other animals symbolizing her motherhood of life. Trains of galli, or emasculated men and boys, painted and dressed like women, ministered to the goddess as priests or prostitutes. At Komona in Kappadokia, as the goddess Ma, she

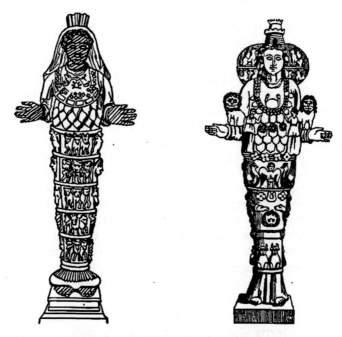

11. Diana of Ephesus, the many-breasted mother of southwest Asia.

was ministered by 6000 eunuch priests and the galli in Phrygia, like those of Ba-al and Ashtoreth, slashed their arms with knives in religious frenzy.

The apparent misuse of the term "virgin" which is applied to Ishtar, Venus, Aphrodite and all of the other great mother goddesses of antiquity is due to the fact that originally the word denoted merely an unmarried woman or maiden. She might even be a prostitute, a term which Ishtar applied to herself. As goddess of generation, she was devoted to loss of chastity and to childbirth, although not to marriage. Unmarried women of the East, whether virgins or prostitutes, wore veils to indicate their unmarried status and when Isis is made to say that no man has lifted her veil she means that she has never been a party to a marriage ceremony.

The hierodouloi or sacred prostitutes who served in the temples of the mother goddesses were likewise called "holy virgins." In Greece, children who were born of unmarried mothers were called parthenoi or "virgin born". Some modern writers are inclined to believe that the traditional virgin birth of Jesus was founded upon a mistranslation of the Greek word "almah", (virgin), meaning a maiden or unmarried woman.[12]

The custom of applying the term "virgin" to the mother goddesses may be traced back to the period when they were more specifically indentified with the moon, which fact may explain why they were represented as virgins. Marriage signifies a lasting union; and as the sun and moon appear to wander eternally through the heavens, widely separated by time and space, they cannot be represented as permanently united. The only time they may be said to meet is during the brief periods when they are in conjunction. This conjunction might, however, be interpreted poetically as a temporary mating, or as a brief tryst between lovers, for such they always remained. So, the moon goddess passed down the centuries as the Great Mother Goddess, who created and ruled all life on earth, yet was never a bride.

In Egypt she was known as Isis, "the nurse", or "the mother"; in India she was Devaki; in Phrygia, Artemis, the "child bearer"; in Carthage she was Tanit; in China, Ching Mon. In Syria she appeared as half human and half fish, under the name of Attar or Athar, and in Lebanon her name was Atergatis. She had traits in common with Demeter, with Hecate, as goddess of the moon (harvest), and with Rhea, goddess of the earth. Her name varied in different times and places but her character remained essentially the same.

In his Metamorphosis, written in the 2nd century A. D., Lucius Apuleius, an initiate into the Egyptian Mysteries, shows that in his day the character of the lunar goddess was the same as it had been centuries before. Writing of the appearance of the goddess to him in a vision, he quotes her as saying:

"Behold Lucius, I am come; Thy weeping and prayer hath moved me to succour thee. I am she that is the natural mother of all things; mistress and governess of all elements; the initial progenitor of worlds; chief of the powers divine; queen of all that are in hell; the principal of them that dwell in heaven, manifested alone and under one form of all

---

12—The correct Latin for virgin is not "virgo" but "virgo intacta." In Hebrew, it would have been more appropriate to use the word "Bethula" for virgin.

the gods and goddesses. At my will the planets in the sky, the wholesome winds of the seas and the lamentable silences of hell be disposed; my name, my divinity is adored throughout all the world in divers manners and in variable customs and by many names. For the Phrygians that are the first of all men call me the Mother of the Gods at Pessinus, the Athenians which are sprung from their own soil, Cecropian Minerva; the Cyprians which are girt by the sea, Paphian Venus; the Cretans which bear arrows, Dictynnian Diana; the Sicilians which speak three tongues, infernal Proserpine; the Eleusians, their ancient goddess Ceres; some June, other Bellona, other Hecate, other Rhamnusia and principally both sort of the Ethiopians which dwell in the Orient and are enlightened by the morning rays of the sun and the Egyptians which are excellent in all kind of ancient doctrine and by their proper ceremonies accustom to worship me, do call me by my true name, Queen Isis."[13]

Proclus, writing in the 5th century, on the Timaeus of Plato, states that the "moon is the cause of nature in mortals and the self conspicuous image of fontal nature."

A distinctive feature of the mother goddesses is their frequent identification with names derived from the root Ma, which in Greek means mother or nurse. Ma is a title of the goddess Bhavani, the Venus of India; Ma or Mah was the name of one of the earliest Sumerian goddesses and was also the title of the great Multimammia of southwest Asia. Mah or Mas is the Persian for moon, and, in the form of Maia, was a name which the Greeks applied to Demeter. In India, the fire god Agni is the offspring of Maya who represents motherhood and creation, being similar to Maria (Maera), who was the wife of the sun god Hephaistos, according to Pausanius. Among the Persians she is the mother of the god Mithra.

According to the Hindus, their goddess Maya Durga denotes "inaccessible" or "non-realizable" or illusion. All existence is ultimately resolved into Brahma and Maya, being and appearance, reality and illusion.

As the mother of Adonis, the name Ma becomes Myrrha. In Arabic it becomes Mizram or Mizraim and is the same

---

13—*The Golden Ass*, being the Metamorphosis of Lucius Apuleius, translated by W. Adlington, 1566. Revised by S. Gaselee, 1928.

as Miriam, the sister of Moses. The names Miriam, Maera, Maria and Mary, the mother of Christ, are all the same.

It may be further recalled that according to myths of the ancient Sumerians, all life on earth derived from Ishtar, daughter of the god Ea, who rose from the ocean each day. Like Ea, Ishtar, the moon goddess, also rose out of the sea, her name probably signifying the star which seemed to rise from the ocean.

Aphrodite was said to have risen from the sea and she was often portrayed rising from the waves or sailing on a sea shell. Venus was frequently called Stella Maris, "star of the sea", and one of the ancient meanings of the name Mary was "star of the sea", for which reason the Virgin Mary was often affectionately called Stella Maris.

The August festival in honor of Ishtar's Descent was paralleled in Greece and Rome by festivals of the Passage of the Virgin on August 13th when the aid of Artemis and Diana was invoked to prevent storms which might injure the maturing harvests. This festival was changed in the 6th century A.D. by the Roman Church to the Feast of the Assumption of the Virgin Mary on August 15th. As in the case of all festivals in honor of pagan gods, the date was of astronomical significance. In the Roman calendar of Columella, August 15th marked the disappearance of the zodiacal constellation of the Virgin. With the Greeks that day was fixed as the day of the Assumption of the Blessed Virgin Astrea or her union with the sun.

During this period the sun passed through the constellation of the Virgin and the bright rays of the sun made the stars of the constellation invisible to the eye. In the Book of Numbers it is related that Miriam was excluded from the Israelite camp and not allowed to show her white, leprous face for seven days, and some writers interpret the account of this incident as an allegory comparable to the period in which the celestial virgin cannot be seen. It is three weeks before the sun makes sufficient progress through the sign of Virgo to enable that constellation to be seen by the unaided eye emerging from the other side. In church calendars this day, September 8th, is devoted to the Nativity of the Blessed Virgin.

At the time of the equinox in March, the Virgin was honored with a festival which originally belonged to Tam-·

muz as the springtime sun. At this time, crescent-shaped cakes or buns were eaten in honor of the goddess just as Christians today eat hot cross buns on Good Friday. In Phrygia the festival was held at the same time in honor of Attis; in Greece and Rome the day was dedicated to Cybele and called Hilaria because of the joy occasioned by the return of the warm rays of the sun at the spring equinox. Later the Roman Church changed the festival to Our Lady Day or Day of the Blessed Virgin.

The baking and eating of cakes at this season in the form of the crescent moon and often containing a cross or representation of the virgin goddess is one of the oldest customs known.

IV

LUNAR AND SOLAR MYTHS

IN ADDITION TO THE myths derived from the ancient belief that the moon was a Generator of Life, Goddess of Motherhood and Regulator of Fate, the moon was the subject of another type of myth in which her monthly changes were thought to be the result of a conflict between deities. It was a contest between the god of light, or the Overworld, and the god of darkness, or the Underworld, in which each contestant triumphed in turn over the other. With the growth of sun worship, the myths which were based upon this theme began to partake of a solar character.

The underlying motifs of the light and darkness myths were growth and decay, life and death, day and night, summer and winter, which seemed to constitute systems of pairs or opposites by which all life and activity in the universe was maintained in a state of balance by the opposition of natural forces.

The mother goddess cults generally deteriorated gradually into sex worship and finally passed from the world's stage, leaving only a mass of myths and superstitions, but the light-darkness myths contained the germ from which developed the great "ethic" religions which now for upwards of 2500 years have played a great part in molding civilization.

The principal feature which distinguished the Light-Darkness stories from religious parables was that they did not convey any moral or deal with good and evil in the modern sense. There was no Heaven or Hell, no future reward for a good life or punishment for an evil one. The myths were simply allegories of the various aspects of the sun and the moon.

Although the earliest known records of the Egyptians show that they believed in reincarnation, a future life was not given as a reward for a good life. The only requirement was that the individual should have appeased the gods with the customary gifts, prayers, and sacrifices. Displeasure of the gods brought punishment, not in the future, but here on earth, in the form of illness, disease, famine, hardship, and poverty.

The Babylonian Underworld was not a place for punishment of sinners but was a cold, gray cavern where the dead, both good and bad, sat around silently until the end of time. It was the product of a philosophy of life similar to that in Isaiah 22:13 which says, "Let us eat and be merry for tomorrow we must die," or the cynical philosophy of Ecclesiastes: "Yea, though he live a thousand years twice told, yet hath he seen no good: *do not all go to the one place?*" (Eccl. 6:6)[1] "Never", said Euripides, "is the good separated from the evil; there must be a mixture of the one and the other."

Light was not in itself a complete entity: it required the Darkness to make it whole, just as the male required the female. As a positive current of electricity is without force unless accompanied by a negative current, so, in early times, the god or power of Light was considered incomplete without the power of Darkness to give it contrast, opposition, force, and completeness.

Opposition or apparent conflict between the ascending and descending phases of the moon provided the underlying motif for the story of the Two Brothers, called the "parted", which, in various forms, is found in mythology all over the world. In the zodiac they are thought to be represented as Gemini, the Twins. In China they appear as Oph and Shichim; in India they are Cristna and Balarama; in Egypt, Sut and Horus. Some students of comparative religion see similar motifs in the conflicts between Abel and Cain and Jacob and Esau.

The descending half of the moon was often depicted as the Dark One, the Deceiver. In another type of myth, the descending moon becomes the Manifester, the Precursor or the sacrificial type and the ascending half is portrayed as the Bringer of Light, the Savior or Redeemer. The full moon is, of course, the Virgin Mother, the Queen of Heaven.

In Egyptian mythology, the ascending phase of the moon as the reflector of the sun's light is represented by the god Horus who is portrayed as the Eye of the Sun. The dark phase is caused by Sut, the demon of Darkness, who steals or wounds the Eye of Horus. On ancient monuments he is shown with the head of a jackal, which fact proclaims him as the night prowler and the thief of light.

Plutarch said that "the festival in honor of the sun was

1—See also *Eccl.* 9:2; 9:5; 2:24; 3:12,13; 5:18; 8:15; 9:7,9.

held on the 30th day of Epiphi, called 'the birthday of Horus's eyes', when the sun and moon were supposed to be in the same right line with the earth".

To ancient Hindus, the sun was the Eye of Varuna and Agni; to Persians, the Eye of Ahura Mazda; to Greeks, it was the Eye of Zeus; and Macrobius said it was the Eye of Jove. Early Teutons regarded it as the Eye of Wotan or Woden, and in Java and Sumatra the sun is called Mata-ari, "the eye of day".[2]

The moon at full is the mirror of light; hence it is sometimes depicted as the mother or reproducer of the sun's light and becomes his consort during the hours of night when the sun is invisible or is in the Underworld. In thus reproducing the light of the sun, she is represented as being the mother of his child. The Egyptian lunar god Taht or Khensu is sometimes pictured with the Eye of Horus, or the new moon, in his hand and the goddess Meri bears the eye upon her head as typical reproducer of the child, the "Bringer of Light".

The lore of many primitive peoples contain countless myths of this nature which appear without meaning until examined from the standpoint of sun or moon mythology. An example is found in old traditions that the Egyptian Sut-Horus, the Hindu Buddha and the Christian Jesus, were all born from the side of their mothers. Again, in the case of both Indra and Jesus, the growing embryo was said to be visible whilst in the mother's womb, which was represented as being transparent. The child Jesus was so represented in Christian pictures of the enciente Virgin Mary.

As these legends are based upon a physiological absurdity, their origin is inexplicable until compared with lunar phenomena. Then, it becomes apparent that the legends had their origin in the passing of the moon from the full to the dark phase, when the round orb decreases in thickness until it assumes the thin crescent shape. As the light portion of the moon decreases, the dark area increases or seems to grow in size; also, due to the reflection of light from the earth's surface, the dark area is dimly visible to the eye. This is the dark little one developing in the womb of its mother, the birth taking place from the side.

2—*Primitive Culture*, Tylor, v. 1, p. 350.

In Hindu legends, Cristna is depicted as having been torn from his mother by a single black hair; and Balarama was similarly torn from his mother by a single white hair. This legend is explained by the fact that as the moon begins to wane, a thin rim of shadow appears on the right side. This may be likened to a single black hair, while, in the transition from dark to light phase, the first thin arc or rim of light may be likened to a single white hair.

One of the titles bestowed upon Ishtar is Goddess Fifteen, because in a solar month of 30 days, the journey of the moon may be said to consist of 15 steps upward and 15 downward. The authors of the apocryphal Gospels of Matthew[3] made this phenomenon the basis of a fable about the Virgin Mary, thus proving that the Babylonian myths were known in Judea at the beginning of the Christian era and that some gospel writers were not averse to using them to their own ends.

It is stated that when the Virgin was a three-year-old infant, just weaned, she was taken by her parents with offerings "therewith to the temple according to the Psalm of degrees, fifteen stairs to ascend". There, according to the Gospel,[4] the infant Virgin readily ascended the steps unaided like an adult.

Another version of this story is repeated in *Protevangelion*,[5] where it is said that when the Virgin was nine months old her mother placed her on the ground and "when she had walked nine steps, she came again to her mother's lap". A similar legend of the infant Buddha credits him with taking a step in each of the four cardinal directions shortly after birth.

In another place it is said that when Mary was three years old her father and mother took her to the temple where she was received and blessed by the high priest and "he placed her upon the third step of the altar and the Lord gave her grace and she danced with her feet and all the house of Israel loved her".[6]

3—In the early years of Christianity there existed a great number of gospels some of which were held in the same esteem as the present Gospels. Many of these were declared Apocryphal or Pseudepigraphical at the Council of Nice and others were eliminated during the Protestant Reformation.

4—*Pseudo-Matthew*, c. 4, v. 20.

5—*Protevangelion*, c. 6, v. 1.

6—*Ibid*, c. 7, v. 5.

That early writers were in the habit of taking an old myth and adapting it, or parts of it, to new uses is illustrated by a Greek myth which relates that Hephaistos ascended from the Underworld riding on an ass or swine, which he made drunk before directing him up to heaven. In the apocryphal Gosepl of James, the author represents the Virgin Mary as riding on an ass when Joseph saw her laughing on one side of her face and crying on the other, probably to identify her with the light and dark phases of the moon. She is lifted from the ass and gives birth to the child of light in a cave.

One type of myth frequently found in Babylonian and Egyptian literature introduces a figure which symbolizes evil in every part of the world. Here the gradual disappearance of the moon in the last half is represented as being due to its being swallowed by a serpent. In sun worship the serpent becomes a water dragon or crocodile which swallows the setting sun as it sinks into the sea.

During eclipses the Chinese rent the air with cymbals, trumpets, and clanging instruments to frighten away the dragon which they believed was swallowing the moon.[7] It was from this superstition that the ascending node of the moon was called "the head of the dragon" and the descending node became known as "the tail of the dragon". In India there is a myth which tells how Vritra or Ahi, the serpent of night, was vanquished by Indra, a great sun god. This myth may allude to the bright light of the sun overcoming the constellation of the Dragon in the northern heavens.

In Australia and in some parts of North America the role of the serpent was taken by a great frog. In Egypt it was the great god Apep which battled with Ra and Horus, both solar heroes. In the Babylonian Epic of Creation the sun hero Bel-Merodach (Marduk) slays the monster Tiamat (chaos and darkness) in a battle in which Bel turns against the open-mouthed dragon a wind storm of such violence that the wind filled its belly and "its belly was stricken through".

Many centuries later the same story was incorporated into the Jewish writings as a historical incident in the life of Daniel. According to this story, the King of Babylonia

---

7—The Chinese word for eclipse means "eat".

had a great dragon which Daniel slew by throwing down the throat of the monster, a fire-ball composed of pitch, causing the animal to burst and die. In the Aramaic language used by Daniel, the word for windstorm reads almost the same as the Babylonian word for pitch, so, in the Biblical version one interpretation of the word was merely substituted for the other.

In the Egyptian Book of the Dead, the power of Darkness is frequently portrayed as a black jackal, fox, or other predatory animal and disappearance of the moon is pictured as due to its being gradually devoured by this evil animal. Eclipses were widely believed to be due to the sun or moon being swallowed by a dragon or jackal. Primitive people in many countries threw stones at the moon or sun in an effort to frighten the devourer away. This practice has been observed by travelers among primitive people in modern times. In ancient Rome, when it was believed, during an eclipse, that the moon was being swallowed, the people shouted "vince luna" to encourage her. In many parts of the world, especially in Scandinavian countries, the devourer is often pictured as a wolf.

In Greek mythology the story of Kronos tearing Uranus into fourteen pieces is but another version of the gradual dismemberment of the moon during the fourteen days of its waning period.

The same motif is also found in an Egyptian myth related by Plutarch wherein Typhon (Darkness), the Evil One, while hunting at night, finds the dead body of the sun god Osiris (Light) prepared for burial and, fearing that in a future life Osiris might again appear to destroy him, tears the body into fourteen pieces and scatters them far and wide. Isis, the consort of Osiris, travels from country to country to find her slain lover. In her wanderings she is followed by scorpions, a feature which betrays the zodiacal character of the story for the star Sothis is the star of Isis, and in the zodiac it is followed by the constellation of Scorpion. Isis finds and assembles the pieces of Osiris's corpse, but cannot restore life to the body because she is unable to find one part, the organ of generation.

The story of Isis wandering in search of her lover follows the pattern of Ishtar's search for Tammuz. Like that of many other gods, the character of Osiris is a hybrid one. In many respects he appears to be a sun god, yet he is the patron deity of agriculture and in many aspects is a corn spirit, while his reign of twenty-eight years and the manner of his death indicates that at one time he was probably a moon god.

During the annual festival of lamentation for the death of Osiris the priests poured out libations of milk each day from 360 vases to denote the days of the primitive year in which the sun pursued its course. At Acanthe, near Memphis, on the Lybian side of the Nile, an annual memorial feast was held in which 360 priests carried water from the Nile and poured the water into a large reservoir, perforated at the bottom, thus symbolizing the days of the year and the ceaseless lapse of irrevocable time.[8]

Osiris died on the seventeenth day of the month Athyr (i.e., in the waning moon), when the sun entered the lower signs of the zodiac which symbolized the Underworld. On the nineteenth of the month the priests proclaimed that Osiris was found. According to the mythic mode of representing the phenomenon, the absence of moonlight for about three days between old and new moon was due to the lord of light in the lunar orb having been swallowed by a monster dragon, or fish, and remaining in its belly for three days.

In the Babylonian pantheon, the water god Ea ruled over the slimy waters of the great "deep" out of which the world was formed. In token of this tradition, a large basin of water was kept in all Babylonian temples. Ancient myths represent Ea as being a friendly deity who rose out of the sea each morning to teach man agriculture, civil government, handcrafts, and other arts of civilization. In early sculpture he is portrayed as half man and half fish and was probably the original Aquarius, the water man in the zodiac, as well as the forerunner of Neptune.

In later versions, Ea appears as Ioannes and, as the fish god Dagon, he was worshiped by the Philistines. According to some interpretations, Ea or Ioannes represented a primeval sun god who spread his benefactions over the earth and, at the close of day, dropped into the sea to spend the night beneath the waves like a fish.

In Hindu Brahmanism, the god Vishnu, in his first incarnation, is alleged to have appeared to humanity in the form of a fish, or half man and half fish, exactly the same

---

8—*Indian Antiquities*, by Thos. Maurice, v. 6, p. 143.

12. *Vishnu as the Matsya or fish Avatar. In India
he is represented as a fish and as being swallowed
by a fish.*

as Ioannes or Dagon was represented among the Chaldeans
and other peoples. In the Indian version, Manu, the Hindu
Noah, was saved by Vishnu who, in the form of a fish,
dragged Manu's boat to the top of a rock. Davkina, the
consort of Vishnu, seems to be the same as Dav-ki or
Damkina, the consort of Ea.

The Greek myth of Hercules and Hesione describes
the slaying of darkness by the sun god. It relates that after
King Laomedon of Troy had bound his daughter Hesione
to rocks by the sea, a sacrifice to Poseidon's destroying
monster (darkness), Hercules (the sun), saved the maiden
by leaping fully armed into the fish's gaping throat and
cutting his way through the monster's belly. The rescue
of Andromeda by Perseus is another version of the same myth.

The story of Jonah being swallowed by a whale and
then thrown on the shore at Joppa, after three days in its
belly, contains several elements which connect it with the
story of Hercules and Hesione. It may also be compared

with Oannes being swallowed by Tiamat, the dragon of darkness, at the time of the winter solstice.

In early Christian centuries, a Greek sculpture of Andromeda's monster was used as a model for Jonah's whale. In Pliny's time, the remains of Andromeda's chains were exhibited on a rock along the shore at Joppa and the bones of a whale were taken to Rome as relics of the monster.[9]

Several other features in the story of Jonah's escape from the belly of a whale point to the mythical origin of the story. After his escape, Jonah went to Nineveh and there told the story. One of the emblems of Nineveh, the capitol of Assyria, was a fish in a basin of water. Sallimannu, "the god of peace", was depicted as a fish god of the city Temen-Sallim, "the foundation of peace". According to Sayce, the royal scribe of Sadikan, now Arbon on the Khabur, was named Sallimannu-nunu-ilani, "Salamannu the fish god is king of the gods".

The name of King Solomon, "the peaceful one", is so familiar in sound and meaning to that of the fish god Salamannu that some writers have suspected the story of Solomon was drawn from a far older source than has been attributed to it. The brazen bowl mounted on twelve bulls which was found in Solomon's temple may have had the same significance as the fish basin in Nineveh. Every Greek temple had a basin at its entrance for the holy water of the fishes and there is a basin of water, called Piscina, in the entrance of every Catholic church.

In the Vedas, the sacred books of the Hindus, the earth is represented as a huge fish which swallows the red sun at the end of day and casts him out again at sunrise, just as the whale cast out Jonah. In Polynesian mythology, the earth is frequently pictured as a huge fish. (See Tylor, *Early History of Mankind*, p. 345).

The story of Jason and his companions sailing away in the ship Argo in search of the Golden Fleece is another type of solar allegory. Jason's 50 companions (some writers say 52) on his travels were drawn from the 50 or 52 weeks of the year in which the sun pursues his celestial course. The Golden Fleece which Jason sought may be an allusion to the fleecy, golden clouds at sunset.

9—*Primitive Culture*, Tylor, v. 1, p. 333.

Clouds are also allegorized as celestial cows and a myth relates that Hermes stole the "cloud cows" of Apollo on the day of his divine birth. In the Rig Veda clouds are called "the cows of Indra".

The numbering of Jason's companions after the weeks in the year is rather similar to a myth of the sun god Helios in which he is said to have had 350 head of cattle (7 herds of 50 each). Likewise, in the Veda, the sun god is blessed with 720 twin children, i.e. 360 days and 360 nights and his chariot is drawn by 7 horses, i.e. the 7 days of the week.

The Biblical account in which 365 kings minister to Nimrod is thought to stamp him as a solar character. Of Enoch it is related that, like the sun gods, he lived 365 years and was a builder of cities. It is not related that Enoch ever died, but "Enoch walked away with Elohim and was no more" (to be seen). Ascensions to heaven are generally acknowledged to be characteristic features of solar myths.

It is said (Gen. 14:14) that Abraham enlisted his 318 trained servants to fight against the Elamites. In the 354-day lunar calendar the moon was considered to be visible on 318 days and this fact has led some writers to suspect that the 318 soldiers who helped Abraham destroy his enemies were the 318 moonlit nights of the year. Attention has also been drawn to the coincidence that at the first Council of the Roman Church, held at Nicea in 325 A.D. there were 318 bishops present.

In some of the Light-Darkness myths night is portrayed as a lustful female who swoops down upon, overcomes or ravishes the sun and saps his energy at the end of day. In others the goddess of dawn is pursued and overcome by the rapidly advancing rays of the morning sun. In the Rig-Veda, a hymn says of Ushas, goddess of dawn, that "she bares her bosom" to entice the sun god to pursue her. Elsewhere, it is said, of the overcoming of dawn by the sun, that "Prajapati loves his own daughter and forces her."

From myths, which represented the setting sun as being devoured by a reptile, there developed another type in which the heroes were pitted against great bulls, dragons or other monsters representing the dark powers of nature. The myths of Zeus, Apollo, Helios, Orion, Kronos, Siegfried, St. George, Hercules, all contain this motif.

As early as the fifth century B.C., Pausanius observed that the Twelve Labors of Hercules represented the annual passage of the sun through the twelve signs of the zodiac. His opinion was supported by the Scholiast of Hesiod which says that "the zodiac in which the sun accomplishes its annual course is the *real career* of Hercules".

The frequent identification of sun gods with goddesses who symbolize fruitfulness and productivity is exemplified by the association of Hercules with Omphales, a goddess of procreation, and with Iole, the daughter of Eurytos, "the copious flowing", a goddess of procreation who is fructified by the heat of the sun.

In another myth, Hercules marries Hebe, a goddess who renews her youth each year. This story was probably inspired by an old legend that the sun (Hercules) renews his strength at the end of each annual journey.

In 1773 Semler stated that the Biblical Samson is, like Hercules, a hero of the sun type and this fact is now recognized by practically all Biblical authorities. He is from the tribe of Dan which means "judge", a title which is often bestowed upon the sun god Shamash. The name Shimsohn (Samson) means "little sun". Although the name identifies him as a solar type, the story of his exploits has many lunar characteristics, a peculiarity which is to be found repeatedly in the adventures of mythical solar heroes.

Another characteristic of solar myths is the miraculous birth of the sun god by a virgin goddess and the account of Samson is, at least, partly in harmony with this tradition. It is related in the Book of Judges (13:3) that an angel appeared before Samson's barren mother and informed her that she would conceive a man child who would be consecrated a Nazarite or holy man. Manoah,[10] the name of Samson's father, is related, cabalistically, to Jahveh and is mentioned several times, but the name of the mother seems to·be withheld intentionally. In the story's earliest, most primitive, form. the mother was probably represented as a virgin goddess. If so, her name was eliminated centuries later, when the story was placed in the Scriptures.

The character of the Samson story is further indicated

10—The name Manoach has a numerical value of 104, which is 4 times 26, the number of Jahveh. See chapter on the Cabala.

13. Marduk in combat with a dragon. From a cylinder seal.

by the fact that all of the central figures in the Hebrew sacred writings from Abraham to Moses were miraculously born. Sarah, Rebekah and Rachel are represented as having been barren and, before the births of Isaac, Jacob and Joseph, an angel appeared before the women and informed each one, in almost identical language, that she would conceive and bear a child. The same story is repeated again in the case of Samuel's birth.

The close connection between some of the feats of Samson and those of Hercules again illustrates the manner in which the adventures of mythical heroes find their way from country to country under different names and guises. The first Labor of Hercules was the killing of a lion, which represented the passage of the sun through the zodiacal sign of Leo. The first feat of Samson was also the killing of a lion. Hercules carried away the gates of Cadiz and Samson did the same thing with the gates of Gaza.

The death of Hercules at Cadiz was an astronomical allegory representing the end of the year, when the sun reached the most westerly point in its annual journey at the time of the winter solstice, in the sign of Capricorn. (See Death and Re-Birth of the Sun Gods). The gateway of the sun was considered by ancient astronomers to be between Capricorn and Cancer, from which the Tropics are named. The gateway was marked by pillars which, according to the myth, stood at the Straits of Gibraltar.[11]

Samson started for Gaza at midnight and did not sleep until morning, which is a lunar characteristic.[12] His death occurred under the pillars which supported a banquet hall in Gaza where a feast was being held in honor of the fish god, Dagon. According to Sir William Drummond, Gaza signifies a goat, the zodiacal sign of Capricorn.[13]

As the Samson story is given in the Book of Judges, he is accompanied on his adventures by 30 companions; he slays 30 men at Ascalon and takes from them 30 changes of clothing, the repeated use of 30 coinciding with the 30 days of the solar month.

When Delilah asks Samson the source of his strength, he tells her that if he is bound with 7 new bow strings, his strength will depart although, when she so binds him, he breaks the strings with ease. Then Delilah binds him with 7 new ropes which also fail to hold him. Next, Samson confesses to her that if his 7 locks of hair are shorn, all of his strength will surely vanish. The story does not speak of an indefinite number of locks; there are 7, no more, no less. Similar stories which tell of the sun being bound by ropes or being retarded in its course are to be found in many lands.

If the story of Samson is read merely as a simple narrative it appears preposterous for it cannot be imagined that Samson would deliver himself into the hands of an intriguing enemy female and tell her how he could be rendered defenseless. It acquires meaning and significance only when considered as a lunar-solar myth. The 7 bow strings then represent the first 7 days of the new moon when it is increasing in vigor and power. Next, the 7 ropes are broken, making in all 14 bindings which fail to hold him. The number 14 indicates the number of days which bring both the moon and Samson to the peak of their power. When the moon is full, the powers of Light have overcome the powers of Darkness, the "Philistines".

11—The Phoenicians settled a colony upon the Straits of Gibraltar at Gadis or Gades, on the western coast of Andalusia, which is the modern Spanish city of Cadiz. According to tradition, there was at Cadiz, in ancient times, a statue of Hercules with a gate on his shoulder.

12—Jud. 11:37,38,39.

13—*OEdipus Judaicus*, Sir Wm. Drummond, p. 360.

But, as soon as the moon passes the full, the dark forces renew the attack and this time are successful because the moon begins to become emaciated and lose strength in the 7 days of the moon's third quarter, symbolized by Samson's loss of the 7 locks of hair.

In the final period, the fourth quarter, the powers of Darkness are in control and the moon is deprived of its light. In like manner, Samson, deprived of his strength, is seized by his enemies who bind him, put out his eyes, and thrust him into a dungeon. But, knowing that the moon will rise again to renew the contest, the authors of the legend, in order to maintain a consistent parallel, inform us that Samson's hair immediately began to grow again, intimating that he would soon be ready to renew the battle.

Luxuriant hair and tremendous strength are symbolic of the productivity of the sun god in summer. Loss of the sun god's hair often symbolizes the winter season, when trees lose their foliage. The earth, on whom the sun pours his fructifying warmth, is the lustful female who saps his vitality, so, when the growing season is over, the sun becomes a weak old man, bound and blind. In the Greek myth of OEdipus, which is somewhat similar to the story of Samson, the unfortunate hero tears out his eyes near the end of his career, the loss of his sight representing the declining period of the sun when the clouds of darkness are closing around him.

Again, like Hercules, Samson is identified with three women, only the name of Delilah being given. Her role of destroyer of manly vigor seems to be indicated by her name which means "longing, languishing", and which may be construed as conveying a sense of weakening or drooping. In this respect her character is comparable to that of Ishtar in the Gilgamesh Epic. In an incident in which Ishtar asks the sun god to be her lover, he charges her with being an enchantress, poisoner, and destroyer of male potency very much as folklore continues to represent the moon at the present time.

Gilgamesh accuses Ishtar of witchcraft, criticizes her for her murderous lust and merciless cruelty and declines to become her consort. She becomes enraged and connives to have Gilgamesh destroyed, but is unsuccessful.

The myths of Ishtar's plotting against Gilgamesh and Delilah's betrayal of Samson employ one of the most popular and widely used themes in all literature; the vindictiveness of the woman who is spurned by the man to whom she has offered her charms. This theme appears in the story of Joseph and Potiphar's wife. Because he refused to accept her invitations, she reported that he had made improper advances to her. The Egyptian Book of the Dead and other early records contain many versions of this story, indicating that in ancient times it was as popular in literature as it is today.

The Babylonian Epic of Creation

(The Seven Tablets of Creation)

This poem, called *enuma elis la nuba samamu,* gets its name from the first words meaning "When on high the heavens were not named." The first fragments of the poem were found in Assurbanipal's library in 1873 by George Smith and are believed to have been adapted somewhat earlier than 2000 B.C. from mythological conceptions of a far older period.

The epic is thought to symbolize the triumph of the springtime sun over the storms of winter or the light of day over the darkness of night. It was probably written for the purpose of glorifying the local god of Babylon, raising him above the older Sumerian gods when Babylon became the political center of Babylonia during the first Hammurabic Dynasty. It reveals how the priests and politicians of Babylonia contrived to alter the ancient pantheon of gods for political purposes. But the particular interest which the poem holds for modern readers is due to an account woven into it of the creation of the universe, which account is strikingly similar to the Biblical story of creation.

The epic begins before creation when the universe consisted of a vast waste of slimy water. Heaven and earth were as yet non-existent, nor had the waters of the bottomless abyss been divided into lake, sea, and river. First, there is the creation of the primeval gods Apsu, Tiamat and Mummu. Then the gods Lahmu and Lahamu, meaning sea serpent, are formed. After many ages, the male god Anshar (host of heaven) and the female Kishar (host of earth) are created. From them are born Anu, Bel, and Ea.

Apsu, Tiamat, and Mummu become resentful of the latter gods and conspire to destroy them; but, after a great

14. Enkidu in combat with the bull of heaven, with Ishtar
watching the fght.

war, all the conspirators are killed except Tiamat, who creates 11 monstrous animals for her protection.

Anu, Bel, and Ea then urge the sun god Marduk to take up the task of destroying Tiamat (the deep), now believed to have represented the Persian Gulf, symbolizing darkness and chaos. Marduk agrees only after he has exacted a promise that, if he is successful, he shall be made supreme ruler of the universe.

The fourth tablet describes the sun god going forth in his chariot to battle with Tiamat. After a terrific struggle, he catches her in his net, kills her with an arrow and splits her carcass in two parts "like a shellfish" and from them makes heaven and earth. He binds her auxiliaries with cords and seizes the tablets of life. He draws off her skin and commands the watchmen to prevent her waters from escaping. Then the skin is stretched and placed as a canopy in heaven, separating the waters of heaven from those of the earth and stars are placed in the heavens as dwelling places of the gods, Anu, Bel, and Ea.

Only 25 lines of the fifth tablet were recovered. It describes how Marduk placed the lights in the heavens and ordained their regular courses, placed the 11 monsters in the heavens as constellations of the zodiac as stations for the gods, divided the year into seasons and placed 3 stars in the heavens to mark each month. He placed his own star in the sky as the star Sirius, the chief light of the firmament; he then caused the moon to shine forth to rule the night, granting it a day of rest in the middle of the month (that is, at the full moon) and made the sun to rule the day.

It describes how the wind blew the blood of Tiamat away to secret places, presumably indicating that it formed the Red Sea. There is a break in the tablet here, but it appears that Marduk placed his net in the sky as a constellation along with his bow, as the Bowstar or Canis Major, the bow of the hunter Orion. The winds are tamed, bound, and placed in the four points of the compass. The tablet ends with a hymn of praise to Marduk which credits him with separating the sea from the land and of creating the vegetable world.

In the sixth tablet, the gods marvel at the accomplishment of Marduk but complain that there exists no one to pay them honor. Marduk then slays Kingu and from his blood a man is formed. The gods of heaven, earth, and lower regions are assigned their several functions. He places 300 of them in the heaven, 300 to manage the ways of the earth, and 50 for the lower regions. Then begins the construction of Marduk's temple at Esagila. After the temple is completed the gods hold a great banquet. They next draft the laws and the fates of men for the coming year are decided by "the 7 gods of fates". The poem closes with the gods in the temple reciting the 50 names of Marduk.

Excavations at Ashur, in Assyria, have made considerable contributions toward completion of the text, but the fifth tablet is still a fragment. Most of the sixth tablet indicates that it was used as a liturgy in connection with the great New Year's festival celebrated annually at Babylon on the first 11 days of Nisan, at the spring equinox, when it was customary for all the gods of Babylonia to be brought in their sacred boats to assemble in Ubshukkim, the Hall of Fates in Marduk's temple. At that time a number of festivals were held, including mystery plays based upon events in the poem. Only a few details of the rituals have been preserved.

The creation of heaven and earth, the division of the waters under the firmament from the waters above the firmament, the placing of stars and planets as lights in the heaven, the division of the days and seasons of the year, the creation of the vegetable world, the making of man on the sixth day and completion of the labor on the sixth day so completely parallel the Biblical version of creation that there can be no doubt the authors of the Book of Genesis were familiar with the Babylonian story and adapted it to fit their own purpose.

The term used in the Jewish manuscripts for firmament means "what is spread out". This description corresponds with the manner in which Marduk stretched the skin of Tiamat over the heaven.

Tiamat, who is used here as a symbol of the chaos and darkness which prevailed before creation, is comparable to the Biblical expression *T'hom* (Gen. 1:2) meaning "the deep". Apsu the consort of Tiamat seems to have been represented originally as the mother of Ea, the god of primeval water. The son and messenger of Apsu and Tiamat is Mummu, meaning "intelligence". The Bible says that "In the beginning" God created the earth, but the Jerusalem Targum says "By His Wisdom", which is the attribute of Mummu.

The large basins of water in Babylonian temples were called "Apsu". These, presumably, symbolize the waste of waters which, according to Babylonian traditions, was the original source of all earthly life and, in this sense, Apsu, the mother of Ea, personified the universal female principle.

In Solomon's temple there was also a basin of "molten brass",[14] the meaning or purpose of which is nowhere mentioned in the Bible, but which seems to have had the same significance as the Babylonian Apsu.

Gilgamesh Epic

Several ancient Babylonian versions of the Deluge have been discovered within the last century, the one best known being that given in the Gilgamesh Epic. It contains two separate narratives, the first being a solar myth portraying in allegorical form the annual course of the sun, rising to its full strength daily at noon and annually at the beginning of summer and sinking gradually to the western horizon to return, in due time, to the abodes of man. It is written on 12 tablets symbolizing the 12 months of the year. The story of the Deluge is contained in the second part and is

14—See *I Kings* 7:23, *II Kings* 25:13, 16,17, and *Jer.* 52:17.

of but minor importance in the poem, which is thought to
date from about 2000 B.C.

Gilgamesh, the hero of the story, is represented as a
king of Erech, a city of Sumeria. He is now thought to
have been a historical character who ruled as the fourth
king of the first dynasty of Erech in about 4500 B.C.

In the first tablet the goddess Aruru creates a kind
of "wild man of the woods" named Engidu to act as a
rival to Gilgamesh whose power and tyranny have begun
to be a burden to the people. In order to get Engidu away
from his desert home and his beasts, a "shamkhat" (joy
maiden) from Ishtar's temple is taken to him. When they
approach Engidu, this woman opens wide her garments,
exposing her charms and yields herself to his embraces for
6 days and 7 nights and gratifies his desire until he is won
away from his wild life. He eventually meets Gilgamesh
and the next three tablets relate their friendship, quarrels,
and adventures, the first of which is a battle with a mythical monster named Khumbaba. After Gilgamesh slays the
monster, they return to Erech where Gilgamesh adorns
himself in kingly robes and receives the acclaim of the
people.

The sixth tablet is interesting because of its reference
to the Ishtar-Tammuz myth, which was inseparable from
that of the Great Mother Goddess. Goddess Ishtar becomes
enamored of Gilgamesh and invites him to be her lover,
promising him great wealth and honor. But he, knowing
the fickle manner in which she has treated other lovers,
scornfully repulses her.

Enraged at being thus humiliated, Ishtar pleads with
Anu to send a mighty bull to slay Gilgamesh and Ea creates
Gudanna, "the celestial bull", which appears to be the constellation Taurus. The tablet, containing a description of
the battle has been destroyed, but it seems that Gilgamesh
finally killed the celestial bull with a sword, while Ishtar
looked on in anger. Gilgamesh dedicated the horns of the
bull to the sun god; after he and Engidu had washed their
hands in the river Euphrates, they returned to Erech,
where they were again received with honors. Then Engidu
died, by means which are not made clear, although one
version indicates that he was poisoned by Ishtar, who had
been offended by him.

15. Gilgamesh and Enkidu are shown at left in a wrestling attitude with a woman between them, probably Ishtar. Two horned goddesses stand at right, one of whom holds a trident. From a cylinder of the Hammurabic period.

Deeply grieved by the death of Engidu, Gilgamesh decides to seek immortality from his ancestor Ut-napishtim and his wife who are the only mortals ever to achieve eternal life. He journeys to a high mountain lying on the western horizon between earth and the underworld, the gates of which are guarded by huge scorpions whose backs reach to heaven and whose fore feet reach down to the underworld. They recognize Gilgamesh as a king by his regal bearing and advise him to turn back. Before him, they say, lies the region of darkness where for 24 hours he must travel before again emerging into daylight. But Gilgamesh will not be dissuaded. After a day's journey he comes upon the wonderful garden of Edinu by the sea, where majestic trees bear lapis lazuli and gems of fruit. Here the sea goddess Siduru, a version of Ishtar, directs him to Adad-Ea, the ferryman, who takes Gilgamesh across the dreadful waters of death to the Elysium where dwells Ut-napishtim.

When Gilgamesh finally meets Ut-napishtim he is too ill to leave his boat but tells his relative the object of his journey. Ut-napishtim sorrowfully tells him that death is the fate of all mankind. Gilgamesh is still inconvinced. Then Ut-napishtim relates how the Babylonian Noah, named Xisuthrus, was warned of the Deluge.

Ut-napishtim mixes a magical compound containing seven ingredients for Gilgamesh which causes him to sleep deeply for seven days. When he awakes, he still requests the secret of eternal life and, at length, is taken to where the plant of life can be found growing at the bottom of the bitter sea, which is apparently the Persian Gulf. On the way back to Erech, Gilgamesh decided to bathe; and, while he was out of his boat, a serpent smelled the plant and carried it away. As the serpent left it cast off its skin and it was the serpent and not man that received the power to renew its youth.

The Deluge

A warning from Ea came to Xisuthrus in a vision, warning him of the coming Deluge and telling him to build a ship or ark, shaped like a cube and measuring one hundred twenty cubits on each side. In it he built six floors, each being divided into seven compartments of nine rooms each. With many men working, the ark was built in four days, laid down on the fifth, loaded on the sixth and finished on the seventh day in the month of Tishri-tu, which would be in autumn. The ark was made water-tight by caulking the outside with bitumen and the inside with pitch.

Xisuthrus gave a great banquet and took into the ship living seed of every kind; all his family and household, his gold, silver, and other possessions, the cattle and beasts of the field, handcraftsmen; all that was his.

Then a storm raged for six days and nights and on the seventh day the flood abated. A swallow was then sent out to find land, then a dove, then a raven. When the raven was seen wading in shallow water, the anchor was thrown out and the ark landed on Mount Nissi, in Armenia. Xisuthrus then released all of the animals to the four winds, set up an altar on the mountain top, and made an offering to the gods, who were drawn like flies to the feast by the sweet smell of burning cedar, myrtle, and the sacrificial offering. After the feast Xisuthrus disappeared and was seen no more.

The story ends with the god Enlil expressing regret for having caused the flood and vowing that never again will he smite every living thing.

The adventures of Gilgamesh are thought by some authorities to be a primitive allegory of the seasons, the

16. Scorpion men of the mountain of Mashu.
From an Assyrian cylinder.

encounters with the bull, lion, and various mythical animals comprising the signs of the zodiac. According to this theory, the monster Khumbaba is Leo, the lion; Ishtar is Virgo; the bull slain by Gilgamesh is Taurus; the Scorpion-men represent Scorpio; the sea goddess Siduru is Capricorn, the fish-tailed goat. The eleventh chapter corresponds to the rainy season in the sign of Aquarius when the Deluge occurred according to Babylonian legends. The return of Gilgamesh to Erech, in the twelfth chapter, may symbolize the renewal of life and vegetation with the return of the sun after completing its annual revolution.

Other tablets have been found containing ancient versions of Creation, the Fall of Man, and the Deluge, one of which relates how Mami, the great primeval mother goddess cast her incantations upon fourteen pieces of clay "seven on the right she placed and seven on the left she placed" and created them "in her own image".

One of the most interesting discoveries was that of a triangular fragment in the British Museum, which was first observed by Professor Sayce and was copied by Stephen H. Langdon in 1912.[15] Later, the missing pieces were found and the six columns of the tablet were practically restored. The tablet gives a description of Paradise, the Fall of Man,

---

15—See University of Pennsylvania, Publications of the Babylonian Section, 1915, Vol. 10, No. 1.

and the Deluge which is about one thousand years older than the Biblical version.

The tablet begins with the earth god Enlil destroying humanity by a deluge, assisted by the earth goddess Nintud under the name of Ninharsag. The flood lasts nine months, during which man dissolves like tallow and fat, but Nintud contrived to save the king and certain pious persons by warning them to escape in a boat.

After the deluge, Nintud is represented in conversation with the hero, who appears to be a king named Tagtug. The god Enki reveals the secrets of the universe to Tagtug and engages him as a gardener in Dilmun which corresponds to Paradise. Enki instructs Tagtug regarding the plants and trees whose fruits the gods permit him to eat, but Tagtug eats of the cassia tree, which is forbidden by Nintud, whereupon he loses the privilege of immortality which he enjoyed before the deluge. Henceforth he is merely a mortal man, subject to toil, illness, bodily weakness, old age, and death.

The Land of Dilmun is a historic land mentioned in several very early records, and is described as being located far south of Babylon along the eastern coast of the Persian Gulf. Ancient Babylonian maps show the world as a flat, circular surface around which flows the Persian Gulf, called the "bitter stream". This corresponds exactly with the river which, in the Biblical version, issued from Eden then divided into four branches. According to the tablet, these branches would be identified as the Indus, the Nile, the Euphrates and the Hiddekel, which flows before Ashur.

Many primitive nations had myths describing the jealousy of the gods toward the creatures they had created and whom they made subject to disease and death because of a "fall" from grace. This is the substance of the story of the Fall of Adam and Eve, who, before their transgression in the Garden, were immortal.

If these Babylonian stories are as old as they appear to be—and no scholars question their age—it is apparent that they were known in Babylonia from 600 to 2000 years before the date assigned to Moses. Possibly Abraham was familiar with them before he migrated from Ur to Canaan.

It has been reported that when discovery of the Deluge story was first announced, one great religious organization immediately leaped to the conclusion that it would be found

17. The temptation of Adam. From a Babylonian tablet.

to refute, for all time, modern critics who denied tne historicity of the Deluge. Learned priests were sent hurriedly to the scene, to make copies of the cuneiform tablets, so that confirmation of the Biblical narrative could be proclaimed to the world. But the project was abandoned quietly when the tablets were found to confirm the mythical origin of the Biblical account.

Recovery of these ancient records, and the discovery that many of the "Mosaic Laws" were derived from the Code of Hammurabi, some of the Laws having been in use for 2,000 years before the time of Moses, have been supplemented by the many other findings of modern research. These discoveries have caused higher ecclesiastics to discard theories regarding the origin and nature of the Bible which had been defended vigorously for centuries.

The far reaching effects of these changes of viewpoint become apparent when it is considered that for over 2500 years the Jews have believed that the first five Books of the Bible were given to Moses on Mt. Sinai, at least part of the record having been written in God's own hand. (Deut. 9:10). According to Bible chronology this took place in 1510 B.C.

Inasmuch as the record came directly from God himself, it must be accepted as perfect in every word, letter, and comma. The slightest imperfection would condemn it as the work, not of God but of man, and the Israelites were warned of the terrible consequences to those who should question the divine origin of the record. When the Chris-

tian Church was founded, the early Fathers acknowledged
the sacred character of the Jewish records and their in-
fallibility became a fundamental article of Church doctrine.[16]

16—"Nothing is to be accepted save on the authority of Scripture
since greater is that authority than all the powers of the human
mind."—St. Augustine, *Commentary on the Book of Genesis.*
"So important is it to comprehend the work of creation that
we see the creed of the church take this as its starting point.
Were this article taken away there would be no original sin,
the promise of Christ would become void, and all the vital force
of our religion would be destroyed."—Peter Martyr.
"The whole of antiquity informs that Hebrew in which the
Old Testament is written was the beginning of all human
speech."—St. Jerome.
"Of all languages Hebrew is the first and oldest; of all is alone
pure and not mixed; all the rest are much mixed for there is
none which has not some word from Hebrew."—Conrad Griner,
16th century Swiss cleric.
"This work (Creation) took place and man was created by the
Trinity on October 23, 4004 B.C. at nine o'clock in the morning."
—Dr. John Lightfoot, 17th century Vice-Chancellor of Cambridge
University.
"We must accept the whole of the inspired autographs or re-
ject the whole," said Rev. E. Garbett in a sermon preached before
the University of Oxford. "The very foundations of our faith,
the very basis of our hopes, all the very nearest and dearest
consolations are taken away from us when one line of that
sacred volume on which we base everything is declared to be
untruthful or untrustworthy."—Bishop of Manchester, England,
in the Manchester Examiner and Times.

V

SUN AND MOON WORSHIP AMONG THE JEWS

EFFORTS OF THE early leaders of Israel to exterminate the sun and moon cults constitute one of the longest and most bizarre struggles in history. Details of the struggle are of special interest to people of Christian countries because the religion of the Jews became the foundation stone of the Christian religion. Had the pagan cults triumphed, the whole course of western civilization would have been far different.

But to assume that all sons of Israel were firm believers in Jahveh[1] and, therefore, unanimous in their hatred of the heathen cults would be far from the truth. The Scriptures make clear the fact that, from the Mosaic period onward, a considerable number of Israelites found the warm, sensuous rites of Baal and the Mother Goddess more attractive than the cold, stern worship of Jahveh. There were serious defections among the Israelites while they were still wandering in the Wilderness.[2]

Later leaders found it necesary to exhort their followers repeatedly to avoid the worship of Chemosh (Shamash), Baal, Moloch, Dagon, Venus, Milcom, and Ashtoreth, the Queen of Heaven, "the whore of Babylon," and their idols, images, sacred groves, and "high places". The Books of Judges, Chronicles, and Kings, particularly, are filled with accounts of the constant, bitter, and bloody struggle to exterminate the heretics.

Moses had assured his people that they were esteemed by Jahveh "above all the nations of the earth";[3] if they worshiped no other god but him, he would help them overcome their enemies and lead them into a land of milk and honey. But many were unconvinced. They admitted that they could not destroy their enemies because the latter were stronger[4] or had chariots of iron[5] and complained of

---

1—The name Jehovah is a mistranslation of the Hebrew name Jahveh or Yahweh.
2—*Exod.* 32:4, *Jud.* 2:12, *I Kings* 11:33, *Jer.* 7:17,31, 44:15,17,23,25.
3—*Exod.* 3:17, *Deut.* 14:2.
4—*Num.* 13:31,33.
5—*I Jud.* 1:19,27,29 to 34.

Jahveh's failure to help them subdue the inhabitants of various parts of Canaan.

Many of the Israelites seem to have considered Jahveh to be a mere tribal god, holding supreme power over them, but powerless against their enemies. Their Syrian neighbors believed that Jahveh was a mountain god who reigned in the hills, but was ineffective in the valleys.[6] Belief in one Supreme Deity, Lord of all the peoples of the earth, was, as yet, far beyond popular comprehension.

With the exception of the forty years during the reign of King David in which the efforts of Samuel succeeded in unifying the people, there was constant "back-sliding" by the men and women of Israel who forsook Jahveh to worship the heathen gods of the Canaanites.[7]

It is evident also that despite the professed hatred of Israelite leaders for all rites and customs identified with the pagan cults and, particularly, anything of Babylonian origin, there were certain notable exceptions. Although Exodus informs us that in the statutes and commandments which Moses gave to his people the death penalty was prescribed for magicians, foretellers, observers of time (astrologers), wizards, sorcerers, necromancers, etc., enforcement of these laws was far from consistent. The pages of the Old Testament contain many accounts of mysteries, miracles and magic; but instead of the exponents of prophecy and magic being vigorously exterminated, they were most often highly honored.

All leaders of Israel either consulted foretellers and magicians, such as the prophetesses Miriam,[8] Deborah,[9] Huldah,[10] and the witch of Endor[11] or they practiced prognostication and magic themselves, Moses being the most famous magician and foreteller of all. Joseph had a reputation as "revealer of secrets" even as a boy. When only seventeen years old he amazed the Pharaoh of Egypt with his feats of prophecy and magic, for which reason he was

---

6—*I Kings* 20:23,28.
7—"And the children of Israel did evil again in the sight of the Lord and served Baalim and Ashtoreth and the gods of Syria and the gods of Zidon and the gods of Amon and the gods of the Philistines and forsook the Lord and served not him." *Jud.* 10:6.
8—*Exod.* 15:20.
9—Jud. 4:4.
10—*II Chr.* 34:22.
11—I Sam. 28:4,7.

given in marriage the daughter of Potiphera, the priest of On, the king's chief astrologer.

From early times, the priests of Israel were called by names which signified they were astrologers or "dividers of the heavens". There was a loosely drawn distinction between true and false prophets and between priestly prophets and lay prophets, but the distinction was not consistently observed, as may be seen in the fact that some of the accepted prophets were women. In general those who made prophecies of an orthodox religious character were approved, while those who resorted to astrological horoscopes and fortune telling for profit were condemned.

Encouraged by Solomon and the many other sunworshiping kings who followed King David and the subsequent disintegration of the monarchy, the worship of heathen gods increased at an alarming pace. The Biblical record for that period states that ". . . now for a long season Israel hath been without the true God and without a teaching priest and without law."[12] The people consulted observers of time, wizards, necromancers, etc.; made molten images, paid honor to the "Sun, moon and stars and all the host of heaven" and worshiped Baal and Ashtoreth "on every high hill and under every green tree."[13]

The spread of the pagan cults to every part of Israel had been facilitated by ancient customs regarding the setting up of altars and offering of animals in sacrifice. Since the days of Abraham these acts of religious homage had been rights exercised, not by the priests alone, but by all sons of Israel. As the customs were based on precedents set by Noah, Abraham, Isaac, and Jacob and the express command of Moses, they bore the full authority of sacred law.[14] Samuel admitted that he was both a prophet (seer), and a worshiper at the "high places" or local shrines.[15] The customs prevailed during the lives of the great prophets Amos, Hosea, Micah, and Isaiah yet none of them dared to question the legality of the local shrines.[16]

12—II Chron. 15:3.
13—II Kings 17:9.
14—Exod. 12:3, 21, 24; 20:24.
15—I Sam. 99:12,19,25; I Kings 18:30,35.
16—Only the people sacrificed in high places because there was no house built unto the name of the Lord until those days. I Kings 3:2.
    And the king went to Gibeon to sacrifice there; for there was the great high place: a thousand burnt offerings did Solomon offer upon that altar. I Kings 3:4.

But the right of every son of Israel to set up altars and make sacrifices wherever he wished also made it easy for back-sliders to practice their pagan rites, unseen by the stern, disapproving eyes of the priests.

The struggle against the pagan cults was made even more difficult by the fact that Palestine lay on the main caravan route between Egypt and Babylonia. Both countries enjoyed great prestige because of their old and mature cultures. Moreover, they possessed great wealth and military power, which Israel had good reason to fear. In 722 B.C., Samaria was invaded by the king of Babylonia who took the "Ten Lost Tribes" into captivity. In 685 B.C. Assyria attacked and made vassals of the northern states. Relations with Egypt were strained and there was constant fear of war. From the north the Scythians swept down into Assyria and, after administering a stunning defeat to the Assyrians, marched on Egypt. Although their route lay along the sea coast, and Palestine was not molested, the danger of an invasion by the Scythians produced consternation in Israel.

Leaders of the Jews faced the possibility of their people intermarrying with the Canaanites and gradually drifting away from their leadership: they also foresaw the danger of their people being absorbed culturally and militarily by their more powerful neighbors to the north, south and east. Israel was therefore between the jaws of a giant nut-cracker which threatened the supremacy, if not the very existence of Jahvehism. If these dangers were to be overcome, the Jews would have to be welded into a nation quickly; thoroughly united by religion and government, and so completely set apart from all other nations that their identity as a people could never become lost. At this critical period, young King Josiah, apparently being deceived by the priests, became involved in a daring act of trickery which was part of a plan for purging Israel of its idolatry.

One day in 621 B.C. it was reported to the king that Hilkiah, the high priest, had found in the temple "the Book of Laws" which had been strangely missing since its reputed promulgation by Moses some 800 or 900 years earlier. The story is best told in the 22nd and 23d chapters of II *Kings*. But, before continuing with the results of this discovery, it is necessary that a digression be made to speak of another important discovery.

While engaged in the preparation of a graduation thesis for the University of Jena, in 1805, William M. L. De Wette, decided that "the Book of Laws" found by Hilkiah was none other than the Book of Deuteronomy. If Moses had placed the Code of Laws in the Book of Exodus, reasoned De Wette, why should he have written another Book treating of the same subject in which he gave commands directly contrary to those contained in the first Book. Yet, in Exodus, every son of Israel had been commanded to set up altars and offer sacrifices whereas, in Deuteronomy, observance of these rites was denied to all but the priests.[17]

After careful study of the spirit and language of the new Book, De Wette observed that it seemed perculiarly well adapted to meet the situation confronting Josiah and, in fact, appeared to have been written, not by Moses, but by a much later author.[18] Continued researches by modern authorities have fully confirmed De Wette's keen deductions and it is now generally conceded that Deuteronomy was written (probably in Babylon) during the reign of King Manasseh or King Josiah.

De Wette's discovery not only threw new light on Deuteronomy, it also made it necessary to reconsider the entire story of the life of Moses. Scholars had long known that many details in the life of the great law-giver were similar to events in the myths of the Greek god Bacchus. Like Moses, Bacchus was born in Egypt, was found floating in a basket and had both real and foster mothers. Like Moses, he made water gush from a stone by striking it with his staff; like Moses, he wore two horns on his head: he became a lawmaker and wrote his laws on two tablets of stone. Moses performed miracles with snakes and Bacchus was always portrayed with snakes. Moses waved his staff and made the waters of the Red Sea turn back and Bacchus did the same thing with the waters of the Orontes river in Syria and the Hydaspes in India.

17—*Deut.* 12:8,15.

18—In 1679 Spinoza observed that in the Pentateuch certain towns and places bore names that were not given to them until several centuries after Moses. Repeated occurrence of such expressions as "the Lord said to Moses" and "Moses said," etc., also indicated that the Pentateuch was written, not by Moses but by another author writing about him. The fact that the Book of Deuteronomy described the death and burial of Moses was seen as final proof of the theory.

For further reference to the authorship of the Books of the O.T. see *Unravelling the Book of Books*, Ernest Trattner, 1931.

It has always seemed peculiar that the so-called Books of Moses give practically no information about the culture of the Egyptians during the four hundred years in which the sons of Israel are said to have lived in Egypt. No mention is made of Egyptian achievements in astronomy, mathematics or architecture nor are the pyramids, the great monuments and temples at Thebes and Karnak even mentioned in the Scriptures.

It is equally strange that the Book of Exodus gives the only record we have of the plagues of Moses and the slaughter of the first-born of the Egyptians. Yet, the sickness, disease and death caused by these acts of vengeance would have brought panic and disaster so extensive as to make it inconceivable that Egyptian historians could have failed to mention them.

Although the Tell-el-Amarna tablets give much information regarding Canaan at about the period of the Exodus, they make no allusions to the Jews in Egypt or to the great catastrophe caused by the events preceding their escape.

In their Exodus from Egypt, the Israelites are said to have assembled right before the eyes of the Egyptians and escaped by night to the Red Sea where, at the command of Moses, the water rolled back and remained suspended in the air until the whole caravan walked across the dry bed of the sea to safety on the shore of Sinai.

The enormity of this miracle can better be appreciated when it is recalled that offspring of the seventy-two descendants of Israel who originally migrated to Egypt increased with such rabbit-like rapidity that their number doubled about every thirty years, so that, when the Exodus began four hundred years later, descendants of the original group numbered 600,000 men; the women, children and servants not being counted. This great army, with its cattle and personal effects, traveling in Oriental fashion, formed a caravan probably more than two hundred miles long. To contrive the escape from Egypt of this great multitude of people, then to make the waters of the Red Sea remain rolled back until all of them had crossed would have been a miracle of miracles.

The conclusions of modern authorities regarding the mythical nature of the remarkable incidents in the life of Moses and the discoveries regarding the authorship of Deuteronomy have been supplemented, in recent times, by the finding of important evidence concerning the authorship of the so-called Priestly Laws, contained in other Books of the Pentateuch. The ideas they contain, and the language employed, closely resemble the writings of Prophet Ezekiel who was exiled to Babylon in 597 B.C. He is now generally looked upon as the spiritual father of all the Priestly Laws, although they were probably compiled by a group of exiled priests in Babylon about 500 B.C. In 444 B.C. they were taken to Jerusalem by Ezra and proclaimed to the people by Ezra and Nehemiah by almost the same method that had been used to proclaim Deuteronomy two hundred years earlier. But, let us return now to Deuteronomy.

When the Book of Deuteronomy was shown to Josiah, he became terrified by the realization that for centuries his people had not been governed by the "true" laws of Moses. After consulting the prophetess Huldah, he assembled all the people at the temple, read the long-lost Book to them and declared that, henceforth, it would supersede all other Books of Law.

The newly-found Book commanded all Jews to forsake the heathen gods, customs, and rites and to pay obeisance only to Jahveh. The death penalty was prescribed for dreamers of dreams, foretellers, observers of time, magicians, sorcerers, witches, enchanters, consulters of familiar spirits, etc. Priests of the pagan cults were to be stoned to death; all images, idols, pillars, groves, high places and altars were ordered destroyed. Then a code of statutes was provided which regulated the daily lives of the people, certain of the statutes being intended forever to discourage marriage and social intercourse between the Jews and the people amongst whom they lived.

The new Book significantly abrogated the right of the people to make sacrifices and set up their own altars. These ancient customs had originated when the Jews were nomadic tribes and the new laws took recognition of their changed status as an agricultural people. Thereafter the temple in Jerusalem was to be the only legitimate sanctuary of Jahveh and it was to be served only by the Zadokite, or hereditary priests. Thus, by one sudden, shrewd maneuver, the authority of the priests was greatly strengthened. Local shrines were declared illegal, pagan cults and practices were outlawed, a line of social demarcation was drawn between the Jews and their pagan neighbors and the ground was prepared for a sweeping reformation. With prophecy discredited and declared illegal, the day of the great prophets, who had played an important part in earlier history, was coming to a close.

After promulgating the new laws, Josiah went about the country breaking down the high places and cutting down the sacred groves. He destroyed the horses and chariots of the sun god which the kings of Judah had kept in the suburbs;[19] he "brake down the houses of the Sodomites that were by the house of the Lord, where the women wove hangings for the groves."[20] "He slew all the priests of the high places that were upon the altars and burned men's bones upon them and returned to Jerusalem."[21] "He killed the priests who burned incense to the sun, moon and to the planets and to all the host (stars) of heaven."[22] Then he killed the wizards, the workers with familiar spirits, astrologers, foretellers, sorcerers, etc.

Even Solomon's temple was purged of idols and images which had long been permitted to contaminate it. During the reign of King Manassah and other pagan kings who preceded Josiah, Baal and Ashtoreth had been worshiped openly in the temple and worship of Jahveh had become secondary. The altars which King Manasseh had built in the two courts of the temple and vessels which had been used in the worship of Baal, the groves and the host of heaven had been permitted to remain in the holy sanctuary up to the very time Deuteronomy was "discovered". The campaign which he launched against pagan worship immediately thereafter was begun for the specific purpose of carrying out the commands supposedly laid down by Moses in the newly-found Book.

In considering the causes which spurred Josiah into such sudden and violent activity it is very important that we bear in mind the fact that other Books of the Pentateuch contain substantially the same statutes against pagan worship and practices that are found in Deuteronomy. The Books of Exodus and Leviticus give repeated warnings of the terrible penalties prescribed for the worship of pagan gods,

---

19—*II Kings* 23:11.
20—*Ibid*, 23:7.
21—*Ibid*, 23:20.
22—*Ibid*, 23:5.

images and idols, for worship at high places, for practicing magic and sorcery, for consulting wizards, witches, etc.[23]

If the statutes contained in these Books were transmitted to Moses on Mount Sinai, they should have been known to every son of Israel, yet Josiah knew nothing of them until he read the Book of Deuteronomy. The priests, judges and kings who had kept graven images, worshiped at high places and consulted witches, wizards, etc. had done so without having appeared to be aware that they were violating the commands of Moses.

Several other discrepancies in the record also require consideration. The Books of Judges, Samuel, and Kings are supposed to cover nearly 1000 years of Jewish history, yet they make no reference to Jahveh's talks with Moses; they say nothing about the miracles Moses performed in Egypt, his passage of the Red Sea or his wanderings in the Wilderness. Nor do they make any illusions to the stories given in Genesis of Creation, Adam and Eve and the Deluge. Although the names of Abraham, Isaac, Jacob and Moses are mentioned a few times, nothing is said about their lives and they are treated as if they were merely obscure, legendary figures.

On almost every page of the Books Amos, Hosea, Micah, and Isaiah the great prophets complain that their people have forsaken Jahveh to worship Baal, Ashtoreth and the host of heaven. They give repeated warnings of the terrible punishment awaiting those who worship the heathen gods but, at no time do they refer to Moses as their authority for such warnings.

It is now generally conceded by Bible authorities that the legends and historical records appearing in the Pentateuch were put into written form about the seventh century, possibly not more than 100 years before Deuteronomy. Thereafter revisions and additions were made in the Books up to the 4th or 3d century. Apparently the Jewish people were not sufficiently awed by the commands given in Genesis, Exodus, Leviticus and Numbers and it became necessary for the priests to prepare a new Book (Deuteronomy), written in clearer and much more vigorous language, that is, the new work put more "teeth" into the

---

23—*Exod.* 20:3,4; 34:12 to 17; 23:24 to 33. *Lev.* 17:7; 19:4,31; 20:2 to 6; 20:27; 26:1: 26:15 to 46.

Laws. Then the new Book was presented to the people with much dramatic fanfare. This was followed immediately by a savage blood-letting which was calculated to instill so much fear into the minds of the people that they would not dare to continue worship of the pagan gods.

De Wette contended that the reason certain laws in Deuteronomy contradict laws in other Books of the Pentateuch is because Deuteronomy was written at a later time, to meet conditions which had not existed when the other Books were written. But, in his effort to disprove the Mosaic authorship of Deuteronomy, he failed to observe that there was just as much reason to doubt the authenticity of all the other so-called Books of Moses.

Despite the successful beginning of the young king's ruthless campaign to eliminate worship of the heathen gods by force, most of its effect was dissipated by a series of tragic events which provided some of the darkest pages in Israel's history. In 608 B.C. Josiah joined the Assyrians in a war against the Pharaoh of Egypt and was killed in Syria. Ten years later the Assyrian King Nebuchadnezzar attacked Jerusalem, pillaged the temple of its treasures and took back to Babylon as prisoners King Jehoiachin, his wives, his court, and ten thousand soldiers and craftsmen.

This severe blow left the Israelites dazed and terror stricken. Their grief, however, was perhaps due more to their moral defeat than to their military debacle. The promise that they would be made supreme over all other people constituted the very keystone of their perpetual Covenant with Jahveh, solemnly acknowledged by the rite of circumcision. Now, at a time of grave peril, his help was not forthcoming.

But, in truth, serious weaknesses in their religious structure had been becoming more and more apparent over a long period. Failure to subjugate completely their neighbors in Palestine after several centuries of continual warfare and their inability to prevent calamitous invasions by Babylonians and Egyptians had already cast a shadow of doubt over their belief that they were under the special protection of Jahveh.

As early as the eighth century, some of the prophets seem to have realized the futility of trying to maintain the narrow, traditional belief that Jahveh was interested in none but the Jews. First, Amos proclaimed Jahveh as the apotheosis of love and righteousness, the supreme ruler, not of the Jews alone, but of all the people on earth. Isaiah, Hosea and Micah spoke in similar spirit and the Book of Isaiah (26:19,21) even announces the coming of a Messiah, the creation of a new heaven and earth following the judgment and destruction of evil.[24]

According to the primitive beliefs of earlier days, Jahveh was a dual personality, combining good and evil natures. Repeatedly the Bible speaks of him as being jealous, wrathful, terrible, and revengeful;[25] of practicing deception and trickery on behalf of the Jews, and of sending destroying angels or his evil spirit against those whom he wished to destroy.[26]

The new concept of the prophets gave to Jahveh a sublime, universal character which was completely lacking in the former nationalistic concept, yet it is not apparent from the Scriptures that the people quickly responded to it, or that they even found it comprehensible. In the first place, the prophets' version of a universal God of love and justice was directly contrary to every premise on which their religion was founded. If what the prophets said were true, it could only mean that Jahveh had repudiated his Covenant with them or that such a Covenant had never existed, and all the claims and promises made by the

---

24—The authorship and date of the prediction of a coming judgment cannot be placed with certainty. Cheyne's Encyclopedia Biblica places it at about 334 B.C. Older theories attributed the whole Book of Isaiah to the eighth century but parts of it refer to events which occurred as late as the 2nd century and modern authorities concede that most of the work is by writers of much later date, with only a small portion of the Book being by Isaiah. "Chaps. 40-66 have no title and make no claim to be by Isaiah. Chaps. 40-48 set forth the reign of Jerusalem and the Exile as having already taken place."—*Enc. Rel. & Eth.*, Article, Isaiah.

25—He (God) is a merchant; the balances of deceit are in his hand; he loveth to oppress. *Hos.* 12:7. .

26—The evil spirit of the Lord came upon Saul. I *Saml.* 18:10.
The Lord sent a lying spirit. I *Kings* 22:22.
I make peace, and create evil: I, the Lord do all these things. *Isa.* 42:7.
Then God sent an evil spirit between Abimelech and the men of Shechem. *Jud.* 9:23.
Behold now, an evil spirit from God troubleth thee. I *Saml.* 16:14.

patriarchs, prophets and leaders, from Abraham to Isaiah, had been a cruel fraud upon the people.

After having it dinned into them and their forefathers for centuries that Jahveh was terrible and revengeful, they were now asked to believe that he represented love and righteousness. After being asked to believe that he cared only for the Jews, they were now asked to believe that he loved their enemies as much as he loved them, even including nations which worshiped other gods and knew nothing of Jahveh.

But some prophets continued to believe that Jahveh cared only for the Jews and as late as the seventh and sixth centuries some of them looked forward to a day of judgment, after which Jerusalem would be the center of Jahveh's kingdom on earth. Some prophets asserted that the coming judgment would be for the Jews alone while others predicted that non-Jews would be either annihilated or made to bow and serve Israel.[27]

From evidence given in the Books of Kings it is apparent that the great drift from Jahveh to the pagan gods which occurred during this period and which Josiah's reformation sought to overcome, was due in great part to the confusion, bewilderment and lack of faith in Jahveh which the revolutionary doctrines of the prophets had produced in the minds of the people.

Their attitude toward Jahveh after Nebuchadnezzar's invasion is revealed by Jeremiah, who warned them that their humiliation (because of the invasion) was due to their having turned their backs on Jahveh, and reminded them that they still practiced their heathen rites and "children cut wood and fathers kindle fires and women knead their dough to other gods."[28]

When Jeremiah warned them that they need not expect Jahveh to help them prevail against the Babylonians merely because they were Jews and that they must earn his help by their righteousness, he was denounced as a partisan of Babylon, thrown into a dungeon, and narrowly escaped death.

When he addressed those who escaped the Assyrians by fleeing to Egypt and urged them to return to Jahveh, they

---

27—*Hos.* 3:5, *Mic.* 5:3, *Is.* 9:1,6, 8:23, 9:5, 11:1,8, *Mic.* 5:24, *Is.* 60:10, 12,14, *Zech.* 8:15, *Joel* 3:4, 1:6.
28—*Jer.* 7:18.

greeted his pleas with scorn and told him that when they baked cakes, burned incense, and poured out drink offerings to the Queen of Heaven they were happy and prosperous but since they had ceased such worship, "we have wanted all things and have been consumed by the sword and by the famine."[29]

In his exile in Babylon Ezekiel also lamented his former days in Jerusalem saying that "then He (God) brought me to the door of the gate of the Lord's house which was toward the north and, behold, there sat women weeping for Tammuz," and at the door of the temple, between the porch and the altar, there "were about five and twenty men with their backs to the temple of the Lord and their faces toward the east, and they worshiped the sun towards the east."[30]

In 586 B.C. Nebuchadnezzar again attacked Jerusalem and broke down the walls, burned, and pillaged the holy city and left it a desolate mass of ruins. King Zedekiah was made prisoner, his eyes were put out and all of the city's most worthy inhabitants were dragged away to Babylon. This time Nebuchadnezzar made sure that destruction of the city was so thorough that there would be no danger of its rising again.

For centuries the prophets had thundered against the abominations of the proud and powerful city on the Euphrates. Now, by an ironic turn of fate, the inhabitants of Jerusalem were forced to march as captives over 800 miles of desert to that center of iniquity.

When the prisoners reached Babylon, the old city was undergoing many changes. Although still the intellectual and political center of southwest Asia, the capital was definitely on the decline. National unity had been strained and weakened by rapid political and religious changes following a series of destructive wars which had brought the Assyrians into power. Fifty years later Babylonia would forever cease to exist as an independent nation.

A great increase in knowledge of astronomy in the preceding centuries had also been gradually undermining the powerful influence of the astrologer-priests and the people were losing faith in gods to whom homage had been paid since the dawn of history. Within a few years the situ-

---

29—Jer. 44:15,18. Ezek. 9:14, 9:16. Also see Amos 5:26. Acts 7:24.
    Jer. 8:2; 7:13,21;44:17,18,19,23,25.
30—Ezek. 8:14,16.

ation was to become further confused by conquest of the city by the Persians who were to bring with them the Indo-Persian religion of Zoroaster (Zarathustra) to challenge the supremacy of the old gods. (For Zoroaster, see Appendix.)

In the comparatively liberal, cosmopolitan atmosphere of Babylon, with its mixtures of Oriental philosophies and mysticism, the Jews absorbed many new theories which amplified and filled gaps in their theological speculations. For the Zoroastrians not only worshiped one supreme deity like themselves, they had a more highly developed religious system which included among its doctrines belief in the existence of a soul, free will, a mediator, a virgin born savior, heaven and hell, purgatory, angels, devils, a day of final resurrection and judgment, baptism and catechisms.

Another significant difference between the religion of the Jews and that of the Persians was that the latter religion was more concerned with the individual whereas Judaism, particularly in its older form, merely looked forward to a time when all of its national enemies would be annihilated, when Israel would be acknowledged ruler of all the world and would enter a perpetual reign of peace and prosperity. Being concerned only with the welfare of the nation as a whole, its history, psalms and so-called Laws of Moses gave no thought to individual immortality and resurrection. The only punishment to the individual, for disobedience to Jahveh, came in the form of poverty, disease or famine during his life on earth.

Despite Jahveh's disappointment with the children he had created, it is not related anywhere in the Pentateuch that he ever warned either Adam, Noah, Abraham or Moses of the end of the present world, or of a day of resurrection and punishment for the wicked. The Fall of Adam and Eve was charged, not to the devil, but to a serpent. The stories concerning these characters had probably become part of Jewish sacred literature before belief in the existence of heaven, hell and the devil was incorporated in their religious philosophy.

The Zoroastrians, however, envisioned all worldly activity as the result of a perpetual struggle between the forces of Darkness and Light. To Ahura Mazda was credited all that was good, just and beneficial to man while, to his brother Ahriman, the Prince of Darkness, was attributed all that was evil or harmful. In the final period, before the end of the world, Ahura would triumph over Ahriman; then would come the resurrection and the reign of peace and happiness on earth.

The despair into which they had been plunged by the Captivity had made the Jews particularly susceptible to dogmas which could be interpreted in a manner which would help them to keep alive the old dreams of a day when their nation would reign supreme. Therefore, when the Exiles in Babylon became familiar with the Zoroastrian philosophy, they were impressed profoundly. Nor could they fail to see that by borrowing certain ideas from the new religion, they would be able to strengthen some weak points in their own.

If Jahveh loved all men, why was life on earth fraught with countless dire inequalities and injustices? Why did he cause some men to be born deaf, dumb, blind, malformed or mentally defective? If he were perfect, how could he create an imperfect man or an imperfect world? Why did he create insects and vermin to harass his children, whom he loved? Why did poverty, floods, famine and disease strike haphazardly the righteous and unrighteous alike?[31]

Zoroastrianism had avoided embarrassing questions of this kind by the appointment of separate deities for good and evil and by the promise of a future day of judgment and resurrection, when all of the injustices and misfortunes of earthly life would be balanced by a life in heaven for the good and punishment in hell for the bad. Ahura Mazda, the god of righteousness, had been further relieved of any responsibility for evil by the doctrine of Free Will which made each individual accountable for his bad deeds.

These ideas soon began to find favor among Jewish leaders and far-reaching changes began to develop slowly in their theology. Back-sliders and doubters continued to be warned that Jahveh was a terrible God of jealousy and vengeance but more and more emphasis was being placed upon his role as the kindly father to whom the weary, the sick, and the down-trodden could turn for help and consolation. Those who found no relief from their pains and troubles in this

---

31—All things come alike to all: there is one event to the righteous and to the wicked; to the good and to the clean, and to the unclean; to him that sacrificeth, and to him that sacrificeth not: as is the good, so is the sinner; and he that sweareth, as he that feareth an oath. *Eccl.* 9:2.

world could still hope for serenity and bliss in the world
to come.

Eventually Deva and Shaitan,[32] the Persian names for
the cause of evil, became transformed by the Jews into
devil and Shatan (Satan) and troops of angels and devils
began going about their appointed duties. Adoption of the
devil as the cause of evil overcame some of the contradictions
in their older theology, but the method by which the Jews
grafted the Prince of Darkness on their religion added some
new and fatal inconsistencies. Satan is introduced in the
Scriptures in a casual manner, without any attempt being
made to rationalize the belief in his existence, or to integrate
him into the religious system. No explanation is made of
the time or manner of his origin or of his relation to Jahveh,
leaving the Book of Genesis as the only source of information
on the subject. And, inasmuch as Genesis states that Jahveh
alone existed before Creation, it must be assumed that he
created the devil during the creation of the universe or
afterward.[33] On this basis, however, the real responsibility
for the creation of evil rests upon Jahveh. On the other
hand, if the devil were not created by Jahveh, that is, if
he came into existence independently, or if Jahveh cannot
curb or destroy him, then Jahveh cannot be omnipotent, and
the universal conception of him as All-Powerful cannot be
maintained.

When King Cyrus permitted the Jews to return to
Jerusalem, worship of the gods of fertility still persisted and
in 444 B.C. Nehemiah promulgated new laws to stamp it
out. Even as late as the Maccabeean period (165-135 B.C.)
many Jews kept pagan idols and wore amulets of pagan
gods. It is related that when Judas Maccabeus and his com-
pany went out to bury some dead soldiers, small images

32—II *Kings* 19:22, *Zech.* 3:1 and *Job* 1:1, 8:6,12 and 2:1,4.
33—Rabbinical literature also mentions Lilith (plural, Lilin) as the
source of all evil. She is represented either as a siren with long
hair or as a night monster who seduced men by evil night
dreams and this union produced devils, ghosts, and evil creatures. The word was probably derived from the Babylonian
demon lilatu whom the Jews worshiped in Babylon as the
goddess of night or as a goddess of the stream. *Isa.* 14:2,3, 34:14
and *Zec.* 5:9 probably refer to Lilith. According to a tradition
prevalent in the Middle Ages, Eve bore demons to male spirits
for 130 years before her union with Adam. Another version
makes Lilith Adam's first wife.

of the pagan gods were found hidden under the coats of every one of them.[34] These were minor manifestations, however, and worship of Baal and the Queen of Heaven were nearly over. By this time new ideas and problems had developed to divert the minds of the people.

By 135 B.C. the Jews were split into warring factions and before peace was restored more than five thousand persons had been killed. On one side were the hereditary priesthood, or the Sadducees, representing the older Judaism. They accepted only the Books of Moses and resented the intrusion of new ideas into the national religion. On the other side were the lay priests, the Pharisees, who defended the new doctrines of a future life, heaven and hell, a resurrection after death, and a day of final judgment. Zoroastrian influence was also reflected in a wave of Pharisaic speculation concerning the coming of a Messiah.

By the end of the century, the end and renewal of the world was an accepted belief of the Pharisees and by the beginning of the Christian era it was accepted by practically all Jews. Then, in order to find justification in the Scriptures for the new beliefs, the rabbis devised new interpretations for obscure passages by stretching and twisting the meaning of words. Later rabbinic literature even rebuked the Sadducees repeatedly for having denied that immortality and resurrection were mentioned in the Books of Moses.

As a result of the adoption of belief in the devil as the cause of evil there was a great increase in magic and demonism and these subjects continued to be conspicuous features of Jewish literature for several centuries. Hallucinations, witchcraft, sorcery, epilepsy, blindness, fevers, in fact every human ailment or misfortune was blamed upon the devil, whose evil spirit was thought to have taken possession of the afflicted person. With this development faith healers and wonder-working holy men sprang up who were reputedly able to drive out devils, cure blindness, heal the sick, raise the dead, and perform many other kinds of miracles. (It was due to its having been born into this atmosphere that Christianity was practically dominated by magic and demonism until well after the Middle Ages. Even today, they continue to be important phases of Christian belief).

34—Maccabbees 12:39,40.

In 70 A.D. the Romans destroyed Jerusalem and dispersed its population. Fear that scattering the Jews over the earth might cause their ancient records to become lost led to the formation of a council of rabbis who met in Jamnia about the beginning of the 2nd century A.D. for the purpose of codifying the holy records and giving them permanent form. The council decided that "divine inspiration" had ceased in the age of Ezra and Nehemiah; therefore, all later writings were excluded and the Scriptures were closed for all time. Since then they have remained in substantially the form in which we have them today. So, at a time approximately coincident with the birth of Christianity the Jewish worship of Jahveh reached its final form. The long fight to destroy the old Babylonian worship of the gods of the sun, moon and stars had ended with the adoption of a new theology and eschatology which would eventually become general throughout the western world.

VI

SUN GODS AND OTHERS

As PRIMITIVE TRIBES gradually turned to agriculture, they gave up their nomadic existence as wandering hunters and shepherds and settled in clusters of rude huts which, in time, grew into towns and cities. With the growing importance of agriculture as the source of their food supply, they became aware that it was the fructifying power, not of the moon, but of the sun which controlled the forces affecting their means of living. This led to the beginning of sun worship.

The power of the sun was apparent, not only in the changes of the seasons and the annual periods of plant growth, but its friendly or unfriendly influence was also seen in the times of drought and rainfall, as well as in the periodic overflows of streams. Most of the earliest great centers of civilization developed in the rich, alluvial valleys of large rivers; therefore an accurate knowledge of the annual floods bringing moisture and deposits of soil to the bottom lands was of special importance. In Egypt, where the growing of crops was entirely dependent upon the floods, the New Year was reckoned from the summer solstice which marked the annual rise of the Nile.

Whereas the computation of lunar periods required only man's ability to count the nights of the moon on his ten fingers, the needs of agriculture made it necessary to reckon time in much longer periods. Both the development of agriculture and the use of solar time were, therefore, dependent upon, and perhaps coincident with, man's learning to count the days in a whole year.

Knowledge of the 365-day solar year appears in the very oldest Egyptian records and seems to have been the basis of the calendar used by the Egyptians as early as 4000 or 5000 B.C. To the end of a 360-day zodiacal year they added 5 intercalary or epagomenal days which were celebrated as the birthdays of the gods Osiris, Isis, Horus, Typhon, and Nephthys. In the seventh century B.C., Thales took the knowledge of the 365-day year to Greece.

Although the Babylonians do not seem to have employed the 365-day year as early as the Egyptians, the change from lunar to solar time, in the reign of King Sargon, is recorded on a clay tablet dating from about 2850 B.C. (some authorities say 3700 B.C.) while the earliest mention of the sun god Shamash is thought to date from about 4200 B.C.

The Babylonians added an intercalary month to their 360-day year once every 5 or 6 years. They observed the solstices and equinoxes which divided the year into seasons, distinguished the planets from the fixed stars, and charted the motions and cycles of Mercury, Venus, Jupiter, Mars and Saturn with surprising accuracy. Their theories regarding the nature and movements of the planets formed an important part of their system of astrology, of which more will be said later.

The Chinese knew the exact, or almost exact, number of days in the year and had a way of determining the solstices and equinoxes as early as the time of Emperor Yaou, 2356 B.C. They also had an intercalary system and some instruments for surveying the heavens. In addition, they had knowledge of the 5 planets, the 12 zodiac signs and probably the 28 stellar divisions.

In the Babylonian time-system, the day was divided into 12 double hours and the double hour was divided into 60 minutes. The unit of time was equal to about 2 minutes of our time and corresponded to the time taken by the sun to traverse a space in the heavens equal to its apparent diameter. Four minutes of our time (1/360th part of a day) was the estimated time required for an average walker to cover 360 double cubits, and a great kasbu (21,600 cubits) required 4 hours or the length of a night watch.[1]

This was the basis of the Babylonian method of reckoning by 60 (1/6th of 360) which gave birth to the sexagesimal system, the division of the circle into 360 degrees and the observation that 1/6th of the circle's circumference is approximately equal to its radius. From the 27-day month and the 360-day year they determined the relative value of

---

1—A double cubit was 10 handbreadths, 60 finger breadths or approximately 39.24 inches, almost precisely the same length as the French meter. The small cubit was one-half the larger unit.
  A walker who covered 360 double cubits in 4 min. would walk at the rate of 3.34 miles per hour.
  Oriental philosophers estimated that a man in health makes 360 respirations in a Ghair (Ghari) time or about 24 min. This is at the rate of 15 respirations per min. or 21,600 per day.
  The earth makes a complete turn of 360 degrees on its axis each 24 hours, therefore it turns 1 degree for every 4 min. or 60 respirations. According to another Oriental system, it was estimated that 15 twinkles of an eye equal 1 minute. The division of the hour into minutes and seconds of our time was probably the work of scholars of the Ptolemaic period, i.e., in the 2nd century A.D.

gold and silver as 27 parts of gold to 360 of silver, or in the ratio of one to thirteen-and-one-half.

Hipparchus (150 B.C.) published a list of ten hundred eighty fixed stars and closely estimated the distance of the sun and moon from the earth. Aristarchus estimated the diameter of the sun to be between 6 and 7 times that of the earth, hence about 300 times its bulk. He estimated the moon's diameter at one third that of the earth and its volume about one-twelfth that of the earth.

Archimedes had made the first machine in which the rotation of the celestial sphere and the changing positions of the stars were simulated by the motion of a wheel.

By the time Alexandria became a part of the Roman Empire, the radius and circumference of both the sun and moon, and their distances from the earth, had been determined.

About 100 B.C., Hero of Alexandria composed a book in which he described the principles of about 100 mechanical appliances, which included a cyclometer, a theodolite, and a double forcing pump.[2]

When Julius Caesar commissioned the Alexandrian astronomer Sosigenes to draw up a new calendar, in 46 B.C., the length of the year was fixed as 365 days 6 hours, the same length as the year in the Babylonian calendar then in use. The leap year was introduced into Egypt during the reign of Pharaoh Euergetes I, in 238 A.D., to absorb the annual difference of 6 hours between solar time and calendar time.[3]

The general development of culture had kept pace with progress in science and, centuries before the close of the pre-Christian period, there had been created many of the greatest masterpieces of art, literature, and architecture the world has ever known.

In view of the crude facilities then at hand, these accomplishments required remarkable intelligence, ingenuity, and keenness of observation. Despite the advanced state of society, and the amazing amount of knowledge which had been amassed regarding the heavenly bodies, popular beliefs lagged far behind and very little of this knowledge was reflected in the systems of worship. When Greek scholars

---

2—*Mathematics for the Million*, Lancelot Hogben, pp. 265-266.
3—The true length of the sidereal day is 23 hrs. 56 min. 4 sec. and our calendar year is 365 days 5 hrs. 48 min. 46 sec.

declared that the sun was not a god, but was a huge ball of fire, they were berated as atheists. Myths and religious beliefs which prevailed at the beginning of the Christian era concerning the nature of the universe, its origin, age, and structure were almost as ridiculous as the naive theories which had prevailed several thousands of years earlier.

Somewhere in the dim past a belief had developed that objects and activities existed in the heavens which were similar in every way to those seen daily on earth. The earth was merely a Microcosm of which heaven was the Macrocosm. First, the sun, moon and stars, the wind, rain, storm, lightning, etc., were personified and deified in the image of man. Then, in order to provide explanations for heavenly phenomena which were beyond their comprehension, the ancients endowed their gods with supernatural powers.

Belief in the ability of gods and demons to transform themselves into birds and animals, to defy the laws of gravity, to change their stature from minute to gigantic proportions, to render themselves invisible, or to perform any other feat that man can conceive, is the oldest and most primitive product of man's effort to think out the ways of the world in which he lives. This presumed ability of the gods constituted a magic formula which enabled mystic priests to provide a solution for any imaginable problem as easily as a magician takes rabbits out of a hat. Once the belief in this supernatural power found its way into the mores of the early peoples, their ability to distinguish between fact and fancy, possibility and impossibility, was impaired and they became susceptible to belief in all kinds of superstitions, myths, magic, and miracles.

With a supernatural explanation provided for all earthly or heavenly phenomena, little incentive remained for seeking their true or scientific explanation. Civilization was thereby immeasurably retarded. As there was no limit to what the gods could do, no story or theory regarding their activities could be disproved, regardless of its apparent absurdity, for who could place limits on the limitless?

Drawing their conception of heaven from the life which they saw about them, the Accadians, in ancient Babylonia, envisioned the sun as a plowman, who yoked oxen to his glittering chariot and plowed his daily path through the heavens. He was even likened to an ox himself, hence the

18. Shu separating Nut, or Neith, (sky) and Seb (earth) at the beginning of creation.

ecliptic was termed the "yoke of heaven," and the god Marduk was sometimes called "the bull of light". The moon was called "Enlil's strong calf". The moon goddess Nana (Ishtar) was called "Anu's young heifer" and was portrayed with horns.

The myths of other very early nations were equally imaginative. In Egypt, the sun god Osiris was worshiped as Apis the bull, and each year a sacred bull was led around the walls of the city or temple every day for 7 days. This was probably the origin of the story of Joshua's commanding the ark to be borne around the walls of Jericho every day for 6 days and 7 times on the 7th day with 7 men blowing bugles. (Josh. 6:3,4).

A cow with a horned moon on her head was a symbol of Isis, who, in one sense, was the moon. This was the origin of the Greek myth of Io, "the chaste virgin" mentioned in the Prometheus of Aeschylus, and accounts for her being represented with a horn on her forehead. Ioh is Egyptian for cow, and Epaphus, the son of Io is derived from Apis, the sacred bull. In the Persian sacred Book of the Avesta the moon is said to be Gao-chithra, that is, possessed of the seed or life principle of the cow which symbolically represents all animal life.

In another account the heaven was a great cow, with her head to the west, the earth between her fore and hind feet, and her under parts studded with stars. According to another version, the sky was a woman bent over, with her hands and feet resting on the ends of the earth. She was sister of the earth god Seb. In the beginning, the sky goddess Nut, or Neith, was locked in connubial embrace with Seb until Shu the air god thrust them apart, whereupon she remained fixed in the sky with the ships of the sun and stars sailing across her body. This legend is similar to the story in the Babylonian Creation Epic in which Marduk split the body of the female Tiamat, using one half. of her body to form the heavens and forming the earth from the other half.

One of the labors of Marduk in the Creation Epic was dividing the primeval waters, forming from one part the waters which were thought to exist all around and under the earth and forming from the other part the great body of water which was believed to constitute the "firmament of heaven".

Over this celestial sea the gods sailed in boats. After dropping to the western horizon at sunset, the sun was said to spend the night paddling his heavenly craft back to the east to repeat his journey the following day. Models of such sacred boats were to be found in Babylonian temples, and in Egypt they were carried in religious processions.

The Biblical accounts of creation seem to echo the Babylonian story of the division of the firmament's waters, and in the early centuries of Christianity the nature of the firmament became a lively subject for speculation. Some fathers of the church believed the firmament was supported by pillars at the four corners of the world. Saint Jerome quoted Ezekiel to prove that God froze the waters of the firmament at the time of creation in order to keep them in place. For several centuries it was the generally accepted view of the church that high over the universe there were solid arches which supported the heavenly waters and that angels opened windows in the firmament whenever the Almighty wished to send rain upon the earth.[4]

In an Indian creation story, the earth was conceived as resting on the back of an elephant which, in turn, stood on the back of a turtle.

In another Hindu version of creation, a lotus is represented as rising from the navel of Vishnu. In the lotus

4—See *History of the Warfare of Science with Theology in Christendom.* Andrew D. White, v. 1, p. 324.

19. The sky represented as Nut, the celestial cow, supported
in the heavens by Shu (air) and minor gods. Shu stands in a
sacred boat.

20. Vishnu with his Sakti on Sesha the 7-headed serpent, contemplating creation. A lotus rises from Vishnu's navel and the
four-headed Brahma sits in the blossom while performing
the creation.

blossom sits Brahma, brooding over the primeval waters and surveying the results of creation.

In early Egyptian sculpture, the sun is represented in human form with the head of a hawk, emblematic of his lofty and rapid flight. In later periods, he is represented in Egyptian, Babylonian, Hittite, and Assyrian sculpture by a disk which is sometimes winged, or surrounded by radiating lines or rays, symbolizing the sun's rays.

Both in Egypt and in India, the sun was sometimes represented differently for the various parts of the year. In Egypt, the sun was represented in spring as a child and in autumn as an old man. Osiris or Atum (Amon) was the sun when it had set and was hid from view. Ra was the midday sun.

In numerous myths the sun god was conceived as flying through the heavens in a chariot drawn by four white horses. (The Hindu version gives the sun god Surya seven green horses.) Because of its rapid passage across the sky, the sun was sometimes called in the Veda, "the quick racer", "the runner", or merely "the horse", and one of the epithets applied to the Greek Apollo is Hippo, meaning horse.

On Assyrian monuments, the sun god is sometimes represented as a man standing on the back of a leaping horse. In some countries, the horse became sacred to the sun, in honor of whom it was burned as a sacrificial offering, and a stable of sacred horses and a golden chariot were often maintained in the temple of the sun god. When Josiah undertook to exterminate sun worship among the Jews, one of his acts was destruction of the chariot and horses which King Solomon had maintained in a suburb of Jerusalem in honor of the sun.

According to Herodotus, during the campaign against the city of Babylon, the Persian King Cyrus exacted a curious bit of revenge against the city for the loss of one of the "consecrated horses of the sun" which was drowned in an attempt to cross the river Gyndes. Cyrus made the stream fordable for his army by dividing it into 360 channels, corresponding to the passage of the sun through the 360 degrees of the zodiac.

The legend of the sun god flying through the heavens in a chariot drawn by a fiery white steed is responsible for

*21. Khnum at his potter's wheel, molding
the first men out of clay.*

the Greek myths in which Phaeton fell from his father's
chariot while driving it across the sky and of Bellerophon
similarly falling to his death from the steed Pegasus. When
the Jewish historians wrote that Elijah was carried in a
whirlwind to heaven in a chariot of fire and horses of fire,
they were merely telling the story in the popular literary
form. (II Kings 2:11).

In a theory of creation found in India, Egypt, Phoenicia, Greece, and among the modern Polynesians and Finns,
the whole universe came from a cosmic egg. In the version
known at Memphis, in Egypt, Ptah (the opener) broke the
egg from which the sun and moon came forth. At Elephantine, the creation of the world was attributed to Knum,
who molded the first man out of the mud of the Nile, like
a potter working with his wheel. Similarly a Greek myth
attributed creation to Prometheus who molded the first man
and beasts out of clay. Emanations of divine fire passed.
into them and became their souls.

At Sais, in Egypt, creation was attributed to Neith, who wove the universe as a weaver makes a piece of cloth. According to one account, the sun god Ra was called "the egg of the cackler", because he was the son of Seb, a word which is equated with "goose". In another myth, Ra was born as a calf of the celestial cow or child of the sky goddess.

According to Japanese mythology, the universe egg was broken by the horns of a bull. Almost every country seems to have had myths asociating a bull with creation and with the sun. He is the same heavenly bull which figures so prominently in Hindu and Babylonian legends, the bull killed by Mithra and who is identified in astrology as Taurus, probably the first sign of the zodiac.

Man's eternal desire to solve the mystery of the origin of himself and the universe led to the invention of equally fanciful accounts of extraordinary acts of the spirits, demons or gods to explain the cause and origin of all phenomena to be seen on earth or in the sky. "Every race has had its legendary accounts of the origin of things, and while creation myths can never be far in advance of the ideas and sentiments of a people, they may and even do, lag far behind. Religious conservatism makes adult nations slow to put away the childish things that faith has once consecrated. If a creation legend has found its *vater sacre,* and been incorporated with the ritual of the altar, scarcely anything short of a miracle is strong enough to charm it away from the popular mind."[5]

For untold centuries, fabulous accounts of creation and the births and deeds of the gods were repeated by magi and priests in thousands of temples, and accepted by the devotees as eternal truths. Uncounted thousands of slaves wore out their bodies building temples and colossal monuments in honor of the great gods and other thousands of worshipers honored them with magnficent processions, ceremonies, prayers, gifts, and the blood of human sacrifices. Man was degraded and made to feel inferior by being taught that all of his vices were his own fault but that all of his virtues, all his accomplishments in his struggle against adversity, were due to the benevolence of a friendly, all-wise, all-powerful deity.

5—*Introduction to History of Religion,* J. B. Jevons, 1896, p. 9.

22. *Ra, as the sun, in his sacred boat ready to begin his daily journey through the heavens. Ra sits in the solar disk. Horus is at the right with a finger to his lips. From an architrave of the entrance to Edfu.*

As the older, cruder beliefs became obsolete through the evolution of society, they were succeeded by newer forms, better adapted to the changing times, but based upon the same old concepts. The magi who read the will and intentions of the gods in the stars, or in the livers of sacrificed animals, were succeeded by holy men of another type, remarkable for the fact that but few of them had normal minds or were educated according to the standards of their times. They were the prophets, seers, ascetics, neurotic reformers, mystic zealots, fanatics, and hermits of the desert who "heard voices", saw strange visions, and were reputedly able to cure lepers, banish fevers, drive out devils, heal the sick, and raise the dead.

Although their teachings varied greatly, the holy men posed as the special spokesmen for the deity, describing his thoughts and appearance and transmitting his commands to the people. Inasmuch as they were esteemed as the very voice of the deity himself, the utterances of the holy men were listened to with great awe and reverence, the very strangeness of their sayings often being accepted as proof of their divine inspiration.

Despite the claims of the holy men to speak for, and in the name of the Supreme One, it is impossible to point to a single instance in which their "divine revelations" regarding the creation and operation of the universe have been confirmed by the findings of science.

No part of our knowledge of the heavens—the age, size, form or composition of the earth, or the origin, species and distribution of animal and plant life on its surface—has been derived from the intuitive methods of the mystics: everything we know about the universe has been learned by the materialistic methods of science.

Probably no people in the ancient world felt the blighting influence of holy men more than the Jews. They were discouraged from studying the causes of natural phenomena because all knowledge which God wished them to know was supposed to be revealed in their sacred scriptures. To question the accuracy of their holy records, or to attempt to peer behind the veil of God's mysteries, was blasphemous, and punishable by death.[6]

As a result of its discouragement of independent thinking, Judea made no discoveries in mathematics or astronomy; its artisans produced no great sculptures, monuments, temples, public buildings, or feats of engineering comparable to those of Egypt, Greece, or Babylon. Development of handcrafts and ability to work in metal and stone in Judea lagged behind that of its neighbors, and the contributions which this small, uncultured country made to western civilization were confined entirely to the field of religion.

When King Solomon decided to build his temple, skilled workers in wood, stone or metal were not to be had in all of Judea, and he found it necessary to appeal to Hiram of Tyre for architects and workers. Traditions say that this building, of simple design, and only about thirty feet wide by ninety feet long, cost eight billion dollars and was the marvel of the world, the envy of all nations. Yet, when Herodotus travelled from Egypt to Babylon, he did not deem it worth while to go by way of Jerusalem to see this marvelous structure. When the invading armies of the Scythians and Alexander the Great came down from the north on their way to Egypt, plundering every city in their path, they marched along the sea coast within a short distance of Jerusalem without considering it a prize worth looting.

6—The secret things belong unto the Lord our God, but those things which are revealed belong to us and to our children forever, that we may do all of the words of this law. *Deut.* 29:29.

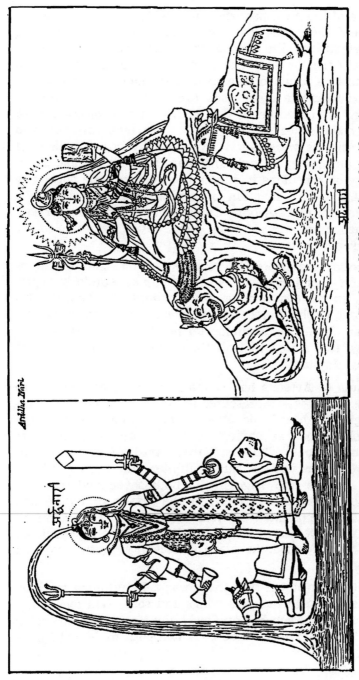

23. *Siva and his Sakti, Parvati, joined as the Hindu Ardha-Nari, his right side being male and his left side female.*

One of the most persistent and widely circulated beliefs in ancient times was that which represented the first gods as bi-sexual. As life among the gods was thought to be similar to that on earth, and as life on earth was seen to result from a union of the male and female, ability of the first god to create other gods (and men) was represented in many myths as being due to his combining both male and female sexes in one body. Ancient mystics and metaphysicians were not handicapped by considerations of earthly physiology or logic and therefore saw nothing extraordinary or ridiculous in such a theory. Its wide popularity is evident in the mention of hermaphroditic gods in the oldest records of Babylonia, China, India, Egypt, and Greece. In time, even minor gods were often represented as combining both sexes.

Apollo was generally represented by the Greeks as male-female and Bacchus was sometimes similarly represented. In his comment on the Timaeus of Plato, Proclus cites some Orphic verses to the effect that "Jupiter (Zeus) is a man, Jupiter is an immortal maid". In the same commentary, it is stated that all things were contained "in the womb of Jupiter".[7]

Diana or Artemis had characteristics of both sexes. In Cyprus, Venus was represented as Aphrodite and was sometimes given a beard and other male characteristics. Diana was looked upon as having existed before Zeus and most of the other gods. The poet Calvus spoke of her as masculine and other writers called Jupiter the mother of the gods. Agditis was originally of both sexes and seems to have been transformed later, in the myths of Cybele and Attis. Damascius cited Orpheus as teaching that, inasmuch as the deity possessed the generative powers by which all things were formed, he was, of necessity, both male and female.

Polyhistor stated that there was a Babylonian tradition that the first men had two wings and some had four wings and two faces. Each had one body and two heads, one being male, the other female. The body had both male and female organs.

7—Jupiter is the king, Jupiter himself is the original source of all things: there is one power, one god and one great ruler, great ruler over all." Proclus, *Timaeus* of Plato, p. 95.

24. Nut as the starry Egyptian goddess of night.

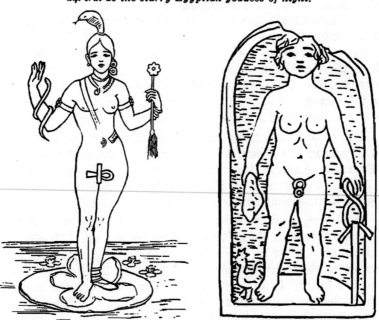

25. Figure at left is from a drawing made by a Hindu Scholar showing Brahma, who, in the act of creation, made himself male and female. In the original the male and female organs are shown united but as they are too gross for reproduction here, they have been replaced by the ankh cross. The figure at right represents young Mercury as being neither male or female. From an ancient Gaulish sculpture.

The Babylonian god Tammuz was consecrated a Qedesha or harlot (I Kings 19:24) and Ishtar sometimes wore a beard.

Porphyry acknowledged that Vista, Rhea, Ceres, Proserpine, Themis, Priapus, Bacchus, Attis, Adonis, Selenus, and the Satyrs were all one and the same. According to the Codex Vaticanus, in the western hemisphere the Mexican bi-sexual deity Ometecutli was worshiped as the creator of the universe.

Egyptian gods were often represented as masculine in front and feminine behind, or human in front and of animal form behind. As the Hindu Ardha-Narisvara or half-woman, Siva and his consort Devi or Kali are united in one body, the right side of which is male and the left side female. In art the right side is usually painted red and the left side is painted black.

The Books of Job[8] and Isaiah[9] represent Jahveh as having male-female characteristics and other evidence indicates that this tradition persisted among the Hebrews from very early times. The first syllable of Jahveh (Jah) is masculine and the second syllable (havvah) is feminine, thus indicating the original conception. According to Prof. Langdon,[10] the name appears to derive from Yāw or Yāh, a pre-historic title of the male-female moon-god among Semitic tribes of South Arabia. The Jews added the female root, making the word Yahweh or Jahvah. Due to an error in translation, the name is spelled Jehovah in the Christian Bible.

Use of the title, however, was not confined to the Arabs and Jews, as it appears in the records of several branches of Semites. Ancient Assyrian texts refer to the same deity as Ja-u or Ja-hu and on Neo-Babylonian tablets the name appears as Ja-a-ma, which is pronounced Jawa.

In the temples of Egypt, Yahweh was worshiped under the titles Y-Ha-Ho; Jao, Iao and Iaw by Gnostic Christians, whose rites and titles were so similar to those used in the worship of Serapis that one could scarcely be distinguished from the other. In fact, Emperor Hadrian in a letter to his Consul, Servianus, expressed the opinion that the Christians in Egypt were worshipers of Serapis.

8—*Job* 21:24; also *Deut.* 32:18.
9—*Isa.* 46:3f.
10—Mythology of All Races, v. 5, p. 5, et seq.

26. At the beginning of the Christian era, Gnostic magicians and faith healers did a thriving business in gems containing magic sentences and monograms like the examples shown above. They were worn as charms or amulets, principally by women, to insure fertility and for protection from evil influences. The name Iaw or Iawhe (Yawheh) frequently appeared with a figure of Priapus, or Horus, and the mystic Gnostic word Abraxas. The figures were usually part man and part dog, snake, cock or lion.

The Hebrew letters (יה) EI (read backward as Yah) are identical with the Greek letters IE which were carved upon the front of the temple of bi-sexual Apollo at Delphi, where priestesses chanted the phrase IEIE IEIE in his praise. Practically the same sound and meaning was conveyed also by the term Yeye Yeye, which devotees sang in honor of Cristna in India, and by the term Euoe Euoe which Bacchantes rendered in honor of Bacchus in Greece.

The word Aleim or Elohim which is employed 2570 times in the Bible as a title of God is also composed of male and female roots and must be considered as having had the same origin and meaning as Jahveh. Al, El, Il or Ilah, meaning lord, was a very ancient title of the sun among Arabians, whence was derived the Mohammedan title of Al-lah. Its equivalent in Hebrew is Eloah which becomes Elohim by addition of the plural termination im. When read backwards, im is pronounced mee, meaning who in the sense of unknown or unknowable. Old Jewish traditions say that the pronunciation of the word is as if one were to say EL HEM, meaning "They are God".

From the tradition that the first gods were male-female came a belief that the first man and woman were also androgynous. As early as 3,000 or 4,000 B.C. oriental creation stories described the splitting apart of the male-female halves of the first androgyne at the time of creation, as previously described in the story of the Babylonian female Tiamat and the Egyptian story of Shu and Tefnut. The first Zoroastrian couple was a two-faced androgyne which was split apart by Ahura-Mazda.

In the centuries immediately before and after the opening of the Christian era, speculation concerning such matters became greatly intensified in the eastern Mediterranean countries. The period is noteworthy both for the great number of mystic religious sects which sprang up and for the extraordinary dogmas which they put forth. To add to the confusion produced by the degeneration of the old nature cults, Jews returning from Babylonian captivity and Greeks returning from the eastern invasion brought back with them a mass of oriental ideas, which produced the greatest plague of theories, mystic sects, evangelists, metaphysicians, healers, and magicians the world had seen up to that time.

*27. Left: A coin from Gaza showing figure of
god Yaw, 4th century B.C.
Right: Coin from Gaza with figure of the androgynous god Ashtart-Yaw.*

A writer in the Talmud says of the creation of Adam
that "when the Holy One created the first man he created
him as a hermaphrodite, as it is written: 'male and female
created he them'."[11] Another account says that "when the
Holy One created the first man he created him with a
double face and then cut him into halves and gave him
two backs, one here, one there."

Many of the strangest anthropomorphisms of the period
were created by Gnostics, Basilideans, and Valentinians and
strongly reflected the influence of Babylonian spiritism,
which made the period reek with angelology, demonology,
witchcraft, devil-chasing and all other forms of magic. Seals
and lockets of these sects contained amulets and charms
with inscribed designs representing Iaw (Jahveh) with
characteristics which identified him with the Egyptian gods
Osiris, Isis, Horus, or Serapis, or portrayed him as part
human and part cock, scarab, dog (Anubis), lion, snake
or other animal—as fanciful and childish in conception as
anything the primitive Sumerians had imagined in 3,000
or 4,000 B.C.

At the beginning of the second century A.D. Elkesai,
the leader of a Jewish Gnostic sect, published a tract in
which he declared the primary man had been "revealed" to
him as a monstrous hermaphroditic being 96 miles high
and 94 miles in breadth and that the male-female halves
were cleft apart to form the Messiah and Holy Spirit.

Several centuries later orthodox Jews were offended by
another work called the Shi'ur Komah (Estimation of the

11—*Bereshith Rabbah* (Midrash Section 5:5). Also see *Jewish Encyclopedia*, v. 8, p. 558. Or *Zohar*, v. 1, p. 11.

Height) written by an Alexandrian Jew who attempted to describe minutely the physical body of God; his neck, beard, right and left eyes, upper and lower lips, ankles, etc. But some of the most learned men of the orthodox faith put forth theories equally preposterous. In one instance the dimensions of Adam[12] are described by a Cabalist as extending from one end of the world to the other and another writer describes a mystic angel called Sandalphon whose "height is a walk of 500 years and who binds crowns for the deity."[13]

Philo Judaeus frequently expressed the opinion that the ideal man was born as man-woman, and Plato believed that man was originally androgynous and had two faces. Eusebius, the Christian Bishop of Caesarea, concurred in this opinion and declared it to be in harmony with the Hebrew Scriptures.

"Other theologians have upheld and accepted this, for example, St. Augustine, de Gubbio (theologian to Pope Paul III at the Council of Trent and Prefect of the Vatican Library) and a minor friar Francesco Giorgio (1522)."[14]

The learned Jewish philosopher Maimonides (12th cent.) thought that Adam was created bi-sexual, with two faces turned in opposite directions, the 'havah or feminine half being separated from Adam during his deep sleep.

Fantastic as these theories are, the boundless credulity which enabled the most learned of men to believe them is even more remarkable. But in things pertaining to the supernatural, time has a way of glossing over and imparting respectability, prestige, and credibility to the wildest products of man's imagination.

Had it been related to either Plato or Maimonides that similar things occurred in their own time and in their own communities, they would doubtless have laughed off the stories as preposterous, but neither of them saw anything ridiculous in believing that such things could and did occur in an earlier period. It does not seem that the great inventors of tall tales ever realized that, if God had the power

---

12—*Zohar*, v. 1, p. 38, translated by Harry Sperling and Maurice Simon. "And this is the mystery of the creation of the first man who was created with two faces (male and female) combined." *Zohar*, p. 11.

13—*Haggada*, 13.

14—*The Night of the Gods*, John O'Neill, 1893, v. 1, p. 240.

to create man and woman at all, he could have done so in a workmanlike manner and not have had to produce fabulous monstrosities. Yet, in extenuation of their superstition, it is only fair to admit that it is no more absurd to believe that the first man and woman were split apart at the time of creation than it is to believe that Adam was made from mud and that Eve was shaped from one of his ribs. The most marvelous things have always been represented as having occurred, not right at home under the eyes of the writers, but in the remote past, or in a distant town or country, and the awe with which people still regard ideas or things which are merely very old or exotic shows no signs of becoming outgrown.

VII

DEATH AND RE-BIRTH OF THE SUN GOD

IN THE FERTILITY MYTHS, the sun was represented as a handsome young god who impregnated the earth with his life-giving warmth and life, thus being the source of growth in vegetation and stimulator of the procreational activity which caused animals to mate and bring forth their young. Everywhere that sun worship flourished, the sun god was honored as the Supreme Deity, the father of all creation.

In the Light-Darkness myths, the sun was portrayed as a powerful blond hero who slew a serpent, dragon or other animal which typified the dark forces of nature, the darkness of night and the cold, dark days of winter.

Features drawn from both the fertility myths and the Light-Darkness myths were represented in a third type which reflected the prevailing theories concerning astronomy and astrology. Where the old fertility myths had depicted the sun god as the lover of a virgin moon or earth goddess, the type now under consideration represented him as the son of a virgin, both his birth and his death taking place at the time of the winter solstice, in the zodiac sign of Virgo, the Virgin.

Because it was believed that the sun regulated the planting and harvesting periods, appointed and distributed the seasons; ran through the climates, swayed the earth, etc., the sun god was looked upon as a legislator, lawgiver, conquering hero. Because the warm rays of the sun were thought to promote cheerfulness and good health, he was called the Bringer of Light and Enlightenment, Wisdom, Peace, Health, and Prosperity, the Good Physician and Savior of Humanity, the Sun of Righteousness who overcame disorder, chaos, strife, sickness and disease.

Probably no myth ever existed which possessed such universal appeal. It was a synthesis of all solar myths. The magnificent temples built in honor of the sun, the colorful festivals, prayers, and rich gifts with which the people of many countries honored him, testified to the implicit faith and fervent reverence of millions of worshipers of the youthful sun hero who died and was re-born to save humanity.

He was generally represented as being born in a cave or cavern, his birth often taking place after a conception of ten months; being born of an undefiled virgin mother of noble family, the birth being heralded by blazing stars and signs in the sky. The infant was said to have been taken by his parents to distant lands to escape from a jealous tyrant who wished to slay him. He amazed his elders by his precocity, grew up in obscurity, healed the sick, and was crucified in the prime of life. His death was marked by earthquakes, lightning and darkening of the sky. He was resurrected in three days and brought light and peace to the world.

Although all of these incidents are not to be found in every solar myth, at least part of them are to be found in the careers of solar heroes of every age and country. Long before the Christian era they were employed in the stories of Tammuz in Babylonia, Attis of Phrygia, Adonis in Phoenicia, Osiris (Horus) in Egypt, Bacchus (Dionysius) in India, Quetzalcoatl in Mexico, Apollo in Greece, Mithra in Persia, Yu in China, and Cristna in India. Some of the motifs, particularly that of virgin birth, may be traced in the careers of Hercules, Prometheus, Aesculapius, Zeus, and in numerous obscure local sun gods of many places.[1]

The sun god legend gave rise to the belief that similar miracles attended the births of all great characters, historical as well as mythical, until, finally, many public men deliberately spread stories of their own virgin birth as evidence of their greatness. Every man who was renowned for virtuous living or for intellectual superiority was supposed to have a portion of the divine mind or essence incorporated or incarnated in him.

Legends developed that miraculous circumstances attended the births of Plato, Pythagoras, Alexander, Augustus, Zoroaster, King Sargon, Amenophis II, Buddha, Socrates, Tamerlane, Pope Gregory, Queen Hathsheput, Scipio Africanus, Caesar, Appollonius, and many others. Even Nero seems to have made some effort to be credited with virgin birth as a token of his greatness, and Emperor Constantine did likewise. A king of Greece found it necessary to issue a decree declaring the death penalty for young, unmarried

---

1—Virgin birth was also attributed to Hermes, Antiope, Auge, Danae, Melanippe, Romulus, Remus, and Saoshyant.

women who attributed the fatherhood of their children to the gods.

Allegory of the Seasons

As the sun appears to recede southward in autumn, the days in the northern hemisphere become shorter and cooler, vegetation withers, fertility of the earth ceases, the sun stands lower in the sky, its warmth and brightness are diminished. Allegorically speaking, the hours and powers of Darkness are gradually winning over the powers of Light.

On December 22nd, in north temperate latitudes, there are twice as many hours of darkness as there are of daylight. For weeks the sun has been growing weaker and weaker. Now is the culminating point, the shortest day of the year. On this day the sun reaches his farthest point southward. In Babylonian mythology this point represented the gates of the underworld, presided over by Nergal, the Prince of Darkness. In the Hercules myth, it represented the arrival of the sun at the Pillars of Hercules, which marked the end of his journey. As the sun sinks below the horizon on this date, the forces of Darkness achieve their victory.[2]

But the supremacy of Darkness is quickly challenged because the virgin goddess (Virgo) gives birth to a new sun which replaces the dead god on the following day, and a new cycle begins.[3] For about three days the length of the day seems to remain unchanged, then it gradually lengthens.

The birth of the sun was personified in Egypt by Horus, the god of light and savior of the world. On the inner walls of the holy of holies in the temple of Luxor, the birth of Horus is pictured in a series of four scenes which are strikingly similar to Christian representations of the Annunciation and Immaculate Conception of Mary and the Birth and Adoration of Jesus. The temple was built by King

---

2—"Having said that a planet entered into a zodiacal sign, the conjunction was denominated a marriage, adultery or incest: having further said that it was buried because it sank below the horizon, returned to light and gained its stage of altitude, it was considered to be dead, risen again, carried to heaven, etc." *Ruins of Empires*, by C. F. Volney, p. 104.

3—According to the Alexandrian astronomer Sosigenes, who revised the calendar for Julius Caesar in 46 B.C., the winter solstice took place on Wednesday night, December 25th at 1:30 a.m. It was reckoned the nativity of the sun because the day then begins to lengthen.

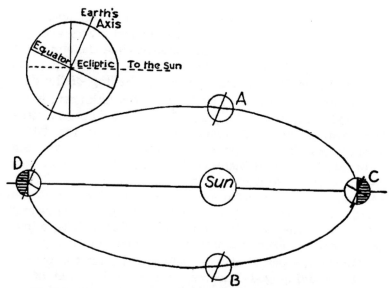

28. *The earth's path around the sun. A and B show position of the earth on March 21st and September 22nd when day and night are of equal length. C and D show position of the earth on December 21st and June 21st, the shortest and longest days, of the year. The small diagram shows inclination of the earth's axis toward the sun on June 21st.*

Amenhept III of the seventeenth dynasty about sixteen centuries before Christ.

In the first scene Taht, the scribe of the gods, announces to the virgin that she will give birth to a son. In the second scene Kneph and the goddess Hathor hold ankh crosses, or keys of life, to the head and nostrils of the mother-to-be, and whose pregnancy is indicated by her swelling form.

In the third scene the mother is seated on the midwife's stool and the new born babe is held by attendants. In the fourth scene the enthroned child is receiving homage from men and gods. The three figures behind Kneph, on the right, are probably the three magi or kings of the legend. Each one holds gifts in the right hand and an anhk cross in the left.

In India, during the Aries age, the passage of the sun into the sign of Capricorn was celebrated during the twelve days immediately following the winter solstice in honor of the Vedic gods Indra and Agni, with the addition (later) of the god Ganesa. Presents were exchanged, cattle were led about with garlands around their necks; all who could do so took purification baths in the sacred rivers and general rejoicing prevailed.[4] At the present time the sun enters the sign of Capricorn about January 15th which is the time of a festival in India marking the lengthening of the days.

Because the date of Christ's birth was unknown, it was combined, until about the year 354, with a baptismal feast which was celebrated January 6th in Rome on the date of an old pagan festival. After that time his birth was generally observed on December 25th and the custom soon spread to the eastern churches. But there was no officially fixed date for celebration of the Nativity by the Roman Church until about the year 530 A.D., when, at the request of the Pope, the Scythian monk Dionysius Erigos, a poet and astronomer fixed the date as December 25th.

During the period shortly before and after the birth of Christ the dying god Dusares, "the only begotten of the Lord" born of the virgin goddess Allat, was worshiped by the Nabataeans in the Syrian cities of Petra, Bostra, and Adraa. He was a god of fertility and was portrayed as a deity of the vine similar to the Greek god Bacchus. His birth was celebrated in December with games and festivities. Allat was pictured with a cornucopia, which identified her as the goddess of fate or fortune. Like Athena, she wore on her head a mural crown with turreted walls, which identified her as the protectress of cities.

A similar festival was held in Alexandria on December 25th in honor of a little known goddess called Kilkellia. In this festival the image of an infant was taken from the temple sanctuary and greeted with loud acclamations by the worshipers who shouted "The Virgin has begotten".

In Alexandria the "Birth of the Aeon" was celebrated by Gnostics on the nights of January 5th and 6th. At this time priests of the cult met in the temple of the goddess Koré who was probably associated with the Greek goddess of the Underworld. A figure of the goddess resting on a bier, seated and nude, with crosses marked on her brow, hands, and knees, was brought up from an underground shrine. After dancing, singing hymns, and carrying the image seven times around the temple, it was returned to its dwelling place below. Epiphanius, who described the

---

4—*Ocean of Story,* Edited by Norman Penzer, v. 8, p. 19.

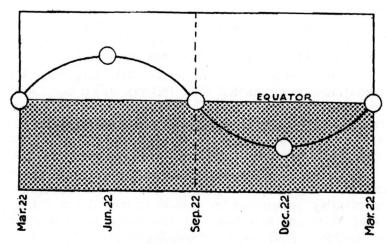

29. *The diagram indicates the six months during which the sun rises north of the equator and the six months when it rises south of the equator, that is, when it is in the "Underworld."*

ceremony, added: "and the votaries say that today at this hour Koré, that is the virgin, gave birth to the Aeon".

Spring

For weeks after the winter solstice, the puny, newborn sun struggles against the powers of Darkness. Myths present the youngster as growing up in obscurity or concealment. But as the weeks pass, the young sun god gathers strength, rising higher and higher in the sky, his brightness increasing rapidly until finally on March 21st, he emerges victorious.

This is the day of the spring equinox, when the sun crosses the equator. It is the turning point, the day of his Passover or Crossification. Night and day are of equal length all over the world on this date, the sun rising at 6:00 a.m. and setting at 6:00 p.m. Now begins a period in which the hours of light exceed the hours of darkness, symbolized as the sun's resurrection from the Underworld (the lower signs of the zodiac) and with its regeneration, life and vegetation can continue; the young sun redeems the world from darkness.

During the Aries (lamb) age, Egyptians celebrated this season by sacrificing a lamb. Three days later they celebrated the resurrection of the young sun god. The Jewish custom of killing the paschal lamb and celebrating the Passover is said to commemorate the Lord's passage over the houses in Egypt when he slaughtered all of the first-born children and animals of the Egyptians.[5]

There is little reason to doubt that, originally, the celebration was an ancient solar festival. With the rise of Christianity, the day and hour on which Jews were commanded to sacrifice the lamb came to be observed as the day and hour on which Christ died on the cross, his Resurrection being celebrated on the third day following.[6]

From the dawn of history, this was the time of the most joyful season of the year. It was deemed the mating and planting season and, in most calendars, it marked the beginning of the new year. As the young sun, Tammuz, rose on the first day of the week, Babylonians closed their places of business and went to the temple of Bel Tammuz for the purpose of offering solemn thanksgiving to the sun god. In Phrygia, Gaul, and, apparently, in Rome, the death of Attis was celebrated at the spring equinox and his re-birth was celebrated on March 25th.

In the Holi festival, held in India at this season, Hindus throw red powder on each other in imitation of the pollen which fructifies flowers and plants. This festival is thought to have been connected, originally, with worship of the sun. In the Roman Church, March 25th is celebrated as the Annunciation of the Virgin Mary, exactly nine months before Christ's birth on December 25th.

Summer

On June 21st, the longest day of the year, the youthful sun reaches the farthest point northward in the ecliptic. On this day the sun rises earlier and sets later than on any other day of the year. On June 21st, the earth's North Pole is inclined 23½ degrees toward the sun, and on December 21st this position is reversed, the North Pole then being inclined 23½ degrees away from the sun.

To the Babylonians the point of the summer solstice represented the gate of Nibbu, the domain of the god Anu,

---

5—The lamb was sacrificed at 3:00 p.m. in the afternoon on the 14th day of Ahib (later Nisan) the first month. It was a full moon festival and was followed by fasting until the equinox, seven days later.

6—The time now fixed for Resurrection Day or Easter is the first Sunday after the full moon following the vernal equinox.

"the point beyond which no man can pass". It marks the very peak of the sun god's virility, when he shines with maximum brilliance and heat. The culminating point is at the full moon which marks the day when the sun mates with Ishtar, the Great Mother Goddess.

It also marks the beginning of the sun's decline, for, having given freely of his energy to restore fertility to the earth, his powers begin to wane, that is, the length of the days soon begin to decrease. In Babylon both the marriage and the decline of Tammuz[7] were celebrated but a few days apart. This was the significance of the statement of Gilgamesh in which he accused Ishtar of being an enchanter, a poisoner and sapper of virility. For his death the people of Babylon and other Chaldean cities were in the habit of mourning and fasting for 40 days prior to the great festival of Ishtar.

In all parts of the world may be found customs and legends relating to the apparent rise and decline of the sun's virility. Some legends relate that the sun is retarded by being bound with ropes. The day on which the sun turns in his course and begins to retreat toward the south has also been marked by celebrations in which the participants lighted and leaped over bonfires and in all ages, fire and fire worship have been closely associated with the sun. In France these fires were called the *feux de joie*: in England, *bon* fires; in Germany, *Johannsisfeuer* (St. John's fire); in Ireland they were called *Baal tinne* (time of Baal's fire).

This custom was observed from Iceland to Spain and Greece in the south. The custom is widespread among the Mohammedans of North Africa, particularly in Morocco and Algeria. It is common, both to the Berbers and to many of the Arabs and Arab-speaking tribes despite the fact that such customs are strictly forbidden by the Mohammedan religion, and despite the fact that the moon and not the sun is the central figure in that religion.[8]

It was from the Druidic custom of burning a whuil or log (from the Saxon word meaning wheel or circle) that we derive the custom of burning Yule logs. It is estimated that the altar stone in the huge circle of stones forming

7—The 10th day of Tammuz (June 25th) was a day of mourning to the Babylonians.
8—*The Golden Bough*, Sir James Frazer, Abgd. Ed., p. 631-2.

the ancient ruins at Stonehenge, England, is so placed that it directly faces the rising sun on the day of the summer solstice.

The turning point of the sun was observed by elaborate ceremonies in Egypt, India, China, Greece, Mexico, and Central America. In the eighth century Christian missionaries in Northern Europe complained that the natives celebrated the summer solstice by assembling on hill tops on the eve of June 21st and at sunrise setting fire to large straw-covered wheels, which they rolled down the hills to symbolize the downward course of the sun at this stage of its annual cycle. Grimm mentions having observed this custom in Germany and Northern France in 1823. Today this season is celebrated on June 23rd as St. John's day and the custom of building St. John's fires has been continued by the Roman Church in some countries down to the present time.[9] The celebration of John the Baptist's birthday exactly at the time when the days begin to grow shorter gives pertinence to his prophetic remark: "He (Christ) must increase but I must decrease".

June 21st was fixed by the Greeks for the celebration of their Olympic feasts, the beginning of which was attributed to Hercules, whose first labor was the slaying of a lion, the zodiacal sign of Leo.

Autumn

On September 23rd the powers of Light and Darkness are again on even terms (day and night being of equal length) and the sun now begins its entry into the Underworld. In Babylonian astrology this period marked the entry of the sun into the six lower signs of the zodiac and the six unlucky or unfruitful months. It was also observed by important religious ceremonies as the time of judgment, the period when men's deeds on earth were weighed in the Balance and, on the zodiac, was symbolized by a pair of scales. At this period Babylonians solemnly celebrated the Festival of Lights with processions of the citizens carrying torches to symbolically light the passage of the dead through the Underworld.

The Jews celebrate the seventh month as a memorial

9—In Sardinia, Sicily, Catania, etc. St. John's Day, June 23rd, is celebrated very much the same way as Adonis (and Tammuz) was mourned in past centuries." *The Golden Bough*, Abgd. Ed., Sir James Frazer, p. 344.

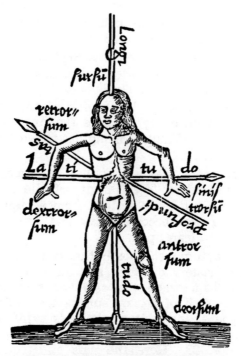

30. *An occult conception of the
Middle Ages showing the Macrocos-
mic man pierced by spears corres-
ponding to the equator and ecliptic.
Reproduced from the* MARGARITA
PHILOSOPHICA, TOTIUS PHILOSOPHIOE
RATIONALIS ET MORALIS PRINCIPIA
DUODECIM LIBRA DIALOGICE COMPLEC-
TENS, *by Joannes Schotus, Prior of
a Carthusian nunnery, Friburg,
1503.*

and the tenth day of the month is observed as the Day of
Atonement. (*Lev.* 23:24,27). On the twenty-fifth of Kislev
(December) they celebrate the Feast of Hanukkah, which
Josephus mentions as a feast of lights. The feast was started
by Judas Maccabbeus, his brothers, and the older congregation of Israel in the year 165 B.C. to celebrate the re-
dedication of the altar in the temple to Jahveh after its
desecration by Antiochus Epiphanes It was usual either
to display eight lamps on the first night of the festival, and
to reduce the number on each successive night, or to begin
with one lamp the first night and increase the number
daily until the eighth night. By tradition, the twenty-fifth
of Kislev was the date of the dedication of the altar in the

time of Moses and probably originated as a solar festival when the calendar was changed from lunar to solar time. The Roman Church celebrates September 14th for St. Michael, the conqueror of Hades. Later in the season comes the observance of All Souls Day.

In Mithraic sculpture the waning of the sun's vitality in winter is symbolized by a figure showing the reproductive organ of a bull (Taurus) being destroyed by a scorpion (sign of Scorpio).

In Egypt there was an annual ceremony after the autumn equinox called "the Nativity of the sun's walking stick", the ceremony being derived from a supposition that the sun, having now become weak and impotent, needed a walking stick to lean upon.

After the autumn equinox,[10] the dark powers steadily increase their mastery over the sun until the final episode on December 22nd when the cycle ends with the sun's death and the birth of a new sun savior. (The death of the old sun god at the winter solstice is typified in a most unusual manner in the sixteenth century drawing reproduced on page 123. Here the axis and equator of the earth form a cross on which is placed the Macrocosmic man, pierced through the heart by a spear which strikes him at an angle of 23½ degrees, the exact angle of inclination of the ecliptic on December 22nd and June 21st).

From the foregoing it will be seen that the dates on which the sun reached the four critical points in its annual journey were the most important dates in the ancient astronomical and astrological systems, the dates on which occurred the principal events in the myth of the sun god. All of the important events of the Old Testament, such as the laying of foundations, dedications of temples and altars occurred on the same cardinal days. The most remarkable events of the New Testament also occurred on the same dates, for instance, the Annunciation and the Assumption of the Virgin Mary, the Birth and the Resurrection of Christ and the birth of John the Baptist.

10—In Egypt the death of the sun god Osiris was observed on the 17th day of the month Athor, which was at the time of the autumn equinox, when the sun entered the six lower signs of the zodiac. An ark was made in the shape of the crescent moon and on the nineteenth of the same month, the priests proclaimed that Osiris was found, his resurrection being on the third day of the moon.

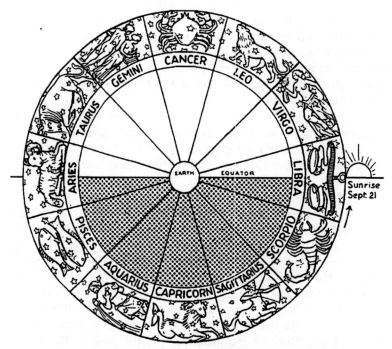

31. *Position of the zodiac constellations at sunrise, September 22nd, in the middle of the Aries Age. The constellations of the six fertile months are above the horizon and those of the six infertile months are below. Libra, the Scales, divides the two periods.*
The constellation of Aries which arose with the sun on March 21st is now sinking in the west. Virgo will rise in the east during the night of December 21st and will be at zenith in the morning when the sun rises in Capricorn.

What the Stars Reveal

In most ancient calendars the year began at the time of the vernal equinox, March 22nd. According to the calculations of some astronomers, the sun rose in the sign of Aries at this season of the year from about 2512 to 360 B.C.[11] It was within this period that astrology, the zodiac, and the sun god myths reached complete development, though the first zodiacal signs were charted in the sky much earlier.

11—The beginning and end of a zodiac age can only be approximated because the constellations or signs are separated by imaginary lines arbitrarily placed on maps by astronomers. Estimates of various authorities for the beginning and end of a zodiac age can easily vary as much as 200 or 300 years. According to recommendations of the International Astronomical Union the Aquarius age will begin in 2700 A.D.

As the earth makes a complete revolution every twenty-four hours, all of the twelve signs or constellations follow each other through the sky with a new one rising over the eastern horizon every two hours. And as the earth advances in its orbit around the sun, the sun appears to rise in a different sign each month.

During the Aries age sunrise was in Cancer at the summer solstice, in Libra at the autumn equinox and in Capricorn at the winter solstice. Several hours before sunrise on December 25th, or about midnight, the sign of the Virgin rose above the horizon. This was the hour of the young god's birth.

The sacrificial lamb (Aries) was in the west at this hour and sank below the horizon with the rising of the Virgin in the east. High in the western sky, in the sign of Taurus, stood Orion, the star of Horus. The three bright stars in the Belt of Orion were the three magi or kings. Directly across the sky from Orion is the Scorpion, which, a myth says, followed him, as indeed it does, in the zodiac. In Taurus is the constellation of Columba, the dove, symbol of the Virgin and the Holy Ghost. At the feet of the Virgin is the herdsman Boeotis.

Within the sign of Taurus there is also a small group of stars called the Stable (Aurega). This is the same Stable of Augeas which Hercules mythically cleansed as his sixth Labor and Justin Martyr proudly boasted that Christ was born on the very day when the sun takes his birth in the the Stable of Augeas in the sign of the Goat (Capricorn). It also agrees with the tradition that the sun god was born in a stable or cave (caves or niches carved in the rocks being sometimes used as stables).

Other figures to be seen in a map of the heavens are Hercules and the Dragon which guarded the Garden of Hesperides. Also to be seen are Castor and Pollux, heroes in the myth of Jason's adventure in the ship Argo in search of the Golden Fleece, as well as the Argonaut or ark.

In the sign of Scorpio is the small constellation of Aquila, the eagle. This bird was identified with the Greek god Zeus, the Hindu Vishnu, the Hebrew Jahveh and was one of the four animals mentioned in Ezekiel's mystic vision. The other animals are the bull (Taurus), lion (Leo) and man (Aquarius). During the Taurus age the four bright stars Aldebran, Regulus, Antares, and Fomalhaut in these four signs, that is, Taurus, Leo, Scorpio, and Aquarius, marked the four cardinal periods of the year.

In the Aries age, Capricorn was followed in January by the sign of Aquarius. The principal festival now marking this period is Epiphany, commemorating Christ's baptism and assumption of the Holy Spirit. It is the essence of symbolism that like qualities go together; therefore, when we read that the baptism of Christ by John the Baptist, occurred on January 6th, the event falls just where we should expect to find it, in Aquarius, the Waterman.

January 6th was observed in Egypt as the day of Nilos, when the water of the Nile was said to be at its purest. Epiphanius wrote that this was the season when water was withdrawn from the river and stored, not only in Egypt but in many other countries. In some places springs and rivers were said to turn into wine on this day. From this tradition a myth developed to the effect that Bacchus (Dionysius) turned water into wine at this very time of the year; and, by one of those "coincidences" which are to be found so frequently in the Scriptures, the turning of water into wine at the marriage in Cana was the first miracle of Jesus.

Two centuries after Epiphanius, Chrysostom commanded that the water be blessed and drawn from the rivers at the baptismal feast. In Catholic communities priests still bestow blessings on rivers and other bodies of water at this season of the year, the practice doubtless being derived from the ancient Egyptian custom.

VIII

SEX SYMBOLISM

T HE MYTHS WHICH WERE WOVEN about the sun gods and mother goddesses were not only astronomical allegories portraying various aspects of the seasons and the fertile and infertile periods in nature, but were also expressions of a philosophy which envisioned the entire universe as a great sexual system. From the observation that creation of life on earth was dependent upon the union of male and female, it was but a simple matter to think of the earth as the mother goddess in whose womb seed was impregnated by the light and heat of the sun, who, therefore, was thought of as the great father of all existence.

All sun and moon cults were, in fact, fertility cults and their principal gods were fertility gods. The difference between sun worship and sex worship was largely one of emphasis.

Greek mythologists were conscious of the traditional relation between heaven (or the sun) and earth when they represented Ouranos and Gaia or Zeus and Demeter, as husband and wife. Belief in this relation still persists in the minds of Hindus, and annually, at spring time, when the sal tree is in bloom, the Orāon people of Bengal celebrate the marriage of the earth goddess Prthivi (meaning broad) to Dyaus, the sky god.

In a treatise on agriculture, Columella, a Roman writer, said: "it is the union of the universe with itself, or with the mutual action of the two sexes; the great secrets of nature, her sacred orgies, her mysteries, which have been portrayed in the initiations with innumerable emblems. From these are derived the ithyphallic feasts and the consecration of the phallus and cteis, or sexual organs, of man and woman in the ancient sanctuaries."

Whereas myths allegorized nature in narrative form, symbols served a similar purpose in a more graphic way. Thus, the spring sun was portrayed in paintings and sculpture as a lusty child, and the winter sun was represented as a feeble old man with a flowing beard.

Many of the earliest languages did not have a neuter gender and everything on earth or in the sky was designated male or female, according to its imagined positive or negative qualities. Every property, condition, or quality, such as directions, metals, gestures, colors, shapes, forms, letters, numerals, etc., acquired a definite significance in the all-embracing scheme. In this universal two-fold system, natural characteristics were classified somewhat as follows:

Male	*Female*
Positive	Negative
Sun	Earth (or moon)
Life	Death
Summer	Winter
Good	Evil
Odd	Even
Fire	Water
Heat	Cold
Vertical	Horizontal
Square	Round
Angular	Curving
Seen	Unseen, and so forth

By association of ideas, wells, pools, lakes, valleys, caves, caverns, clefts, and fissures in the earth were likened to the matrix and esteemed as places of special veneration. In these places the emblems of maturity were sacrificed to Astarte. This seems to have been the custom referred to in Isaiah 57:5, where mention is made of mothers "slaying children under the clefts" of the rocks. Early Christians denounced such places as *cunno diaboli* (Devil's Yonies),

Holes or fissures in the earth from which sounds, vapors or gases escaped were esteemed as sacred oracles. The great Greek oracle at Delphi was such a place, the name itself being derived from *delphus,* meaning womb. When spelled *delphis,* the word means dolphin. Aphrodite, the goddess of love is associated with fecundity and birth and, as *delphis,* the dolphin, is associated with *delphus,* the womb, or birth place, Aphrodite is often represented as seated on a leaping dolphin.

Round or dome-shaped rocks or mounts, hills and "high places" were likened to the breasts of nature, or to the navel of the earth, which connected the old with the new. Such places were anciently the favorite locations for sacred altars and edifices. Artificial mounds and pyramids were similarly esteemed and their remains, in various sizes and styles, are to be found in all parts of the world. In Sparta, cakes shaped like breasts were carried in wedding processions by women who followed the bride and sang her praise.

The mountain on which Apollo was born was called Titthonia, meaning "the nipple". "When round towers were situated upon eminences fashioned very round," said J. R. Bryant, "they were, by the Ammonians, called Tith. They were so denominated from their resemblance to a woman's breasts and were particularly esteemed to Orus and Osiris, the deities of light; hence the summit of Mount Parnassus was named Tithorea from Tith-Or." The symbolic relationship between rounded objects and the female principle was probably the source of the ancient custom of placing a boss, mount, or navel in the center of buns or sacred cakes, and of building low, round domes on Oriental temples.

From *omphe, om-pi,* or *am-be* was derived the Greek word omphalos or umbilicus, and the mountain where oracles were delivered was called Har-Al-Ompi or merely Olympos. The *ompi* at Delphi was called Omphi-El, or oracle of the sun; while the moon was designated Olympias. At the temple of Amon, in Libya, an emblem of the god, described as an umbilicus of immense size, was borne in a boat carried on the shoulders of 80 men.

The wife of Siva, the Hindu god of creation, is called Parvati, and her ompi, boss, or navel is one of the particular "jewels" to which her worshipers pay adoration. As the full-breasted mother, "the lady of the mountain" or "the mountainous one", she is the great omphalos of all creation, a term which was also applied to Ishtar.

The temples of the Babylonians were built on mounds of earth or brick, sometimes raised many feet above the plain and called "mountain of the world" or "mountain of the gods".

In Palestine, from the days of Abraham, the sacred altars were built on hills or "high places". During the reign of King Solomon the country was covered with statues and phallic emblems and mounts, or high places, for Chemosh (Babylonian sun god Shamash) and Moloch, the god of fire.

These shrines remained throughout the monarchy until Josiah broke them down.[1]

Early Chaldeans believed their "holy house of the gods" stood in the exact center of the universe. Egyptians visualized the world in the form of a human figure in which Egypt was the heart and Thebes was the center. For Assyrians the center was Babylon, for Hindus it was Mt. Meru, and for the Greeks it was Delphi.

Before Mohammedans made Mecca their holy city, they looked upon Jerusalem as the center of the universe. Prophet Ezekiel declared Jerusalem was in the middle of the earth, and it became a general belief among the Jews that Mt. Moriah, in Jerusalem, the site of Solomon's temple, was the "navel" of the universe. St. Jerome accepted this view and it became the orthodox position of medieval churchmen, who quoted Ezekiel as their inspired authority. The round hill of Mt. Tabor, which Christians called "the Mount of Transfiguration", is still called by Mohammedan fellaheen the "umbilicus" of the great mother Terra.

The most important part of the Church of the Holy Sepulchre in Jerusalem is the nave east of the rotunda. Here the floor is not occupied except for a short column, probably an ancient symbol representing the tree of life and marking the center of the world.

According to an old Irish belief, the navel of the world was on the boundaries of Meath where five provinces meet and was called Uis-Neach, where tradition said the sacred fire was lighted. The Arch Druids called it Midhe and the spot was marked by a large stone called Cul-na-mireann, that is, "stone of the parts".

The medieval practice of seeking Scriptural authority for questions of geography was the source of a belief that not only did the site of the cross on Calvary mark the geographical center of the earth, but that on this very spot had stood the tree which bore the forbidden fruit in the Garden of Eden.[2] This belief prevailed until after Columbus demonstrated that the world is round. In modern usage the "nave" of a church is its hub, center, or navel.

1—Yet have I set my king upon my holy hill of Zion. *Ps.* 2:6.
And he heard me out of his holy hill. *Ps.* 3:4.
2—*History of the Warfare of Science with Theology*, Andrew D. White, vol. I, p. 98.

The sacred omphalos among the holy images in the temple of Apollo was closely related to Python, the sacred snake of Delphi and to the cosmic egg which various myths describe as the original source of creation.

The omphalos was generally represented as a conical stone resembling the shape of half an egg standing on a low quadrangular base, but sometimes it took the form of a whole egg merely flattened at the bottom to enable it to stand on the pedestal. In this form, its appearance is quite similar to the loop, or handle, of the Egyption ankh cross, which, in its numerous forms, symbolized the female principle.

Sometimes the omphalos appeared bare and at other times it was draped with hanging fillets or covered with cross-hatched lines represented either as plain ribands or as tied tightly at regular intervals to resemble a string of eggs.

In China the earth is visualized as square and the heavens as round. In harmony with this conception, the sacred temple of the moon (identified with heaven) is round. This relation is also observed in the Chinese "cash" or coin, which is a thin circular disk with a small, square hole in the center. The union of circle and square, heaven and earth, male and female, represented to the Chinese the divine source of all things. It was probably for similar reasons that the square and compass, the instruments employed to make these forms, became symbols of Freemasonry.[3] The custom of tonsuring the heads of Roman Catholic priests was derived from Egyptian priests, who shaved a circular spot on the tops of their heads to represent the disk of the sun.

In countries where women are separated from men in the household, the zenanas or female quarters are considered the womb of the house, and certain ancient writings refer to these quarters in terms which may be translated as "the

---

3—"On account of the circle and square, the Sabbaths here referred to come under the injunction of the word 'keep' used in the second verse of the Ten Commandments (*Deut.*, Ch. 5.). (The circle and square were used by Cabalists to symbolize the three highest Sephiroth in the Cabala). The Lord's sanctuary is situated in the center (of his palace) and which is most to be averted is the penalty of penetrating into the place of the circle and square, treading on the spot where the central point is situated." *Zohar*, vol. 1, p. 23, Translated by Harry Sperling and Maurice Simon.

between the thighs" of the house. The "holy of holies" was the womb of the ancient temples.

Throughout the world, the east or sunrise point was the prime direction and signified light, life, and birth. The west and southwest were the land of the dead. Temples, cathedrals and churches were oriented to the sunrise point at the vernal equinox, to the sumer solstice, or to the sunrise point on the day sacred to the saint to whom the church was dedicated. In China, however, the temple of the sun at Pekin was oriented to the sun at the time of the winter solstice. The great temple of Ishtar in Babylon was built at the northeast corner of the wall surrounding the city, at the point toward the rising sun at the vernal equinox.

At the great Egyptian temple at Thebes, there was a long avenue, lined on each side with statues of ram-headed sphinxes. The avenue was so oriented that on the twenty-first day of June, at the precise moment when the sun reached its farthest point northward, its rays spread down the long avenue, passed through the narrow temple entrance and, for a brief moment, illuminated the sacred image in the holy of holies. This symbolized the impregnation of seed in the womb of the great earth mother by the sun.

The orientation of the temple of Isis is described by an inscription which reads: "She (the star of Isis) shines into her temple on New Year's day and she mingles her light with that of her father Ra (the sun god)". The particular star of Isis was Sothis, or Sirius (the Dog star), and it has been determined by calculation that a conjunction of Sothis and the sun took place in 700 B.C. This was the very date on which the great zodiac was constructed in the temple of Osiris at Denderah, so, it was built as a memorial to the conjunction of Isis and Osiris or Ra.[4]

The Jewish historian Josephus wrote that as early as Solomon's day the temple at Jerusalem was oriented to the east and at the vernal equinox, the rays of the sun passed down an open passage to the holy of holies which the high priest entered only once each year.[5] It was open to the east and closed to the west. There is evidence that the entrance of sunlight on the morning of the spring equinox formed part of the ceremonies.

4—*Dawn of Astronomy*, J. Norman Lockyer, 1894, p. 194.
5—*Ibid*, p. 92.

Many English churches are oriented so that the sun shines through the window above the high altar and worshipers face the sun. St. Paul's Cathedral and Westminster Abbey in London, Notre Dame in Paris, St. Peter's in Rome, and the Cathedral of Milan are oriented to the vernal equinox.

"In regard to St. Paul's at Rome," says Lockyer, "we read that so exactly due east and west was the Basilica that on the vernal equinox the great doors of the porch of the quadriporticos were thrown open at sunrise and also the eastern doors of the church itself and, as the sun rose, its rays passed through the outer doors, then through the inner doors and penetrated straight through the nave, illuminating the high altar."[6]

In the East, the dead were always buried facing toward the rising sun. This practice also became widespread in Europe. The orientation of churches in Christian countries began within the first four centuries. Despite protests against the custom in the Middle Ages, it continued; and until recent times, all churches were more or less oriented, particularly the Roman and English churches.

"In baptism, the catechumen was placed with his face toward the west, then commanded to renounce Satan with gestures of abhorrence, stretching out his hands against him, or smiting them together and blowing or spitting against him thrice. The ceremony and significance are clearly set forth by Jerome: 'In the mysteries (meaning baptism) we first renounce him who is in the west and dies to us with our sin and so, turning to the east, we make a covenant with the Sun of Righteousness, promising to be his servants'."[7]

Orientation was never a law of ecclesiastical architecture, yet it became dominant in early centuries. The author of the *Apostolic Constitution* gives directions for building churches toward the east and Vitruvius stated that churches should be oriented toward the east.[8]

Orientation of lodges of the Freemasons is similarly observed, the seat of the Master being placed on the side toward the rising sun and the seat of the Senior Warden

6—*Ibid*, p. 96-98.
7—*Augustin de Serm.*, Dom. in Monte 2, 5 cited by Edw. B. Tylor, *Primitive Culture*, vol. 1, p. 428.
8—*Ibid.* p. 427.

being placed on the western side, which is dedicated to the moon.

Among Babylonians and other Semites, the north was associated with heaven, the overworld, the region presided over by Anu, supreme god of the heavens. Jewish records show that they regarded the north as the dwelling place of the Lord,[9] and animals sacrificed in the temples were killed "on the side of the altar northward before the Lord". (Lev. 1:11).   ·

There is a slight contradiction to be noted here which probably arose through the astrological system, because while the north, the region of Anu, is considered the overworld, or heaven, it is also the region farthest removed from the south, the region associated with the sun. The north is therefore associated, in a sense, with hell, the region of darkness.

The customs, which prevailed in many countries, of performing dance movements clockwise, or sunwise, and of passing wine and playing cards in the same direction, probably originated in primitive sun worship. It was customary, in the Orient, for worshipers to face the sun during their morning prayers, and this placed the left, or female, side of the body toward the north. It was perhaps due to this association of ideas that the entrance and meeting place for women was on the north, or dark, side of the temple. Ezekiel complained because the Jewish women gathered there and sat mourning for the sun god Tammuz.[10] There also was located "the seat of the image of jealousy"[11]; and, although the Bible makes the image somewhat of a mystery, there can be but little doubt that it was a phallic image, probably an ashera.

In medieval England the north doors of churches were reserved for the passage of suicides, criminals, and condemned persons and the northern parts of cemeteries were believed to be gathering places for evil spirits. In China the side of an object on which the sun shines is considered as male, and the sunless or dark side, as female. Accordingly, the north sides of mountains, buildings, etc., are designated as Yin, or female.

9—I will sit also upon the mount of the congregation on the sides toward the north. *Isa.* 1:13.
10—Ezek. 8:14.
11—Ezek. 8:3,5.

There is an old custom in the Scotch Highlands, of "making the deazil", walking sunwise three times, around a person to whom it is desired to wish good luck. Walking around the person in the opposite direction, or "withershins," brings bad luck.[12] In the west of England it is said that "if an invalid goes out for the first time after an illness and makes a circuit, the circuit must be with the sun: if against the sun, there will be a relapse. In Devonshire it is believed that blackheads or pinsoles may be cured by creeping from east to west on hands and knees or through a bramble three times".[13]

In China, Tibet, and India the stupas or shrines have raised platforms around them for circumambulation of pilgrims. A similar custom prevails at the Ka'bah at Mecca and the holy sepulchre at Jerusalem.

Almost universally, the right hand has represented masculinity and good fortune; the left is associated with femininity and bad luck. This is exemplified by our word "sinister," which originaly meant left-handed, evil, unlucky, and by the word "dextrous," meaning right-handed or lucky. To Arabs and Abyssinians the right hand is "the hand of honor", the right side is the side on which distinguished guests are placed; the left hand is "the hand of dishonor", for which reason the left hand is used to perform all acts which are considered unclean. The Jews also preserve this custom. In performing ceremonies in Jewish temples "every turn must be made to the right of the way" (Yoma 15 B) and left-handed persons are disqualified from becoming rabbis.

Similar ideas prevail in India, where the worshipers of Sakti are divided into two leading branches, the Daksinacharis, or followers of the right hand, and the Vamacharis, or followers of the left hand ritual. The Vamis adopt a form of worship contrary to that which is usual, and they worship Durga, the Sakti or divine energy of Siva, in all her terrific forms.[14]

It is customary for a Brahman to pass persons or objects so that the right hand is always kept toward them\ Among the Vasavadatta it is customary for the devotee to walk around an object with the right hand toward it during the

---

12—*Romances & Drolls* of West England, Hunt, p. 418.
13—*English Folklore*, Thistleton Dyer, p. 171.
14—*Sacred Books of India*, vol. 26, p. 1012.

marriage ceremony. A similar custom appears to have existed among the Romans and Celts. In accordance with a law of Manu, a bride in the Vasavadatta ceremony must walk three times around the domestic hearth, or she and the groom may walk around the central pole in the marriage shed, or a sacred building, tomb, or sacrifice.[15]

In all ages the hand has been the symbol of strength, power, authority, and creative activity. The raised hand may represent a warning or a sign of protection. During the Middle Ages, the hand of God was often used in this sense in Christian art. In India, the raised right hand is a sign of Siva and is often found engraved on sacred stones, village gateways, and sacred groves. Egyptians often used the hand as a symbol of the creative power of the sun. One account tells us that a colossal right hand of the mighty god Anu was mounted on the summit of the Tower of Babel. Hindus and early Mexicans impressed the hand, covered with blood or vermillion, on the doorposts of their temples, that is, on the delphus or door of life.

A divine hand with the thumb and two forefingers resting on a cruciform nimbus was an Egyptian symbol of Isis. The first finger, which is the only one which can stand alone, is the symbol of the creator, divine law, and wisdom; the middle finger represents the Holy Spirit.

A side view of the hand with the thumb and forefinger forming an O and the other fingers raised, is a male sexual symbol. It may also be read as 1 and 0 or 10, a Cabalistic number for the creator.

One hand pointed upward and the other pointed downward is a sign of heaven and earth, called in India the Sign of the Witness. It is common in China as well as in all other countries where Buddha is venerated.

Examples of the heaven and earth sign have been found in Babylonia; in Greece they have been found on articles connected with the Eleusinian Mysteries. During the 14th, 15th, and 16th centuries this sign was much used in Europe.

Hands crossed downward signify the cross of the equinox, or St. Andrew's cross. In Christian art it represents the burial and resurrection of Christ.

15—*Ocean of Story*, vol. 1, p. 190.

The sign of the vesica piscis is made by raising the first two fingers and bending the third and fourth fingers over so as to meet the thumb. Jewish priests make a similar sign when pronouncing benediction, except that they raise the three middle fingers. The significance of the mystic poses of the hands of Jewish rabbis shown in Plate 32, Figs. 7, 8, 9, is best revealed by comparing them with the hands of a Hindu dancer shown on the same page, and with various symbols of the matrix.

Horns are indicated by holding the first and little fingers erect while the second and third fingers are closed in the palm of the hand, with the thumb being thrust against the first finger. When the thumb is bent so as to touch the middle fingers lightly it makes a combined sign of the vesica and horns.

The horn sign, originating in moon worship, became a sign of divinity. Horns of the bull or cow, typifying honor, power, and royal dignity, were placed over doors as talismen of good luck. Ishtar, Cybele, Isis, Diana, and other mother goddesses possessing moon characteristics were usually portrayed with a crescent moon over their heads. The Egyptian goddess Hathor, the world cow, was often portrayed as having the head of a vulture surmounted by a crescent or horned moon and a solar disk. Today, in Italy and other countries, superstitious people make the horn sign to avoid the evil eye. In Greek art, the cornucopia, or horn of plenty, was associated with the gods and goddesses of vegetation.

All of the early mystery religions used secret signs, gestures, and passwords for the identification of members. As the pagan cults began to disintegrate several centuries before the Christian era, numerous minor sects sprang up, such as the Essenes, Therapeutae, Gnostics, etc., which maintained many of the old secret rites and practices. Long before the Christian church was founded, the general pattern of religious organization had become well established by tradition. As the new religion took form, it adopted many of the rites as well as the secret handclasps, signs, and passwords of the older cults. In Rome their use was particularly widespread because of opposition to the new religion during the first three centuries of its existence. Unbaptized persons were not permitted to be present at the Holy Communion, and even now certain

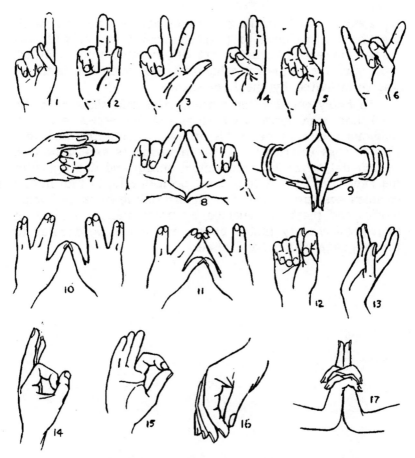

32. *Hand signs: Fig. 1 is a sign of the creator. 2, Holy Trinity.
3, gesture of Catholic and Episcopal priests in giving benediction. 4, benediction (Jewish). 5, vesica discis. 6, sign of the
horns. 7, phallic sign. 8, 10, 11, mystic signs of Jewish rabbis.
9, hands of a Hindu dancer. (Compare with forms on Plate
48.) 12, sign of the fig. 13, yoni sign. 14, same as No. 7. 15,
16, yoni signs. 17, union of male and female.*

secrets of the mass are made known only to the priests. In
the Greek Orthodox Church a curtain is drawn across the
sanctuary so that the consecration cannot be witnessed by
those outside the priesthood.

In early Christian religious art great attention was
given to the pose and arrangement of hands, heads, and
costumes of the saints, virgins, and other figures portrayed,
so that the statues or images would fully typify the persons

represented. In time the making of holy images and paintings became reduced to a mechanical formula, with the result that early Christian art degenerated into a stilted, unimaginative formalism which was not overcome until art was rejuvenated by the Renaissance.

In every country and period, grips and signs with the hand and arm have been employed by secret societies, religious bodies, trade guilds, thieves, prostitutes, and robbers to pass information between members and associates. In Oriental countries, pantomimic acting and dancing with the hands, arms, and body have been developed into highly complex systems, which are almost unknown in the west. Stories and plays are enacted by poses and movements of such great variety that a book could easily be devoted to the language of the hand alone.

IX

SEX SYMBOLISM

(Continued)

In the language of symbolism, everything in creation that resembled the presumed creator, whether in name, character, function, or shape, was supposed to represent the deity. As gods were invariably anthropomorphic, it followed that the creative powers of the gods were of the same form and character as their human models.

Differences in physical structure which distinguished the human male and female were employed to denote the male and female gods. In their grosset forms these symbols consisted of realistic representations of the generative organs: in their most refined, esoteric, or abstract form, they consisted of a mere circle or oval for the female and an upright shaft or pillar for the male. (Plate 33).

These two basic forms were used, either separately or in conjunction, and in an endless number of variations, to signify not only male and female characteristics but to represent as well the generation and production of life and the gods who ruled over these functions.

In simple combination the pillar and circle appear as 10 which may be read either as Io or the number ten (10). Symbolically, ten is the number of perfection, completeness, and divinity; and for many ancient peoples it symbolized the supreme deity. Both the number ten and Jod, the tenth letter of the alphabet, were assigned to Jahveh by the Jews.

Characteristics attributed to the gods were indicative of their personality and functions: their titles contained allusions to the sun as the source of creative energy and to the masculine emblem. They were esteemed to be powerful, high, erect, firm, bright, happy, upright, large, noble, hard, mighty, able. Generally they were associated with animals which possessed similar characteristics, such as the ram, goat, bull, ass, elephant, and lion which were noted for their strength and lustfulness. Large, powerful men resembled the prevailing conception of a god and were called "men of god" and "god-men." Strong animals were

141

called by such terms as the "bull of god" or the "ram of god". Female deities were designated by titles which alluded to the moon and the beauties and functions of women.

Advantage was taken also of the tripliform character of the male generative organs to effect a further refinement in the primary symbols by arranging three things so that one should stand between and above the other two. Sometimes a bar was placed across the end of an upright shaft, thus forming a cross like a "tau" or T. In its Ethiopic form the tau (T) is the exact prototype of the Christian cross and some writers have asserted that the cross was derived from the tau. Proselytes of Mithra were marked on the forehead with the tau and at Eleusis, initiates were marked with this sign before they were admitted to the Mysteries. According to the Vulgate translation of Ezekiel 9:4, the ancient form of the Hebrew tav (T) was stamped on the foreheads of the men of Judah who feared the Lord, and was the sign which was drawn in blood on the doorposts of the Israelites in Egypt. (Exod. 12:22).

To the primary two-fold symbols representing the generation and production of life there was thus added a third form signifying the three-fold character of the male. This form, combined with the female unit, made a total of four, which number symbolized the foundation of nature and the root of all things.

The three-fold character of the male symbol becomes much more significant when considered in connection with the fact that all of the great creative deities of antiquity were personifications of the genital powers and were always arranged in groups of three. This appears to have been the origin of the Trinity, three gods in one, one god is three, which will be treated at length in a later chapter.

The principal gods of the Assyrian triad were Asshur, (Assur, or Asher), Anu, and Ea. The name of Asher, the supreme god, signifies in its various spellings "to be straight", "upright", "the erect one", "fortunate", "happy", "to be united in love". Similar words with equivalent meaning are eshek, "a stone or testicle", "he presses or squeezes into"; Jasher, "he is upright"; Jashar, "he is straight". Asher, the central upright member of the trinity, was therefore identified with the three-fold sexual symbol. Sir Henry Rawlinson stated that as well as he could determine from his long study of Babylonian relics, the right testicle rep-

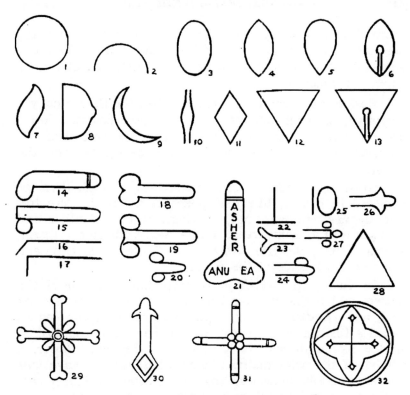

33. *Figs. 1 to 13, variations of basic female symbol.*
Figs. 14 to 28, variations of basic male symbol.
Figs. 29 to 32, combination of male-female symbols.

resented Anu (fire, heat, light) and the left represented Ea
(water). With Beltis, the goddess representing the female
unit, they made up the Arba or Arba-il, the four great gods
of the quadrilateral, the perfect earth. This was in harmony
with an ancient belief, once widespread in the East, that
male offspring came from the right testicle and the right
side of the womb and that females came from the left.[1]

Widespread use of the cross as an early sexual symbol
does not justify the conclusion that it had no other meaning.

1—In the holy records of the Brahmans, Siva asserts that Brahma
was born from his right testicle and Vishnu came from the left.
Traces of similar beliefs have been found among primitive
tribes in modern times. A Hottentot woman will refuse to marry
a man unless one of his testicles has been removed. This is
done to prevent the birth of twins which is considered a bad
omen. A similar custom prevails among the natives of Ponape,
in the Caroline Islands and elsewhere, the operation usually
being performed when the males are 7 or 8 years old.

More than 300 variations of this symbol have been found throughout the world, many of them dating from the Stone Age and it appears to have had different meanings at various times and places.

Beside the T or tau cross, also called the St. Anthony's, Egyptian, or crux immissa (T), the most common forms are the Greek cross (+), called the crux commissa, St. Andrew's cross (X), called the crux decussata; and the Latin cross (†).

Greek, St. Andrew's and tau crosses, in plain form or enclosed in circles, like the spokes of a wheel, were frequently used in paintings, carvings, pottery, textiles and sculptures of ancient Greece, Rome, Sicily, Phoenicia, Egypt, Persia, China, Assyria, North and Central America, and some of the islands of the Pacific.

In India, the wheel is an important emblem of the chariot which the sun was believed to drive across the sky each day. A disc with an equilateral cross in the center, called a Chakra, is a weapon which the Hindu god Vishnu hurled like a discus. It is related to the lotus flower, a symbol of the solar matrix. Some wheel crosses have four spokes, possibly indicating the four seasons or four points of the compass, and others have twelve spokes, representing the twelve months.

The Latin cross appears on many ancient designs from Egypt and on seals representing Ishtar and the Phoenician goddess Astarte. Pagan Greeks used the cross as a symbol of Bacchus and Apollo and modified it to represent the features of the life-giving goddesses Aphrodite, Harmonia, and Artemis of Ephesus. It was commonly worn by temple prostitutes in India as a symbol of life-giving power.

The Hammer of Thor, the Scandinavian god of rain, lightning and fertility was derived from the T cross. In Freemasonry the T or tau is used in the ritual of the Third Degree and three T's in the form of a crown form the jewel of the Royal Arch Degree. (See Plate 37, Fig. 14).

Appearance of the cross wherever sun and fertility worship flourished has led some to believe that the intersecting bars of the cross originally symbolized the rays of the sun which impregnated the earth with its life-giving power. The cross has also been believed to represent the solstice period when the sun crosses the equator, the day

*34. Development of the ankh cross. Fig. 1 is a primitive god
called Taht. 2 to 8, evolution of the Taht symbol. Figs. 19 to
42 show use of circle or oval and its incorporation with upright pillar to form the ankh cross. 31 is a peculiar Taht with
face of Osiris showing between bars. Above the Taht is an
ankh cross with outstretched arms holding a solar disk. 43,
ancient medal found in Cyprus resembling a cross and rosary.
44, T-cross over female symbol, from a mark on the breast of
a mummy in University College, London. 45, 46, figures holding Tahts and ankh crosses from Egyptian paintings. 47, 48,
Greek lamps showing Egyptian influence.*

it is said to be on the cross. Point is given to this theory
by the ancient method of crucifixion in which the condemned person was transfixed on a tree with the arms and
legs outspread in the form of a cross.[2] This would suggest
a form similar to the cross of Jupiter Ammon. In fact, some
ancient cross devices show a solar disk placed at the
intersection of the bars, representing the sun on the cross.

2—The name of Salivahana, an Avatar or Savior of India, means
tree-borne or one who is supposed to have suffered death on
a tree.

Another theory is that the cross was derived from the ancient method of pressing one stick against another and twirling it rapidly until the resulting friction created fire. This method is still employed in making the sacred fire in Hindu temples.

The high development of pictograph writing in Egypt produced the greatest variety of forms and meanings of the cross to be found anywhere. The principal form of the cross in that country, called the ankh or key of life, consisted of the T cross and an oval or loop representing the matrix. When combined they signified eternal life and immortality. Sometimes the ankh cross is called the crux ansata, or handled cross.

In this case we have the rare opportunity of tracing from ancient paintings and sculptures the evolution of a symbol from its beginning to its final stage. First there is a little known predecessor of Osiris called Taht, Tat, Dad or Dud, a primitive god of fertility, procreation, and life, who wears a peculiar headdress containing four cross bars, possibly representing the four quarters of the earth or the four provinces of Egypt. In his hands he holds a whip as a symbol of authority and a crook or staff as a symbol of magic, divination, and ruler of fate.

Figures 2 to 18, Plate 34 show the evolution of the figure of Taht, first to an upright bar or pillar. A similar bar with cross strokes was also a symbol of the meter used to measure the waters of the Nile and was regarded with great reverence by the Egyptians. Figure 31 is a peculiar one and shows a Taht with the face of Osiris in it and above it there is an ankh cross with two arms holding a solar disk.

With the development of the Osiris legend and his worship as a god of fertility, this upright bar appears to have represented the phallus of that deity, as a symbol of his life-giving power, although Sir Ernest A. W. Budge, a noted Egyptologist, surmises that it may have represented the *os sacrum* or lower backbone of Osiris.

The upright and horizontal bars are again shown in combination with the circle, oval, or loop, which forms were employed with several different meanings, including the sky, sun, mouth, the god Ra, and as a genetrix signifying the universal mother principle. Occasionally a triangle is substituted for the oval or circle and, in some instances, the horizontal bar is shown as a scroll of fate.

35. *The figure at left shows a Catholic priest wearing a pallium with an ankh cross, from a Venetian Book,* MISSALE ROMANUM, *1509. The female figure is wearing a modern nun's costume.*

As a symbol of life and immortality, the ankh was carried in the hands of deities, kings, and honored souls who were quartered in the Hall of Judgment. Sometimes it was shown being held to the nostrils of one on whom it was desired to bestow the breath of immortality or to restore life to the dead.

Use of the ankh emblem spread from Egypt to North Africa, Sardinia, Phrygia, Palestine, Phoenicia, and Assyria, and has been found in those countries on bas reliefs, tombs, pottery, jewelry, coins, and seals. The British Museum possesses a large stone figure from Easter Island on which an ankh is carved in bas relief. Before the Latin cross became a Christian symbol, the Egyptian cross was often used by Christians and was incorporated in the priests' pallium. The drawing reproduction on Plate 35 which depicts a monk wearing a pallium with an Egyptian cross on it is from an old papal book, *Missale Romanum*, illustrated by a Venetian monk in 1509. The female figure wears a modern nun's costume.

During the latter years of the pre-Christian period, another cross was used in Egypt as a symbol of Harpocrates or Chr Amon (Horus), the god of light. Horus was usually portrayed with a curving lock of hair on the side of his head representing, according to general opinion, a sign of youth. This curved form was attached to the upright bar of a cross and, eventually, developed into a loop. This form is sometimes called the handled or sword cross and also appeared in India and Mexico.

A similar cross of Greek origin consisted of the Greek letter P (the English R) joined with X (the Greek letter Chi). It was called the Chi-Rho[3] symbol and appeared on Graeco-Bactrian coins in the 2nd century B.C. and on Herodian coins in the 1st century B.C. From the letters X and P (Ch-R) came the word Χρης or Chres meaning Lord, then Chrestos, then Christ. Emperor Constantine placed the ☧ sign on his labarum in 312 A.D., during the war with Maxentius and the emblem was soon adopted by Christians as a monogram of Christ.

As early as the 2nd century, Christians began making the sign of the cross with the hands and Tertullian says: "at each journey and progress; at each coming and going out; at the putting on of the shoes; at the bath; at meals; at the kindling of the lights; at bed times; at sitting down at whatsoever occupation engages us, we mark the brow with the sign of the cross." Illiterate monks employed the cross as their signature and it remains today the legal mark for those who cannot write.

The Latin cross was first used as a Christian symbol in the 3rd or 4th century. It was not employed as a crucifix, that is, it did not have the body of Jesus upon it, but was accompanied by the figure of a lamb. In paintings and sculptures, the lamb was shown upon or in front of the cross, or was represented with one foot lifted as if it were holding or bearing the cross. In some cases, the lamb was portrayed as bleeding from wounds in its side and feet. Fourth century sculptures show a lamb performing miracles such as raising Lazarus from the dead or multiplying the loaves and fishes.

The association of the sun, cross, and lamb originated in the ancient custom of celebrating the Crossification or

---

3—Compare the pronunciation of Chi-Rho with Cairo.

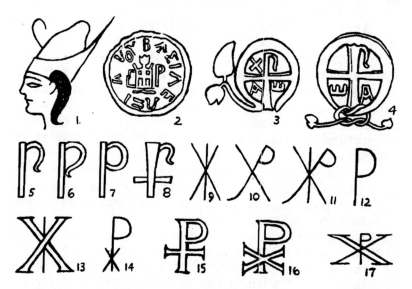

36. *Fig. 1, head of Horus showing symbolic lock of hair. 2, Chi-Rho symbol on copper coin of Herodes. 3, 4, cross monograms on doors of houses in Returze and Serdjilla. 5, 6, 7, 8, variations of the curved form. 9, Assyrian thunder-bolt held by Marduk. 10, 11, 12, sword crosses with handle forming the Greek letter R. 13 to 17, examples of the Chi-Rho cross.*

Passover when the sun crossed the equator at the spring equinox and passed into the zodiac sign of Aries, the lamb. Lambs were used in sacrificial rites of the Babylonians, Egyptians, and Jews and a lamb was sacrificed in the rites of Bacchus, the animal being represented before a cross with sun rays or a solar disk encircling its head.

In early Christian dogma, it was the blood of the Lamb of God which took away the sins of the world. Long after the beginning of Christianity, however, many people continued to believe that, instead of being accepted as a historical fact, the crucifixion should be viewed in the old pagan sense, that is, symbolically. While the church vigorously proceeded to establish its doctrines and authority, it preferred to avoid making the crucifixion a subject of widespread controversy and, for almost seven centuries, it forbade the placing of Christ's figure on the cross. None of the paintings in the Roman catacombs shows him on the cross and, in the holy sepulchre, the savior is represented by the figure of a lamb.

At the Council called *In Trullo*, held at Constantinople in 692 A.D., this policy was finally reversed and thereafter all crucifixes bore the figure of Jesus, although the lamb continued to be shown, usually at the foot of the cross. At first Jesus was represented fully robed, standing calmly before the cross with outstretched arms; later he was placed on the cross and finally, represented undraped, bleeding, and tortured by pain from wounds, as he is represented on crucifixes today.

During the Middle Ages waxen representations of a lamb before the cross were believed to possess miraculous power for prevention of hail-storms, tempests, high winds, thunder-bolts, lightning, conflagrations, enchantments, and pestilences, and thousands of them were purchased by the faithful. In the reign of Pope Urban this amulet, called the Agnus Dei (Lamb of God), was blessed by the Pope himself, and special rules and rites were provided for its consecration. By a Papal bull of 1471 manufacture of the amulet was monopolized by the Pope, to whom it furnished a great source of revenue.[4]

The hooked cross, or swastika, has been used even more universally than the tau. It is sometimes called the gammadian cross because it consists of four Greek letter gammas radiating from a common center. From the Bronze Age to the present this swirling symbol of motion has been scratched, drawn, or molded on coins, tools, utensils, ornaments, weapons, and fabrics all over the world. As an architectural motif in temples and palaces it appears singly in meander bands, and in mosaic patterns on walls, pediments, lintels, cornices, and floors.

The word swastika was thought by Max Muller to be derived from the Sanscrit word *su*, meaning "well", and *asti*, meaning "it is". When the limbs face toward the left the device is called sauvastika, and is a female symbol. It was conjectured by Count Goblet D'Alvielle that the sauvastika, being female, was an unlucky emblem. This theory seems to be disproved by the fact that on objects from India and the ruins of ancient Mediterranean cities the design faces either right or left, although examples in which the limbs turn to the right are much more numerous.

4—*History of the Warfare of Science with Theology*, Andrew D. White, vol. 1, p. 343.

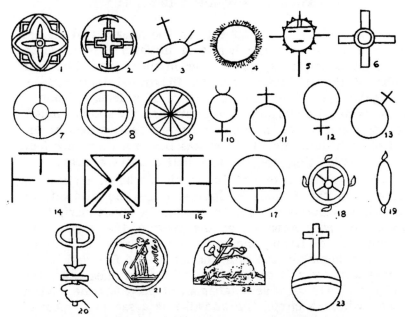

37. Fig. 1, symbol of Babylonian sun god Shamash. 2, Hindu cross with arrow heads. 3, solar disk with rays and cross. From Troy. 4, solar disk with rays. 5, sun cross of Dakota Indians. 6, cross as a solar emblem of the Gauls. 7, 8, 9, wheel crosses. 10, 11, 12, 13, symbols of planets Mercury, Earth, Venus and Mars. 14, Tau crosses forming the crown jewel of Freemasonry. 15, Taus transformed into a Maltese cross. 16, Tau crosses forming base and axis of the Great Pyramid. 17, Tau cross in a circle. 18, 19, Chakra of Vishnu (front and side views). 20, cross ornament held in hand of Ishtar. From sculptured design on a rock at Yazili Kaia, in Anatolia. 21, Ashtoreth with cross, on prow of a boat. From a Sidonian coin. 22, Christian Agnes Dei. 23, Christian symbol of sovereignty and power.

The swastika represents health and happiness and Hindus believe that it has the power to scare away evil. It is therefore branded on cattle, especially the village bull, whence it has, perhaps, the significance of general fertilizer. Swastikas are sketched in white or red over the doorways and steps of city homes. In country villages, as soon as the morning cleansing with earth and dung is completed, the mistress of the house sketches the sacred emblem in front of her house, garden gate, etc.

In China the sign may be seen everywhere; on medicine wrappers and sweetmeats, on the stomachs or chests of idols, on the flanks of animals, on bare walls and various other places. To Buddhists of China, India, Tibet, Mongolia, Korea, and Japan it symbolizes the "ten thousand truths" of Fohat or Buddha. It appears on the images and statues of Buddha and over the hearts of initiates as well as on Buddhist inscriptions, coins, and manuscripts. The four limbs of the Buddhist swastika illustrated terminate in triangular feet. On each limb there is a female symbol: in the center the male and female symbols are shown united. The sun and moon in conjunction are represented at the end of each limb and in the spaces between there are four swirls representing fire, the sun, and creative energy.

The swastika is one of the mystic marks which may be counted on the famous sculptures called Buddhapada or footprints of Buddha. The *Ramayana*, the Hindu scriptures, say there. was a swastika on the prow of the sacred bark or sun boat of Rama, the seventh incarnation of Vishnu. It is also found on the sun chariot of the fire god, Agni. Parsee jewelers and bankers in India sometimes place the design on their safes as a talisman of good fortune. When placed within a circle, the swastika is a sacred symbol of the fire worshiping Jains, to whom it represents the four grades of existence of souls in the material universe.

The triquetra is a three-legged figure closely related to the swastika. It is a very ancient symbol and appears on the official seals of the governments of Sicily and the Isle of Man. The triquetra, or fylfot, sometimes represents a three-headed rooster instead of a human figure, but it is significant that the three-legged or three-footed one is always male, the upright central limb representing man's "weapon", the phallus. The word "foot" is a very ancient slang term for the sexual parts of man. In both Egyptian and Sanscrit, the heart, phallus, and euphemistic foot were emblems of identical meaning. In the Jewish version of the Bible Isaiah 7:20 reads "the hair of the feet" and in II Kings 18:27 and I Kings 14:10 the original text reads "the water of his feet". In all of these instances "feet" is a euphemism for genitals.

The three-legged cross is used in India by bankers, residents of Madras, various Punjab sects and by most all Hindus during the licentious fete for Durga's consort. In Japan, the ever-present three-legged Tomaye is one of the most common ornaments.

In excavating the site of the ancient city of Troy, Dr. Heinrich Schliemann found the swastika on a vast quantity of pottery and other objects of Trojan, Mycenaean, Lyca-

38. Development of the swastika. Fig. 1 is called a "sun snake."
9 is Thor's Hammer. 10, 11, 12 are from Gaulish coins. 17 is an
American Indian symbol of the four winds. 18, interlaced Greek
letter Zeta. 24, a Runic swastika from Sweden. 25, the Buddhapada or footprints of Budda, with swastikas. 26, a Buddhist
swastika containing male-female symbols. 27, interlaced cross
and swastika from a Chinese design.

39. Upper: Figs. 1 and 2 show Sicilian fylfot or triquetra. 6 is
an architectural motif. 7 and 8 show use of heart and lingam
motifs among the Teutons.
Lower: Figs. 1, 2, 3, 5 show variations of the Vajra, a three
pointed symbol of Buddha. 4 and 6 show the trident of Siva.

onian, and Thracian origin. It has been found on coins in Gaza, Syracuse, Leucus, and Iberia, on Celtic funeral vases, on jewels in the royal tombs of Nycenae, and in the mosaic on the floor of the royal palace gardens at Athens.[5] It appears on ornaments, probably as symbols of fertility, on ancient figures of the mother goddesses Nana, Artemis, Hera, Demeter, and Astarte.

Other examples have been discovered on the walls of Roman catacombs, on coins, ceramics, pottery, and sculptures from Greece, Lapland, Crete, Cyprus, Rhodes, and other islands in the Mediterranean. Further examples have been found in Germany, Scandinavia, Mexico, Yucatan, Peru, Uruguay and on pottery and textiles of the Pueblo, Dakota, and other Indian tribes in North America. Strangely enough, this device does not appear to have been in general use in Phoenicia, Egypt, or Babylonia, although examples of the swastika have been found in those countries.

R. P. Greg, an authority on the swastika, thought it was the emblem of the supreme Aryan god, Dyaus or Zeus, and later of Indra, the rain god of India; of Thor or Donnar among the early Scandinavians and Teutons; of Perrun or Perkun among the Slavs. Dyaus, originally the "bright sky god", came more especially to mean the god of both sky and air and the controller of rain, wind, and lightning as in Jupiter Tonans and Jupiter Pluvius. Mr. Greg thought it not improbable that the emblem itself, resembling two Z's or zetas placed crosswise, may have been the letter z of the early Greek alphabet.

The illustration on Plate 40 leaves no doubt, however, that from the beginning of history the swastika was a symbol of life or procreation. This reproduction was made from a peculiar small leaden figure, probably of Artemis, on which a crude swastika appears on the vulva. The idol was found by Dr. Schliemann in the ruins of the ancient city of Ilion (Troy). The extreme antiquity of the idol is attested both by its very primitive workmanship and by the fact that it was recovered from an excavation twenty-three feet below ground level.[6]

5—*Ilios, the city and country of the Trojans*, Dr. Heinrich Schliemann, 1880, p. 352. Also see *Troja, results of the latest researches and discoveries on the site of Homer's Troy*, Dr. Heinrich Schliemann, 1883, p. 122 *et seq*.

6—*Ilios, The City and Country of the Trojans*, Dr. Heinrich Schliemann, 1880, p. 337.

*40. Primitive idol,
made of lead, with
a swastika. From
the ruins of Troy.*

As ancient mathematicians and astronomers began to master its principles, geometry was assumed to be a divine science which would unfold the forms and proportions the Great Architect had employed in the creation of the universe and certain geometrical forms were accredited a mystic importance wholly apart from their mathematical properties. Consequently, many ancient symbols were derived from geometrical forms among which the square, circle, and triangle and their secondary forms, cube, sphere and pyramid or cone were particularly reverenced as containing the key to secrets of the construction of the universe. These forms served as the basis for many of the most sacred symbols of the early religious and secret orders.

Because of the great importance of the number five in the mystic scheme in China, the forms were there expanded from three to five to include the air and ether. Stupas containing these five basic or mystic forms may be found in Buddhist monasteries and public places in China, Tibet, and

Japan where they signify the five sources from which all things come and to which they return.[7]

In this system of Oriental imagery, the earth was conceived as occupying the center of the universe, with the sun, moon, and other planets spread around it in concentric circles like the segments of an onion.

In Hindu symbology a point or • purm represents the deity, self-existent; a circle represents Brahma and eternity. A triangle within a circle is the emblem of the Trinity in Unity: a circle inscribed within a triangle means the reverse. A sun disk within a crescent moon represents the "conjunction of the divine power".

The Egyptian Aakhu device represented the disk of the sun on the horizon and symbolized life after death and resurrection. When worn as an amulet, it was supposed to give the wearer the strength and power of Horus or Ra. (Plate 42, Fig. 5).

Because of the great variety of forms and proportions of the triangle, its repeated occurrence in natural forms, and identity of its three sides with the sacred number of the gods, it was widely used in amulets and emblems. Some of its properties and applications will be considered in the chapter on the Cabala.

An equilateral triangle with the apex pointing downward approximately corresponds to the shape of the hirsute fringe which adorns the *mons veneris* (Mount of Venus), and is a symbol of water and the female principle. When the apex is pointed upward it represents fire and the male principle. The letter daleth of the Phoenician alphabet and the Greek letter Delta (Δ) are analogous forms and signify the door of a tent or the outlet of a stream.

7—The Chinese recognize 5 colors, 5 elements, 5 fruits, 5 directions, 5 tastes, 5 cardinal virtues, 5 notes of music, 5 punishments, 5 classics. The human body has 5 constituents and the trunk has 5 organs. See *The Sacred Five of China*, Wm. E. Geil, 1926.

According to notions current in India, there are 5 precious jewels (ruby, sapphire, pearl, emerald, topaz); 5 beauties of women (hair, flesh, bone, skin, youth); 5 trees of paradise, 5 great sacrifices, 5 sacred flowers, 5 emblems of royalty; mankind has 5 senses; the Brahmans worship 5 products of the cow; Siva has 5 aspects; the Dravidians recognize 5 divine foods; the Assamese 5 esentials of worship and the Avesta doctrine recognizes 5 divisions of human personality.

There are 5 words of the evil eye among Mohammedans and the number 5, being considered lucky among the Romans, entered into their wedding ceremonies. *Ocean of Story*, vol. 2, p. 307n. Also see chapter in this book on "Symbolic Meaning of Numbers".

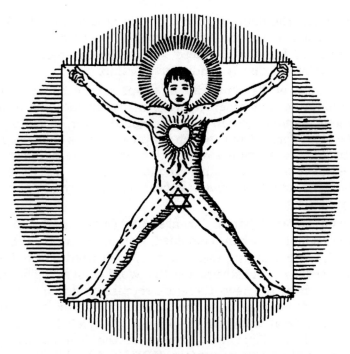

41. A Hindu conception of Macrocosmic man, with interlaced triangles representing the male and female creative powers.

· In India the first triangle is a special emblem of Vishnu, representing the female, and the second one is an emblem of Mahadeva or Siva, representing the male. When combined they are called the United Symbols of Vishnu and Siva, the Sherkun or Six-Points. This is the well-known "Star of David". It is still used in all Oriental countries and, in Masonry, is a symbol of the Royal Arch Degree. The six-pointed star is also a symbol of fire-water or "burnt water" and has been used by taverns to indicate a license to sell alcoholic liquors.

When the apices of the two triangles are joined, there is formed a double triangle, which was the symbol of the gods Horus and Sut; also of north and south Egypt. The double triangle with a serpent placed across the intersecting bars is a Buddhist symbol denoting wisdom or sexual desire. Figure 9, Plate 42, shows the use of the triangles in a Hindu emblem called the Srí Iantra. The outer circle represents the world; the large triangles represent the male and female.

When used, the figure is placed on the ground with Brahma to the east and Lakshmi to the west. A relic of a saint or an image of Buddha is placed within the inner circle, and the complete shrine is ready for worship.

Because of its similarity in shape to the honey comb, the snowflake and other crystals, many mystics see a tremendous significance in the six-pointed star, deeming it to be the form from which nature weaves her sacred mysteries. As a symbol of creative nature the number six is identified with the Mother Goddess and with the six days or ages of creation which appear in the mythologies of many nations.

The Hebrew letters for fire אש (male) and מים for water (female), when combined, form the word אשמים, Aeshmim or Shamayin, meaning heaven, a word which Jews often used as a substitute for the word Jahveh. The six-pointed star of the Jews therefore represents fire and water, male and female, as does the symbol of Vishnu and Siva. The four lateral triangles yielded by the symbol are sometimes used cabalistically to represent the four consonants comprising the Tetrogrammaton JHVH and read "with God".

Instead of pronouncing Jahveh's name the Jews often referred to him as *The Name*, spelled *ashm*. Here the letters אשם are equivalent cabalistically to air, fire, and water, the three elemental substances anciently thought to compose the universe.

Bisecting a three by four rectangle with a diagonal line gives two triangles in the proportion of three, four, and five, the famous right-angled triangle of Pythagoras and the forty-seventh problem of Euclid. To Pythagoras this triangle symbolized marriage, the perpendicular signifying the male; the base, female; and the hypotenuse, the child. It appeared in conventional representations of the Eye of Horus which were used in Egypt and elsewhere as charms against the evil eye. An equilateral triangle was also used as a symbol of the deity, its three sides representing his three-fold power. To the Hindus an equilateral triangle symbolizes AUM, a mystic term representing the sum of all existence.

An eye within a triangle is a Masonic symbol of the Great Architect and may be found on the Great Seal of the

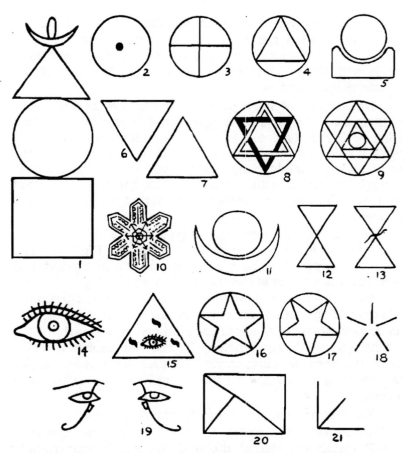

42. Fig. 1, side elevation of a Chinese stupa. 2 may be interpreted as the earth surrounded by celestial regions or as the cosmic egg containing the germ of all existence. 3, symbol of heaven (circle) and earth (cross). 4, symbol of the Trinity. 5, Egyptian aakhu device, representing solar disk on the horizon between mountains of the east and the west. 6, inverted triangle; a symbol of Vishnu, water, and the female principle. 7, upright triangle; symbol of Siva, fire and the male principle. 8, Male and female triangles joined, the familiar "Star of David." 9, the Sri Iantra, a Hindu variation of interlaced triangles. 10, six-sided snow flake. 11, sun and moon in conjunction. 12, double triangle; a symbol of Egyptian gods Horus and Tut (light and darkness). 13, Buddhist symbol of wisdom and sexual desire. 15, All-seeing Eye in an equilateral triangle, with three "Jods." 17, inverted star, a symbol of witchcraft. 18, star-shaped Egyptian hieroglyphic meaning "king." 19, Egyptian udjats or eyes. 20, three by four rectangle bisected to form two right-angled triangles and the Golden Section. 21, Bisected triangle; a symbol of Isis and Sakti.

United States, which appears on the dollar bill. Early Christians used a similar device as a symbol of the Holy Spirit, and Jews sometimes placed the all-seeing eye in a circle with three letter Jods representing JHV, one of the mystic monograms of Jahveh.

Natives of Polynesia paint the mystic eye on the prows of their boats for protection against bad luck. The Egyptian triad of Osiris, Isis, and Horus was sometimes represented by a triangle within a circle. Hindu worshipers of Sakti, the female principle, mark their vases with a right angled triangle, bi-sected with a line, and worshipers of Isis used to mark the vessels necessary to her rites in the same manner.

In its original form the Egyptian eye or udjat was worn as an amulet as shown in Plate 42, Fig. 19. The eye was supposed to be a very potent charm against bad luck and the wearer of the udjat felt assured of good health, protection, and general well-being. Twin udjats represented the eyes of the sun and moon, that is, the two eyes of Her, an ancient form of the goddess Hathor. It was painted on coffins and mortuary articles. In the Babylonian creation myth the hero, Marduk, carried between his lips an amulet in the form of an eye when he set forth to battle with Tiamat.

The badges distinguishing the three orders of Egyptian priesthood were the Greek theta (Θ), signifying the sun, the T signifying eternal life and the equilateral triangle signifying pleasure.

The important feature of the celebrated ring with which King Solomon was said to perform feats of magic was a five-pointed star or Pentacle, formed by two over-lapping triangles and sometimes called the "Seal of Solomon". When placed right side up the star was a powerful amulet of white magic but when inverted, it was a symbol of witchcraft, black magic, sorcery, and an omen of bad luck.

To Pythagoreans and others, the Pentagram was a symbol of the universe, or perfection. It has been found on early Syrian pottery, on earthenware from Ur in Chaldea, and is believed to be an older design than the hexagon or Star of David. In India it is a symbol of Siva as well as of the ten Avatars of Vishnu. Egyptians employed a five-pointed star as a hieroglyphic for their gods.

This star is so common today that it seems impossible it could ever have been thought to possess magical properties, but in an age when people looked for symbolic meanings in everything, it had many significant associations. In astrology the five points represented the 5 planets Mercury, Venus, Mars, Jupiter and Saturn. Mathematically, the five points form ten angles of one-hundred eight degrees each and there are five lines equal to the extreme ratio. It contains ten lines equal to the mean ratio, and when the sides of the center part are added to the mean ratio, they equal the given line.

There were one hundred-eight days in four Babylonian twenty-seven day months. Ten times one hundred eight days equals one thousand and eighty, or three years in the astrological calendar. In India one hundred eight is the number of Brahma, the god of light, and is of great magical significance. Brahmans consider the potential length of human life to consist of twelve divisions of nine years each, or a total of one hundred eight years. The ideal human figure is divided by canon into one hundred eight parts and the making of images and statues is a highly formalized art. The length of two human lives (216 years) is the number of metempsychosis or reincarnation. This is the mystic six times six times six.

The rosary or Rudraksa beads worn by Brahmans number one hundred eight and "by putting on the Rudraksa beads, persons become the Rudras . . . incarnate in the flesh and body . . . by these all sins arising from seeing, hearing, remembering, smelling, committing prohibited things; talking incoherently, doing prohibited things are entirely removed with the Rudraksa beads on the body. . . . The one hundred eight signifies the number of Vedas and Brahma, the source of wisdom".[8]

8—*Sacred Books of the Hindus*, vol. 26, bk. 11, ch. 3, p. 1063. The number 108 has a mystical meaning to Buddhists as well as Brahmans. At Gautama's birth the number of Brahmans summoned to foretell his destiny was 108. There are 108 shrines of special sanctity in India; there are 108 Upanishads; 108 rupees is a fair sum for a generous temple or other donation. In Tibet and China 108 is a sacred or mystic number in connection with architecture, ritual, and literature. (See Yule's *Marco Polo*, vol. 2, p. 347, London 1903). The number of beads in both Tibetan and Burmese rosaries is usually 108. This number appears on documents before the name of the Maharajas or high priests of the Bhatti caste. *Ocean of Story*, vol. 1, p. 242 and vol. 6, p. 14, 231 and 280.

X

SEX SYMBOLISM

(*Continued*)

MORE THAN ANY other people, Orientals have always liked
to speak in metaphors and parables, describing one thing
when referring to another. In the development of their
custom of viewing everything as male or female in character, bowls, cups, basins, baskets, windows, arches, doors,
bells, bags, sacks, boxes, arks, boats, and hollow things of
all kinds became emblematic of the womb, even the palm
of the hand being considered female because of its hollow-
ness. Circles, rings, ovals, horseshoes and other objects
of like character symbolized the pudendum.

Poles, posts, pales, trees, pillars, columns, obelisks,
spires, towers, swords, spears, clubs, mountain peaks, and
other projections were considered masculine and, in India,
various kinds of stone, metals, and trees were classified as
male or female according to their characteristics. Some
objects, such as a pestle and mortar, lock and key, or the
egg and dart design, combine both male and female symbols.

Objects are also classified according to their functions.
A hoe or plow, for instance, is male because it opens the
earth to receive the seed for planting and is called an
"opener". By similar reasoning, a furrow or cleft is designated female and the field or meadow itself is of the same
sex. The Latin word *vomer* signified both plowshare and
phallus.

The signatures of some Indian princes contain ideographs of a plow to indicate that they are earthly representatives of the creator. At marriage ceremonies, a plow is
set up under a canopy as a harbinger of fertility.

In ancient drawings and bas reliefs, male figures were
often acompanied by female symbols and female figures were
either given male symbols as hair ornaments or articles
of dress or such objects were placed near the figures as if
the scene were not complete unless both sexes were rep-

43. *Left: Egyptians hoeing. Right: The hala or Hindu plow converted to a war weapon.*

44. *Fig. 1, androgynous deity with male and female serpents at left and right. Opposite the male serpent there is a lozenge-shaped female symbol and opposite the female there is a six-pointed sun symbol. Overhead is a crescent moon. Below the female there is a cup and below the male there is an amphora, representing .fructification of the earth by the sun.*
Fig. 2, Male and female figures dancing before the mystic palm tree, representing the tree of life. Opposite the male animal there is a pointed oval or female symbol. Opposite the female there is a fleur-de-lys, or male symbol.
Fig. 3, worship of male-female symbols. Above is the female moon and the male sun. Opposite the worshipper are a pointed oval, triangle, barred cteis and palm tree. From sculpture on white agate stone in Calvert's Museum, Avignon.

resented.[1] It was probably for a similar reason that priests sometimes wore female garments and priestesses were garbed in male attire. This custom has continued in the Catholic and Episcopal churches to the present time.

The drawings on Plate 44 illustrate this use of the male

1—"In the *Bhavagata Purana* (2nd Skanda) Mahadeva is described by Brahma as 'the Parabrahman, the Lord of Siva and Sakti who are the seed and womb respectively of the universe'. The import of this is that the male and female are forever inseparable and are found together in cosmic evolution". *Elements of Hindu Iconography*, vol. 2, Pt. 1, p. 58, J. Gopinatha Rao.

and female symbols and were originally reproduced by Layard.[2] Figure 1 is from a Babylonian seal. The central figure represents an androgyne deity with an erect male serpent on the left and a female serpent on the right. Opposite the male there is a lozenge shaped female symbol and at his feet is an amphora which signifies Ouranos, or the sun, fructifying Terra the earth, by pouring from himself into her. Over the female serpent there is a crescent moon and opposite the serpent there is a six-rayed star representing the sun. At her feet is a cup which apparently represents the female element in creation.

Figure 2 is from a gem cylinder in the British Museum. It represents male and female figures dancing before the mystic palm tree. Opposite a particular spot on one figure there is a diamond or oval and on the other, a fleur de lys, the symbol of the male triad.

Figure 3 is from a sculpture on white agate stone and represents an act of worship before symbols of the male and female creators arranged in pairs. Above are the sun and moon. Below are the male palm tree and the barred cteis identical in meaning with the sistrum as a symbol of the virgin female. Next comes the male emblem, the cone and the female symbol, the lozenge.

Plate 67, Figs. 1 and 2, show designs taken from ancient Assyrian tablets in which the female symbol is placed near the male and the principal worshipers are shown holding bags, typical symbols of the womb. To Hindus, Bhaga-vata or Parvati, the mother of mothers, is the "Lady of the Sack" whom Florentines called Madonna Del Sacco, but who is now called Dea Immacolata, or simply St. Bride or Bridgetta.

The interdependence of the male and female in the scheme of creation is rooted deeply in Chinese philosophy. As described by Major General James G. Forlong[3], who spent many years studying the subject, male and female symbols form the basis for the Chinese ideograph signifying man. Figure "A" represents Ti, called "the pillar god", "supreme monad", "the one", but lacks the power to create because the female symbol is missing. "B" is an inverted V repre-

---

2—*Recherches sur les Culte, les symboles, et les attributs, et les Monu-mens, Figures de Venus,* Paris, 1837, p. 32 *et seq.* and figured in Plate 1.

3—*Rivers of Life,* vol. 2, p. 551 *et seq.,* Maj. Gen. James G. R. Forlong.

A   B   C   D   E

senting zan, yang, or man; with phallus or knotted stick accompanied by Shang, "the heavenly dot", as the moon poised over the waters and representing the female principle. The combined ideographs signify power to create life. "C" represents a god-man or double phallused one. It is the Le or Ti by virtue of which the Shang generates life; but, as the female half is missing, the god is powerless to create. "D" is the dual form of Shang-Ti, Sing Le, or Shin Le, the creative god accompanied by the female ark or womb. "E" is an Akkadian cuneiform character representing the letter "A", called zikaru, "the male thing", or "the sword", and by the Jews, called zakar; "that which pierces or penetrates". In Assyrian it represents As or Asher, the phallus.

When a boy is initiated by the Naojote ceremony of the Parsees in India, and invested with the Sudra and Kusti, or sacred shirt and thread, the priests make a long vertical mark of red lead on the forehead of the initiate. If the child is a girl, a round mark is made. The vertical mark signifies the fertilizing or conceiving rays of the sun and the round mark represents Chandra, the moon, which is fertilized by or receives the conception from Surya, the sun. Brahman devotees of Parvati paint three vertical strokes on the forehead. The outer strokes are white or

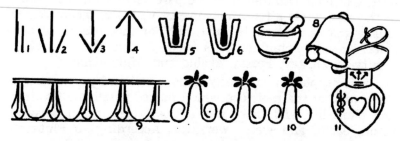

45. *Figs. 1 to 6; Hindu caste symbols. 7, 8, pestle and mortar and the bell, symbols of male and female. 9, egg and dart design, containing male and female symbols. 10, the limbus, a male ornamental repeat design. 11, the bulla, an ornamental loin cloth worn by Oriental children in lieu of clothing.*

yellow and the center one is always red. This represents
the matrix of Bhavani.

The modern *naman,* or emblem, which Hindu followers
of Vishnu paint or draw upon their foreheads as a symbol
of creative power is a white U-shaped mark, in the center
of which is a vertical stroke in red. (See Plate 45, Figs.
5 and 6). Another symbol of similar character, and possibly of the same origin and significance, consists of a V
(v and u were formerly the same) roughly forming an
arrow head pointing up or down (↑ ↓). This was an
ancient method of representing the letters I and V which
formed a sacred monogram of JHVH. The letters IU were
joined with *pitar* (father), to form the name of the Roman
Iu-piter (Jupiter). Wide arrowheads are still. stamped on
articles owned by kings as symbols of their sovereignty.

The crescent moon was once a common and widely diffused feminine symbol, and to the present day, amulets in the
form of a crescent moon are regarded as especially appropriate for virgins and pregnant women. They were popular
among many people of western Asia and signified to them the
strength and protection of the *waxing* moon. Moon amulets
were fastened on the necks of camels to protect them from
the evil eye. A Greek epithet for the moon was Cynthia,
from Cynthus (k and c being the same: likewise u and y)
and, as a goddess of fecundity, Cynthus was the same as
Kunti, the wife of the sun in India and Kun or Kiun
(queen) of the Jews.[4]

The two supreme Rajah families of Hindustan, the
Suryabans and Chandrabans, are called the children of the
sun and moon. When Indian poets wish to describe the
beauty of male children they compare them with the beauty
of the sun, while girls are compared with the moon; hence,
to say that a woman is "mah rui" or moon-faced is considered a high compliment. A moon face is also a mark of
beauty in Turkey, Persia, Arabia and Afghanistan.

The people of many early nations believed the moon was
the source of the moisture which makes possible all animal
and plant life, and there was a close relationship between
moon, earth, and water worships. According to Plutarch,

4—From *kunya,* a small well; *kund,* a basin, pool, pitcher or spring;
kundi, one who carries a water pot, pitcher, or chain for fasten-
ing a door; *khunta,* a wood or iron pin or peg; and *kunta,* a
spear.

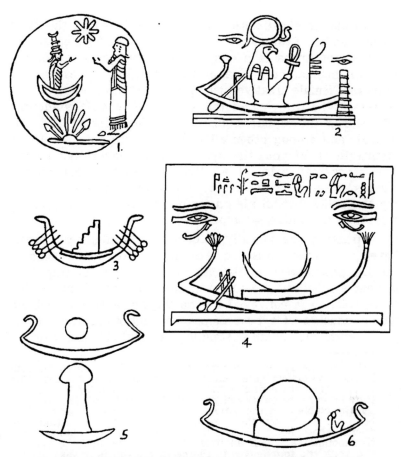

46. Fig. 1, *moon god standing in his crescent-shaped boat; a Chaldean conception. 2, hawk-headed Ra in sacred boat, protected by all-seeing eyes. 3, sacred bark of Egyptian sun god with steps or stairs for ascending the heavens. 4, sun and moon in conjunction on a sacred boat. 5, sun boat with serpentine ends. It rests on a phallic pillar. 6, solar bark with sun on the horizon (the aakhu symbol.)*

Egyptians regarded the moon as the mother of all the world and believed her to have both male and female natures. Prophet Ezekiel complained because the women of Jerusalem revealed themselves as moon worshipers by wearing the saharon, an ornament made of gold or other metal in the form of a crescent moon.

By transition a crescent becomes an arc or ark, which term is cognate with the argha, a boat-shaped vessel used in India as a ceremonial vessel. (Plate 48, Figs. 37 and 38).

Numerous modifications of this form are used in the caste marks which Brahmans paint upon their foreheads. To Hindus, the argha is a conventional representation of the yoni or matrix, but, in a deeper sense, it represents the universal female creative principle. The round object in the center of the drawing of the argha (Plate 48)* symbolizes Mt. Meru,[5] the Indian equivalent of Mt. Moriah and Mt. Ararat, and among other allusions, it represents the Great Mountain of Vishnu, the symbol of his generative power. The story that pairs of all living creatures were aboard Noah's ark appears to have been a symbolic way of expressing the belief that all life on earth came from the argha, the womb of the universal mother.

Speaking symbolically, a boat is a cradle, nest, home, haven, or womb; thus the crescent-shaped sacred boats of the Egyptians were emblematic of the matrix. A ship with a mast symbolized the union of the male and female. The same relation is conveyed by the lingam, a Hindu emblem which consists of a boat-shaped conventionalization of the yoni, with the phallus standing upright in the center.[6]

5—"Meru is the sacred and primeval linga and the earth beneath is the mysterious yoni, expanded and open like a lotus. The convexity in the center is the *Os Tineoe* or navel of Vishnu and they often represent the physiological mysteries of their religion by the emblem of the lotus; where the whole flower signifies both the earth and the two principles of its fecundation: the germ is both Meru and the linga: the petals and filaments are the mountains which encircle Meru and are also the type of the yoni: the four leaves of the calyx are the four vast regions toward the cardinal points and the leaves of the plant are the different islands in the ocean around Jambu and the whole floats upon the waters like a boat. . . . It is their opinion, I do not know on what authority, that at the time of the Flood the two principles of generation assumed the shape of a boat, with its mast, in order to preserve mankind". Captain Francis Wilford in *Asiatic Researches*, the Royal Asiatic Society of Bengal, vol. 8, p. 273.

6—The Deluge allegory as described by Hindu Puranics: "Satyavrata having completed the ark, the flood increasing, he made it fast to the peak of Naubandha (on Mt. Meru, from Nau, a ship and bandha, to make fast) with a cable of prodigious length. During the flood Brahma, or the creative power, was asleep at the bottom of the abyss. The generative powers of nature, male and female, were reduced to their simplest elements, the linga and yoni, assumed the shape of the hull of a ship since typified by the argha; whilst the linga became the mast. In this manner they were wafted over the deep. under the great protection of Vishnu. When the waters had retired, the female power of nature appeared immediately in the character of Capoteswari, or the dove, and she was soon joined by her consort, in the shape of Capoteswara". Captain Francis Wilford in *Asiatic Researches*, the Royal Asiatic Society of Bengal, vol. 6, p. 522.

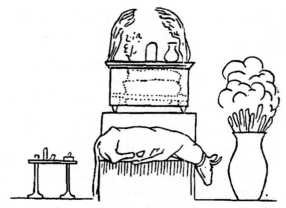

*47. The Jewish sacrificial altar, shewbread
and cherubim.*

Sometimes Mahadeva is represented standing in the center of the argha, like the mast of a boat. In India lingams are to be found everywhere, varying in size from household ornaments a few inches high to outdoor monuments several feet in height. A large crescent-shaped boat, pointed at each end and called the omphalos or umbilicus, was carried in procession in the Greek religious services at Delphi.

In Hebrew, the letters P and B are interchangeable, therefore *Pith* or *Peth* signifying womb, door, or entrance, and *Bith* or *Beth* meaning house, are synonymous. The ark of Noah was called *The-bith* or *Tebah*, and as *Bith* preceded by the article *the* signifies sacred or consecrated, the word *The-bith* denotes the consecrated ark or womb from which all life came. To Egyptians the city of Thebes signified the tebah, womb, ark, or navel of the universe.

The tabernacle of the Jews was designated the meshken, or birthplace. The holy of holies contained the ark, the holiest of all symbols. It was the place of salvation and safety, the sacred receptacle of divine wisdom and power; hence, the ark was the holy abiding place of the Tablets of the Law which were given to Moses by the Lord.

In speaking of this incident, the Book of Exodus calls the Tablets the "Testimony of Jahveh", and describes in detail the construction of the ark which was built especially for their safe keeping.

The circumstances surrounding the receipt of the "Testimony" by Moses are quite mysterious. Statements made elsewhere in Exodus show that the Jews possessed what they believed to be the "Testimony" before Moses was given the stone tablets. In Exodus 16:33, 34 it is stated that Moses commanded Aaron to take a pot of manna and lay it up before the Lord; "so Aaron laid it up before the Eduth (Testimony) to be kept". This occurred before Moses had his famous conference with the Lord; in fact, before Moses had even arrived at Mount Sinai.

The text indicates plainly that the Testimony was an idol representing Jahveh and as this Testimony was treasured by the Israelites *before* the Sinai incident, it is evident that adoption of the Tablets of the Law marked the overthrow of an old form of worship and the beginning of a new one.

Mohammedans also recognize the Old Testament as part of their holy records and the most holy object in their Ka'aba,[7] at Mecca, is a stone phallic image. From Rome to Japan early nations possessed similar arks, chests, coffers, or arghas for holy objects, which were usually symbols of male and female pudenda. The ark of the Egyptians contained what they believed to be the symbols of the true creator, the phallus, the egg, and the serpent. The first represented Osiris as the sun, the male generative principle and active creator; the second, the preserver or passive female principle; and the third, the destroyer or reproducer.

If the Jews adopted the idea of an ark from the Egyptians, as the evidence seems to indicate, it was doubtless for a similar purpose and contained similar objects. The ark itself was a female symbol, therefore the Eduth or Testimony must have been a male image, probably of unhewn stone, representing Jahveh the increaser, the generator of life. Probably the ark also contained a brazen serpent, the ubiquitous Egyptian symbol of life and creative energy.

According to another Jewish tradition, there was no evil until Eve's curiosity led her to partake of the tree of life (or knowledge) and the consequent opening of her womb brought forth all that is evil in the world. In Greek mythology, curiosity also led to the opening of Pandora's

---

7—Compare Ka'aba with the Hebrew word kobah, meaning vulva. Furst's Hebrew Dictionary translates kobah as anything hollow or arched like the Ka'aba which signifies the ark or vulva, cup, kob, al-cova or alcove. The Greek for kobah means female parts.

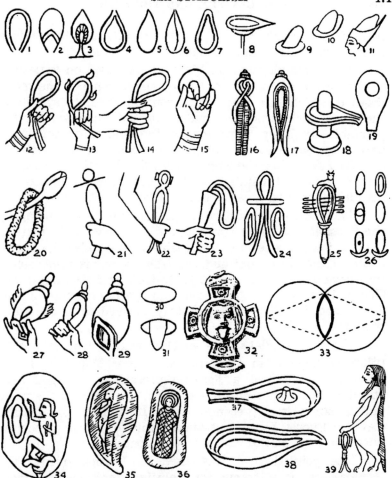

48. The loop or yoni symbol. Figs. 1 to 8 are common variations of the loop in design. 9, 10, 11, evolution of hat of Osiris from male and female forms. 12, 13, 14, cord carried in left hand of Siva. 15, ring on finger of Siva, representing union of male and female. 16, 17, the "pasa", an ornamental loop of ropes carried by Siva as "binder of fate". 18, 19, side and top views of Hindu lingam, combining male and female forms. 20, cloth garland hung on twigs in springtime by Hindus, the bud and cloth loop symbolizing union of male and female. 21, 22, 23, 24, Egyptian symbols thought to insure protection, happiness and long life. 25, sistrum. 26, Hindu caste marks. 27, 28, 29, conch shells. 30, the oval as a symbol of the mouth and voice; also a yoni symbol. 31, mouth with protruding tongue symbolizing union of male and female. 32, design on ancient Mexican calendar stone showing figure with an extended tongue pointing to yoni symbol below. 33, geometrical method of forming a vesica piscis. 34, ancient gem found at Nineveh showing figure (probably Horus) seated on a lotus and contemplating the female ovoid at left. 35, Gestation of Harpocrates (Horus). 36, Detail from an 8th century Italian painting from Cyprus showing the infant Jesus in the "door of life". 37, 38, boat-shaped arghas or ceremonial vessels. In the center of 37 is a small formalized linga of Mahadeva, identified with phallus of Vishnu and Mt. Meru, the Hindu equivalent of Mt. Ararat. 39, Egyptian deity with device insuring happiness and long life.

box, chest, or ark with a similar result, and the hidden symbolism in both cases is basically the same.

The forms pictured on Plate 48 are based on variations of the oval and are intended to illustrate some of the many ways in which this shape has been employed to symbolize the argha, ark, ankh, or matrix of the universal mother principle. In Egypt variations of the oval as an unfringed phallic eye were painted on temple walls, doors, peristyles, etc., as a symbol of the ever-virgin Isis. In various arrangements, it is still painted on the foreheads of millions of people in India as a caste mark. (Plate 48, Fig. 26).

The female generative organ is called, in India, by the Sanscrit word yoni (pronounced yun or yn). The letters i, j and y were once interchangeable as were also the letters u and o, therefore yoni and the Hebrew words *iune,* meaning dove (a female symbol), Jo-nah, and Jo-annes; the Greek titles Io, Iona, and Ionia; and the Latin names Ju-no, Jo-ve, and Ju-piter, were probably derived from the same primitive root.[8]

Figure 4 on Plate 49 is an 11th or 12th century phallic pillar or linga from a temple at Ambar Māgālam, India, on which is carved a figure representing the god Siva standing in a yoni with pointed ends. In Figure 5 the same god is similarly represented on a linga from Dasāvatāra Cave, at Ellora. In ancient Mexico this form was associated with the rites of the savior Quetzalcoatl.

The pointed oval was used in Europe during the Renaissance as a frame for paintings and stained glass windows. One of the current popular encyclopedias describes its origin as having been due to the custom of artists drawing halos or rays of light around the heads of Virgin Mary, Christ and the Apostles. The halo was gradually enlarged, it is said, until it enclosed the whole figure and the German artist Albrecht Durer devised an improved method of making it by drawing two overlapping circles as

---

8—"The assumed pronunciation of the Hebrew deity is Jahveh but as the first letter may be read i, ja, ya or e and the third u, v or o while the second and fourth are the soft h, the word may be read as Jhuh, similar to the Ju in Jupiter, as Jehu, the name of a king of Israel; as Yahu it appears on Assyrian inscriptions; like Jeho in Jehoshaphat; Ehoh which is analogous to the Evoe or Euoe associated with Bacchus or as Jaho, analogous to the Gnostic Jao. The Greek fathers gave the word as if equivalent to Yave, Yaoh, Yeho, iao." *Ancient Pagan and Modern Christian Symbolism,* Dr. Thomas Inman, Pref. xii, fn.

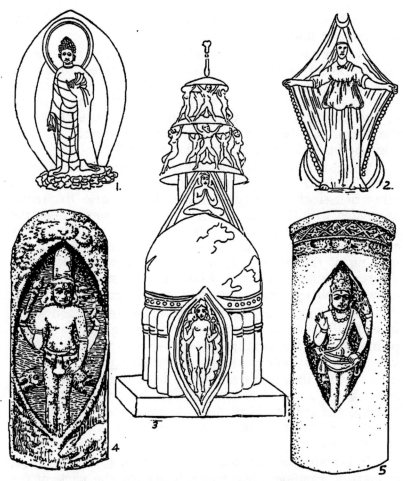

49. Fig. 1, Maityna Bodhisatwa in a vesica piscis shaped like a horseshoe. 2, a figure from Bryant's ANCIENT MYTHOLOGY, probably taken from a Greek coin representing Selenitus with the sacred peplum (veil). 3, Buddhist dagoba in the Jumnar Cave, Bombay Presidency. Supporting pillars, dome and other details are phallic symbols. Dagoba is from Dhatu (relic) and Garbha (womb). 4, stone linga (badly worn) with floral wreath and figure of Siva standing in a vesica piscis. 5, linga from Daśāvatāra Cave, at Ellora, with Siva in a vesica piscis.

illustrated (Plate 48, Fig. 33), the overlapping parts becoming the aureole or vesica piscis (fish bladder), as it is popularly called.

Despite this polite myth, however, the several illustrations here reproduced show unmistakably that the symbol had the same significance to Renaissance artists and ecclesiastics that it has had to people throughout the Orient for three or four thousand years.

The Virgin Mother, particularly, was often represented as standing in a frame of this shape. Figure 2, Plate 50 was drawn from a subject on which the wording was practically illegible, but it appears to have been a medal of the sort worn by Christian pilgrims to the shrine of the Virgin of Amadon and commonly described as "the holy mother and child in the door of life".

The fish is a well-known religious symbol, sacred, originally, to Ishtar, Isis, Venus, the Japanese Kwan-non, and other deities of the sexual nature. It was also frequently associated with the sun. In the opinion of some writers, the fish became a symbol of abundance because of its fecundity and, also, because its mouth was thought to resemble the opening of the uterus. It was a symbol of the Egyptian goddess Hathor and was worn as an amulet to bring domestic felicity, abundance, and general prosperity.

Inasmuch as every detail in ancient paintings and sculptures had a definite meaning, there is more than a remote possibility that the peculiar fish-shaped eyes which Egyptian artists gave to their paintings of female figures originated in the belief that fish were symbolic of the sexual nature. Substance is given to this thought by the fact that in India, Parvati, the mother of mothers, is sometimes described as *minakshî* or fish-eyed in the sense that she is *kimakshî*, or amorous looking.

In Scandinavia, the fish was a common symbol of Frija, goddess of marriage, from whom is derived the name of the sixth day of the week. In China, wood, metal and ceramic representations of fish (usually the carp) are placed on roofs of pagodas as talismen of fecundity and good fortune. The Biblical Joshua is described as the son of Nun, a word which, in Hebrew, signifies fish and woman, or rather the sexual parts of woman.

The custom among Semitic peoples of eating fish on Friday seems to have been associated, in remote times, with the belief that the eating of fish promoted lustfulness and virility. Arabs, Jews, and other Semites considered Friday to be woman's day, the day particularly dedicated to Ishtar, Astarte, Mylitta, Beltis, Venus, Isis, and other goddesses of fertility.

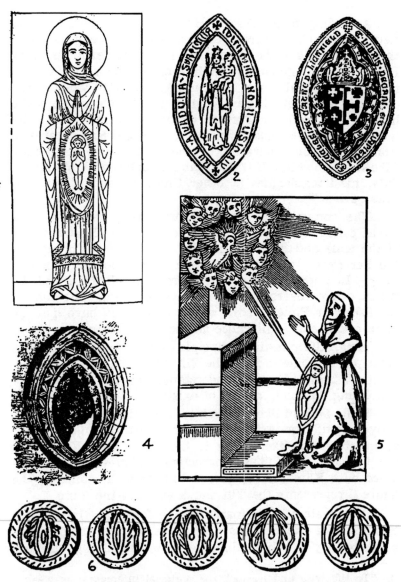

50. Fig. 1, the infant Jesus in a flamboyant aureole or vesica piscis. From a painted window (French) of the 16th century. 2, a medal probably representing the Virgin of Amadon. 3, seal of the Cathedral of Litchfield, England. 4, window of Dumblane Abbey, near Stirling, Scotland. 5, the "overshadowing" of Virgin Mary by the Holy Ghost in the form of a dove. 6, carved medallions containing vesica piscis, from a church in San Fedele, Italy.

According to Sir Austin Henry Layard, the Druses of
Lebanon, in their secret vespers, offer a true worship of
the sexual parts of the female and pay their devotions every
Friday night. Mohammedan husbands who failed to ful-
fill their conjugal duties on this day not only violated the
code of Mahomet; they risked a disruption of domestic
harmony as well. A Turkish canon proclaimed that "the
wife has only conclusive claim to her husband's caresses
from sunset on Thursday to the same hour on Friday
(Turkish Sabbath). If the husband complies with his family
duty, his irregularities at other times are not of material
consequence."[9]

The conventional design representing two fish in a
circle, called the Great Monad, is one of the oldest symbols
of the male and female principles and is found throughout
the Far East. In India and China, it is called the Yin and
Yang. In Japanese, the characters are called In and Yo
which, when reversed and joined, read Yo-ni. The sign of
the fishes, or Pisces, in the zodiac appears to have had the
same origin and significance as the Great Monad.

Yang, the positive principle, and Yin, the negative
principle, combine to form the Yih which stands for the elements of being. He who understands the Yih is capable of
expressing all combinations of existence.

Yang is lord-like, heavenly, masculine, light, strong,
active, rigid; Yin is feminine, dark, earthly, mild, pliable,
submissive, wife-like. Yang is the Great Sun; Yin is the
Great Moon. In Chinese characters, Chien (heaven) combined with K'un (earth) means Universe. In numerals the
figure 6 represents the Yin and 9 signifies the Yang.

In a system of divination to be found in the Chinese
Yi King *The Classical Book of Changes,* the Yang is rep-
presented by a whole line (————) signifying strength

9—"To the wise and learned, the material intercourse is weekly,
from Sabbath to Sabbath. The Sabbath night is the night on
which the "evil power", being supplanted by the "beneficent
power", roams about the world accompanied by his many hosts
and legions and peers into all places where people perform their
conjugal intercourse immodestly and by the light of a candle,
with the result that children born of such intercourse are epi-
leptics, being possessed by the spirits of that "evil power" which
are the nude spirits of the wicked called demons (ashedim):
these are pursued and killed by the demon Lilith. As soon as
the day is sanctified, the "evil power" becomes weakened and
withdraws into hiding during the night and day of Sabbath".
Zohar, p. 60.

51. Christ in a vesica piscis. From a carved ivory of the 11th century. In the corners of the design are the Four Beasts of Ezekiel.

and unity, and the Yin is represented by a divided line (— —), signifying weakness and disunity. The creator of the system is not definitely known, one tradition crediting its invention in about 3322 B.C. to Fu hsi, who is said to be the founder of the Chinese nation, while another tradition credits its creation to King Wan and his son Kau in the 12th century B.C.

From the 2 regular or primary lines were formed the Hsiang or emblematical symbols, thus, ═ ═ ═ ═
The same 2 lines placed successively over these Hsiang formed the 8 trigrams or Kwa which served to determine the good and evil changes or events and from this determination there ensued the prosecution of the great business of life. The 8 trigrams represent 4 Yang objects or qualities and 4 Yin objects or qualities.

Addition of the Hsiang to the trigrams produces 16 figures of 4 lines each. This process is continued to 32

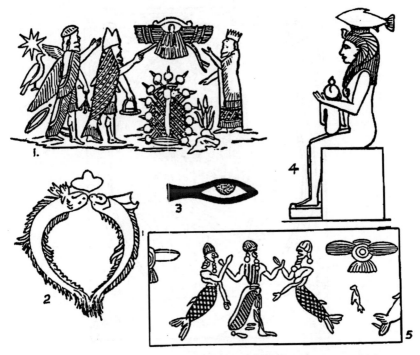

52. *Fig. 1, Assyrian priests adoring a sacred "grove" above which is an eye with wings and tail, forming a symbol of the male triad and female unit. The fish-god holds a basket, a female symbol; the winged figure holds a symbol of the male triad. Behind him is a pointed oval and eight-pointed star, both female symbols. 2, two fawning fish forming a mystic yoni, the Sakti of Mahadeva. Above them is a rudimentary fig leaf representing the male triad, or triune father Siva, or Asher, united with Anu and Ea. (A Buddhist conception from the Journal of the Royal Asiatic Society, vol. 18, p 392). 3, fish-shaped eye from Egyptian painting. 4, Isis with fish symbol on her head. 5, Oannes, or Bel, flanked by two fish gods. Dagon, the fish god of the Philistines, probably resembled the fish gods shown above.*

figures of 5 lines each and further progression produces 64 trigrams, each of which possesses a special meaning. The significance of the trigrams is explained in a series of 64 essays.

Trigrams contain the 3 powers heaven, earth, and man which are considered to be one and the same. In the mixed groups the lower line represents man and the upper lines represent water, fire, wind, mountains, and the sea. Three whole strokes represent the Khien, the Great Yang and 3 divided strokes represent the Great Yin. Other trigrams represent the first, second and third son and the first, second and third daughter, making a family of 8.

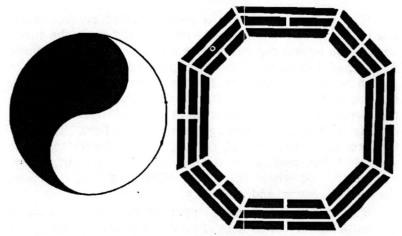

*53. Left: Yin and Yang, Oriental symbols of male and female.
The white area is male.
Right: Chinese Yih symbol.*

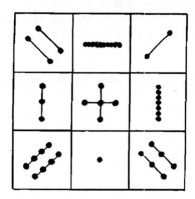

54. Chinese magic square.

Minor trigrams, which contain but one whole line, belong to Yang and represent 1 ruler and 2 subjects, symbolizing authority. Those which contain 2 divided lines belong to the Yin and signify 2 rulers and 1 subject, or weakness and inferiority.

The 8 trigrams are often arranged to form an octagon in imitation of the carapace of the sacred turtle. The version of the trigrams given in the illustration is according to the system of King Wan.[10]

10—Sacred Books of China, James Legge, 1882, 4 vols.

The Chinese also have a much simpler symbol called the magic square which is likewise derived from the turtle shell. The legend regarding it is that after Yu, the Chinese Noah, had tamed the Flood by persuading the waters to return to their 9 channels, he saw a turtle floating on the surface of the river Lo.[11] On its shell there was a square composed of 9 smaller squares in each of which a series of dots formed magic arrangements of numbers. This was the first map of the world, devised by the deities to divide and allot the surface of the earth. The central square, number 5, was where the king resided and was, therefore, the seat of power and authority.

The design which first appeared on the upper shell of the primeval turtle now appears on modern turtles, the luxurious passenger ships, where it is painted on the decks for shuffleboard players. It will be noted that the numbers on the squares add to 15 in any direction. In past ages many magic squares of this type were used by Orientals, Gnostics, Cabalists, and other mystics as amulets and talismen, the key number in each case having a special mystic significance.

11—*The Sacred Five of China*, Wm. E. Geil, 1926, p. 170.

XI

SEX SYMBOLISM

(*Continued*)

Dragons, turtles, serpents, crocodiles, and salamanders have occupied a paradoxical position in symbology and constitute a class of the oldest and least understood of all symbols. Because many species of reptiles make their homes both in the water and in the earth, they were everywhere associated with the female principle and the dark forces of nature. They were, therefore, identified with evil, destruction, and death as well as magic, sorcery, and witchcraft.

In Spain and certain other Spanish-speaking countries, the fear and superstition regarding them is so great that the word "snake" is never spoken. When superstitious natives wish to speak of this reptile, it is indicated by making a wriggling motion with the hands. Yet, serpents were anciently esteemed as guardians of graves, sanctuaries, and households and were kept or represented there—by symbol. They were considered to be the embodiment of wisdom, and the water god Ea, of the ancient Sumerians, was commonly called a "serpent god". They were also identified with sacred groves and tree worship and ancient tablets and seal cylinders which picture the tree of life almost invariably show a serpent near, or coiled around, the tree.

In China, the dragon is a symbol of clouds, floods, rain, and the gods of water. Clouds are called the breath of the dragon and when it rains, the dragon is said to be in the sky. The dragon is one of the four sacred animals of China and represents royalty, power and sovereignty.[1] The throne upon which the emperor formerly sat was called the throne of the dragon and a yellow dragon was embroidered on his robe.

There is an old tradition, of unknown origin, that the salamander is able to endure fire. Benvenuto Cellini described an incident of his childhood when his father pointed out to him a salamander in the fireplace and remarked that such an instance had never been seen before.

1—The sacred animals are the unicorn, phoenix, tortoise, and dragon.

According to Pliny and Aristotle, the animal not only resists fire, but actually extinguishes it.

The serpent, particularly the cobra, is one of the oldest and most widely used of all ithyphallic symbols. The ability of this Oriental species of serpent to puff up its cape, to raise its head erect and weave it from side to side caused it to be associated with the phallus as a symbol of life, procreation, and wisdom. Turtles have somewhat similar characteristics, for which reason they, too, were identified with life and procreation in Egypt, India, China, and Babylonia.

As a symbol of continuity, circularity, infinity, and immortality, the serpent was frequently pictured with its tail in its mouth, that is, without beginning or end. It was believed to be self-created, self-existent and therefore, hermaphroditic. Snake charms were popular amulets of fecundity and procreation because of the animal's reputed ability to renew its life. This reputation is believed to have been given the serpent because of its ability to slough off its old skin and thereby regenerate itself. It was probably due to these characteristics that the serpent was, at an early period, associated with medicine, health, and healing and became sacred to Hippocrates, the father of medicine, as well as to Aesculapius, the healer and divine physician, in whose honor snakes were kept in Greek temples and fed by naked priestesses.

The Greeks portrayed Hygeia, Medusa, and Apollo with serpents. Serpents encircled the body of Athene. Demeter had as her attendant at Eleusis the snake Kychreus, who was probably an ancient snake god. As goddess of the Phigalians, in Arcadia, Demeter had snakes twined in her hair or encircling her body and her chariot was drawn by snakes.

Priestesses at the great oracle at Delphi were called Pythonesses, or snake women, and Clement Alexandrinus wrote that a snake was the consecrated symbol of the Bacchic orgies. Snakes were kept in Apollo's shrine at Epirus and fed by naked priestesses. They were said to be descended from Pytho and were playthings of the god. Zeus was identified with a snake as Zeus Ktesios, the fertility god, and it was in the form of a serpent that he violated Persephone. In a Roman myth, Bona Dea was violated in similar manner by her father Faunus and, in her ritual, a consecrated serpent was placed beside her image.

55. *Figs. 1 to 6, serpent symbols from Egyptian gems and seals. 7, Eshmun, "the healer", from a coin of Elagabalus. 8, the head of Osiris in his sacred boat, guarded by a serpent. 9, A Naga or serpent altar (India). 10, phallic pillar with entwined serpents. The small figures represent a lingam and the sacred bull Nanda. 11, nymphs and priests in adoration before a linga, encircled by serpents. 12, the woman, the circle and the serpent. From sculpture of an ancient Gaulish deity on the portals of a temple at Montmarillon, France. (Redrawn from Thomas Maurice's* INDIAN ANTIQUITIES).

The uraeus (cobra) was placed on the foreheads or crowns of Egyptian kings and was shown united with the solar disk whenever it was desired to depict the life-giving power of the sun. Representations of the cobra were painted on royal standards and were carried in processions by the priests of Ra. The cobra was also a special emblem of Isis and Nephthys and, eventually, became identified with all of the goddesses.

The serpent was identified with the flaming eye of the god, hence "eye" and "asp" became synonymous and two eyes, or serpents, were called "daughters of the sun". Serpents were often mummified and, in later times, they became very popular motifs for jewelry designs, two of them usually being represented together; one with the head of Serapis and the other with the head of Isis. The serpent, crocodile, and dragon were associated with Buto and Nekket, the guardians of upper and lower Egypt.

Vishnu, the second member of the Trinity, in India, is portrayed sleeping on the body of Ananta, the world-serpent. Nagas, or snake gods, are an important feature of the Nayar tribe and old paintings show women performing certain phallic rites of an obscene nature with the snake god, which indicate, unmistakably, that the serpent is a symbol of the phallus. A snake throne or kavu, abode of the snakes, is an indispensable adjunct of some branches of the tribe.

On a vase of the Babylonian high priest Gudea, dating from 2700 B.C., there is a design showing two snakes entwined on a rod in what is thought to be the mating position. This is probably the origin of the caduceus which is shown in early prints. as two snakes entwined on a T-cross surmounted by a solar disk which rests upon a crescent moon, the snakes, T-cross, circle, and moon being symbols of life. The caduceus is associated with Mercury and Aesculapius, and is a modern symbol of medicine and health.

The serpent's identity with healing may be seen also in the incident in which Moses, although a reputed hater of images, idols and magic, nevertheless changed his staff into a brazen serpent. An image of the brazen serpent, called Nehushtan (II Kings 18:4) was kept in the holy of holies and incense was burned before it until the temple was cleansed during the reign of King Hezekiah which proves that serpents were particularly sacred to the Jews before the 7th century B.C.

Every nation had its legend of a Garden of Paradise, a tree of life and a serpent. In Genesis, Chapters 1 and 2, this legend has been confused by the manner in which two conflicting accounts of creation have been patched together. In the first version, a primitive, naturalistic one, man is urged to "thrive and multiply" but, in the second, a rather labored effort is made to connect procreation with shame and evil. Elsewhere, the older parts of the Bible do not contain a trace of evidence that intercourse between the sexes was condemned. Abraham was promised by Jahveh

56. *Buddhism mixed with serpent worship. Worshipers are in adoration before the footprints of Buddha and serpent gods. Serpents also appear in the headdress of the priests.*

that he would have seed as "numerous as the stars of heaven for multitude". Prophets and lawgivers alike consistently represented Jahveh as promising abundant offspring, large flocks and herds as blessings to those who worshiped none but him. For a man or woman to be without a mate or childless was the most tragic of misfortunes.

In the *Avesta*, the Persian scriptures, there are, however, numerous references to continence or "purity of life"; and in the *Bundahesh*, the scriptures of the Parsees, it is related that Mashya and Mashyoi, the first man and woman, were seduced by Ahriman in the form of a serpent or lizard, and their descendants thereby became tainted with the original sin.

Whether the Jews adopted the Adam and Eve story from the Persians; whether the latter took it from the Jews, or whether both adopted it from old Babylonian sources is a debatable question. But, inasmuch as both the Persian and Babylonian cosmogonies were much more highly developed than that of the Jews, there was very little for the former to gain from the latter. On the other hand, it is well known that the Jews derived many ideas from their masters. Circumstances indicate, therefore, that the story of the Fall of Adam and Eve was probably borrowed from Persian sources during the exile, and included in the holy records.

When the compilers of the Bible adopted the story, it was doubtless evident to them that Adam and Eve merely exercised powers and desires which had been given them at creation and which the creator intended that they would be unable to resist. For that reason it would not appear consistent or just, to say that when "Adam knew Eve" (sexually) he and she were punished because the act itself was sinful. Therefore, contrary to the candid, unequivocal manner in which the Jewish record usually speaks of such incidents, the transgression of Adam and Eve is described in symbolic language which admits of different interpretations and avoids stating directly that they committed a sinful act.

The real nature of the offense is revealed in Gen. 3:22. It was the partaking of the fruit "in the midst of the garden" which gave Adam knowledge of his ability to create life, thus making him "as one of us", that is, equal to the creator. But for Jahveh's children to be endowed with powers equal to his own could not be tolerated, therefore it was necessary that Adam be degraded and made mortal "lest he put forth his hand and take also the tree of life *and eat and live forever*". St. Jerome, Clement Alexander, and other early Christian fathers affirmed that the garden in which the seed is planted is mother earth, that is, Eve, and the serpent is sexual desire. The name of Aphrodite, the Cyprian mother goddess, has the same meaning as the Persian word paradesa or garden. The Hebrew word GN, gan or garden appears to be closely related to the Greek word gune, meaning woman, and in some ancient languages it is used as a metaphor for woman.

The name Eve gives a further clue to the origin of this myth. The word Eve (pronounced Hawwa in Hebrew), when aspirated, is the same as the Aramaic word Hawwē, denoting a serpent. The word *nagash*, written n-g-sh without vowels, also signifies a serpent in Hebrew and is pronounced almost exactly the same as the word n-c-sh, meaning sexual intercourse. The association of Hawwa, the woman, with Hawwē, the serpent (the cause of her "fall"), is, therefore, a play upon words, a practice which was very popular with Oriental myth makers.

57. *The tree, pillar, serpent, conch, and caduceus on ancient coins as symbols of life-giving power.*

Compare חוה , Chavach, a serpent

הוה , havah and hauah, to breathe, also to burn with passion

חוה , cleft or fissure

הוה , chucha, a thorn or piercing object

As ה and ח are interchangeable, we have havah, Eve or Eva; the yoni, the mystic mother.

Phoenicians honored as queen and mother goddess, a deity named Hawwat who was associated with serpent worship, and there are indications that other early Semitic people worshiped the same figure under the name of Hawwa.

Babylonians associated Ishtar with serpent worship. The sign used in writing her name seems to represent a serpent coiling about a staff. Nintud, a form of Ishtar, is represented as having scales like a serpent from her girdle to the soles of her feet. Babylonians identified her with the Greek Serpens, or Hydra, as goddess of birth. The hissing sound of *ts* or *tch* is represented in Egyptian hieroglyphics by the ideograph of a snake.

Nintud-Aruru was a Babylonian goddess who was associated with Marduk in the creation of the first man. A tablet says, "Aruru fashioned the seed of mankind with him (Marduk)". Jewish records have Eve saying practically the same thing, i.e., "I have gotten a man with Jehovah" (Gen. 4:1). All of which points to the probability that Eve is a survival of an ancient Semitic mother goddess who was transformed, under Babylonian influence, into a goddess of childbirth and who, as the first mother, naturally became the spouse of Adam, which in some Oriental languages means phallus.

The lotus or lily rivaled the serpent as a symbol of fecundity, immortality, and self-creation in Egypt, China, India, Japan, and in Greece and Rome as well. It was particularly identified with the gods because it was both a male and female symbol, the bud being male and the blossom female. The lotus seed has the unusual characteristic of developing completely with roots within the seed pod. It is therefore born alive, like an infant.

The capitals of the pillars Jachin and Boaz which stood in front of Solomon's temple were decorated with lilies and pomegranates, both being symbols of fertility. (I Kings 7:19, 20). Brahma is portrayed in India as springing from a lotus flower, which, in turn, rises from the navel of Vishnu. The lotus is also a special symbol of the self-existent Buddha. In Egypt it was venerated as a symbol of Isis, who was described as "the white virgin". In early Christian centuries, the lily was a symbol of immortality.

The fleur de lys was used as an early Christian symbol of the Trinity and, as the illustrations herein have already shown, was originally a symbol of the male triad.

The almond (or luz) and the apricot were reverenced as female symbols in Egypt. The fig was another ancient and widespread sexual symbol. The fruit of the fig tree was looked upon as a symbol of the virgin uterus, in contradistinction to the pomegranate which represented the *gravid uterus;* the leaf was a male symbol because its three lobes suggested the male triad.

The fig tree was considered more sacred when entwined with the palm and the two were constantly planted together around temples in the East. This custom still prevails in India. When trees are thus embraced, Hindus say that Kalpa is developed, for the fig is her female energy and the embrace causes the revolution of time.

In India and China a tiny plate of gold, shaped like the leaf of the Indian fig tree and representing the male genitals, is tied to a woman's neck at her marriage. When Catholic missionaries attempted to substitute the cross for the fig leaf in the 18th century, they met with such vigorous re-

58. *Left: Female worshiper placing an offering to Priapus on a phallic altar. Atop the pillar is the god, bearing a thrysus with pine cones and streamers. The youth at right carries in one hand a pine cone and, on his head, is a basket of fruit, with a representation of a phallus. Around the base of the altar appears to be a peculiar serpent with an ass's head, both of which are phallic symbols. (From Maffei's* GEMME ANTICHE FIGURATE, *vol. 3, Pl. 40, Rome, 1707).*
Right: Male and female in conjunction, holding a fleur-de-lys. From a gem of unknown origin, but apparently Babylonian.

sistance from converts that they were forced to compromise by permitting the fig leaf to be worn with a cross engraved upon it.

Fico or fig is, in Europe, a very old, vulgar slang term for the male organs. In cases of sudden or suspected treachery or other danger, men, women and children of Italy and other Mediterranean countries make the sign of the fig by closing the fist with the thumb protruding between the first and second fingers. (Plate 32). Amulets representing the hand thus clenched are made of gold, silver, ivory, coral, crystal, or semi-precious stones. The gesture became, in southern Europe, a kind of insult and Italians call it "to make" or "do" the fig. In England during Queen Elizabeth's time, it was called "to give a fig" and writers of that period called it "the fig of Spain". In America the expression "I don't care a fig" is still used occasionally by persons who probably have no idea of its original meaning.

Another gesture of similar form and meaning is made by extending the middle finger and closing the other fingers. To show the hand in this form is considered a most contemptuous insult because it is understood to intimate that the person so addressed is addicted to unnatural vices. Nevertheless, this sign is looked upon as a protection against magical influence, and jewelry representing the gesture is carried on the person as an amulet.

Like the lotus, the conch shell or *concha veneris* is especially venerated by the devotees of Vishnu as an emblem of the female genitals. The conch and the crescent moon were once commonly worn in Italy to assure fertility, but within the past century the practice has been discouraged by the church.

The conch is oval in form, has a conical or phallic top, and is often represented as winged like the hat of Osiris. The illustration on Plate 48 shows a concha held in the hand of the creator god Siva with a finger pointing directly to a diamond in the palm of his hand. The smaller figure shows a concha in the hand of the Sakti of Siva, the goddess who presides over the wombs of women as "the mother of all mothers". This symbol is often found on religious garments and church architecture.

It is believed that the sound of a conch shell can frighten away demons. It is still used in India as a trumpet in churches. Although both the gong and bell are also used, the conch is the choice of the strictly orthodox and, at certain solemn rites, it is indispensable. The Greek goddess Aphrodite was born out of the sea and, in art, is frequently represented as riding on a sea shell or scallop, another female emblem.

One of the most unusual results of the ancient practice of attaching symbolic meanings to things was the adoption of a bird as a symbol of both the Holy Spirit and female creative power. The Holy Spirit was the activating force and driving power which lifted the gods out of their passive state and made them create. Because of this ability, the spirit was considered to be of female character. As this concept developed in India, the primary gods Brahma, Vishnu, and Siva were thought to be accompanied by goddesses who aroused their creative faculties and spurred them into activity, for which reason their female consorts were called Saktis, meaning "energy".

The Holy Spirit, however, was not confined to the corporeal body of a god but was free to roam through the air like a bird whenever and wherever it wished. It was doubtless because of this similarity that pagan nations generally chose a bird as a symbol of the Holy Spirit.

59. Virgin Mary with six doves, representing attributes of the Holy Spirit. Seven doves are usually shown, representing fear, strength, piety, wisdom, science, council, and intelligence.

The oldest Hebrew symbols of the Spirit were the pair of strange, hybrid, winged creatures called cherubim. After the Exile they were succeeded by angels, which the Jews borrowed from the Persians. Angels are now usually referred to as being of neuter gender but in the Old Testament they are described as of male sex, this being one of the few instances in which the active agent of the creator is not represented as female.[2]

When the Bible says that Noah sent out a dove from the ark at the time of what might be called the second creation, it is in perfect conformity with the usage of symbology. The Spirit is Ruach, spelled RKH, and when the letter A is prefixed, it spells Arkh, the womb from which all life originated.

2—*Gen.* 16:7, 8; *Jud.* 13:6, 16, 21; II *Sam.* 24:16.

As a symbol of the female creative principle, the dove was identified with Ishtar, Semiramis, Astarte, Venus, and Virgin Mary. A black dove was the symbol of the oracle at Delphi. A Hindu myth says that Iswara, a form of Siva, and his consort Parvati, transformed themselves into doves and it was in this form that they appeared immediately after the Flood.[3]

Both doves and pigeons were highly reverenced by the Jews and were the only birds which they deemed worthy of sacrifice. With the beginning of Christianity the dove was adopted by the new religion as a symbol of the Holy Spirit. In some eastern languages, the word for dove is synonymous with yoni, the matrix, and it has been imagined by some writers that the sound of a cooing dove bears some resemblance to a libidinous invitation in Hebrew.

In Egypt a hawk took the place of the dove as a symbol of Isis and the same bird was used frequently to represent the ka or Holy Spirit of Osiris. An ancient Egyptian painting represents Osiris impregnating Isis, who broods or hovers over him in the form of a hawk. Even though the great god lies dead upon his bier, the presence of his spouse can still arouse his creative faculties. Hindu sculptures of the linga likewise frequently show a bird hovering over or sitting near this symbol of male creative power.

Doves were called flutterers or brooders, and when the authors of the Bible wrote that the Holy Spirit hovered or brooded over the face of the waters at creation (Gen. 1:2) they seem to have concealed their thoughts in symbolic language, the real significance of which could be understood only by the initiated. Isis in the form of a hawk brooding over Osiris and a dove, as the Sanctus Spiritus, brooding over the waters on the day of creation seem to be but different ways of expressing the same concept.

The Tjet is a female symbol which was as ubiquitous in Egypt as the serpent and ankh cross. It is sometimes erroneously called the buckle or girdle of Isis. It was not a buckle, but a simplified representation of the vagina, uterus, and connecting ligatures of Isis. It was carried in the belts of self-creative gods and was supposed to bring to the wearer, living or dead, the virtue, strength, and power of the goddess. When placed on the neck of the dead on the

3—The name of the Hindu goddess Parvati signifies dove. See footnote to page 168.

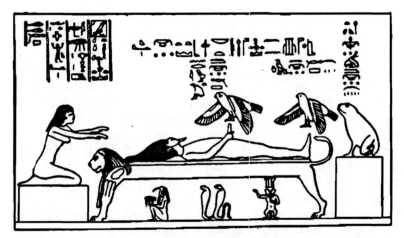

60. *The dead Osiris impregnating Isis, who hovers over him in the form of a hawk. The second hawk is Nephthys, a sister of Isis. At the head of the bier sits Hathor. The frog-headed Heqet sits at the foot. From* OSIRIS & THE EGYPTIAN RESURRECTION, *by Sir E. A. T. W. Budge.*

day of the funeral, the Tjet was supposed to open all hidden places and procure the favor of Isis and her son for the soul's journey through the Underworld. Tjets were made of red jasper, red glass, wood, porcelain, carnelian, agate, red sandstone, gold or gilded stone.

The sistrum was another of the many objects identified with Isis. It was a musical instrument which was used in the temples connected with her worship and symbolized the virgin uterus, the bars across the fenestrum indicating that the door of life had not been opened.

The bricks upon which women couched in giving birth were called, by Egyptians, the meshkent, meaning "life", "birth" or "birthplace". The meshkent was personified by the goddess Meshkenet who wore a conventionalized, bicarnate uterus on her head, this being an ideograph representing the cow goddess Neith.

Meshkenet succeeded the primitive frog-headed goddess Heq or Heqet, a patron of gestation, who assisted in the birth of kings and sometimes took the place of the ankh as a symbol of life. Her frog head represented life in embryo as the frog by the growth of its feet after birth, typified strength from weakness; it was worn in the form of an amulet for recovery from disease and for health and long life.

The Egyptian hieroglyphic Ra (O) is a formalized representation of an open mouth. As the source of the voice or breath, it is related to the Holy Spirit. Because it is a form of opening or entrance, the mouth is also a female symbol. An open mouth with a protruding tongue is a symbol of shame or astonishment, but it once had the same significance as the Hindu yoni and linga. In some parts of the East, natives still stick out the tongue as a token of servility or submission in a sexual sense. Typical portrayals of the Hindu goddess Kali show her, with extended tongue, standing on the prostrate body of her husband. In the legend, her gesture is said to be due to excitement after killing a dangerous giant, but the Hindu Tantras explain her victory as having been of a sexual nature.[4]

Bells are very old sexual symbols, the hollow bowl being female, the clapper or tongue male. Oriental maids wore bells until marriage to signify virginity. In Biblical times Jewish girls wore bells; and, about or slightly above the knees they wore a light chain. The custom caused Prophet Isaiah to complain that impudent maidens walked through the streets of Jerusalem with tinkling bells and a mincing gait. (Isa. 3:16).

Dr. Thomas Inman[5] states that the custom arose through a belief that violent movements of the body in walking briskly or clambering over objects would break the delicate membrane called the hymen which was evidence of virginity. Therefore, chains were worn about the knees, forcing the maidens to take very short steps so that they might retain until marriage their "token of virginity". Bells were worn as ornaments and their tinkling sound proclaimed that the wearer was in the market as a virgin. In the East, bells were also hung around the necks of camels for protection against the evil eye because their sound was thought to frighten evil spirits away.

Moses may have had the symbolic aspect of pomegranates and bells in mind when he commanded that a row of them be woven around the hem of Aaron's robe in blue, purple, and scarlet. The seedy pomegranate serves as a symbol of fecundity in the myth of the goddess Nana,

4—Against whom do ye sport yourselves: against whom make ye a wide mouth and draw out the tongue? Are ye not children of transgression, a seed of falsehood? *Isa.* 57:4.
5—*Ancient Pagan and Modern Christian Symbolism*, Dr. Thomas Inman, New York, 1915, p. 22.

61. Figs. 1 to 8, hieroglyphics and symbols of Meshkenet. The figure of Meshkenet in the center seems to be derived from the ankh cross. Figs 10, 11, 12 show head of a goddess, probably Hathor. Arrangement of the hair seems to be a conscious imitation of the Meshkenet symbol. Assyrian sculptures of Ishtar also exhibit this same hair arrangement.

the mother of Attis, who becomes pregnant by placing a pomegranate in her bosom.[6]

The bell was a symbol of early Christianity and was looked upon not only as the "call of Christ" but as the sign of Christ himself. In Europe during the Dark Ages, it was thought that if they were consecrated by baptism, bells would prevent hail storms, tempests and lightning, and banish demons.[7]

Such beliefs developed during the reign of Charlemagne, and in 968, Pope John XIII gave them ecclesiastical sanction by baptizing the bell of the Lateran in Rome and christening it with his own name. Soon afterward church bells everywhere were being given consecration ceremonies.

6—"And they made bells of pure gold and put the bells between the pomegranates upon the hem of the robe, round and about and between the pomegranates". "A bell and a pomegranate, a bell and a pomegranate, round about the robe to minister in as the Lord commanded Moses". *Exod.* 39:25, 26.

7—A bell at Basle bears the inscription "Ad fugandos demons". Another, at Lugano, reads, "the sound of this bell vanquishes tempests, repels demons, and summons men". Another in the cathedral of Erfurt declares that it can "ward off lightning and malignant demons". A bell in the Jesuit Church at the University town of Pont-a-Mousson bore the words "they praise God, put to flight the clouds, affright the demons and call the people". *History of the Warfare of Science with Theology*, Andrew D. White, vol. 1, p. 345.

The ringing of church bells during funeral services was believed to drive away the devils who waited to seize the soul of the deceased.

In Japan the peach is the symbol of the yoni, therefore peachwood staves were used in the demon-expelling ceremonies on the last day of the year. At the phallic festival of the *Sahe no kami*, or phallic deities, held at the first full moon of the year, boys went about striking young women with pot sticks used in making gruel. This practice was believed to insure fertility. A similar custom has prevailed in various parts of Europe within modern times. In the vicinity of Roding, in the German Palatinate, a bride is struck with willow or birch twigs as she walks from the church door to her place at the marriage ceremony.

The universality of the language of symbolism is well shown in the drawing, made early in the 18th century for Dr. Engelbert Kaempher's *History of Japan,* and reproduced on Plate 62. It represents the Chinese and Japanese fertility goddess Kwan-non or Kwan-yin, whose name signifies the yoni of yonies.

Ancient philosophers described her as the daughter of Chong-wang, that is, Chong the phallus, or king of phallic worshipers. Myths say that, like Ishtar, this yoni goddess refused offers of marriage, and in consequence descended to hell, which, because of her presence, lighted up like a paradise to the horror of its lord, who thereupon returned her to life on a lotus. Then she conferred youth and health upon her aged father by flesh taken from her own arms and ever since she has been shown with a thousand arms and every earthly blessing.

Kwan-yin is equivalent to Kaiwan of the Ethiopians and Egyptians; the Chiun or Kiun of the Hebrews; Kun, Kusi or Kunti of the Hindus; and the queen, quean, qwan, coinne or cwene of Europe. She is the great watery principle, queen of heaven, lady of plenty; the virgin goddess of a thousand arms who reigns throughout the world under a thousand different names.

Dr. Kaempher said she is at times pictured as the multi-mammia and, occasionally, is depicted with a mass of babies who seem to grow out of her fingers, toes and, indeed, her whole body. At other times she is a snaky fish goddess, in which guise she is represented as worshiping the phallus and moving in a sea of all things phallic.

62. *Kwan-non, Japanese mother goddess with symbols.*

The goddess sits on a lotus shrine over the primordial waters. On her forehead is the heavenly dot or Shang, the star of life. She has yoni ornaments in her hair, which is gathered up in yoni loops. Above her is her lord Ti Shang or Thi'an with a solar disk, supported by two arms of his Ruach or Holy Spirit, without which nothing is or can be. In her lap is the typical symbol of the womb and yoni, and immediately above it is what appears to be the tree of life. On the throat of the goddess there is a winged sun and, suspended from the wings, are two inverted tau cross pendants. The pose of the hands before her chest has a phallic significance.

In the hands of the goddess may be seen many of the typical symbols representing the properties or characteristics of male and female principles, among them being fruits, flowers, the budding branch, the chakra or solar wheel, the book of fate, a gate or entrance, a bethel, sword, arrow, axe, oar or paddle, shuttle, censer of sacred fire, bow of life, the mirror of Venus, Isis or Maya, a womb-shaped vase with cruciform head, and numerous other symbols.

XII

SEX SYMBOLISM

(Continued)

THE SANCTIFICATION AND WORSHIP of stones was a manifestation of animism or spirit worship, sharing with tree and
serpent worship the distinction of being one of the most
general and ancient forms of worship. It was particularly
widespread among Semites, and the rock or stone (Tsur of
the Bible) was the real, old god of the Arabs, Jews and
Phoenicians. Later, when the old forms of worship were
superseded by sun worship, many of the old beliefs were
absorbed by the sun cults, and sacred serpents and stones
became identified with the phallic aspect of the solar gods.

In Greece a stone was frequently set up along the
roadside in honor of Hermes or Mercury and as each
traveller passed he paid honor to the deity by adding a stone
to the heap or by anointing it. From these stone heaps,
called baety-li (Hebrew Bethel) there later developed the
sculptured boundary stones or "Hermes" of the Greeks and
Romans. From their identification as phallic symbols, the
word Hermes became synonymous with phallus. Even today
travellers in the East often come upon heaps of stones and
passersby walk quietly around them in order to avoid
disturbing the local spirit which is supposed to dwell there.

In the oldest books of the Bible, God is referred to as
a local spirit who sometimes dwells in rocks. It is related
that Joshua set up a stone as a witness to God (Josh. 24:26),
and set up twelve stones in a circle, or Gilgal, where the
Israelites crossed the Jordan. (Josh. 4:20).

On an occasion when Jacob dreamed that he heard the
voice of the Lord, he decided, when he arose in the morning,
that the voice he had heard came from the stone which he
had used for a pillow. Thereupon, he anointed the stone
with oil and set it up as a bethel, or house of God, saying,
"Surely, the Lord is in this place: and I knew it not".[1]

1—*Gen.* 28:22; *I Sam.* 10:8; *II Kings* 4:38; *Jud.* 3:19; *Hos.* 4:15;
I Sam. 7:12.

Moses set up twelve stones for the twelve tribes of Israel near the foot of his altar at Mount Sinai.[2] When Jacob and Laban made a covenant they set up a heap of stones and a pillar of stones as a witness of the Lord.[3] (Compare with pillar and circle or boat and mast). The Biblical phrase "The God of Abraham and the God of Nahor, the God of their fathers judge betwixt us"[4] seems to indicate that Jacob and Laban believed in different gods, therefore they compromised by using the god of their fathers on whom both could agree.

Even after the primitive belief in local gods had been superseded by belief in one Supreme God, the old term "Rock" remained in use as a title of God. When Christ said of Peter, "Thou art a Rock" he employed an expression which had been significant for over two thousand years.[5]

Conical stones which apparently served as idols have been found at Golgi, in Cyprus. A white, upright, conical stone was a symbol of Aphrodite at Paphos. Square stones were used by the Greeks and Arabians as a symbol of Venus. At Peiga, in Pamphylia a conical stone was the emblem of Astarte. Diana of the Ephesians was represented by a stone. In 204 B.C., during the war with Hannibal, the Romans took from Pessinus to Rome a large black stone sacred to Cybele and worshiped it with great ceremony.

Chemosh of the Moabites was worshiped in the form of a black conical stone. To the Nabataean Arabs of Syria, a large stone was a symbol of the god Dusares and the great mother Alla. Suidas, a Greek writer, says that Dusares was worshiped in the form of a black stone four feet high which stood on a gold base.

Square blocks of stone seem to have formed an intermediate stage between rough, unhewn stones and realistic, carved statues. In Greece, there was a square image of Zeus Teleias. During the dominance of Greek religion a rectangular *cella* constituted the central part of the Greek temple. The temple was sometimes extended at front and

---

2—*Gen.* 31:52.
3—"This heap be a witness and this pillar be a witness." *Gen.* 31:52.
4—*Ibid.* 31:46.
5—The Lord is my Rock. *II Sam.* 22:2, 3, 32.
　　For their Rock is not our Rock. *Deut.* 32:31.
　　. . . of the Rock that begat thee thou art unmindful. *Deut.* 32:18.
　　Where are their gods, their Rock, in whom they trusted. *Deut.* 32:37.

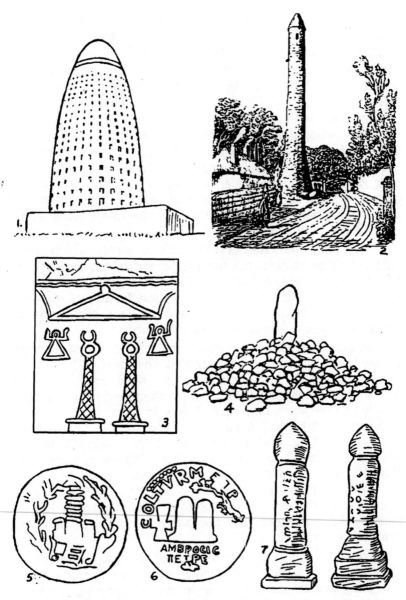

63. *Phallic pillars. Fig. 1, Siva lighthouse, Suwal, India. 2, round tower in Ireland. 3, Carthaginian design probably from a coin, showing Baal and two horned pillars. 4, "a pillar of stones and a heap of stones" such as Jacob erected for Jahveh. 5, an ancient coin showing a baetyl (Bethel). 6, colonial coin of Tyre with two pillars. 7, phallic pillars from Pompeii.*

back with additional chambers, or surrounded by single or double rows of columns. The holy of holies in Solomon's temple was constructed in the form of a cube.

The lares and penates which Romans kept as household fetishes were small stone images representing male and female figures. The Latin word pena-tes suggests that the images were of phallic significance.

The Persian god Mithra was thought to have been born of a rock, to have married a rock, and to have been the parent of a rock. Before the rise of Mohammedanism Byzantine writers regarded the worship of Aphrodite as the principal cult of Mecca. The idol of the goddess was a white stone and that of her son was the small black stone now in the holy Mohammedan Ka'aba.

The dual character of the creative forces which were thought to be responsible for life on earth was symbolized by pillars, obelisks, columns, and similar forms. During the time of Hosea, pillars were an important feature of religion, and the prophet thought that ephods, pillars, and teraphim (images) were essential to proper worship.[6]

Pillars representing the male and female principles were to be found at temples throughout the East. They were not incorporated in the structure but stood in front of the entrance, the columns forming a symbolic gateway, or door of life. There were two such pillars in front of the temple of Hercules at Gades. A pair of pillars stood in front of the oracle at Dodona and pillars flanked the approach to the entrance of most temples in Egypt. Pillars typified life, strength, and protection in the same manner as the linga and yoni in India. The two pillars, Jachin and Boaz, which stood before the temple of Solomon, had male and female names and doubtless had the same significance as such symbols elsewhere.

In addition to the pillars placed at the entrances of temples, single pillars and towers, which are thought to be of phallic origin, are still to be found in many parts of the world. In Ireland there are many towers of this type. Usually they were not erected on the tops of hills, as would be expected if they were intended as watchtowers, nor were they usable as fortresses. It is widely believed therefore that they were merely phallic monuments. These

---

6—*Hos.* 3:4.

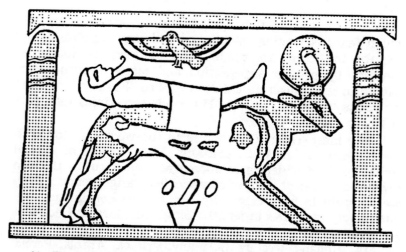

64. *The body of Osiris borne on the back of the sacred bull Apis. Osiris has been embalmed for burial and the pail contains his viscera. Over Osiris a hawk hovers, representing his* KA *or spirit. The sky is supported by two phallic pillars.*

towers vary in height from fifty to one hundred fifty feet and are from twelve to twenty feet in diameter at the base. They are empty inside and most of them are divided into from 3 to 8 lofts or stories by rests or projecting stones.[7]

Large stones which stood alone or at a distance from any rocky formation seem to have excited the curiosity of people in early times as they do even today, and in many places they became meeting places where councils, festivals, and religious rites were held. In time legends were created about them and they often acquired a sacred or semi-sacred significance.

Most stone monuments, however, were transported to their final sites and erected for specific purposes, the most common of the monuments being single, huge, upright or slanting stone slabs called menhirs (long stones). In many instances the menhirs were surrounded by ovals or circles of stones, thus forming the familiar pillar and circle symbols of the male and female. These are called dolmens (from Breton *dol*, a table and Welsh *men*, a stone). Some of them have peculiar mystic designs scratched or carved on them.

The greatest number of menhirs are found in France, where there are between three and four thousand. Around

7—*Round Towers of Ireland*, H. O'Brien, pp. 511-515.

such monuments, gatherings of various kinds were held which featured singing, dancing, and kissing. In France and neighboring countries, phallic virtues were attributed to menhirs by popular superstition and maids desiring marriage and wives desiring children rubbed themselves against the rocks to insure fertility. Husbands sometimes took part in the ceremony.

The most celebrated menhirs in the world are found in the vicinity of Carnac in Brittany. They consist of several series, each of which is composed of from four to thirteen rows or avenues of upright stones called "alignments". They are thought to have originally formed one continuous avenue nearly two miles in length. Single menhirs and dolmens are also found in Morocco, Algeria, Spain, Portugal, Great Britain, Holland, western Germany, Crimea, Arabia, Persia, India, and other parts of Asia as well as in Australia and Peru.

Today the word cromlech denotes merely a leaning stone, but originally it signified a stone containing either a natural or a man-made hole or aperture. It also denoted a group of stones placed close to each other and enclosing an area sufficiently small and narrow to be roofed over by one or more capstones, thus forming a rude chamber. This chamber was sometimes partly or wholly imbedded in a mound of earth or stones presenting, to outward appearances, the form of a tumulus or cairn. In rare instances cromlechs consisted of two single standing stones supporting a third and forming a passageway or door of life so that persons seeking purification could pass through and be regenerated.

The Gaelic word klachan or clachan denotes either a church, a stone, or a sacred meeting place. When villages and churchyards were built around the sacred stones, they too were called klachans. An Irish expression for going to church also signifies "going to the stone" and in northern Scotland the word klachan is still used for "house of God".

In 567 A.D., the Council Board of Tours (France) felt obliged to issue a decree against "the worship of upright stones" and in the 5th and 7th centuries similar warnings were issued from Canterbury.

In the British Isles there are ruins of more than two hundred monuments formed by circles of stone, the best known of them being the great monument of Stonehenge

65. Cromlechs. Fig. 1, St. Michael's Mount, Land's End, Cornwall.
2, Kit's Coty house, Aylesford, Scotland. 3, leaning menhir in
Brittany. 4, holy stone, Constantine, Cornwall. 5, holy stone,
Lochaber, Scotland.

on Salisbury Plain, which is believed by some authorities
to have been erected in the Stone Age, probably about
2000 or 1800 B.C. Stonehenge originally consisted of an
outer circle three hundred feet in diameter and an inner
circle one hundred six feet in diameter, inside of which
there was another series of smaller stones in the form of
a horseshoe. Inside this there was a second, smaller horseshoe, near the central curve of which there was a large altar
stone fifteen feet high.

In the east side of the outer circle two stones formed an entrance leading to the great stone altar. Outside the larger circle there was a circular furrow, ditch or rampart which was intentionally broken at the point where it intersected the east-west axis of the monument. At this point stood a large stone called a sacrificial stone, but which some authorities have called a pointer, or linga.

It has been conjectured that Stonehenge was built by the Druids as a temple of the sun, the entrance stone and altar being so placed that on June 21st the first rays of the rising sun shine upon the huge pointer, then pass directly through the entrance and strike the great stone altar.

Another great monument at Abury consists of a central circle enclosed by a great circle of stones which is approached by two long serpentine rows of upright monoliths forming an avenue over half a mile in length.

Even more than large quaint rock formations, natural cavities and fissures in the earth have always been peculiarly fascinating for superstitious people and have been regarded with a mixture of fear and wonderment. Ancient beliefs regarding the significance of caves, caverns, and clefts led to the custom, which still persists in certain parts of the world, of passing children (and adults as well) through openings and crevices as an act of purification and re-birth from the womb of Mother Nature.

When the rulers of Travancore, in southern India, ascend the throne they are transformed from the Nayar caste into Brahmans by passing through a golden cow or lotus flower, which then becomes the property of the Brahman priest.[8]

On the island of Bombay there is said to be a rock containing a natural cavity, with an upper and lower entrance, which is used by the Gentvas as a means of purification. This, they say, is effected by going in at the lower opening and emerging from the upper opening.

8—For the purpose of regeneration, it is directed to make an image of pure gold of the female power of nature in the shape either of a womb or a cow. In this statue the person to be regenerated is enclosed and dragged out through the usual channel. As a statue of pure gold and of proper dimensions would be too expensive, it is sufficient to make an image of the sacred yoni through which the person to be regenerated is to pass." Captain Francis Wilford, *Asiatic Researches*, Royal Asiatic Society of Bengal, vol. 6, p. 535.

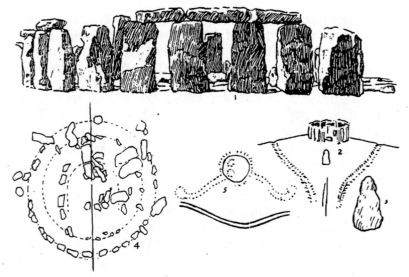

*66. Stonehenge as seen from the east. Figs. 2 and 3
are distant views showing the stone pointer and ram-
parts. 4, is a ground plan of the east-west axis. 5,
ground plan of Abury.*

In Nepal, India, small perforated stones, generally
about the size of an orange, and called salagrama, are regarded as sacred to Vishnu. By a very peculiar coincidence,
similar stones called salagrana, are wrapped in red woollen
and carried in the pockets of persons in Tuscany, Italy,
who practice sorcery.

Old adoption ceremonies still survive in some parts of
the world in which the adopted person is symbolically
re-born. Among the Berawas of Sarawak, when a woman
wishes to adopt a child or adult, a feast is arranged and the
adopting mother is seated on a raised and covered seat. Then
the adopted person crawls from behind and between her
legs, thus imitating childbirth. Among the early Jews a
childless woman became a foster mother by merely having
a real mother sit upon her knees during birth of the child.[9]

In ancient Greece any man who had been erroneously
supposed to be dead and for whom funeral rites had been
held during his absence, was treated as dead to society until
he had gone through the form of being born again. Dio-
dorus wrote that when Zeus persuaded his wife Hera to

9—And Rachel said, Behold my maid Billah, go in unto her and
she shall bear upon my knees that I also have children by her.
Gen. 30:3.

adopt Hercules, the goddess got into bed and, clasping the
hero to her bosom, pushed him through her robes and let
him fall to the ground in imitation of real birth. In Dio-
dorus's day the same mode of adopting children was practiced by the Barbarians and is still used by Bulgarians and
Bosnian Turks. A woman will take a boy whom she intends
to adopt and push or roll him through her clothes. Ever
afterward he is regarded as her son.[10]

In passing to the underground chamber where the
sacred rites of the Mithraic Mysteries were conducted, it
was necessary for the initiates to pass through a narrow
entrance leading to the cave or underground chamber, as if
entering a womb. Above the chamber a bull was sacrificed
and its blood flowed down through a wooden grating on
to the initiate. This was the Tauribolium ceremony in
which the initiate was purified and reborn in the blood of
the bull.

Purification, regeneration, and re-birth are certain to
have been important features of the Mysteries in Egypt,
where the initiates appear to have been placed in a "cradle
of skin", or symbolic womb, from which they emerged,
simulating the process of gestation and being thereby re-
created and purified. The rite was probably in imitation of
a myth which alleged that the sun god Ra was born in the
form of a calf from the cow Nut or Neith, the mother goddess of heaven, the initiate thus becoming identified with the
· sun god. Both Plutarch and Apuleius state that in the
procession of Isis a wooden image of a cow was borne upon
the shoulders of the priests. It was probably an image of
Nut, the divine cow mother of the gods, from whose womb
the initiates were symbolically re-born.

The Mystery of Osiris and Isis was generally considered
the most ancient of Mysteries, being already in existence
at the beginning of recorded history. Those who were admitted to the Lesser Mystery were denominated mystae or
veiled while those who were initiated into the Greater
Mystery were epoptai or seers.[11]

10—*Golden Bough*, Abdg. E., Sir James Frazer, pp. 14, 15.
11—In Egypt, in order to represent gestation and re-birth, either
a statue or mummy was placed inside the hide of a sacrificial
animal, or inside a wooden cow, and a priest would let himself
within the hide on the night of the funeral as a substitute for
the dead man. Next morning the priest was considered to issue
from the skin as from a womb. *Kings & Gods of Egypt*, Alex.
Moret, p. 186.

The ancient rite of purification, death, and resurrection has been continued as an initiation rite in certain religious orders down to modern times. After passing through several preliminary grades, novice monks and nurs, clad in white, are placed in coffins in front of the altar while the mass is sung. This is when the novices become "professed".

Owing to their secret nature, very little information has come down to us regarding the rites of the Mysteries which for many centuries before the Christian era were practiced by natives of Eleusis, Samothrace, Bilbos, and other places along the eastern shores of the Mediterranean. From what is known of their beliefs, however, it is safe to conclude that the rites included a symbolic dramatization of the processes of nature; conception, birth, growth, death, and resurrection.

The Eleusinian Mysteries, which took place in the Greek village of Eleusis, were probably the most elaborate. They covered a period of eight days and were divided into the Lesser and Greater Mysteries, with the final act taking place in the temple of Demeter. The annual periods of plant growth and death were probably symbolized by a dramatization of the abduction of Persephone by Pluto and the efforts of her mother which resulted in Persephone being restored to the earth for half of each year.

XIII

SEX SYMBOLISM

(Continued)

Determination of the symbolical meaning of trees is complicated by the fact that in various periods and places they have been features of spiritism and totemism as well as phallicism. As a phase of primitive spirit worship they were placed in consecrated ground near altars and "high places" as representatives of the deity and as his dwelling place. This seems to have been the belief of Abraham when he sought God in the oaks and tamarisks of Mamre and when he planted a tree at Beersheba "and call(ed) thereon the name of the Lord, the everlasting God". (Gen. 21:23).

It was an expression of totemism that made oak trees sacred to Jupiter and Zeus and caused the Druids to hold the oak and yew sacred and use hollow oaks for burial of the dead.

Early Spartans laid the dead upon olive leaves and palm branches. The male palm tree was a necessary accompaniment of all phallic and solar festivals and was used prominently in temple decoration. It is found repeatedly on ancient coins and tablets, always with seven branches. In Egypt a palm branch was an emblem of Taht, the scribe of the gods. The branches were carried in religious processions as symbols of self-creation, time, and perpetuity because they were said to add one new frond with each change of the moon. In the Book of Revelation palms seem to possess the same significance.

Because it retained its verdure throughout the year, the pine tree was an emblem of immortality and was often represented on Assyrian monuments and Etruscan funeral urns. The pine cone was a symbol of Venus and Astarte. During the Thesmophoria festival in Greece, images of phalli and snakes were made of dough and, together with pine cones, were dedicated to the goddess as emblems of fertility. Pine cones may still be seen on gateways in Italy where they are regarded as emblems of fecundity, good health, and good fortune. In the Phoenician myth of the sun god Attis, it was under a pine tree that the hero died and was re-born the following spring.

To Chaldeans, the cedar represented not only the tree of life but the "revealer of the oracles of earth and heaven" as well. The name of Ea, god of wisdom, was supposed to be written on its core and Nin-gish-zida was "master of the Tree of Life".

The laurel or bay was the victor's crown, the wreath of Mars and of those to whom their fellows wished to pay honor. It was sacred to Apollo. The first temple at the oracle of Delphi was built of laurel. The chewing of bay leaves was thought to give one the ability to make prophecies.

Holly trees are both male and female, the prickly species being male, the non-prickly being female and there is an old superstition to the effect that whichever kind of holly enters a house at Christmas time determines whether the husband or wife shall dominate in the coming year. According to another tradition, the maiden who wishes to see her future husband should pin the holly on her night dress over her heart and go to sleep with three pails of water in her room. If further prophecy is desired, leaves of the female holly must, on the night of Venus' day (Friday) be tied in a handkerchief and slept upon in perfect silence until Saturn's morn.

Within the past century a custom prevailed in Europe of cutting hawthorne and elm twigs and wearing them during the month of May. Together, they were called May and persons who did not wear them during this month risked being thoroughly ducked in water. Because of the great social changes which have taken place in modern times, many old customs of this kind have practically vanished, except in more or less isolated communities. In outlying districts of the British Isles, for instance, there is a very old belief that the rowan, or mountain ash, is a protection against evil; and it has been the custom to place a staff of ash over door posts to ward off malign influences.

Scotch shepherds drive their flocks to the hills with ash staffs and on Beltane, or May Day, sheep and lambs are passed through hoops of ash. Ash trees are always planted near holy places such as churchyards and stone circles or klachans. Pious persons are in the habit of wearing crosses of ash on a certain day of the year. A fertility god formerly worshiped in northern Europe was called Yggdrasil, meaning ash tree.

In Suffolk, England, it is a custom to split a young ash tree lengthwise and pass a naked child through it three times head first (but some say feet first) to cure rickets and rupture. The child is then turned around and, as the Celts say, passed deaselwise, that is, with the sun, after which the cleft in the tree is bound up. If the tree heals, all is supposed to go well with the child.

The tree should be split about five feet as nearly as possible from east to west, and just as the sun is rising in the early spring before vegetation begins. In Suffolk the operation is called "drawing". In Cornwall, passing through the cleft of a tree has the same significance as passing through an aperture in a rock, or "threading the needle", as it is called. In Killarney, the operation is said to be of a fertilizing nature and brings "a saving of pain to women in a certain way".

In Oxford, an old custom of like meaning is practiced with "groaning cheese", a piece of which, cut in circular or oval form, must be kept ready at birth to pass the newborn babe through. Afterward, the cheese is cut like a wedding cake and given to girls to sleep upon to "excite pleasant and expressive dreams".

In Scandinavia the hazel tree was formerly sacred to Thor and in Bohemia hazel groves were favorite spots for temples. In Bavaria, batons of office were always made of hazel wood and divining rods were made of hazel. Bohemians believed that wherever there were nuts, there were wasps and women were fruitful; also, that wherever nuts were found, illegitimate children abounded. Should a snake bite a hazel rod, the rod was believed to turn at once into a bluish stone, which if thrown into water, would cure an animal of snake bite.

Pliny observed that the Romans hung colored rags and other offerings on sacred trees. Travelers in the East have mentioned the same custom in modern times. In India, according to Fergusson,[1] rags in the form of yoni-like loops

---

1—*Tree and Serpent Worship*, James Fergusson, 1868.

are hung from budding twigs and branches, the branch and loop symbolizing the union of the male and female creative powers. (See Plate 48, fig. 20).

The rite of tree marriage still survives in India as a conventional symbol of totemism. Sacred trees are circumambulated by Nayar women desiring children, and by men who wish to avoid the evil influence of Saturn, under which they are supposed to suffer during some part of their lives.

Phallic poles may still be found near temples and in villages in the Orient, adorned like our Maypoles with brightly colored banners or streamers. Sometimes the figure of a rooster, an emblem of the sun and fecundity, or some other phallic figure is placed at the top of the pole.

The custom of children dancing around a Maypole is derived from the ancient custom of dancing around a tree, tree trunk, or pole, in springtime, in token of the annual resurgence of the generative powers of nature.

England was once noted for its Maypoles. In writing about the general let-down of morals which marked the May time celebrations, Philip Stubbes, a Puritan writer of Queen Elizabeth's time, made it clear why May was often called the month of bastards. Stubbes said that with the arrival of May, men, women and children assembled from every parish, town, and village and went to the hills and forests where they spent the night in pleasant pastimes. In the morning they returned, carrying birch branches and the trunk of a tall, young tree. They painted the tree in various colors, decked it with flowers and banners and set it up on the village green. In some instances small trees were fastened securely in boxes and placed at the top of the poles.

Every morning during May, the parishioners of St. Andrews-under-shaft in London, set up a shaft which was higher than the church steeple and after their ceremony, they carefully put it away under the eaves of the church, which were built so as to protect it. Puritans took offense at the custom and cut the pole to pieces. In 1644 Parliament passed an act for the suppression of Maypoles.

The worship of trees as symbols of male generative power was widespread among ancient nations; and it was in this sense that trees, tree trunks, posts, and pales became prominent in the worship by the Jews in Canaan, of gods of fertility. On ancient Babylonian tablets and seal cylinders, trees are represented as symbols of the tree of life, or the euphemistic tree which creates life. It is the same tree which, in the story of Adam and Eve, is disguised as the "tree of knowledge". To people of the East, wise in the language of symbolism, the meaning of the tree of life, which flourishes in a paradise or garden, is perfectly obvious.

Conventional representations of the tree of life, in the form of upright wooden pillars or tree trunks, and called asherim (translated "groves" in the Bible), were special symbols of the Syrian god Baal and often had obscene designs carved on their surface. Even in the temple at Jerusalem there stood an upright ashera, the emblem of Baal-Peor, the phallus or priapus of the Jews. (I *Kings* 23:6). The "image of jealousy" which Ezekiel said could be seen upon looking north through the inner gate of the temple was undoubtedly an ashera. (Ezek. 8:3).

Baal corresponded to the Assyrian god Asher and was represented as being either male, female, or both; therefore an androgyne. Although he is nominally male, Baal is called "the lady" in Hos. 2:8 and Zeph. 1:4. At his licentious rites men wore female garments and women wore male attire.

The feminine form of Baal was called Beltis, Astarte, or Ashtoreth, and was represented by a feminine form of wooden emblem called asherah or asharah, signifying the door of life, and was probably similar in appearance to the Assyrian type shown on Plate 67.

The relation of pillars and poles to phallic worship is further indicated by the Hebrew word phalash,[2] or palash, meaning "to break or cut through", "to open up a way"; by the Latin word *palus* or *pales;* and the German *pfale,* signifying a pale, which is a universal symbol of the phallus. Pala is a word for spade or the broad part of an oar (the part which cleaves the water), both being symbols of the male organ of generation. The names *Phyllis* and *Philip* mean "love" or "loving". According to this construction,

---

2—Compare with Phallu, the son of Reuben (*Gen.* 46:9), signifying "a distinguished one", "he splits, divides", "he is round and plump".

67. *Fig. 1, Assyrian sculpture showing eagle-headed figures before
an asherah representing the female "door", with symbolic tree of
life in the center. The figures hold pine cones and baskets as
symbols of the male-female. Fig. 2, a king and his son or suc-
cessor with attendant genii before an ashera. Again the pine
cones and baskets are present. Note the king's hand making the
sign shown in Plate 32, Fig. 7. Fig. 3 shows the closed fist, the
dagger, the bull, the tree of life and the "door of life" with
the tree within it.*

Palestine, the land of the Philistines, would denote the land
of worshipers of the phallus.

Asherim and groves or gardens were prominent features
of the procreation rites which back-sliding Israelites practiced at their "high places". The groves or gardens might be
either single trees or clusters of them, under or near which
altars and images of Baal were placed. Ezekiel complained
that Jewish women spent much of their time "making hangings for the groves" (Ezek. 16:16 and II Kings 23:7) where
they engaged in adulterous practices, in tents or booths, in
their worship of the gods of fertility. The sacred high places
which had existed since Abraham's time had become corrupted by heathen practices copied from the Canaanite
followers of Astarte. Later prophets made it clear that

worship of images and gods of fertility was rampant throughout the land. Perhaps it was only due to the bloody reform
of Josiah that worship of Jahveh survived at all.[3]

3—She (Judah) committed whoredom with stones and with stocks
(trees). *Jer.* 3:9.
Saying to a stock (tree) thou art my father and to a stone, thou
hast brought me forth. *Jer.* 2:27.
A people that provoketh me to anger continually to my face;
that sacrificeth in gardens and burneth incense upon altars
of brick. *Isa.* 65:3.
They sacrificed upon the tops of mountains and burned incense
upon the hills, under oaks, poplars and elms, the shadow thereof
is good, therefore your daughters shall commit whoredom and
your spouse shall commit adultery. *Hos.* 4:13.
They that sanctify themselves and purify themselves in a
garden behind one tree in the midst, eating swine's flesh and
the abomination and the mouse shall be consumed together.
Isa. 66:17.
Thou hast built them high places at every head of the way
and hast made thy beauty to be abhorred and hast opened thy
feet to every one that passed by and multipled thy whoredoms.
Ezek. 16:25.
For they shall be ashamed of the oaks which ye have desired
and ye shall be confounded for the gardens that ye have
chosen. *Isa.* 1:29.

XIV

SEX SYMBOLISM

(*Continued*)

THE RELIGIOUS EXALTATION created by worship of the forces which generate life caused the rites and ceremonies of primitive people to assume an extreme and violent form. With the impulsive, passionate people of the East, particularly, nature worship frequently took an erotic form, with the religious side of the ritual being overshadowed by sacred prostitution, phallic worship, self-mutilation, and other extremes.

The growth of Christianity was due, in part, to a repugnance which thinking people had begun to feel against the orgies and obscenities of fertility cults. In its movement away from these debasing practices, the pendulum swung to the other extreme and, whereas the old religion was devoted to worship of the powers of procreation, the new one developed a profound abhorrence of sex, its members believing the creation of life to be innately sinful and a cause of human degradation.

St. Paul repeatedly recommended to his listeners an Essenian rule of conduct which, if it had become general, would have resulted in the depopulation of the world. Paul spoke with pride and joy of his chastity and urged that young men and women forego marriage. Men and women who were already married were asked to abstain from sexual acts.

To avoid the temptations of life, emotionally unstable members of the new religion abjured human society and became ragged beggars or hermits, living amidst filth and vermin in secluded caves, wells and mountain crags. In their contempt for the human body, some early leaders of the church, like Origen and Melitto, went so far as to resort to self-mutilation, a practice which, the Gospels say, was sanctioned even by Christ.[1]

1—". . . and there are some eunuchs, which were made eunuchs of men; and there be eunuchs, which have made themselves eunuchs for the kingdom of heaven's sake. He that is able to receive it, let him receive it." *Matt.* 19:12.

The avowed celibacy of religious extremists sprang from a pre-occupation with the sexual idea. The history of monastery and convent life during the Dark Ages attests the fact that human resistance frequently broke down under the physical and mental strain occasioned by a life contrary to nature. The celibate often yielded to the temptations he had sought to avoid.

On the other hand, there was, among nature worshipers, a complete absence of sex inhibitions, and their most honored gods were those that were believed to regulate the mysteries of the life cycle from germination of the life-bearing seed, in animal or plant life, through birth, growth, and death. Next in sanctity to the gods who created all life were the instruments with which they performed their holy miracles. As early as the building of the pyramids, long before circumcision was practiced by the Jews, the Egyptians dedicated the sexual organs to the god of generation by the rite of circumcision. For priests and soldiers circumcision was compulsory. In Madagascar it is still necessary for soldiers and officials.

Circumcision prevailed among the early Ethiopians, Phoenicians, Syrians, Idumeans, Moabites, and Ishmaelites. In more recent times it was known to the early Mexicans, South Americans, Fijians, Samoans, Australians, and other primitive people. Among some peoples, such as the Turks and Malays, the legal and social status of a man is determined by circumcision. In certain African tribes uncircumcised persons are refused the rights of inheritance and are not admitted to the tribal councils.

The sanctity of the generative organs in Biblical times is revealed by an incident where Abraham, wishing his servant to swear "by the Lord, the God of heaven", commanded the servant to place his hand under the patriarch's "thighs" in order that the physical representative of Jahveh's generative power might be a witness to the oath. (Gen. 24:2, 9). Israel commanded his son Joseph to swear in the same manner (Gen. 47:29) and, when Solomon ascended the throne, all princes and mighty men "gave their hand under Solomon". I Chron. 29:24f).

The words sacrifice and sacrament are from the Latin word sacer, meaning sacred. Sacer appears to be cognate with the Hebrew word zakar, meaning phallus. The words test, testify, and testimony are derived from the ancient

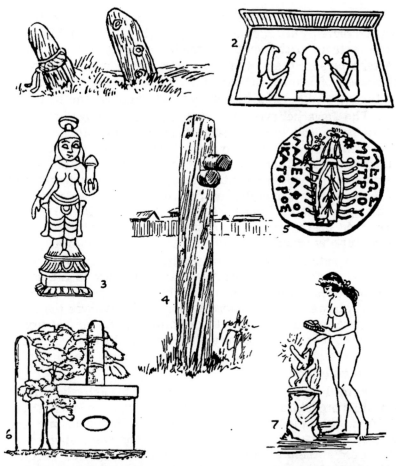

68. *Fig. 1, modern Fijian phalli or sun stones. 2, Egyptian deities worshiping the male emblem. 3, Hindu goddess of fertility holding a phallus. 4, modern phallic pole erected before a Mongolian monastery to frighten away a female demon. 5, Syrian medal representing Baal holding a staff and surrounded by phalli. 6, nymphaeum found in excavating for the Barbarini Palace, Rome. The monument presents both male and female symbols. 7, a worshiper offering a sacrifice to Bacchus.*

practice of swearing by the testes and the custom has prevailed among Arabs until modern times. Writing in the last quarter of the 19th century, Dr. Inman stated that every female in the Lebanon district considered it her duty, once each year to salute with her lips the reverenced organ of the sheik.[2]

2—*Ancient Pagan and Modern Christian Symbolism*, Dr. Thomas Inman, Introd., p. xxviii.

In India, worshipers of Siva reverently touch the testes of the sacred bull Nanda as they begin their worship. No more solemn oath could be made by a Hindu, or other eastern person, than by making him swear with a hand on the testes of Nanda, nor could a son or servant give a more enduring pledge than by placing his hand on the testes.

The Jews believed that only the sexually perfect were fit to serve the lord of generation and the Mosaic Laws provided that a man who was "wounded in the stones", emasculated or otherwise sexually imperfect, could not serve as a priest, nor could he enter the house of the congregation.[3] If a woman were guilty of injuring the sacred organ of a man, one of her hands was cut off. (Deut. 25:12). Saul preferred death by falling on his sword to the degradation of capture by uncircumcised Philistines.. (I Sam. 31:4).

The extent to which the Biblical injunction regarding physical perfection of priests is observed today in the selection of popes is known only to higher ecclesiastics. Roscoe[4] tells us, however, that before Roderigo Borgia was installed as Pope Alexander VI, he was examined in the holy of holies of the Vatican to make sure that he was in every sense a man, although he was already known to be the father of several children.

According to early, primitive concepts, Jahveh himself was the progenitor par excellence and when sixteen thousand captive Midianite virgins were distributed among the victorious Jews, thirty-two of the maidens were allotted as the Lord's tribute and reserved for his special service. (Num. 31:40). Long after the Jewish religion began to assume an ethical character, the role of Jahveh continued to be predominately that of a god of fertility, whose worship was expected to assure full reproductive ability to men and women.

Repeated references are made in the Bible to phallic idols, images, and worship, but they have been so thoroughly disguised in translation that they give the average reader no understanding of the beliefs and practices to which they refer. Many of the names of people and places mentioned also have a phallic significance, which is not revealed by standard Bible Concordances.

3—*Deut.* 23:1.
4—*Life and Pontificate of Leo the Tenth*, Wm. Roscoe, 6 vols., 1846, 2nd ed., vol. 1, p. 180.

Jeremiah complained that his people set up pillars in the form of bosheth, translated under the word "shame"[5] which, like the words "thigh" and "loins", is used as a synonym for phallus. To the Jews the word bosheth was so common in ordinary speech that both Saul and Jonathan gave the name bosheth to their sons.[6] The idols to which the Israelites made sacrifices at Baal-Peor were bosheth, Baal, the god of generation, being rendered interchangeable with bosheth. The word Peor means opening or womb and worship of Baal-Peor was worship of the male and female principles. Elsewhere the words "abdominable thing", "filthiness", and "nakedness" are the terms most frequently used in the Bible when speaking of the sex organs.

Jacob wrestled with the Lord and called the place Peniel because, according to the Bible translators, there he saw the Lord's face. (Gen. 32:30). This, of course, cannot be accepted in a literal sense for it is inconceivable that Jacob could have actually struggled physically with an omnipotent creator. "Faces" is a mystic term frequently employed to denote the different attributes or aspects of God. The face Jacob saw was Peni-El. El is a title of God and the first part of the word needs no explanation.

The idols which Rachel stole from Laban (Gen. 31:24); the images which the Danites took from Micah (Jud. 15:5, 18, 24); and the idol which David's wife, Michal, put in her bed to deceive Saul's messengers (I Sam. 19:13, 16), appear to have been male or female images with exaggerated sexual parts representing the god or goddess of fertility. Maachah was deposed as queen for making an idol of this sort in a grove (I Kings 15:13), and it may be remembered that Abraham's father Terah was a maker of images.

The worship of phalli by the women of Jerusalem was sternly condemned by Ezekiel 16:17: "Thou hast also taken

---

5—Thy nakedness shall be uncovered, yea, thy shame shall be seen. *Isa.* 47:3.
Pass ye away thou inhabitants of Saphir, having thy shame naked. *Mic.* 1:11.
. . . and separate themselves unto that shame (phallic image). *Hos.* 9:10.
And ye set up altars (phalli) to burn incense to Baal. *Jer.* 11:13.
Also *Exod.* 32:6, 25, and *Num.* 25:3.

6—The name of Ish-bosheth, son of Saul and Mephi-bosheth, son of Jonathan, were called alternately Ish-Baal and Mephi-Baal. Gideon was alternately called Jerub-bosheth and Jerub-Baal.

thy fair jewels of my gold and of my silver, which I had given thee, and madest images of men and didst whoredom with them".

Models of the phallus were hung around the necks of Greek children as a defense against and a defiance of witch-craft and the evil eye. Even in modern times, they have been used as common amulets by men, women, and children in Italy and other Mediterranean countries, and by natives of the Celebes Islands. The significance of the phallus in ancient mythology still endures in Japan where, in the Shinto religion, it is a symbol of vigorous animal life, the enemy of disease and death. On the island of Ambon, in the Celebes, when men are quarreling one of them will sometimes uncover his sexual parts as a challenge to and defiance of his opponent.[7]

In early times the mere exposure of the naked body was apparently thought to put the gods of fertility in a happy or favorable state of mind. King David danced nude before the ark of the Lord (II Sam. 6:20) and, when the Israelites became restless because of Moses' long absence on Mt. Sinai, they called upon Aaron to make them a god to go before them. Aaron set up an image of the Egyptian bull calf Apis, to which the people sacrificed and feasted, then rose to dance nude and to play. (Ex. 32:6, 25). The words which are translated "to play" refer, in the Hebrew version, to the kind of play which caused the fall of Adam and Eve.

Arnobius wrote of a myth in which the goddess Ceres was described as wandering over the earth in search of her daughter Proserpine until she arrived grief stricken, at the hut of an Athenian woman named Baubo, who offered her a refreshing drink called Cyceon. The disconsolate goddess refused to accept the token of hospitality and Baubo was much distressed by the turn of events until she conceived an odd plan to end the awkward situation. She shaved the hirsute fringe from her genitals, then exposed herself to the goddess, who laughed heartily, immediately forgot her sorrow, and accepted the proffered beverage.

Pliny states that in his day it was believed that storms could be driven away by a woman's simply uncovering

---

7—G. A. Wilken, *Verspreide Geschriften*, Hague, 1912, 111, 318.

69. *Worshipers adoring a stone pillar or linga with tree of life carved upon it, with flame-like branches; three male symbols in one. On the throne are the symbols of earth and water. The foot prints of Buddha appear on the base of the throne and his vajra appears at the top of the pillar. From a Hindu sculpture of the 1st or 2nd century A.D.*

herself, and remnants of this old superstition still survive. When droughts occur in Morocco, women of the Tsul tribe are said to gather in a secluded place and, entirely nude, play a kind of game with a ball and ladles, to bring rain.

In parts of Russia, peasant girls are said to drag a plow around their village at midnight as a safeguard against cholera. In modern times the girls have observed the custom barefooted, with loosened hair and wearing a chemise as a concession to modesty but, doubtless, in an earlier, more primitive day, the chemise was not worn.

When floods overflow the banks of pools and streams in southern India, men stand naked on the shore and beat drums to drive away the rain demons. In some parts of Java it is thought that the yield of the rice field will be greater if, at the beginning of the planting season, the farmer and his wife run around the field naked then unite in a conjugal embrace. When the rice is harvested, bundles of rice ears are tied up to represent a bridal pair, and the harvest is carried out with the ceremonies of marriage.

From the time when Babylonians baked them in honor of the goddess Ishtar, cakes, usually in the form of male or female organs, were served annually during festivals of the gods and goddesses of fertility. At Syracuse, on the day of the Thesmophoria, and at marriages, cakes of sesame and honey representing female pudenda were carried in procession and offered to the gods. They were eaten by women on the Holy day and were probably part of the ceremonies in the Eleusinian Mysteries. In Jerusalem, cakes were baked in honor of Baal and Astarte, and Jeremiah complained that the "children cut wood and the fathers kindled fires and the women knead their dough to their gods". (Jer. 7:18).

As late as the end of the 4th century there existed in Rome a body of women called Collyridians who worshiped Cybele as the *Mater Creatoris, Dei Genetrix,* mother of creation, mother of God; and judged it necessary to appease her anger and seek her favor by libations, sacrifices, and oblations of cakes.

Dulaure states that in his time a festival called *La Fête des Pinnes* was held at the town of Saintes, in France, on Palm Sunday, in which women and children carried in the procession phalli made of bread and called *pinne*. These were attached to the ends of palm branches as symbols of fertility and regeneration. The *pinnes* were blessed by the priest and carefully preserved by the women during the year.[8]

In his *Remains of the Worship of Priapus,* Richard Payne Knight says that in Saintonge, near La Rochelle, cakes in the form of phalli were baked at Easter time and formed part of the Easter offerings. Afterward they were distributed to the homes.

A similar custom existed at St. Jean d'Angely where small cakes, made in the form of the phallus and named *fateaux,*

8—*Des Divinites Generatrices,* J. B. Dulaure, Paris, 1825.

were carried in the procession of the Fete-Dieu or Corpus Christi. Dulaure, who describes the custom, says that shortly before the time of writing, (1825), the practice was suppressed by a new prefect of the district. In Brives and nearby towns, cakes were made in the form of the male organs while in Clermont and other places, they were of female form. In some of the older French books on cookery, recipes are given for making cakes in these forms, which are named without concealment.

In addition to the great variety of rather abstract or formalized symbols of procreative power, realistic representations of the phallus were used by nature worshipers for a great many purposes and in many forms and sizes, the most lifelike type being statues or models of the nude male or of the phallus alone, which was generally of unnatural size.

As the creation of life, in a sense, overcomes or offsets the ravages of death, both abstract symbols and literal representations of the sexual organs came to be associated with life, fertility, health, and good fortune. They were the holy sacraments which nature worshipers displayed in temples. When carried in processions, they were believed to have the same power to ward off devils and malign influences which, in Catholic countries is attributed to the Holy Sacrament, for which reason the Host is paraded around shrines and towns. Upon it the most solemn oaths are taken, for a "corporale oath" means an oath on the corporale or linen cloth surrounding the Corpus Domini. To touch the altar cloth is a blessing and to take an oath with one hand on the altar stone is as binding as when Abraham's servant placed his hand under the thighs of his master or when Jacob swore on the *pachad* of his father Jesse.

Phallic symbols were used in Spain, France, Ireland, Scandinavia, Egypt, Greece, Rome, Syria, Persia, and Asia Minor; among the mound builders of North America, in Mexico, Central America, Peru, Haiti, in the islands of the Pacific and in Africa. Many of the literary references, paintings, and sculptures relating to the subject which have come down to us are so direct and realistic that they cannot be printed.

In the annual festival in honor of Isis and Osiris in Egypt, processions of women carried phalli to which strings were attached to permit of their being moved up and down.[9] Sometimes the phalli which were used in temples and carried in religious festivities were of tremendous size. In a procession during the reign of Ptolemy Philadelphus, a phallus was carried which was covered with gold and was one hundred twenty yards long. Before the temple of Venus at Hierapolis, there stood two phalli which were one hundred eighty feet high, upon which a priest mounted annually and remained for seven days. On the walls of the temple at Thebes, Egyptian gods and kings are portrayed with the phallus erect, and the great temple at Karnak abounds with such figures.

In Greece and Rome the god of fertility was worshiped under numerous titles and his phallic image was an important feature of the Liberalia, May Day, Floralia and other festivals to celebrate the regeneration of life at springtime. As Liber, he presided over domestic animals, the cultivation of vineyards, and harvest, and was symbolized by the phallus. His female counterpart, Libera, was identified with Ceres and Venus and represented in the temples by the image of the female organ.

Effigies of the phallus were anointed with oil, removed from the temples, decorated with flowers, and carried or drawn in carriages through the streets, followed by a cheering throng. During the spring festival in honor of Venus, women took the image of the sacred phallus from the hall of the Quirinal and carried it in procession to the temple of Venus, where it was united with the goddess with appropriate ceremonies.

Licentiousness reached its peak about the first of May in the celebration of Floralia, when the riffraff of the town

---

9—At this festival, women used to go about singing songs in his praise and carrying obscene images of him which they set in motion by means of strings. The custom was probably a charm to insure the growth of crops. A similar image of him, decked in the fruits of the earth, is said to have stood in the temple before a figure of Isis and in the chambers dedicated to him at Philae, the dead god is portrayed lying on his bier in an attitude which indicates in the plainest way that even in death, his generative virtue is not extinct, but only suspended, ready to prove a source of life and fertility. Hymns of praise allude to the mighty side of his nature. *Golden Bough*, Abgd. Ed., Sir Jas. Frazer, p. 391.
"In Egypt, they carried the statue [of Osiris] in human semblance, holding the sexual parts prominent and fecund". Again, "They displayed the emblem and carried it around, having the sexual parts threefold". *Isis and Osiris*, Plutarch.

and its neighborhood, called together by the sound of horns, mixed with the multitude in perfect nakedness and excited their passion with obscene motions and language until the festival ended in a scene of mad revelry in which all restraint was laid aside. One of these festivals was witnessed by the younger Cato, who was noted for his grave manner, and he left the scene when the revelers seemed to hesitate in stripping the young women naked because of his presence.

By reason of its reputed power of enchantment and witchcraft, the phallus became synonymous with the name of the Roman god Fascinus, also called Mutunus or Tutunus and later identified with Priapus. Fascinus was attended by Vestal Virgins, and victorious generals carried his symbols through Rome on their cars or chariots in triumphal processions.

The words fascinate and fascinator were derived from Fascinus because his symbol, when worn about the necks of women and children, was supposed to possess magical power which not only enabled its wearer to influence others, but protected them from magical or other influence from without.

The first mention of medieval worship of Fascinum occurs in an ecclesiastical tract of the 8th century entitled *Judicia Sacerdotalia Criminibus* which directs that whoever performs incantations to the Fascinum, or any incantations whatever, except the Creed or the Lord's prayer, shall be made to do penance on bread and water during three Lents. A council in Chalons, France, in the 9th century prohibited the practice in almost the same words, and the Bishop of Worms repeated the warning again in the 12th century. In 1247, the statutes of Mans decreed a punishment for any one who sinned to the Fascinum, and the same provision was adopted and renewed in the statutes of the synod of Tours, in 1396; nevertheless the practice continued until well after the Middle Ages.

Of all the titles under which the god of procreation was worshiped, perhaps none was so widely known as that of Priapus. Under this name he was associated with the goddess Isis in Egypt before the days of Cleopatra. Erotic statues, pottery, coins and gems representing him abounded in Greece: his attributes and activities were portrayed on gems of the Gnostics, Basilideans, and Manicheans at the beginning of the Christian era. From Rome, where he was particularly popular, his worship was carried to the Roman colonies in Gaul, Belgium, Germany, and Britain.

Priapus was the beneficent deity who increased herds of cattle, watched over fruit trees, and cared for bees. He was the patron of maidens seeking marriage. Brides were required to sit upon his statue and sacrifice their virginity to him.

Designs have been found on many coins, statuary, pottery and other articles recovered from the ruins of Pompeii and Herculaneum, on which Priapus is portrayed with large phallus, either alone or in the center of groups engaged in sexual acts. Frequently he is represented by the figure of a phallus alone; thus the adjective "Priapic" became a general term denoting any object or practice of a lewd, obscene nature. During the annual carnival at Trani, in Italy, a Priapic effigy called *il santo membro* was paraded through the streets.

His symbol was carved over doorways or on door jambs. It was used as an idol or amulet in houses and gardens, in front of blacksmiths' forges, under chariots, and in ancient tombs where it was thought to guard the dead against evil influences. It was also a favorite decorative motif for lamps and other household utensils and was often carved on the exterior or interior walls and doorways of churches and other public buildings. Representations of the phallus usually had wings: sometimes they were encircled with flowers and often they were attached to human or animal legs.

Pins, brooches and other objects in the form of the male organ, sometimes with rings attached for hanging about the neck, were worn as personal ornaments or carried as amulets to insure fruitfulness, health, and protection from one's enemies or drive away devils and other evil influences. Many such objects have been recovered in modern times from excavations on the sites of ancient buildings, and examples of them may be found in many European museums and private collections. Drawings made from many of these relics are reproduced in the scholarly works on phallicism, printed privately, by Richard Payne Knight[10] and Thomas Wright.[11]

10—*Remains of the Worship of Priapus*, Richard Payne Knight, 1786.
11—*Worship of the Generative Powers During the Middle Ages of Western Europe*, by Thomas Wright,, 1865.

In France and Belgium, ithyphallic saints were offered favors to obtain children, or to cure impotency or sexual disease. The most famous of these saints was St. Foutin, who is reputed to have been the first bishop of Lyons. When Protestants seized the town of Embrun during the Reformation in 1585, they found among the relics of the cathedral one which was said to be the phallus of the famous saint. It had become stained deep red by the libations of wine which had been poured upon it by supplicants who usually caught the wine in a cup or jar as it dripped from the relic, then let the wine stand until it soured. This "holy vinegar" was drunk by women who considered it an effective method of insuring fertility. The famous saint was also worshiped at Porigny, in the diocese of Viviers; at Vendre, in the Bourbonnais; at Auxerre; at Puy-en-Velay, in the convent of Girouet, near Sampigny; and elsewhere.

Wax models of both sexes were offered to St. Foutin at Varailles, in Provence, in the 16th century. The models were suspended from the ceiling of his chapel and were so numerous that when the wind stirred them they struck against one another and disturbed the congregation.[12]

At Bourg Dieu, near Bourges, Belgium, local inhabitants worshiped a phallic figure called St. Grelichon, or Guerlichon, which had persisted from Roman times. Barren women flocked to the abbey to seek the saint's aid and to celebrate a novena in his honor. The supplicant would recline upon the relic at full length and then scrape particles from the phallus of the image. These scrapings, when placed in water, were supposed to make a miraculous draught.

At Brest, the same saint was honored under the name of Guignolet, and a similar sculptured figure called Ters appeared over the gateway to the church of St. Walburga, in the Rue des Pecheurs at Antwerp.[13]

St. Giles, in Brittany; St. Rene, in Anjou; St. Regnaud, in Burgundy; and St. Arnaud, near Brest, were similarly worshiped, except that in the latter case the symbol of fecundity was covered with an apron which was only raised in favor of sterile women. Its mere inspection, if accom-

12—*Des Divinites generatrices*, J. A. Dulaure, Paris, 1825, p. 205.
13—*Des Divinites generatrices*, p. 204f.

panied by true faith, was considered sufficient to effect miracles.[14]

At Isernia, near Naples, Italy, Saints Cosmus and Damiano were believed to be highly effective against all sorts of disease. At their feast, on September 27th, their relics were carried in procession and the phallus of Cosmo was exposed to view for the benefit of the celebrants. A three day fair was held on the occasion, at an ancient church about a mile from the town, the fair being visited by people from the surrounding villages. During this celebration, those who had any kind of bodily ailment could buy waxen images of the affected part. After presenting an image and an offering at the vestibule of the church, the supplicant presented himself or herself to the priest at the altar and uncovered the part affected. The priest then anointed the part with a miraculous "oil of St. Cosmus" which was believed to be particularly efficacious for ailments of the loins and adjoining parts. Although waxen effigies for various parts of the body were offered for sale, the greatest demand was for phalli, the buyers of which were mostly women. The building of a new road through the town, in 1780, gave the community better contact with the outside world, and news of the local custom soon reached the government in Naples, which immediately ordered that the "great toe" of the saint should no longer be displayed and the sale of phallic images be discontinued.[15]

Phallic emblems have been found carved or scratched on ancient Roman buildings in England, on the doors of the cathedrals of Toulouse, Bordeaux, and other cities in France, and on the walls of Alati, near Rome. In graves of Vikings in Norway, large stones of phallic shape have been found, some of which are preserved in the Museum of Christiania. In Japan, the detached phallus is often used as an emblem of the Shinto religion.

On Trendle Hill near the village of Cerne Abbas, in Dorset, England, there is (or was) cut in the turf, an ancient nude figure one hundred eighty feet long, with distinct sexual parts. As an emblem of fertilizing power the image

---

14—*Ibid*, p. 204f.

15—Excerpts from a letter of Sir William Hamilton, K.B., His Majesty's Minister at the Court of Naples to Sir Joseph Bank, Bart., then President of the Royal Society, published in *Remains of the Worship of Priapus*, Richard Payne Knight.

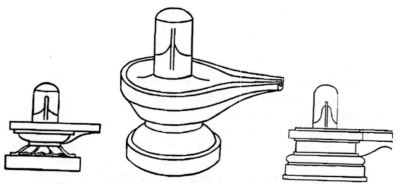

70. *Types of lingam. The base represents Brahma, the Creator; the bowl, Vishnu, the Preserver; and the pillar, Siva, the
Reproducer and Destroyer.*

was a protection against sterility, disease, and death, and was also a guardian of fruit trees and vineyards. If an unmarried girl at Cerne Abbas became pregnant, it was said of her, "she has been sitting on the giant".

By an odd reversal of practice, the position which the male symbol occupied on buildings in Europe was, in Ireland, filled by a crude figure of a woman directing attention to her matrix. Sculptured figures of this kind were placed over the portals of ancient churches and castles, most of which have long been torn down.

To Irish antiquarians these peculiar sculptures are known as Sheila-na-Gig which is said to mean Julian the Giddy, but their prominent positions over doorways indicates that, despite their trivial name, they were symbols of great importance.

Such a figure was carved over the doorway of Cloyne Cathedral. Similar figures were on an old church at Rochestown, and on Ballinahend Castle, both in Tipperary. An example from an old church, which formerly stood in the County Cavan, is now preserved in the Museum of the Society of Antiquaries, in Dublin. In the Museum of Dublin there is another which came from the White Island, in Lough Erne, County Fermanagh. One from Killoa Castle, Westmoreland, is in a London private collection.

In the Orient small phallic images were often placed by the roadside; in front of dwellings; beneath trees in sacred groves; and the ground on which the emblems stood was regarded as holy. As prayers to the god of fertility were thought more likely to be answered if they were offered while in contact with the image, it was customary for the supplicant to raise her clothing and sit upon the image while praying. This custom is still practiced by girls and women in some parts of the world, to invoke divine aid.

In India, under the Hindu name of linga, the phallus has been a special emblem of Siva, the Reproducer, for countless centuries. Some of these linga, made of marble, granite, or rare woods, are many feet in height and are found, decorated with flowers and other offerings, in the temples. Miniature models of gold, silver, ivory, crystal, or wood are worn in the hair or on the arm or breast as amulets or charms. Many linga temples are found on the banks of the Ganges, especially near Calcutta.

Members of the Sakteyan sect pay special homage to the vulva, which is honored as the symbol and incarnation of Parvati, the female counterpart of Siva, the creative deity. Under the name of lingam, the male and female symbols, represented in union, are the most widely used images in India. Throughout southern India they are found in temples and homes, in a great variety of designs. Making of the various types of lingams is a highly specialized art, the proportions and materials used in their construction being minutely regulated by an ancient canon called the Agama.

Almost every village has a public lingam consisting of an oval shaped flat stone and a round, upright stone two or three feet high. The monument is visited early in the morning by women and girls, who sprinkle it with water from the Ganges, deck it with flowers, and rub their bodies against it while reciting prayers to insure motherhood.

In recent times, phallic statues have been found in the East Indian Archipelago, New Guinea, Sumatra, and Ceylon. Both male and female figures had exaggerated pudenda. On the eastern and western sides of a house in Dorei, New Guinea, there were, some years ago, two pairs of rude wooden statues, each pair representing a man and woman in the conjugal act. Beside the door, on the western side, there was an image of a child lying on its back. Other parts of the building were also adorned with suggestive carvings.[16]

In the Celebes islands, representations of women's breasts and sexual organs were to be found on the posts of

---

16—G. A. Wilken, *Verspreide Geschriften*, Hague, 1912, 111, 213f.

houses erected in honor of fallen warriors. On a temple at Langgadopi, the organs of both sexes were shown in union.[17]

In Africa, tree, serpent and sex worship have existed in their vilest forms within the present century. Here the ancient tree of life is still anointed with oil and the drippings from it are believed to be a sure cure for all the ills of man or woman. Fetiches in phallic form are often used in the African Congo and, at Dahomey, along the Slave Coast, a gross figure of a man with exaggerated sexual parts is worshiped under the name of Legba or Egba. Phallic statues may be seen in front of houses, on the streets, and in public places.[18] In one Legba shrine, a male and female figure of the fertility god Obatala was shown and opposite it were the male and female organs represented in union.[19]

17—de Zwaan, p. 18, 62 citing Adriani & Kruift, De Bare'e—*Sprekende Toadjas*, Hague, 1912.

18—*Das Weib*, Leipzig, 1891, i, 439. H. H. Ploss citing without reference Bastian; Ellis, *Yaruba-Speaking People*, p. 411f.

19—*Il Pentamerone, or Tale of Tales*, 2 vols., Rich. F. Burton,, 1893.

XV

SEX SYMBOLISM

(Continued)

Religious Prostitution

IN ADDITION TO the gifts and prayers which were given as offerings to the ancient goddess who bestowed the blessings of fertility upon womanhood, she was repaid in kind by sexual offerings in the form of religious prostitution in early Babylonia, Syria, Phoenicia, Arabia, Egypt, Greece, and Rome. A similar custom prevailed in Central America, West Africa, and other parts of the world. The custom was not confined to consecrated women, or temple prostitutes who served the Mother Goddess, but was regarded as a solemn religious duty of all women.

Sir James Frazer has described the custom as a form of sympathetic magic, undertaken in a belief, once widely held, that like produces like and that a desired result can be achieved by simply imitating it. Sympathetic magic was practiced by the sorcerers of India, Babylonia, Egypt, Greece, and Rome, and is still employed by witch doctors among primitive people. Sir James describes many forms of sympathetic magic and says: "Among the Bataks of Sumatra, a barren woman who would become a mother will make an image of a child and hold it in her lap, believing this will lead to the fulfillment of her wish", and "The North American Indians believed", we are told, "that by drawing the figure of a person in sand, ashes or clay, or by considering an object as his body and then piercing it with a sharp stick, or doing it any other injury, they inflicted a corresponding injury on the person represented".

"When an Ojibway Indian desires to work evil on any one, he makes a little image of his enemy and runs a needle into its head or heart, or shoots an arrow into it, believing that wherever the needle pierces or the arrow strikes the image, his foe will, the same instant, be seized with a sharp pain in the corresponding part of his body".[1]

1—*Golden Bough,* Abgd. Ed., Sir James Frazer, p. 13.

In every age it has been believed that a person could be injured or destroyed by injuring or destroying an image of him. When a Babylonian wished to destroy witches or evil spirits, he burned wax images of them.

For similar reasons it was believed that imitating the acts of the gods by consorting with a consecrated woman, the earthly representative of the goddess of fertility, it was possible to assure the birth of children, increase of cattle, and fruitfulness of fields.

While there may be instances in which the custom originated in these beliefs, religious prostitution was probably more often a sacrifice of virginity at puberty; a sacrifice which was looked upon as the most personal and most important a woman could make to the goddess in order to consecrate her life to motherhood. It was doubtless related to the widespread custom of dedicating the first born child to the deity as "first fruits of the womb".

In Cyprus, Heliopolis, Syria, Lydia, Armenia, Phoenicia, Babylon, and elsewhere, every woman was required to undergo a period during which she sat before the temple as an offering to the temple goddess, whose name varied from city to city, but whose character remained essentially the same. In Babylon every woman was required, once in her life, to prostitute herself at the temple of Mylitta to the first stranger who threw a silver coin in her lap, and to dedicate to the goddess the wages earned by this sanctified harlotry. Surrounding the temple of Bit-Shaggathu was a gallery behind which women gathered daily. Cords attached to them were broken when visitors made their selection.

The custom must be judged as the product of an age when women were everywhere regarded as soulless chattels whose sole purpose and duty was motherhood; when barrenness was looked upon as the work of an evil spirit, and spinsterhood was condemned as a rejection of the god of generation. This was the attitude of Jephthah's daughter who, when told that she was to be sacrificed, asked only that she be given two months in which to wander up and down the country bemoaning, not the fact that she was to be sacrificed, but that she would meet her death in a virgin state. (Jud. 30:30, 39). The story seems to have been connected, at least in later times at Mizpah and perhaps elsewhere, with a ceremony which consisted originally in mourning for the death of the virgin goddess. Jephthah's name means "(God) opens the womb", a title which was often bestowed on fertility gods.

As different groups or cults came to exercise a preference for worship of either of the creative powers, they became known as worshipers of the male or female power. In Egypt, the religion was devoted to both male and female. In India, devotees of Vishnu particularly honor the female and Sivaites worship the male. Early Babylonian worship of the female changed under Semitic influence to worship of the male. During the period of Assyrian domination, even the great goddess Ishtar was given military and other masculine characteristics.

The markedly inferior status of Jewish women, and the fact that they had no part in the national religion, caused them to become worshipers of Baal-Ashtoreth and Baal-Peor. Ezekiel described them as being even more dissolute than whores for, whereas the latter demanded pay for their services, Jewish women made gifts to the men who accepted their favors. (Ezek. 16:33, 34).

With full, red lips and eyes rimmed with kohl; bedecked with tinkling bells and spangles, gold and silver ankle and leg ornaments, bracelets, earrings and nose jewels, they sauntered forth to stalk men on the highways. Around their elbows they wore large "tires" puffed out like pillows; on their heads, unmarried girls wore kerchiefs denoting the season of women and the full moon. (Ezek. 13:18, 21).

"High places" were located in every street and women tore up their garments to make gaily colored hangings and couch covers for the Succoth-Benoth, or tents, in which they paid honors to the god of fertility. (II Kings 23:7 and Ezek. 16:16).

The Scriptures do not distinguish between prostitution as a religious rite and as a social vice, but it is evident that, in both forms, the practice flourished in Judah and Israel throughout the Biblical period. Repeated references to rape, incest, seduction; the enactment of laws forbidding that Jewish women and men should become whores and Sodomites;[2] statutes to insure virginity of brides; the regulation

---

2—There shall be no whore of the daughters of Israel nor a Sodomite of the sons of Israel. *Deut.* 23:17f.

71. *Egyptian goddess Qetesh or Kenit, holding lotuses and serpents as symbols of fertility. Qetesh is equivalent to the Biblical Qadesh (prostitute or consecrated woman) and Babylonian kadishtu. She is the only Egyptian goddess shown full front view. Her position on the lion is thought to be an astrological allusion, representing Virgo over Leo.*

of prostitution, concubinage, and the taking of plural wives; point to the fact that unbridled sexual gratification was a social problem of the first order.

The pagan temple of Queen Jezebel alone had four hundred devotees and Hosea (4:14f) affirms that not only did many women of Israel commit harlotry, but that the leaders of the nation and its priests offered their sacrifices with the sacred prostitutes. Whores and Sodomites were quartered in houses adjoining the temple (II Kings 23:7) and even the precincts of the temple itself were invaded by the prostitutes. The Book of Samuel (2:22) shows that the harlots assembled at the north door of the temple where the image of jealousy was located: "Now Eli was very old and heard all that his sons did unto all Israel and how they lay with the women that assembled at the door of the tabernacle of the congregation of the Lord".

As a consequence of their practicing the rites of Baal-Peor with Midianite women, a great number of Israelites were smitten with an incurable disease, probably syphilis. As a sanitary measure, all captive Midianite women who had "known men by lying with them" (Num. 31:16, 17) were put to death.

Twenty-four thousand sons of Israel died from disease contracted in practicing the rites of Baal-Peor with the women of Moab (Num. 25:9). Men of the nation were warned that they would be smitten "by the botch of Egypt, and with the emerods, and with the scab, and with the itch, whereof thou canst not be healed" (Deut. 28:27) and their bowels would fall out. (II Chron. 21:13, 15).

The Book of Genesis (38:14, 16) bears testimony that religious prostitution was known to the Jews at a very early period, for we are told that Tamar deceived her father-in-law Judah by veiling herself after the manner of the temple women, and sitting before the door where Judah saw her and went in unto her. Tamar was able to entice Judah because he thought she was a temple harlot with whom it was permissible to associate.

Isaiah (6:18) took note of the prostitutes who, in his day, sat with cords about them like the temple prostitutes of Babylon. As late as the first century A.D., the author of the *Epistle of Jeremy* wrote, "women also, with cords about them, sit down in the streets to burn bran as incense but if any of them, drawn by some one of the passersby, lie with him, she reproacheth her neighbor that she was not also thought worthy like herself, nor her cords broken".[3]

At the festival of the Semitic mother goddess Attar, at Hierapolis-Bambysis (Syria) women prostituted themselves and maidens vowed their virginity to prostitution, probably indicating both temporary and permanent hierodouloi, "sacred women", or "vowed women".

At the feast of Bastel, at Bubastis (Egypt), women became temporary heirodouloi and Herodotus (11, 60) says that men and women went to the festival in large barges. At each village they went ashore to sing and dance and frequently the women lifted their garments to display their charms to the villagers.

A similar festival was held at Mendes, where women who seem to have been temporary hierodouloi carried, in

---

3—*Book of Baruch, The Apocrypha of the Old Testament*, Edw. Cone Bissell, 1880, v. 43.

procession, images of the god with the generative member very much enlarged and arranged so that it nodded as it was carried about.

Strabo wrote (c. 17, i, 46) that at Thebes "a very beautiful girl of the most distinguished lineage was consecrated to Zeus (Amon) and played the concubine and had intercourse with whomsoever she desired until the natural purification of her body (i.e., until the expiration of the month) then, after her purification, she was given to a husband".

Before marriage, all women in Cyprus were obliged by custom to prostitute themselves to strangers at the temple of the goddess and Greek inscriptions indicate that the custom was practiced there as late as the 2nd century A.D.

In India the temple prostitute has enjoyed a privileged position for thousands of years. Every important temple of the Sakteyan sect formerly had a number of consecrated women connected with it. When very young, these girls are chosen by the priests for their beauty, health, and grace, and parents feel highly honored to have a daughter selected for consecration to the god.

Saktis are worshipers of reproduction and their secret rites are grossly physical. The rites celebrate worship of the goddess, personified by a naked girl who is supposed to be in a state of hypnotism or trance and unconscious of what occurs during the ceremony. She is called a yogini or female yogi (wandering ascetic), that is, a Kunti, or personification of the yoni.

After reaching puberty the girls are initiated into the mysteries and duties of their profession, after which marriage is forbidden and their children become wards of the temple. British influence has caused the custom to decline in modern times, but it lingers on, principally in southern India.

Within the past half century religious prostitution has also been found on the Gold Coast of West Africa. Ellis has stated that in some communities, the best looking girls were selected when from ten to twelve years old and given three years of instruction in learning the chants and dances to the gods. At the end of this period they were initiated as religious prostitutes.[4]

4—*The Ewe-speaking people of the Slave Coast of West Africa,* London, 1890, p. 140 *et seq.* and *The Tshi-speaking people of the Gold Coast of West Africa, London,* 1887, pp. 120-138.

XVI

THE SYMBOLIC MEANING OF NUMBERS

THE SCIENCE OF NUMBERS was believed by the people of many ancient nations to be a potent form of magic and was reverenced as an invention of the gods. Quite apart from their numerical and mathematical values, numbers were esteemed as symbols which revealed to the learned the divine order of the universe.

The identification of numbers with universal order is linked with the name of Pythagoras (6th Cent. B.C.), who brought existing notions regarding the meaning of numbers into an orderly system and modified and enlarged the system with many theories of his own. Acording to Aristotle the Pythagorean system, in its original form, regarded numbers not merely as predictable relations of things, but as actually constituting their essence or substance. Numbers, he says, seemed to the Pythagoreans to be the first things in the whole of nature and they supposed the elements of numbers to be the elements of all things and the whole heaven to be a musical scale and number.

The system was based upon an association of ideas or upon certain philosophical conceptions concerning the nature of the universe. Numbers were divided into odd and even, limited and unlimited, one and many, right and left, rest and motion, straight and curved, square and circular, light and darkness, good and evil. To the Pythagoreans the equilibrium of the universe was maintained by the relation of its opposites. The numbers 1, 3, 5, 7, 9 were called heavenly numbers and 2, 4, 6, 8 and 10 were earthly numbers.

Pythagoras was one of the most learned and most travelled men of the classic Greek period. Probably no other man comprehended so much of all the learning of his time. After being initiated into the Eleusinian Mysteries, Pythagoras went to Egypt, where he was initiated into the Mysteries of Isis, and is said to have been taught the secret meaning of numbers by an Egyptian priest named Huramon

(Horus Ammon)[1]. In Phoenicia and Syria he learned the Mysteries of Adonis. In Palestine he is said to have spent some time with a mystic sect at Carmel. In Babylon he learned the Mysteries of the Chaldean priests. From Babylon he went, by way of Persia, to Hindustan, where he spent several years as a pupil of the Brahmans.

Although Pythagoras was known as a great mathematician and philosopher, his greatest discovery was, perhaps, that of the dependence of the musical intervals on certain mathematical ratios of lengths of string at the same tension; 2:1 giving the octave, 3:2 the 5th, and 4:3 the 4th.

The following notes are not particularly intended to describe the numerical system of Pythagoras, but rather to indicate the general method by which the symbolic values of numbers were determined.

1. Represents unity, origin, the source of all things. It is identified with the point and is thus a unit having position and magnitude. Identified with reason (intellect) because it is unchangeable.

2. In one sense two signifies male and female, father and mother, the cause of increase and division. It is identified with opinion because it is unlimited and indeterminate. On the principle that the universe consists of a dual system in which all existence is composed of pairs of opposites, this figure is considered a female or negative symbol. As the Zoroastrians interpreted this idea, the universe was divided between the two spirits of good and evil called "the twins which were in the beginning". In India the same thought is expressed in the doctrine that all existence is resolved into Brahma and Maya, being and appearance, reality and illusion.

3. Is identified with creation and resurrection or renewal, the third member of the trinity. The pantheons of nearly all nations were presided over by three superior gods, or by gods grouped in triads of related deities. (As in Egypt, Greece, Rome, Babylonia, Persia, India, China, Japan, etc.).

1—Huram embodies ChR, the eternal light and AUM representing the creation, preservation and destruction of life or childhood, manhood and old age. Ben Aur, whom Moses requested to build the temple, means son of light, or son of Horus. Hiram of Tyre to whom Solomon appealed for craftsmen to build his great temple, is another rendering of Huram.

Three is identified with the triangle by which the deity was symbolized everywhere. The ineffable name of the Jews was depicted in a triangle with each of the three letters JHV representing a different phase of his being or manifestation, and the three-branched letter Shin was inscribed on the phylacteries which were worn by the Israelites.

It is the number of the whole because it has a beginning, a middle and an end. It also signifies the 3 vertical divisions of the universe: heaven, earth, and the subterranean waters which, in the Babylonian system, were ruled by Anu, Bel, and Ea.

Three is the number of knowledge, music, geometry, and astronomy; the essence of celestial and terrestrial forces.

4. The primordial number and the root of all things; the foundation of nature and the most perfect number. As 2 represents the line and 3 represents the surface, 4 is identified with the solid. This number typifies the cube and square, consequently it is the sign for all mathematical combinations. It is related to the organic world, as three is related to the spiritual world, and represents organization and dominion. Because of its many attributes Pythagoreans gave 4 special values beyond its ordinary meaning.

Four is associated with justice because it is the first square number, the product of equals. Is identified with the material world and its divisions; the 4 corners and 4 winds of the earth, the 4 rivers of Eden and the 4 rivers of the old Babylonian mythology. The mysterious Pythagorean Tetractys or 4 rows of dots* increasing from 1 to 4 was symbolic of the stages of creation. To add a row of dots gives the next "triangular" number with 5 on a side and so on, showing that the sum of any number of the series of natural numbers beginning with 1 is a triangular number. The sum of any number of the series of odd numbers, beginning with 1, is similarly seen to be a square, that is 3 and 5 added successively to 1 each give a figure of this kind. In the case of even numbers the sum of any number, beginning with 2, makes an oblong.

•—   .
    .   .   .
  .   .   .   .

The Tetractys was probably associated with the four-lettered word for the Jewish divine name JHVH. By adding 4 to the preceding numbers 1, 2, and 3, Pythagoras produced 10 which is the consummation of the Decad and the number of completeness. It was formerly the arrangement of soldiers in Chinese military tactics.

5. Represents marriage because it is the union of the first masculine and first feminine numbers 3 and 2 (unity not being considered a number). Among the Greeks it was a symbol of light, health and vitality. It is called the equilibrium because it divides the perfect number into 2 parts. Other numbers multiplied by themselves produce other numbers. Only 5 and 6 multiplied by themselves represent and retain their original numbers as the last figure in their products.

Five is identified with fixed traditions; with order and law, both divine and earthly. It is an important number among the Chinese to whom custom and law carry great force. The Hindus and Chinese recognize 5 as the number of qualities: 5 virtues, 5 basic forms, 5 senses, 5 elements, 5 colors, etc. To the Israelites it was the number of military organization.

6. Is the number of completion, typified by the 6 days in which the world was created and symbolized by the Jewish 6-pointed Star of David, and the Chakra, or Wheel of Vishnu. In both the East and the West a belief long persisted that the history of the world would be divided into 6 ages after which would come destruction and renewal of the world on a higher plane.

To Pythagoras, 6 represented the perfection of all the parts, the form of forms. It sometimes appears as a symbol of marriage because it is formed of two triangles, one masculine, one feminine. It is identified with time as the measure of duration and is a key number in ancient calendar systems. It represents health because it is the balance number both calendrically and symbolically.

The number 6 is associated with work, effort, and creative energy, both human and divine.

7. One of the most venerated and most magical of numbers, the number *par excellence* among the nations of antiquity. Pythagoras called it "the vehicle of life". It contains body and soul, spirit and matter, since it contains the triangle and the square.

In the Bible, 7 is the number of the holy or divine day. All of the great festivals are related to 7 days, weeks or years. In the East 7 is associated with oaths or covenants. The divine mysteries and the activities of the Holy Spirit are 7 in number. Most of the associations of 7 have reference to some direct relation of the divine and human. It is therefore the number of religion.

It is called the number of life because of the belief that 7 month babies usually live while those born in the 8th month do not. It is sometimes called a virgin number because it is the only number between 1 and 10 which cannot be produced by either dividing or multiplying another number. It has been called motherless and fatherless; and virgin, or Minerva, because it was not born of a mother but was generated out of the crown or back of the father, the mind.

Seven is an important lunar number identified with Ishtar, Aphrodite, Virgin Mary, and other holy mothers.

8.   Is identified with the cube because it has 8 corners. It is the only wholly even number under 10 ($1 \times 2 \times 4 = 8 = 4 \times 2 \times 1$); that is, 8 is divided by 2 4's, each 4 is divided into 2 2's and 2 is divided into 2 1's.

Eight is identified with man's elevation to a higher life or his deliverance from the evils of the present life. On the 8th day came the final act in the sacred drama which was part of the Eleusinian Mysteries. Clement of Alexandria said, "Those in whom there is no guile do not remain in the 7th, the place of rest but, are promoted to the heritage of the divine beneficence which is the 8th grade". Some of the early Church fathers thought there were 7 gradations in heaven and that the highest place was with the father in the 8th.

In the Jewish scriptures, 8 is associated with salvation, purification, and cleansing. There were 8 persons saved in Noah's ark; circumcision took place on the 8th day; 8 days were required for the purification of women. The Feast of Tabernacles was on the 8th day. Eight is connected with the Chinese tradition of the Deluge and is an important number in their cosmogony. It is called the little holy number.

9.   Is the first square of an odd number (3×3) and sometimes appears as a ratio of a mystic 3 times 3. It is

associated with failure and shortcomings because it falls one
short of the perfect number 10. It is looked upon as an evil
number because it is an inverted 6.

In the Eleusinian Mysteries it was the number of the
sphere through which the consciousness passed on its way
to birth. It is the number of the ruling and controlling
government of God, and the number of man because of the
9 months of his embryonic life. It is also deemed the limitless number because there is nothing beyond it but the
infinite 10, and it is identified with the ocean and horizon
because they are boundless.

10.   Completes the symbolic alphabet of numbers and
denotes completeness and finality. Pythagoras considered it
"the perfect number". It represents the deity, man, and
the universe because it contains the sum of the 4 prime
numbers, includes all mathematical and musical proportions
and defines the system of the world.

The Decad is called both heaven and the world because
the former includes the latter. It was used by Pythagoreans
to denote things concerning age, power, faith, and necessity and was considered unwearied because it was tireless.
The Pythagoreans divided the heavenly bodies into 10
orders.

The Iota, "Jot" or Yod is the 10th letter in the Hebrew
alphabet and is sometimes used as a symbol of Jahveh. It
is the first letter of the name of Jesus, therefore the number and letter were his sacred symbols. The symbolic use
of this letter may be observed in the Apostolic Constitution
(*Ante-Nicene Lib.*, p. 58): "Thou hast known the Decade
and hast believed in the Iota, the first letter of the name
of Jesus". The letter X, which stands for Christ, represents,
in the Greek alphabet, the number 600, the number of years
in the reign of each Avatar or Savior in India.

Many of the early fathers of the Christian Church believed that numbers were frequently used in the Bible in
a symbolic or esoteric sense. Jerome observed that in the
Old Testament the number of Books according to the Jewish
divisions (5 Books of the Law: 8 Books of the Prophets: 9
Books of the Hagiographa) equaled exactly the 22 letters of
the Hebrew alphabet. There are 5 double letters in the
Hebrew alphabet and there are 5 double Books in the Bible,
namely 2 Samuels, 2 Kings, 2 Chronicles, 2 Ezras (which

we call Ezra and Nehemiah), and 2 Jeremiahs (which we call Jeremiah and Lamentations).

The fact that part of the Book of Proverbs (Chapter 31: 10,31), the whole of Lamentations and Psalms 25, 34, 37, 111, 112, and 155 are acrostics founded on the Hebrew alphabet led Jerome to suppose that there was some mystery in the 22 letters from which are formed all of the words connected with the Scriptures.

The Jews always considered their alphabet to be a divine invention and much significance was seen in the fact that there were 22 generations from Adam to Jacob: in the first 6 days of the world there were 22 acts of creation (Book of Jubilees 2:2,22), and observance of the Sabbath began at the close of the twenty-second generation.

XVII

THE SYMBOLIC MEANING OF NUMBERS

(*Continued*)

*Cabala**

THE MOST EXTENSIVE mystical and symbolical use of numbers is to be found in the system of Scriptural interpretation known as the Cabala. In a branch of the Cabala called Gematria the numerical equivalents of letters are asserted to reveal a hidden meaning in the Biblical text. For instance, if the second word of Genesis, be added to the first, the result is 1116 which is equivalent to the numerical value of the Hebrew words "In the beginning of the year it was created". This is interpreted as meaning that the world was created in the beginning of the year, or in autumn. Again, in the first and last verses of the Jewish Bible the letter Aleph (A) appears 6 times and Cabalists interpret this as meaning that the beginning and end of the world will embrace a period of 6000 years.

Despite the obvious weakness of this method of interpretation, the Cabala was in great vogue among European scholars during and after the Middle Ages, and Raymond Lully, Pico della Mirandola, John Reuchlin, Guillaume Postel, Athanasius Kircher, Paul Ricci, Rev. Francis Buddaeus, the Rosicrucians, Rev. John Lightfoot, Baron von Rosenroth, and many others declared that it had been handed down by the patriarchs.

Paracelsus, Cardinal Nicolas Cusanus, Jacob Bohmen, Cardinal Aegidus of Viterbo, Pope Sixtus IV, Theophilus Gale, Ralph Cudworth, Sir Isaac Newton, Spinoza, Schopenhauer, Hegel, and Sir Francis Bacon were students of the Cabala and testified to its validity.

Having been conceived solely as a system of religious interpretation, the Gematria was originally employed only with the Hebrew, Aramaic, and Greek texts of the Hebrew Scriptures but by the 17th century it was applied to Latin texts and even to non-religious subjects. The belief of kings that they ruled by divine order caused the Gematria to become, like astrology, a toy of royalty. Cabalistic diagrams

---

*—See Appendix: Cabala.

were prepared of the names, titles, and important events in the lives of kings, such as the birth of an heir or the winning of a military campaign, the results being interpreted as evidence that the king acted under divine guidance.

In recent times, mystics have revived the Cabalistic system by combining it with the Pythagorean theory of numbers, and have dressed it up with terms borrowed from modern science under the name of Numerology. Its adherents would have us believe that all numbers vibrate to the rhythm of the universe; that each letter of the alphabet is related to a number, and every condition or quality has its own peculiar vibration. So, by virtue of the magical power of Numerology, the man who wishes to be a successful banker or the girl who wishes to win fame as an actress must own or adopt a name with a numerical combination which pulsates in harmony with the proper cosmic vibrations. Of course it is essential that one should know just what names are in tune with the particular profession or skill one wishes to pursue. This is where the Numerologists come in, for they profess to know the answers.

While the Gematria makes use of some of the theories of Pythagoras, the conditions which led to its development were at hand with the creation of the alphabet. When the use of letters superseded hieroglyphics and cuneiform script in Asia Minor, sometime between 1500 and 1000 B.C., there were no separate characters for numerals, therefore each character in the alphabet came in time to represent both a letter and a number. This made it possible for written texts to contain two meanings, one an open, literal, alphabetical meaning, the other a hidden, numerical meaning.

Hebrew Alphabet with Numerical Equivalents

aleph	beth	gimel	daleth	he	vau	zayin	cheth	teth
1	2	3	4	5	6	7	8	9
א	ב	ג	ד	ה	ו	ז	ח	ט

jod	coph	lamed	mem	nun	samech	ayin	pe	zade
10	20	30	40	50	60	70	80	90
י	כך*	ל	מם*	נן*	ס	ע	פף*	צץ*

koph	resh	shin	tau
100	200	300	400
ק	ר	ש	ת

* Indicates final letters.

Other circumstances also favored the development of such a system. Although there were perhaps as many tongues spoken then as there are today, it is probable that most languages were sufficiently similar that the people of one tribe or nation could understand those of another as well as or better than Portuguese today understand Spaniards or Chinese understand Japanese.

For instance, the word for Jah or Yah has its equivalent in Ie, Ieu, or Ieue, which is similar to the root of the Greek word Iaw, Iao, or Ju-piter. In the Targum* ii is always used for the creator instead of IEUE. Over the door of the Greek temple at Delphi the same word EI (written backward) was inscribed in honor of Apollo.

Ieue Nissi, a Biblical title for God, is cognate with Dios Nyssos or Dionysius, a title of Bacchus. The Greek letters IHΣ (IHS), the monogram of Bacchus, also came to be used as a monogram for Jesus. It is widely used in Catholic churches and monasteries, being claimed by Catholics to mean Jesus Hominum Salvator or In Hoc Signo. By a slight change in pronunciation, the Hebrew ח becomes ה giving the sound of the Latin or Greek E and IHS becomes IES which, with a Greek suffix us or ous, becomes Jes-ous.

In Hebrew, Jesse the father of David is written ישי ishi, meaning existence. As written in English it reads Jes from which was derived Jesse which also becomes Jesus upon adding the Greek suffix. The feminine form is אשה isha, ishshah, or woman, and probably means the same as the Egyptian name Isi-s.

Grammar was still only partially developed; the spelling of words had not been systemized and each writer developed his own system of orthography. In some instances writing was from left to right, in others it was from right to left as in Hebrew and Arabic. Sometimes writing was from right to left then back to the right as a farmer plows a field. In other instances, as in Hebrew, there were no spaces between words and, in order to make reading less difficult, when certain sounds appeared at the ends of words, they were represented by different characters than were used for the same sounds in the middle of words.

Letters of a certain class or quality were interchangeable, thus making it possible for a word to have more than one spelling, more than one meaning and more than one

---

*—See Appendix: Talmud.

numerical value. For instance, the letter Jod may be read
as either 1 or 10 and the letter Shin may stand for either
3 or 300.

The Hebrew letters were not merely abstract designs
but each letter had a secondary significance in addition to
its alphabetical value. Thus the letter ו vau, 6, represented
a nail or hook or, in another sense, the womb; while the
letter Jod or Yod י, 10, represented the hand and the phallus.
The letter was also pronounced Ja or Ya as a shortened
form for Yahweh or Jahveh.

Greek Alphabet with Numerical Equivalents

Aα	Bβ	Γγ	Δδ	Eε	F*	Zζ	Hη	Θθ
1	2	3	4	5	6	7	8	9
Iι	Kκ	Λλ	Mμ	Nν	Ξξ	Oo	Ππ	Q*
10	20	30	40	50	60	70	80	90
Pρ	Σςσ	Tτ	Yυ	Φφ	Xχ	Ψψ	Ωω	ϡ*
100	200	300	400	500	600	700	800	900

*F, Q, ϡ numerals only.

The verbal היה hayah, or eye, means to be, to come
to pass, while חיה means to live, to make live. The letters
i, j or y in these words are interchangeable with the letter
vau or w and the words may be read as hvh or hih without
change of meaning. The first becomes havah or heva with
a numerical value of 565 and the second becomes chavah
or ch-v-e, 865, the 2 forms being so similar in meaning that
the words may be used interchangeably. The first literally
means Eva while, as a substantive, the second means mother
and is, in fact, the proper name given in Genesis to Eve,
the mother of all being. The deity name J'havah is a compound of י or Jah and hevia, evah or hevah, thus the
word Jah-evah or Jah-eve has the primary significance of
hermaphroditic existence as male-female.

Apply the methods of the Gematria to a Biblical passage
of which the meaning seems to be strange or mysterious,
such as Genesis 49:11; "He washed his garment in wine". The
Cabalist interprets this passage as follows: The word wine
has a numerical value of 70 and the word sod, meaning mystery, has the same value. This is taken to mean that Judah
was clothed in the Sacred Mysteries, meaning Wisdom or
the Law. This entire chapter of Genesis is evidently sym-

bolical rather than historical. The description of Jacob's sons is really a description of the 12 signs of the zodiac and, in fact, the entire account of Jacob's life is filled with incidents which, apparently, must be interpreted as mythical or symbolical. The phrase "until Shiloh come" (49:10) is sometimes interpreted as referring to the coming of the Messiah and it is pointed out that the numerical value of Shiloh, 345, added to "I AM THAT I AM", 543, gives 888, the number of Jesus, (IHSOUS-888).

This example would be much more successful, however, if the words Messiah and Shiloh had the same numerical values, but the number for Messiah is 355 or 358.

The Hebrew spelling for the word meaning fish is נון or Nun, which has a numerical value of 565. Nun, the mother of Joshua (meaning savior), is therefore equal in numerical value to, and consequently identical with, Eve, the woman or hovah, the feminine part of Jahveh.

Place the numerals over יונה the Hebrew word for dove, John, or Jonah, and they read 5-50-6-10, which figures when added total 71, an important mystic number. In the description of the Flood this word is mentioned five times, which makes three hundred fifty-five (71 × 5), the number of days in the lunar year. Ten is associated with Jahveh; six is the number of creation and the five is composed of 2 × 3, that is the first male and female. Divide thirty by the numbers 10-5-6-5 successively and it produces 365-6 or 365 days 6 hours, the length of the solar year.

The ineffable Tetragrammaton which the Jews used for YHVH, or 10-5-6-5, adds to 26, the sacred number of Yahveh. In the Cabalistic Tree of Life (See Appendix), the Sephiroth in the central pillar total 26, i.e., 1 + 6 + 9 + 10 = 26. When placed in pyramidal form, the sacred monogram produces 72, the great number of God.

$$
\begin{array}{lll}
\text{I} = 10 & & 10 \\
\text{HI} = 10 + 5 & & 15 \\
\text{VHI} = 10 + 5 + 6 & & 21 \\
\text{HVHI} = 10 + 5 + 6 + 5 & & 26 \\
\hline
& & 72
\end{array}
$$

Add the numbers 1 to 12 inclusive and the sum is 78. This represents the eternal creative power which was, is, and will always be; attributed by the Brahmans to Brahma, by the Egyptians to Isis, by the Greeks and Romans to Zeus and Jupiter and by the Jews to Jahveh. This sum is also 13 times 6, the number of the Great Mother.

Manoah, the father of Samson, a mythical solar hero, has a numerical value of 104 which is 4 times 26, the number of Jahveh. The name Solomon contains three different titles of the sun (Sol-Om-On), the three syllables probably representing the sun in the morning, at noon, and at sunset. The name of the Babylonian king Shalmanesar breaks down to Shalmanu-Sar which was an epithet applied to the sun god Bel and is equivalent in meaning to the Hebrew name Solomon. The Jews turned Shalmanu-Sar into Sar-Shalom, or prince of peace.

The Hebrew word Shalom or Salem, is equivalent to "Sal-aam", an Oriental word of greeting which originated as a designation of the sun god. Each syllable of the Biblical name Om-On-Al or Emanuel also contains a title of the sun and the word probably originated in the same manner as the name Solomon.

The first sentence in the Bible reads *"In the beginning God created the heavens and earth"*. In Hebrew it reads *B'Rashith* and is really two words in one, the *B* being a participle meaning *by*. Both as a word and as a number the first word may be interpreted as meaning Wisdom, the first Sephira of the Cabala. Many Cabalists have contended that this was the true meaning of the word and have pointed out that it is the interpretation used by the Targum of Jerusalem. By this interpretation the first sentence should read "By wisdom" and not "In the beginning" God created the heavens and earth.

In the same chapter of Genesis the word which translators have interpreted as God or Jehovah reads אלהים Aleim, or as modern Jews prefer to pronounce it, Elohim. El is both Lord and a primitive title of the sun, being of the same meaning and origin as the Arabic word Al in Al-lah.

The value of the letters for Yahweh (JHV) in the Pathagoras triangle is 543. This is also the number of Moses and for Al Shaddai (AL ShDI), one of the titles of God. The name by which God designated himself in Exodus 3:14 is AHIH ASHR AHIH or "I AM THAT I AM" the value of which is 543, or the reverse of 345. The numbers 345 and 543 may therefore be read as meaning JHVH.

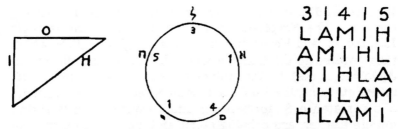

72. Left: A 3 x 4 x 5 triangle as the symbol of Isis, Osiris and
Horus.
Center: The word Alhim (Aleim) in a circle, producing the
numerical value, 31415.
Right: An anagram of the name Alhim giving the same result.

The God name Elohim, or Aleim, has the radical El
as the stem masculine with an *he* attached, giving a feminine
quality, El-h. Numerically Al has the important value of
31 and the addition of *he* makes the value 36. Further, the
word Aleim forms an anagram in which the values of the
letters in the top line, when read without ciphers, give
31415. This may be read as 3.1415, the famous "Pi" proportion or the relation of a circle's diameter to its circumference and identifies the word Elohim with the circle or
female quality. (Plate 72).

One of the most significant of all geometrical forms is
the famous 3-4-5 triangle of Pythagoras which was called

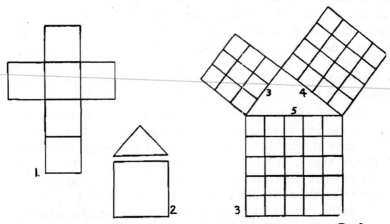

73. Fig. 1, the six sides of a cube unfolded to form a cross. Reading horizontally there are 3 squares and vertically there are 4.
Fig. 2, the 3 and 4 represented as a triangle and square, symbolizing spirit and matter.

the Eye of Horus, aur or Hor, meaning light and typifying the sun. The Egyptians called the 3 sides of the triangle Isis, Osiris, and Horus and the 3 letters IOH or JVH which they applied to the triangle were the secret formula which contained a key to the universe. According to one of its interpretations, the 3-4-5 form symbolized the 3 components of all existence, 3 representing infinite spirit, 4 representing infinite matter, and 5 being spirit and matter manifested in material form.

According to the Cabala, each manifestation of God is divided into 3 principal phases which form the bases of the 3 triads of Sephiroth in the Cabalistic Tree of Life. In one sense, matter is divided into gases, liquids, and solids and, in another sense, the essence of existence is derived from the 3 elements air, fire, and water (earth is believed to be derived from water, therefore is not counted). This is revealed in the first verse of the Bible where the word Aeshmim (heavens) contains the 3 mother letters; Aleph representing air; Shin representing fire and Mem representing water. Again, the 3 branches of the letter Shin symbolize the 3 phases of light or divine fire.

Square the figures 3, 4, and 5 and they produce 9, 16, and 25 which add to 50, the number of Admh or Adam. If a 3 × 4 rectangle be divided by a diagonal line each half will be a 3-4-5 triangle. Divide the 3 × 4 shape vertically into 3 parts and draw a diagonal for one of the sections and its angle will be approximately 23½ degrees, (See Plate 74) which is the angle of the earth's axis to the ecliptic and further reveals the three divisions of the material world. Add 3, 4, and 5 and they produce 12, the number of months in the year and the divisions of the zodiac.

After drawing the diagonal of a 3 × 4 rectangle, draw a second diagonal from a corner to the intersection of the first diagonal and it produces 3 triangles, the areas of which are in the proportion of 3, 4, and 5. The angle of the second diagonal is 52 degrees, being almost exactly the same as the slope of the Great Pyramid. Bisection of the 3 × 4 form was believed to provide a key to the solution of the ancient problem of squaring a circle. A triangle of 3 × 4 × 3 gives the basis for constructing a square and circle of approximately equal area and a 4 × 5 × 4 triangle

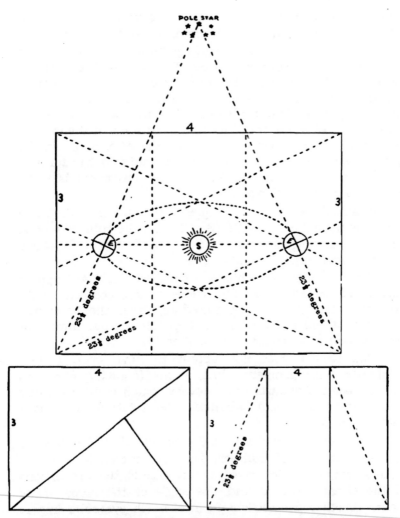

74. *The 3 x 4 rectangle as the basic form on which the world was constructed. At lower left the rectangle is divided diagonally to form two triangles in the proportion of 3 x 4 x 5. The second diagonal forms the Golden Section of the Greeks.*
At lower right the rectangle is divided vertically into 3 sections. The diagonal of each section has an angle of 23½ degrees. The drawing at the top shows the earth's orbit in a 3 x 4 rectangle with the earth's axis inclined 23½ degrees toward the sun.

gives the proportions for making a square and circle of approximately equal circumference. (Plates 75 and 76).

To the Cabalist, a series of significant relations is also exhibited by the sides of a cube. The cube of 6 equals 216 (6 × 6 × 6) which is also the number of DBIR (debir) the holy of holies in the tabernacle and in the temple. According to ancient traditions, the cube was the proper form for the abode of the Holy Spirit and some of the ancient stone idols of the gods were in the form of a cube. In the Babylonian Deluge myth, the ark was built in the form of a cube and in Revelations 21 the New Jerusalem is to be a cube of 12000 furlongs.

Again, the cube of 6 is equal to the cubes, of 3, 4, and 5, that is the cube of 3 = 27 (3 × 3 × 3); the cube of 4 = 64 (4 × 4 × 4) and the cube of 5 = 125 (5 × 5 × 5) which add to a total of 216.

If the 6 sides of a cube are unfolded, they will appear as a cross or tau form. The center square combines with both the vertical and horizontal bars, hence the horizontal counts as 3 and the vertical as 4, giving another important combination of spirit (3) and matter (4).

The Cabala does not appear to have been linked, originally, with geometry; but, as the following examples show, modern Cabalists have devoted much effort to trying to invent symbolic and Cabalistic interpretations of various geometrical forms.

The proportions of a 5 × 8 rectangle (5 + 8 + 5 + 8) produce the YHVH number, 26. This rectangle will enclose a triangle which gives almost exactly the proportions of the Great Pyramid and the angle of the slope of its sides.[1] Another geometrical form of much symbolic import is the trapezoid in the proportions of 10 + 5 + 6 + 5 which again total 26. The angle of the tapered ends is approximately 23½ degrees, or the angle of the earth's axis to the eliptic.

Change the proportions of the trapezoid to 10 + 10 + 10 + 6 and the diagonals produce the angle of the slope of the pyramid; the dimensions add to 36, the number of the sun, and the over-all shape is the same as that of the Masonic keystone.

1—The exact angle of the sides of the triangle is 52°: the angle of the sides of the pyramid is 51° 52′.

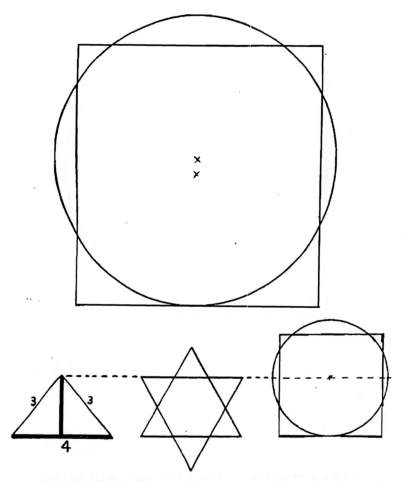

75. *A triangle in the proportion of 3 x 4 x 5 as the basis for making an inverted tau cross, a Star of David and a circle and square of approximately equal area.*

The angles 23½, 38½, 47, 51½, 66½, 77, and 103 degrees recur repeatedly in the simple divisions of rectangles in the proportions of 3 × 4, 4 × 5, 4 × 7, 4 × 9, 5 × 8, and 7 × 8 as well as in such natural forms as the snowflake and crystal. All over the world these natural forms and proportions may be found in designs on pottery, seals and coins, in sculpture, arches, windows, floor plans and elevations of ancient temples and monuments as if their designers had recognized in them some mysterious affinity with the geometry of the universe. These angles and pro-

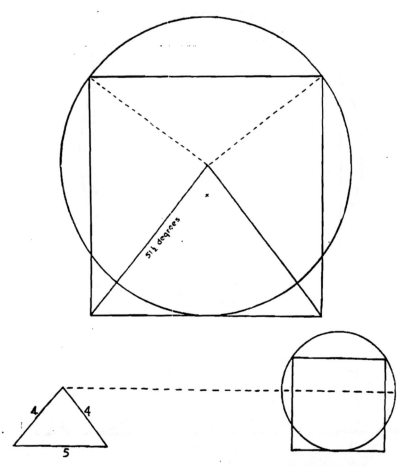

76. *A 4 x 5 x 4 triangle as the basis for making a circle and square of approximately equal circumference. Lines from the center of the circle to the lower corners of the square have an angle of 51½ degrees which is almost exactly the same as the sides of the Great Pyramid. Dotted lines in the large square at the top give the proportion of the flap on the apron of the Freemasons.*

portions occur in the symbolism of Freemasonry and may convey a suggestion as to why Masons speak of the Creator as the Great Architect of the Universe.

The mention of Peter having caught 153 fishes (John 21:11) has often been thought to be of secret significance, therefore this number has been a popular one with Cabalists. Hundreds of Cabalistic formulae have been devised for producing this number from Biblical words and verses, a few of which are here given as examples.

In Greek the word ΙΧΕΘΥΣ meaning fishes has a numerical value of 1224, or 8 times 153. The name of the fisherman, Simeon Peter (in Hebrew, Shimeon Jonah) gives the number 153. The phrase Beni ha Elohim ("sons of God") equals 153. The number for the phrase "The seed of Jacob" is 459, or 3 times 153. The words "house of Israel, my people" (Ezek. 34:30), in Greek, total 1530 or 10 times 153.

One of the many names applied to Christians in early Rome was Pisiculi, or Little Fishes, and the fish symbol in the form of either a single fish or of 2 fishes has been found scratched or drawn in many places on the walls of the catacombs.

In the eighth book of the *Sibylline Oracles*, which appeared in Rome during the first century B.C., the first words, reading Jesous Xristos Theos Oios Soter formed an acrostic in which the initial Greek letters IXTOS (fishes) were thought to prophesy the coming of Christ.

Maria, the Greek name for Christ's mother, has a numerical value of 152. The numerals 1, 5, and 2 may be transposed so as to form 888, the number of Christ, when added either vertically or horizontally, thus

$$152 = 8$$
$$521 = 8$$
$$215 = 8$$

$$\overline{888}$$

Another famous number is 666, called the number of Anti-Christ or "the number of the beast" which is referred to in the Apocalypse. In Latin, "anti--theos esti" meaning

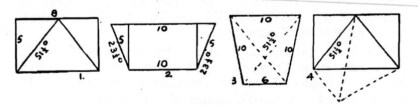

77. *Fig; The Great Pyramid contained (approximately) in a 5 x 8 rectangle. The sides of the rectangle add to 26, the number of JHVH. Fig 2 gives the number of JHVH and the angle of the earth's inclination to the sun. The sides of Fig. 3 add to 36, the number of the sun. The diagonals give the angle of the sides of the Pyramid. Fig. 4 is similar to Fig. 1.*

"he is Anti-God" has the value of 666. Rev. Walter Begley has published more than 100 examples containing this number, most of them being from the Latin.[2]

The sum of all numbers from 1 to 36 added together is also 666, the grand number of the sun. The Hebrew name for the sun is Shamash, the number of which is 640. Add 26, the number of YHVH and it gives 666. This is also the numerical value of Shechem Bar Hamor, the seducer of Dinah in Gen. 34:2. By one interpretation this act foreshadowed the seduction of Israel by Anti-Christ. The numerical value of Shechem is 360 and that of Ben Hamor is 306, thus giving the same number, when added, as is given by the 2 words Nero Caesar, who has been thought by many writers to be "the Beast" referred to.

While the controversy between the Lutherans and the Roman Church was at white heat, the Lutherans formed many Cabalistic combinations on the Beast number which were directed at the Popes, such as the following one given by Rev. Begley: *Id Bestia Leo* = 666.

By Gematria, the slave or concubine offspring of Leah and Rachel also add to 666.

Leah	36		
Zilpah	122	Bilhah	42
Gad	7	Dan	54
Asher	501	Naphtali	570
	666		666

In the phrase "I am Alpha and Omega, the beginning and the end", the first letter of the Greek alphabet has a value of 1 and the value of Omega is 800, or a total of 801, the number of Salvation. The name ADoNAY totals 65. When added to 26, the JHVH number, it gives 91 which is the equivalent of Amen 91.

If space permitted, a great number of curious and even surprising Cabalistic combinations could be given but the examples shown are sufficient to demonstrate the arbitrary and unscientific nature of the system.

In order to prove that the Bible is a symbolic, esoteric work of divine origin, the Cabalist takes the numerical value of a word or phrase then looks for another word or phrase

---

2—*Biblia Cabalistica*, Rev. Walter Begley, London, 1903, p. 119.

with the same value. But when this has been accomplished, no hidden secrets have been revealed and any new meaning that may be derived from the text will be completely dependent upon such arbitrary conclusions as the Cabalist chooses to draw from it. All the system proves is that two or more words or phrases may have the same numerical value. It is not only possible, however, to find a correlative for practically any word or phrase in the Bible: in some cases many correlatives may be found, including some whose associations are utterly dissimilar and unrelated in any conceivable way. For instance, the Hebrew word ro'ah meaning evil is spelled exactly the same as the word friend and presumably this would signify to the Cabalist that friends are evil. CHYShM, Messiah, has a value of 358 and ShChN, Nachash, meaning serpent, has the same value.

The ability of the Gematria to cut both ways like a sword is unintentionally demonstrated by the *Zohar*. It describes an incident in which a certain Ramma bar Chamma was asked why it was that Satan could not accuse people on the' day of Atonement and the Ramma replied that the number of Satan (NTShH-ha, Shatan) was 364 therefore he could accuse people on 364 days of the year but on Atonement, the 365th day, the devil could not accuse. Had the Ramma carried his reasoning a trifle farther, he would have seen that JHVH Adonai, a title of God, has a value of 91 which, when multiplied by 4, gives the same number as Satan, that is, 364. In fact, according to the Cabala, God and Satan can be proven even more decisively to be one and the same for the very word God has a value of 364 (GUD = 3 + 6 + 4).

The fact that the pretensions of the Cabalists can be refuted by such simple demonstrations makes one wonder how Sir Isaac Newton, Bacon, Spinoza and many other brilliant scholars and scientists could have found merit in what is obviously so utterly fallacious. But, history has often shown that when brilliant men dabble in mysticism their critical faculties become numbed and they cease to reason objectively. Being desirous of confirming their religious beliefs, they give undue importance to all favorable evidence and minimize, or ignore, anything to the contrary, with the result that they sometimes fall victims to nonsense which should be apparent as such to even ordinary minds.

Before leaving this subject, some mention should be made concerning significant developments in Cabalistic research which have occurred within recent years through the discovery of many peculiar relations in the proportions of geometrical figures. Some of these developments are of genuine mathematical interest and had they not been linked with Cabalism, probably would have received more serious attention.

The first discovery was made by John A. Parker, a New York mathematician who found a more perfect relation between the diameter and circumference of a circle, the proportions being 6561 for diameter and 20612 for circumference. Later, it was learned that Peter Metius, a Dutchman, had, in 1585, discovered a slightly less perfect relation of 113 for diameter and 355 for circumference.

The fact that these 2 sets of figures were equivalent to the numerical value of certain Biblical words and the further belief that the figures were related to the architectural proportions of the pyramid, gave rise to a theory that these geometrical phenomena were not accidental but were the result of divine laws inherent in the structure of the universe. This coincidence, it was thought, was conclusive proof that the Bible and the systems of letters and numbers are of divine origin, intended by the Great Architect of the universe to reveal to those worthy of the knowledge, the physical structure of man and the universe.[3]

Omitting the Cabalistic references for the moment, the theory is based upon the following proposition: If the length of the side of a square is 81 inches, feet or other units, the area will be 6561 (81 x 81). This sum is equal to 9 x 9 x 9 x 9 and the figure 9 and its multiples are the basis of the calculations. (Reverse 6561 and it gives 1656, the number of years from Creation to the Flood). A circle of the same diameter will have an area of 5153.

By the Pythagorean formula, the circumference of a circle is equal to 3.1415 times its diameter, expressed Pi x Diam. = Circumference. Therefore, a circle which has a diameter of 6561 will have a circumference of 20612 (6561 x 3.14159 = 20612). Multiplying the area of a circle by 4 will give the same product as multiplying the diameter of the circle by 3.14159.

3—See *Key to the Hebrew-Egyptian Mystery*, J. Ralston Skinner, David McKay Co., Philadelphia.

78. The three Jahvehs represented by the 3 sides of an equilateral triangle; by 3 Jods and a tau cross in a circle and by the 3-pronged crown.

If the side of a square equals	81	=	6561	equals area		
" diameter of a circle is	81	=	5153	"	"	
" " " " " "	6561	=	20612	"	circum.	
" the side of a square equals	5153	=	20612	"	"	

If the letter Jod, 10, is taken as the radius of a circle, the circumference will equal (approximately) the circumference of a square measuring 16 on each side. The 16 is equal to 5 + 6 + 5, being equivalent to Ha-Va-Ha (HVH), Havvah or Eve.

If the length of the side of a square is 81, its diagonal will be 114.591498, which figure is equal to the diameter of a circle with a circumference of 360. In other words, the diagonal of the square of 81 is a proportional between values of circumference and diameter of the circle.

Divide 114.5914 by 2 and the product is 57.2957499. Take a circle of any size and draw an arc within it which is equal to the radius of the circle. The angle of the arc will always be 57.2957499 degrees.

Again, the perpendicular of an equilateral triangle whose sides are 81 will be the same as the side of an equilateral triangle within a circle whose diameter is 81.

Now, let's see how these mathematical relations were applied to the Cabala. Omitting ciphers and reading from right to left, the letters of the Hebrew word *aish* (man) are 113: when read from left to right and including ciphers the word has a value of 311. This is also the value of the Hebrew words *the woman*, (h-aish) 5-1-300-5 (or, if reversed, 5-300-1-5), so that numerically, 311 may be read as either man or the woman, while 113 is man. (If the 355 days of the Hebrew lunar year be considered as a circle, its diameter will be 113). The term stands 113-311, which reads either way. But the term *aish* is a form of Adam (1 + 4 + 40) or 144, which may be read as 144-441.

Omitting the article *h*, 5, gives the figure 531-135; woman as 135 and its reverse 531. Thus, there are 3 forms, all connected under the name of man, the woman and Adam which can be placed as

311-113
441-144
531-135.

Adam and woman joined give the figure 531-441 while adding the numbers of the woman, 531 and 135 produces the famous number 666.

A square, the side of which is 81 will, when cubed, give the figure 531441 (81 × 81 = 6561 × 81 = 531441). The solid content of a sphere with a diameter of 81 may be found as follows. One-sixth of 3.14159÷6 (.5235990448) multiplied by the cube of 81 (531441). 531441 × .5235990448 makes 278262 which is precisely the same as 20612 × 135, the number of woman. (Convert this to a time equation and it gives the exact length of the lunar month in days, hours, minutes,— 27 days, 8 hrs. 26 min. 2 sec.).

So, while the area changed into a cube becomes 531441, the solidity of the contained sphere is 20612 × 135 or 278262, showing a continued integral relation where the solid content of the sphere is the circumference multiplied by 135, the solid of the containing cube being expressed by the reversed form of woman—Adam or 531-441.

This is set forth as showing that there is an integral relation between the area of a circle inscribed in a square to the area of that square and between the linear diameter to circumference of a circle, and it is claimed that this harmony with many others (size and shape of the Garden of Paradise, the Flood, the Ark, the temple, the holy of holies, etc.) proves, according to the geometrical school of Cabalists that these relations are the true natural ones from eternity to eternity and are ones on which the Bible is built.

It is further claimed that these mathematical phenomena explain the origin and significance of the great pyramid of Khufu in Egypt, and a cult of Pyramidists has sprung up that professes to see in the dimensions of the pyramid, prophecies of practically every great event in history, both ancient and modern. The hypotheses have gen-

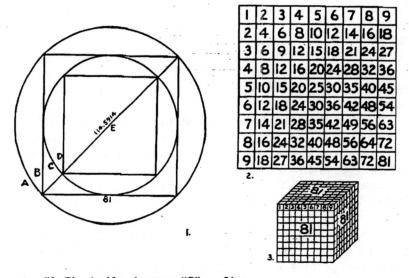

79. Fig. 1, side of square "B" = 81
diagonal of square "E" = 114.5914
circumference of circle "A" = 360
area of circle "A" = 5153
area of square "B" = 6561
Fig. 2, Pythagorean multiplication table
Fig. 3, Cube of 81. The number of facets on the 3 visible
sides total 243

erally been founded upon the assumption that every line
and angle of the great monument was based upon some
deep fundamental truth or law. (Of course the claim that
the pyramid was constructed by ancient Freemasons and
that it contains many secrets of that fraternity is well
known.)

Deep and important meaning has been read into every
angle and dimension of the pyramid's passages and chambers, including the arrangement of the paneling on the
walls and the stone slabs forming the roof of the chambers. The length in inches of certain passages, for instance,
has been claimed to represent a certain number of years in
history: the circumference of the base or of a chamber
has been thought to agree with the exact length of the
day or year. Even the number of stones in the sides of
the base has been thought to possess a deep astrological
and religious significance.

Since Napoleon visited the pyramid during his Egyptian campaign in 1799 a score of scientists have measured

the length of its sides, its height and angle of slant and every dimension of its interior chambers and passages. Although it was constructed at least 25 or 30 centuries before the oldest parts of the Bible were compiled and is nowhere mentioned therein, its dimension are thought to be Cabalistic figures agreeing with and proving the divine origin of Cabalistic mysteries in the Bible.

Some enthusiasts have claimed that the pyramid provides a key to the interpretation of numerous Old Testament prophecies; the date of the Exodus of the Jews from Egypt; the birth, death and resurrection of Christ; the principal events which occurred before, during and after World War I; the outbreak of World War II and the events which were to follow.

The relationship of the volume and area of the triangle, pyramid, square, cube, circle and sphere, it is maintained, reveal the periods of the revolution of the planets, the length of the day, month and year, a perfect system of measures of distance and volume, the distance of the earth from the sun, and other astronomical facts which are not supposed to have been known until many centuries after the pyramid was built. Furthermore, these values are claimed to be found in the teachings of the Bible as well as in the proportions and dimensions of ancient temples and monuments.

The interior and exterior dimensions, by their proportions and relationships, are held to have been designed to provide for future initiates a secret record of the mathematical relationships between all basic geometrical forms.

CHAPTER XVIII

ASTROLOGY

ASTROLOGY ORIGINATED IN Chaldea (Babylonia) where it reached a higher state of development than anywhere else in the ancient world. From Chaldea it spread westward to Syria and Egypt, and later, by way of Greece and Rome, to western Europe, where it continued to influence religious and astronomical speculation for centuries after the great civilization of Babylonia had ceased to exist.

Up to a hundred years ago practically all of our knowledge of Babylonian astrology was derived from the *Observations of Bel,* consisting of 70 books or parts. After the invasion of the East by Alexander the Great, these books were translated by Berossus, a priest of Babylon. This work has been lost, but excerpts from it have been preserved in the works of other writers. These early fragments of the work of Berossus have been enormously supplemented by the many discoveries made within the last century.

Having observed a relation between the positions, movements, and other aspects of the sun and moon, the varying length of the days, changes of seasons, periods of growth, movement of tides, some primitive peoples believed that all life and activity on earth were influenced or controlled by these heavenly bodies, which were personified as deities.

This belief led almost inevitably to the development of astrology, or the art of foretelling events by the positions and movements of the stars. As the phases of the heavenly bodies were believed to be related to events on earth, it was thought a knowledge of these phenomena would reveal the moods, humors, and actions of the ruling deities and make possible the foretelling of events.

Babylonian astrology was based upon the belief that the earth is but a small scale counterpart of the heavens. Everything that exists or occurs in the heavens was believed to be duplicated in the objects and events on earth.

Each part of the heavens was thought to be related to a corresponding part of the habitable world. Part of the labor of Marduk, in the Creation Myth, was to divide the heavens and to place stars and constellations in the various divisions to represent each city or country of the known world. Signs seen in a certain part of the sky were significant for a special city or nation. The most important factors in this attempt to foretell the future were the sun, moon, and 5 inferior planets; the zodiac, meteors, comets, and meteorological conditions. Almost all the signs of the zodiac must have been arranged in approximately their present position by 2800 B.C., and some of the constellations had probably been determined by 5000 B.C.

The planets were believed to be deities, or temples in which the deities resided, and man-made temples on earth were regarded as copies of their heavenly prototypes. Prayers might be addressed to the deities in their earthly temples and communications might be received from their celestial temples by one who was competent to interpret the signs. The very name of Babylon (bab-ilu, gate of the gods) denotes a city copied from the heavenly model.

The most important yearly event was the 11-day festival held at the beginning of the year when the gods assembled in the great Hall of Fates in Babylon to assist the supreme god Marduk in deciding the fates of men for the ensuing year. Associated with Marduk were the gods Shamash, Sin, Ishtar, Nabu, Ninurta, and Adad, who had been supreme in various cities before the ascendency of Babylon. This council of gods determined the future weal or woe of kings and states. Each of the council members represented some special characteristic and the complete council was merely a thinly disguised representation of Marduk in his various manifestations. During this period of Babylon's greatest glory, astrology was employed only for religious purposes or by the king for affairs of state. There was no thought of separating astronomy and astrology from religion because they were essential parts of the religious system.

The city of Babylon itself was laid out in 7 concentric squares in imitation of the supposed disposition of the planets about the earth. According to Herodotus, the wall about the city was 360 furlongs in length, corresponding to the number of days in the ancient astrological year, although, according to Ctesias, the wall was later lengthened to 480 furlongs in order to equal that of Nineveh.

Observations of the heavens were made from the tops of ziggurats, or towers with external stairways. At Borsippa, across the river from Babylon, Sir Henry Rawlinson discovered, in 1845, the ruins of a square 7-storied ziggurat of Nabu, 272 feet square and 140 feet high. Its antiquity is revealed by the fact that it was in ruins in the seventh century, B.C., during the reign of Nebuchadnezzar, who restored it. The lowest stage was colored black, for the planet Saturn; the 2nd orange, for Jupiter; the 3d red, for Mars; the 4th gold, for the sun; the 5th white, for Venus; the 6th dark blue, for Mercury; and the 7th was silver-tinted, for the moon.

Some of the Chaldean ziggurats contained 8 stories, the upper one being dedicated to the supreme god and equipped for his occupancy when he visited the earth. There he had his golden altar, furniture, treasures, and a model of his sacred boat. The only human visitor to this temple, according to Herodotus, was a virgin selected as the earthly consort of the deity and who climbed the winding passageway to the temple each evening to await the coming of the heavenly visitor.

The duty of reading the intentions of the gods and predicting events was assigned to the priesthood, which consisted of a distinct and important hereditary class, constituting a sort of Freemasonry each member of which was required to be free from any physical blemish or imperfection, and to pursue a prescribed course of study. Their duties included the recitation of prayers, the presenting of offerings, writing music for the temple ceremonies, and making prophecies. They were also the astronomers, dividers of space and time, as well as the architects and builders of the temples, which were carefully oriented to the regions of the earth and designed in imitation of the supposed likenesses of the temples in the heavens.

In time the court which surrounded the temple became the financial center where priests, acting as lawyers and bankers, loaned money at exorbitant rates, acted as public scribes in drawing up and notarizing contracts and deeds and arranging for the barter and sale of all kinds of merchandise.

Forewarnings of such catastrophies as floods, famines, or military defeats enabled the rulers either to make preparations to avoid them or by prayers, gifts, and sacrifices to wheedle and flatter the gods into changing their plans. For the priests it was a heads-I-win-tails-you-lose system in which no war or other important undertaking was initiated until the good will of the gods had been determined by astrology and insured by the offering of gifts and prayers to the temple gods. If disaster followed, however, it was accepted as evidence that the gods were extremely angry, and that more prayers and greater gifts were necessary. It was, therefore, to the interest of the priests to maintain the belief that all phenomena on earth were under the ruling power of the deities, whose wills and actions they, the priests, could reveal.

In addition to astrology, the priesthood employed numerous less important methods of divination. These included the interpretation of dreams and the forecasting of events from the actions and movements of birds and animals, from the appearance of misbirths in humans and animals, from the configuration of the liver of a sacrificed ox or sheep, and from the pattern made by drops of oil floated on water in a divining bowl. It was with such a divining bowl or cup that Joseph amazed the Pharaoh of Egypt, and statements in the Bible indicate that liver divination was not unknown to Moses. [1]

Their exclusive possession of all astronomical knowledge and their position as intercessors with the gods enabled the priests to command vast wealth and power which even the king was bound to respect. To maintain their power, they jealously guarded their knowledge and handed it down from generation to generation to only a small group of initiates. A tablet in Assurbanipal's library reads: "The wise shall teach it to the wise: The unlearned shall not see it."

The term "Chaldean" itself denoted a priest, a tribe, or a prophet. In Greece, where astrology was later practiced, the term denoted a tribe or mathematician and, eventually, a charlatan. Our word "magician" comes from Magi, meaning priest or worker in magic.

In the earlier period, astrology was almost entirely empirical; astrologers were not yet able to predict celestial phenomena accurately and reckonings of the moon's phases

---

1—*Exod.* 29:13,22 and *Lev.* 3:4,10,15; 7:4.

show that positions of the sun and moon were not fully understood.

The use of mathematics in astrological calculations began about the eighth century B.C. Thereafter, knowledge of astronomy advanced rapidly and records of that period reveal notations concerning the spring equinox, new moon, eclipses, positions of the planets, and the rising of the fixed stars. The first eclipses observed in Babylonia, and mentioned in the Almagest, are from 721 to 720 B.C.

In the fourth century, the Saros or 19-year cycle was discovered and in the third century, Kiddinu, the greatest of Babylonian astronomers, discovered the precession of the equinoxes; and the year, day, and hour of eclipses were predicted, the precise extent of the eclipse being given.

About 200 B.C., Kiddinu constructed tables of great accuracy, giving positions of the stars. In this work he utilized a vast collection of observations which were said to have been gathered over thousands of years. These records were intended as reference works for reading the fate of men and the determination of the favorable moment for beginning new ventures. To ascertain the significance of any celestial phenomenon, particularly in later times when the archives had become extensive, it was necessary only to consult the records and to observe what formerly followed a similar phenomenon. But, despite the numerous records and the elaborate methods employed, the ability to foretell events on earth failed to keep pace with the great progress made in determining the movements and cycles of the stars.

Comprehensive studies of the correspondences between individuals and celestial bodies were made at birth and calculations were drawn from the configuration of the stars at the time. The calculations were usually based upon many arbitrary or immaterial correspondences between the planets and the lives of the persons for whom they were made. Thus, the approach of Mars to Scorpio was an omen that a prince would die from the sting of a scorpion.

When a certain event on earth had followed a certain phenomenon in the heavens, a similar earthly event was expected to recur at the same time in the following heavenly cycle. Therefore, because eclipses had occurred on certain days of the month, or because a change in the moon's phase seemed to augur good or evil on several occasions, some days were declared propitious for certain pursuits; others, unpropitious. The appearance of the new moon earlier than expected was regarded as an unfavorable omen, indicative in one case of defeat, in another of death among the cattle, on the theory that anything that occurred prematurely was an augury of an unfavorable event.

After beginning as a mere adjunct of astrology, astronomy finally emerged as a science in its own right. While the fame and prestige of the priests as astronomers were greatly enhanced by developments in mathematics which made it possible to predict eclipses, conjunctions, and the positions of the stars and planets with considerable accuracy, these same developments eventually led to the discrediting of astrology.

From its very beginning, astrology had thrived on the belief that affairs on earth took place in a haphazard manner at the whims of gods who could be cajoled into withdrawing their harmful decrees. But when it became evident that such appeals were useless; that the movements of the sun, the moon, and the planets followed certain definite and inexorable laws regardless of the appeals of priests to their gods, and that these movements could be predicted with accuracy, there was no longer any reason to bribe the deities with gifts and flatter them with prayers.

The first real triumph of scientific astronomy over the mumbo-jumbo astrology of the priests occurred in 601 B.C., when, for the first time in history, Thales, a Greek philosopher, successfully predicted an eclipse. This was the opening contest in the war between science and "revealed" supernaturalism. Soon afterward astrology was undermined from another direction. In 539 B.C. the Persian King Cyrus captured Babylon and spread the Zoroastrian doctrine of one Supreme God who ruled by an infinite law of compensation. In the new system there was no place for vengeful, jealous deities who ruled by caprice.

As the power of the astrologers declined in Babylonia, their reputation increased in the West. About this time the Greeks began to penetrate the East and the fame of Babylonian astronomy and astrology was soon carried back to Greece, whence it spread over all of Europe.

Greek astrology is first mentioned in the *Prometheus Vinctus* by Aeschylus, 525-465 B.C., after which the Greeks showed an increased interest in, and knowledge of heavenly phenomena. Further impetus was given to Greek astrology in the fourth century by the conquest of the East by Alexander the Great, at whose request Berossus translated the Babylonian astrological texts. Although astrology never achieved the popularity in Greece which it formerly had held in Babylonia, the Greek astrologers enlarged its scope until they had brought practically all of the known sciences under its influence and had given it substantially the form it has today.

Unlike the Babylonian system, Greek astrology was mathematical from the beginning. Furthermore, it was practiced by laymen instead of priests and was concerned with the individual, whereas the Babylonian astrologers did not begin making individual horoscopes until they were compelled to do so by reduced circumstances, caused by the disintegration of the nation.

In Rome, astrology was held in high honor and, during the period of the emperors, the games of the Circus were an allegory representing the sun, moon, planets, and other bodies of the heavens. The following description of the games is from Dupuis:

"The sun had its horses which, on the race course or hippodrome, imitated the career of the luminary in the heavens. The Olympic fields were represented by a vast amphitheater, or arena, which was consecrated to the sun. In the midst of it there stood the temple of that god which was surmounted by his image. The East and West, as the limits of the course of the sun, were traced and marked by boundaries and placed toward the remotest part of the Circus. The races took place from east to west until seven rounds were made, on account of the seven planets. The sun and moon had their chariots the same as Jupiter and Venus; the charioteers were dressed in clothes the color of which was analogous to the hue of the different elements.

"The chariot of the sun was borne by four horses and that of the moon by two. The zodiac was represented in the Circus by twelve gates; there were also traced the movements of the circumpolar stars or of the two Bears.

"Everything was personified in these feasts: the sea, or Neptune, the earth, or Ceres, and so on, the other planets. They were represented by actors contending for the prizes.

These contests were instituted, they said, in order to illustrate the harmony of the universe, of heaven, of the earth
and of the sea. The institution of these Games was attributed to Romulus by the Romans and I believe that they
were an imitation of the races of the Hippodrome of the
Accadians and of the games of Elis".[2]

In India and China, belief in astrology became extremely widespread and it still flourishes more in those
countries than anywhere else. From birth to death, the
life of a Hindu or Chinese is guided by the positions of the
planets and even minor activities are postponed unless the
horoscope indicates the time is favorable.

Astrology was extensively practiced in Egypt during
the periods of Greek and Roman domination. In the
seventh and eighth centuries it was further developed by
the Arabs, who still place great faith in it.

It was largely through the Moors of Spain that astrology
was introduced into France and other European countries,
where in the 14th and 15th centuries it attained a tremendous vogue. Nearly every ruler had his official astrologer; and at the courts of Italy, Spain, France, Germany,
and England it became customary for the members of the
court to take oaths, not in the name of God, but in the
name of the planets. Courses in astrology were given at
the universities of Cracow, Warsaw, Algiers, and Cairo. It
became the fashion for women of high birth to retain a
"baron", who guided their activities by the positions of
the planets.

In the United States, where people proudly proclaim
this age to be one of science and speak disdainfully of
superstitions, there has been a noteworthy revival of interest in astrology during recent years, and many heads of
great industries who are proud of their shrewdness have
become as credulous in accepting the predictions of the
astrologers as have their housemaids. The publication of
books, magazines, horoscopes, charts and daily newspaper
articles on astrology has become a fairly important business. Divining by drops of oil on water has been replaced
by the pretended gypsy who reads fortunes in tea leaves
or coffee grounds. If some enterprising person will begin

2—*The Origin of All Religious Worship*, Charles Francois Dupuis,
New Orleans, 1872, p. 44.

making predictions from sheep livers, we will be able to foretell the future as well as the Babylonians did.

Interpreting the Zodiac

Inasmuch as astrology was based upon the relative positions of the sun, moon, the 5 planets (Mars, Mercury, Venus, Jupiter, and Saturn), and certain constellations of fixed stars, it was essential for the astrologers to be able to determine the positions of these bodies at all times. Therefore, the heavens were divided into 12 sections, each identified by a constellation of fixed stars, whose order of appearance in the sky is marked in the chart called the zodiac.

Present day star maps show approximately 120 constellations, many of which have been mapped by astronomers within recent centuries. The Greeks had 48 constellations and the Babylonians had even more, but only 12 of these are of astrological significance; therefore all others will here be ignored.

The Babylonians, Chinese, Hindus, Ceylonese, Egyptians, Arabians, and Persians also had lunar zodiacs which, in certain cases, originally contained 27 signs but were later increased to 28. These divisions corresponded to the course of the moon; the 27 or 28 lunar stages were used in observing the stars surrounding the Pole Star when they cross the meridian. During the period when the sun was in the sign of Taurus, the rising of the star Aldebran in Taurus and the setting of Antares in Scorpio, at the spring equinox, provided a means of dividing the heavens into 28 moon stations; 14 in the Overworld and 14 in the Underworld.

Because of the daily rotation of the earth on its axis, every part of the globe is turned toward the heavens every 24 hours. Of course this does not imply that all constellations may be seen from any part of the earth during that time because the stars which are overhead in the daytime are rendered invisible by the sun.

If we were to observe the heavens every evening, always at the same hour, we would see a new zodiacal constellation appear above the eastern horizon each month. At the same hour, 90 days later, this constellation would have risen 90 degrees, to appear on the meridian. At the end of another 3 months it would have disappeared below the western horizon, not to be seen again until 6 months later. This statement applies to all stars in the northern hemisphere except the stars which are near the Polar Star and are visible throughout the year. Because of the earth's daily rotation, these stars seem to move around the Pole every 24 hours.

A few bright stars seem to run counter to this orderly process. They do not retain their relative positions in the sky with respect to each other or to fixed stars: some of them change positions greatly from day to day; others move more slowly. These are the planets, or wandering "stars".

The constellations of the zodiac (path of the sun) lie in what is known as the "ecliptic", a belt in the heavens about 16 degrees wide, marking the path of the earth, or, as it appears to us, the path of the sun.

With the exception of the Balance (Libra) all the signs of the zodiac are named after real or imaginary animals. The relation, however, is purely mythological or allegorical, as not one of the star groups suggests by its shape the animal for which it is named.

Although the zodiac divides the heavens into 12 equal parts, the constellations representing the various signs are not equally spaced nor are they of the same size. Some are crowded together; others are very much spread out. For instance, Leo, Taurus, Pisces, and the Virgin occupy 36 to 48 degrees in the heavens whereas Cancer, Aries, and Capricorn occupy from 19 to 23 degrees. The reason for these variations is that the zodiac was not charted or devised during one period, but, like Topsy, "just growed" over a period of some two or three thousand years.

When a constellation rises with the sun, the sun is said to be in that zodiacal sign. The 12 signs, therefore, correspond to the 12 constellations which were regarded as "houses" or "mansions" occupied by the sun in its travels during the 12 months of the year. This correspondence is made clear in the Babylonian calendar, the names of the 12 months being the names of the 12 signs of the zodiac. In the astrological period the year began at the vernal equinox, which occurs about March 21st.

The 12 signs were divided into 2 parts composing 6 favorable signs and 6 unfavorable signs. The first 6 were those which the sun occupied during the months of warmth,

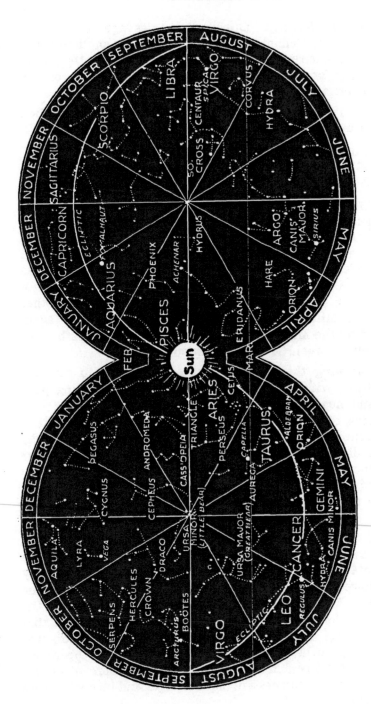

80. *Astrological chart showing position of the constellations of the zodiac on March 21st, at the beginning of the Pisces Age.*

growth, and fertility. During the Aries age, these were Aries, Taurus, Gemini, Cancer, Leo, and Virgo. The 6 unfavorable signs represented the cold, wet months, the period of sterility and death, when the sun was south of the equator or, allegorically, in the Underworld.

The 12 signs were assigned to the 3 gods Anu, Bel, and Ea in this order:

Anu ruled over Taurus, Gemini, Cancer and Leo.
Bel   "   "   Virgo, Libra, Scorpio and Sagittarius.
Ea   "   "   Capricorn, Aquarius, Pisces and Aries.

The last 4 constellations, lying between Sagittarius and the Pleiades and forming the path of Ea, are what are called in Job 9:9 the "chambers of the south". Along this path of Ea lay, according to Babylonian symbolism, the entrance to the Underworld; hence the constellation Sagittarius was called "Ka-sil" (opening of the earth). Where the path of Ea begins (between Sagittarius and Capricorn) another path, the Milky Way, intersects the ecliptic. It is again crossed by the Milky Way at the point where the path ends, precisely between Gemini and Orion.

Following the ancient practice of seeking to combine everything with its opposite, to form pairs possessing positive and negative, or male and female qualities, the first six signs of the zodiac were considered male, and the 6 unfavorable signs, female. The sign of the Balance (Libra) is the dividing point between the favorable and unfavorable months. In the Babylonian religion, Libra was the time of a solemn feast marking the period when the souls of the dead were weighed in the balance.

In the system of Ptolemy, A.D. 139-161, the same thought was carried out in a slightly different way. In the latter system, the odd numbered signs were male and the alternate or even numbered signs were female, "as the day is followed by night and as the male is coupled with the female". Astrology contains many such differences in the interpretation of signs, and it should be remembered that the meaning attributed to any celestial phenomenon was not decided in a scientific manner but was the theoretical product of many different minds. The development of this art took many centuries and such changes and inconsistencies were natural.

Four regions of the earth were distinguished: East, West, North, and South. The rising of the bright star Aldebran, in the constellation Taurus, at the spring equinox, marked the East; Antares, rising in the autumn, marked the West; Regulus, rising in the summer, marked the North; Fomalhaut, rising in the winter, marked the South.

The habitable world was also divided to correspond with the divisions of the heavens. The earth was divided into 7 zones and sometimes into 4 triangles. Each of these triangles was under the influence of 3 zodiacal houses, according to location. Each triangle was divided into 2 parts, an outer and an inner. The outer part was near the limits of the habitable world, while the inner part was near the point of intersection of the diagonals, with Babylon placed in the center as the "navel of the universe".

Sometimes the inner part of the triangle stood under the influence of the opposite triangle. The houses were also united to form geometrical figures such as triangles, rectangles, and hexagons, the first and last figures being good signs, whereas rectangles were unfavorable.

In the Babylonian system each house of the zodiac was assigned to a planet, the sign of Cancer being related to the moon, Leo to the sun, Gemini and Virgo to Venus, Aries and Scorpio to Mars, and Aquarius to Saturn. In each case, the presiding planet was the Lord of the mansion. Furthermore, the sun, Jupiter, and Saturn were associated with the day: the moon, Mars, and Venus with the night; Mercury was associated with both day and night. The sun, Jupiter, and Mars were male: the moon and Venus were female, and Mercury might be of either sex.

The signficance of the planets changed as their latitude increased or decreased. Their influence depended also upon their position relative to each other. Moreover, the astrological significance of each planet was determined by its intensity, speed, heliacal rising and setting, the house of the zodiac in which it rose and set, its position in the constellation, and its proximity to the other planets.

Of the fixed stars, those comprising the constellations of the zodiac were of the greatest importance because it was in them that the sun and planets always rose and set. Other stars, however, were not without significance. The most important positions were the rising, culmination, setting, and the lowest points of the various houses. The heliacal rising was especially important because it aided astrologers in dividing time into uniform periods.[3]

The zodiac signs were further designated according to their assumed resemblance to the 4 elements, earth, air, fire and water. Taurus, Virgo and Capricorn were cold, heavy, and dry signs; Cancer, Scorpio and Pisces were moist, soft, and cold; Aries, Leo and Sagittarius were hot, dry, vehement signs; Gemini, Libra, and Aquarius were light, moist, and hot.

Planets were called "lu-bat" (wandering sheep) or "revealers" and "disposers". Seven "mashu" stars north and south of the ecliptic had "lu" written before them to indicate that they were shepherds guarding the planets lest they wander too far north or south.

Because of their small orbits, Mercury and Venus always appear near the sun, being visible shortly before sunrise or shortly after sunset. Their appearance close together, like a family, caused them to be termed, father, mother and son. Because Mercury and Venus appeared both as evening and morning stars, they might be regarded as good or evil influences.

The three outer planets, Mars, Jupiter, and Saturn formed another triad and appeared to the observer as less under control of the sun than Mercury, Venus, or the moon. Jupiter, in the middle, was kind. The sun, being the giver of life and light, was likewise good; it followed that Mars and Saturn were evil. Mars, with his turbulent, short period of revolution, was the youthful demon, while the slowly revolving Saturn was pictured as the hoary-headed begetter of evil.

Despite his evil aspect, Saturn, or Bel, was regarded as the highest and most distant planet and was the most honored. It was the chief revealer. Saturn was also considered the bellwether sheep among the planets because it appeared to move slowly and steadily. Because of its contrast in speed with Mercury, the two were associated so that Saturn could receive the epithet which properly belonged to Mercury. Mercury was also called the "messenger" because of its rapid movement.

3—A star visible for a few minutes shortly after sunset may disappear then reappear 24 or 30 days later as a morning star. Its disappearance in the west was termed its heliacal setting and its rising in the east was its heliacal rising.

Jupiter was believed to be a good omen when it darkened other planets, but evil if it were darkened. When it appeared in the sky its earthly city, Babylon, might expect prosperity.

Aries was regarded as the leader ram because, in the age when the priests of Babylon were creating the system, it rose heliacally at the beginning of the year.

It was believed that mock suns, which are visible under certain atmospheric conditions, indicated by their number how many days of rain were to follow.

Halos of the sun were relatively unimportant, but a halo of the moon indicated that she was shepherding the stars, and the number of stars within the circle was carefully noted. It was also important to note whether the ring was light or dark, continuous or broken and, if broken, on which side the break appeared.

When a planet entered into a zodiacal sign, the conjunction was considered as marriage, adultery or incest. When it vanished below the horizon and rose again to the meridian, it was thought of as having died, risen again, and been carried to heaven.

Because of its rapid change of position and appearance, the moon was generally considered of prime importance and took precedence over the sun, even in texts which were not astrological.

The moon was likened to a tablet on which the gods wrote their decrees, thus revealing the essence of astrological knowledge. In the Annals of King Assurbanipal, a priest is represented as reading the decrees which have been written on the disk of the moon.

The waxing, waning, and the first and last appearances of the moon were very important; likewise the 7th day of the moon. The priest, Gudea, gives the 7th day as one of rest. No one was struck with a whip; the mother did not chastise her child; the householder, overseer, and the laborer ceased to work; the dead were not buried; the courts were closed; physicians did not treat the sick; it was inappropriate to make a wish; the "Kaba" played no psalm; wailing women sang no dirges.

The 28th day of the moon was a day of lamentation, marking the passing of the old moon into the power of the dragon. The full moon normally appears on the 14th day but texts permitted a margin of 5 days (from the 12th to 16th day) for its appearance. An abnormal appearance was an evil sign. Positions of the stars in relation to the moon were sources of omens. Being on the left side of the moon was regarded as unfavorable.

Eclipses of the sun, the moon, and the planets visible during eclipses of the moon were significant. The extent of the eclipse was important, as well as the part of the moon's face covered by the shadow and the direction in which the shadow disappeared. An eclipse was regarded as a sign that the eclipsed body was being swallowed by a dragon and special prayers were prepared to be recited while the shadow crossed the face of the moon or the sun.

Thunder was the voice of Adad, the god of storms, whose influences were either good or evil, because some rain is necessary for the growth of crops, but too much is destructive of life and property. The significance of thunder depended also on whether it was accompanied by rain. If heard in the month Ab, it portended both good and evil. A thunder storm, in the month Tisri, without a rainbow, was an evil sign. Lightning in a cloudless sky foretold a flood.

Meteors and comets rarely appear, therefore but few omens were attributed to them but their appearance was generally interpreted as an evil omen.

As the Greeks developed astrology, all the known sciences were brought under its influence—botany, chemistry, zoology, mineralogy, anatomy, and medicine.

Colors, metals, plants, drugs, and animal life of all kinds were brought into relationship with the planets. In the system of Ptolemy, the planet Saturn was associated with gray, Jupiter with white, Mars with red, and Venus with yellow; while the color of Mercury varied with circumstances because of its changeable character.

Of metals, the sun was associated with gold, the moon with silver, Jupiter with electrum, Saturn with lead, Venus with copper, and Mercury was associated with quicksilver because of its changeable character as a liquid or solid.

In casting individual horoscopes, the signs of the zodiac were assigned spaces in a square divided into 12 parts (Plate 81) and representing the following values:

1st house	Aries	— life, owner of the horoscope.
2nd "	Taurus	— wife or husband, riches; also poverty.
3rd "	Gemini	— brothers.
4th "	Cancer	— parents, ancestors.
5th "	Leo	— children.
6th "	Virgo	— health, service, or, by another interpretation, pain.
7th "	Libra	— marriage.
8th "	Scorpio	— death.
9th "	Sagittarius	— religion.
10th "	Capricorn	— dignities and offices.
11th "	Aquarius	— friendship.
12th "	Pisces	— enmity.

Spaces 8, 9, 10, 11, and 12 in the horoscope chart are in the upper world, the boundaries of which form the Egyptian hieroglyph for the sky, shown in Plate 82, Figs. 1 and 4. The earth is represented by the same figure inverted. (Fig. 3).

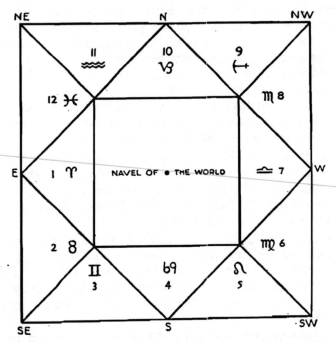

81. *Ancient horoscope chart as a map of the world, giving positions of the signs of the zodiac.*

NE, NW, SE and SW represent the 4 pillars upon which the heavens are supported. From this basic figure also was derived the alchemist's symbols of fire, air, earth, and water, and the directions north, south, east and west.

Each of the planets was associated with a different part of the body. Various schools of astrology had conflicting theories regarding the functions of the organs in men and animals. Later, the signs of the zodiac came to be associated with organs of the body and the constellations of the zodiac became as important as the planets in determining individual horoscopes.

The zodiac was regarded as the prototype of the human body, the divisions of the zodiac corresponding to 12 divisions and 36 subdivisions of the body, each of which was under the influence of a planet. The 1st was the head; 2nd neck; 3rd shoulders and arms; 4th heart; 5th flanks; 6th bladder; 7th buttocks; 8th pubis; 9th thighs; 10th knees; 11th legs; 12th feet. The influence of a planet upon an individual was contingent, not merely upon the planet which happened to rise at the time of his birth or conception, but also upon the relationship between the place of birth and the position of the planet and between parts of the body and certain signs in the zodiac. Venus ruled over the genital organs; Mars presided over the bile, blood, and kidneys; Mercury's domain was the liver. In other systems the liver was controlled by Jupiter or Venus. Many diseases and disturbances were attributed to the influences of the planets or as due to conditions observed in a constellation or in a star's position.

According to Manlius, in the poem *Astronomicals,* written 2,000 years ago, the sun presided over the head, Mars over the right arm, Venus over the left arm, Jupiter over the stomach, Mars the parts below; Mercury ruled over the right leg and Saturn over the left.

Albert the Great (1206-1280 A.D.), assigned rule to the stars as follows: Saturn over science, buildings and life changes; Jupiter over honors, riches, and cleanliness; Mars over war, prisons, marriages, hatreds; Mercury over debts, commerce, etc.; the moon over wounds, dreams, larcenies.

In one system, the days of the week governed by the different planets were: Sunday by the sun; Monday by the moon; Tuesday Mars; Wednesday Mercury; Thursday Jupi-

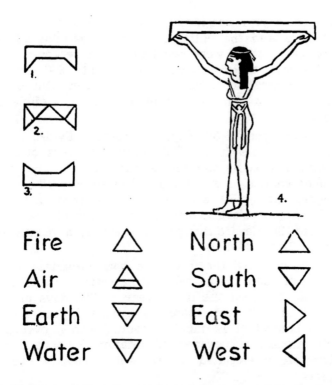

82. *The upper half of the astrological chart, adopted by the Egyptians as a hieroglyph for the sky, or upper world. The figure at the right illustrates the use of this symbol. The lower half of the chart was used as a hieroglyph for the earth, or underworld.*

ter; Friday Venus; Saturday Saturn. In another system Sunday was ruled by the sun; Monday by the moon; Tuesday by Jupiter; Wednesday by Mars; Thursday by Mercury; Friday by Venus; Saturday by Saturn.

Divisions of Time

The day was divided into 12 double hours, each hour representing the time which the sun spent daily in each sign of the zodiac. The nychthemeris (day-night period) was further divided into 6 watches; 3 for the day, 3 for the night. The passage of the sun through the signs of the zodiac, beginning with its position at the beginning of spring, suggested the division of time into years. The spring and autumn equinoxes and the summer and winter solstices further divided the year into 4 seasons.

The solar year was incorrectly calculated as consisting of 360 days and the entire calendrical, astrological, and astronomical systems were based upon this reckoning. The zodiacal circle, therefore, was divided into 360 parts or degrees, 1 degree for each day of the year. Out of this theory developed also the custom of dividing a circle into 360 degrees.

The solar year of 360 days was further divided into 36 decans of 10 days each and 72 dodecans, or weeks, of 5 days each, with a separate star representing each 5 day period. Sometimes each sign was further divided into 12 parts of 2½ degrees each, with a planet presiding over each small part. In the astrological texts it was assumed that every month had 30 days although, in practice, a month may have been 29 or 30 days.

As the sun and the moon are both important factors in the life of man, it was believed necessary to establish a relationship between the moon year of 354 days and the solar year of 360 days; therefore a normal year was declared to consist of 12 months, each presided over by a god. But a solar year exceeds 12 lunations by several days, therefore an intercalated month was necessary every 2 or 3 years.

The 360-day year became so firmly established that, for centuries after the true length of the year became known, a calendar period of 12 30-day months was employed, with 5 extra or intercalary days inserted in order to keep the seasons from gradually receding. In Egypt these 5 extra days were religious holidays for the gods Osiris, Horus, Set, Isis, and Nephthys. In Babylonia an extra month was added every 6 years and named for the Raven. This month was so named because, being an extra month, it was considered an omen of bad luck. Sometimes the 13-month year was called the female year.

Precession of the Equinoxes

As the earth revolves around the sun, it wavers very slightly on its axis like a rapidly spinning top. Therefore, if a line were drawn through its axis from pole to pole and projected toward the heavens, it would not point forever toward the North Star. Because of the earth's wobbly motion the line thus projected would in the course of about 25,800 years describe a circle in the heavens.

As a result of this motion, each year the earth's equator cuts the ecliptic 50.25 degrees westward of the point where it intersected it the previous year. This slight eccentricity of the earth caused no end of trouble and confusion to early astronomers, astrologers, and calendar makers; and even makes difficult the calculations of present day astronomers.

Another way of describing this action is to say that just before the earth has completed a circuit of the sun, it will have reached the starting point in its orbit as regards the stars. In other words, the sidereal or star year on which our calendar is based is shorter than the real solar year defined by a complete circling of the sun by the earth. The difference is 1/25,800th part of a year or 20 min. 23 sec.

Slowly the equinoctial point falls back so that in about 3 years a whole hour is lost; in 71 years, 8 or 9 months, the loss amounts to a whole day. In 25,800 years an entire year is lost, the earth revolving about the sun but 25,799 times in 25,800 years.

To the astrologer, this means the sun does not appear in the exact position relative to the zodiac year after year, but passes slowly through the zodiac, its rate of passage being about 50" 9¾"' each year: 1 degree in 71+ years: 5 degrees or days in 360 years: 30 degrees, or one whole zodiac sign, in 2,152 or 2,153 years and in about 25,800 years the sun will have passed through the full 360 degrees of the great zodiacal circle. Ancient astronomers erroneously calculated the length of time required for the sun to pass through a zodiac sign as 2,160 years, or 25,920 years for the 12 signs.

According to calculations of the astronomer Cassini, the sun rose in the 5th degree of Pisces at the beginning of the Christian era. Allowing 2,160 years for the sun's passage through a zodiac sign, this would place the entrance of the sun into the sign of Taurus about 4,680 B.C. and Aries about 2,520 B.C. In the early centuries of Christianity the Church decided to ignore the Precession of the Equinoxes; therefore, most calendars still show the sun in Aries although it passed out of that sign many centuries ago and is now entering Aquarius.

The antiquity of astrology and the common origin of the ancient religious systems is indicated by the fact that the bull (Taurus) was associated with practically every ancient religion, either as an object of worship or as a sacrificial offering to the gods. During the age when the spring sun rose in Taurus the sun gods were almost uniformly portrayed in sculpture as having the head or horns of a bull, or as being identified with the bull. After the sun passed into the sign of Aries many of the figures became ram-headed.

According to Indian tradition, a great religious war occurred about the time of the change from the Taurus to the Aries period. It appears that when the Ram was elevated to the position previously held by the Bull, for reasons which were understood by the priests only, the populace became divided in their allegiance and cruel civil war ensued.

As the portion of the heavens occupied by each zodiacal constellation was not sharply defined by ancient astronomers, estimates of the exact date of the sun's entry into the Taurus, Aries or Pisces signs might easily vary by several hundred years. Some estimates of the beginning of the Pisces Age have even placed it approximately as late as the opening of the Christian era. At that time the ancient tradition which associated the births and deaths of gods with the signs of the zodiac still prevailed; and certain writers have seen reason to suspect an attempt by early Christian mystics to make the life of Jesus harmonize with the astrological tradition.

The coming Messiah is called, in the Talmud, Dag, the fish, who was reborn of the fish goddess Atergatis. It has been pointed out that the story of the life of Jesus from childhood onward repeatedly calls attention to incidents relating to fish and fishermen as if the incidents had an inner arcane significance. During the first four centuries, Christians were called Pisiculi or Little Fishes and Jesus was called the Big Fish. Representations symbolizing Jesus as a fish appeared on religious and household objects, also on the walls of the Roman catacombs. In the second century Clement urged Christians to have a fish engraved upon their seals to distinguish themselves from the pagans.

CHAPTER XIX

AGES OF THE GODS

HAD THE ANCIENT ASTROLOGERS returned to earth early in the year 1940, they would have seen heavenly spectacles of tremendous interest. On February 18th there was a triple conjunction of Mars, Saturn, and the crescent moon. Two days later there was a conjunction of Venus and Jupiter. Then, for about a week, beginning February 28th, there appeared a phenomenon so rare that its like had not been reported since astronomers began to keep records of celestial phenomena.

Half an hour after sunset the 5 planets Mercury, Jupiter, Venus, Saturn and Mars could be seen in the southwestern sky, forming an almost straight line, rising at an angle of about 30 degrees from the vertical and extending from the horizon toward the zenith like a Jacob's ladder.

The simultaneous appearance of several planets in the same part of the heavens is a very rare sight. There are only 2 instances in history in which all of the planets known to the ancients are said to have appeared in the same region in the heavens at the same time. The first is merely a calculation by the astronomer Bailly that a conjunction of the 5 planets took place February 18th, 3102 B.C., exactly 5042 years before the beautiful spectacle of 1940. This, according to Hindu tradition, was the date of the Flood and the beginning of their present Kali yuga, or Grand Period.

The second appearance of such a spectacle is reported in *The Annals of the Bamboo Books* as having occurred in the Chinese constellation called Yin Shih, during the reign of Emperor Tsuan Hsu, 2,513 B.C.

During the many centuries in which all events were interpreted by astrology, the tradition prevailed that the appearance of any unusual phenomenon in the sky was evidence of a great stirring among the gods, and an omen of important events to come. The births of illustrious men were heralded by the appearance of "signs and wonders" in the heavens. On the other hand, the deaths of great men were marked by thunder, lightning, heavings of the earth, comets, eclipses of the sun or moon, and many other phenomena. Shortly before the time assigned for the birth of Christ there was a conjunction of the moon and the planets Jupiter and Saturn, and there is a legend that Magi were guided to the infant's birthplace by a strange star.

It seems to have been believed almost universally that the total destruction of the world would be marked by a conjunction of the sun, moon, and all the planets, the theory being that in the beginning of the world, the sun, moon, and planets stood in conjunction at the initial point of the zodiac and would return to the same point at the end of the age.

As the theory was understood by the Babylonian priest Berossus, destruction of the world would come by fire when all of the planets stood in a direct line in the zodiacal sign of Cancer (a fiery sign). If this event took place in the sign of Capricorn (a watery sign), the world would be destroyed by water. (In 1940, the planets were grouped in Pisces, also a watery sign.) The Babylonian belief has been found in Egypt, Persia, India, China, Mexico, and among the tribes of South America. It was in Babylonia that the Jews are believed to have received the legend that the world would be destroyed once by fire and once by water. According to the allegorical treatment of mythology, the Flood occurred in the watery sign of Aquarius at the winter solstice point. This would place the event about 3,100 or 3,200 B.C.

If, according to the ancient astrologers, eclipses of the sun or moon foretold fearful events on earth, what great catastrophe would the singular phenomenon of 1940 have foretold to the mystic star gazer? Would it have been considered an omen that the world would be consumed by fire in the great war that has recently engulfed the whole earth? Would it have been an augury of the rise of a great destroyer-dictator?

It has been shown that astrology was based upon the belief that all life and activity on earth are determined by the movements, conjunctions, and other aspects of the sun, moon, and stars and, as these phenomena were known to recur in regular cycles or periods, the events on earth which these phenomena caused were also believed to be repeated in cycles.

The seasonal changes upon earth from summer to winter, with their repeating periods of growth and decay, were believed to have their parallels in the celestial days,

Courtesy of American Museum of Natural History

83. Ladder of planets as they appeared soon after sundown,
February 28th, 1940. Reading downward they are Mars,
Saturn, Venus, Jupiter and Mercury.

weeks, months, years and ages of the gods. Therefore, it was believed that a knowledge of the celestial cycles would not only reveal future events on earth, but would, likewise, reveal the birth, death and rebirth of the gods and the beginning and end of the universe itself. The determination of these cycles then became a matter of deep interest to astrologers, priests, and philosophers. Every country had legends regarding the duration of the world.

In some cases the beginning of the world was represented as a period of pristine purity, a Golden Age, in which man lived in a state of perfection, with the world becoming increasingly degenerate as time passed. The "fall" of Adam and Eve is a variation of the Golden Age myth. Other theories gave a more hopeful picture; the beginning of the world was represented as a period of darkness, disease, and anarchy, with man eternally struggling upward toward perfection.

The Brahmans in India divided the supposed duration of the world into 4 great time cycles, or Ages of the Gods, as follows:

Krita yuga	1,728,000	years
Trita yuga	1,296,000	"
Dvapara yuga	864,000	"
Kali yuga	432,000	"
	4,320,000	" = 1 Maha yuga.

The unit whereby yugas are calculated is 1200 years of the gods, each of which consists of 360 solar years, or 72 periods of 6,000 each, making a total of 432,000 years. One thousand Maha yugas make a Kalpa, or Great Age, at the end of which the destruction and regeneration of the world is to take place. A Kalpa is called a day of Brahma, and his night is of equal length. Three hundred sixty of such days and nights make a year of Brahma and 100 such years constitute his life time. This longest period is called a *para*.

The Kalpa is further divided into 14 Manvantaras, each of which consists of 71+ Maha yugas. The present is the 7th Manvantara of this Kalpa, ruled over by Manu Vaivasata, who is accepted by eastern Buddhists as the outbreathing of the creative principle, the period of cosmic life which lies between 2 *prolayas*: a day of Brahma.

The first, or Krita, yuga was the Golden Age in which man lived 4,000 years; when there were no quarrels or wars; when laws were obeyed and virtue reigned. As time progressed, the Ages became shorter and the state of the world grew increasingly worse, with the Kali or present age representing the complete degradation of man and the coming end of the world. The Kali yuga began February 18th, 3102, B.C.

According to another reckoning, the 4 Ages are supposed to be in the proportion of 4, 3, 2 and 1:

Krita yuga or Age of Gold	24,000 years.
Trita " " " " Silver	18,000 "
Dvapara " " " " Brass	12,000 "
Kali " " " " Iron	6,000 "
	60,000 years.

Each period of regeneration is marked by the coming of an Avatar[1] or Savior. The best known Avatars are those of Vishnu, which are said to be countless.

Berossus, following an older Babylonian system, sought to make history harmonize with it by predicating

466 Seroi (3,600) 4 Neroi (600) = 1,680,000 years of Creation

120   "   432,000   "   of Antediluvian time (10 periods).

10   "   36,000 years of Post-Diluvian time (from the Flood to Alexander the Great).

3   "   2 Neroi   =   12,000 years to the end of days,

1—Avatar: a Sanscrit word meaning "descent", especially used in Hindu mythology to indicate incarnation of a deity visiting the earth for any purpose. The 10 best known Avatars of Vishnu are: 1 fish; 2 tortoise; 3 hog; 4 half man and half lion; 5 dwarf; 6 Rama; 7 Rama; 8 Krishna; 9 Buddha. The 10th is to come and will be in the form of a white winged horse (Kalki) who will destroy the world.

making a total of 2,160,000 years for the duration of the world.[2] .Each cycle is thus a *ner* of Seroi: 600 x 3,600 = 2,160,000 years. This period is equal to 60 x 36,000 years or 9 x 240,000. Of this time, creation lasts 7 x 240,000 years or 7 days of cosmic time. The 2,160,000 year period is a sixth of the important Babylonian number 12,960,000 which is 60 x 60 x 60 x 60. According to another theory, the Babylonians reckoned the period as 144 Saros or 518,400 years.

The 10 kings of Babylon who ruled before the Flood, according to Berossus, are

Alor	10 saros	36,000	years.
Alasper	3 "	10,800	"
Amelon	13 "	46,800	"
Aminon	12 "	43,200	"
Matalan	18 "	64,800	"
Daon	10 "	36,000	"
Evidorach	18 "	64,800	"
Amphis	10 "	36,000	"
Otiartis	8 "	28,800	"
Xisusthrus	18 "	64,800	"
	120 "	432,000	years.

Babylonian influence may be seen in the time which Jewish tradition gives for the period from Creation to the Flood. Xisusthrus, the 10th patriarch, is the Noah of Babylonian mythology as Noah is the 10th patriarch of the Bible. The Jewish tradition of 1,656 years for the 10 patriarchs from Creation to the Flood is equal to 72 periods of 23 years, each period consisting of 1200 weeks, or 8400 days (365.24 x 23 = 8400). In other words, the Babylonians calculated the time from Creation to the Flood as 72 x 6,000 years, whereas the Jews calculated it as 72 times 1200 weeks. It should be noted, however, that the Jewish calculation is based upon the true length of the year, or 365.24 days. This period was certainly not known to the Jews during the sixth or seventh century B.C., when

2—From the Flood to the first Babylonian dynasty, the time was reckoned at 34,800 or 33,091 years, which would make a period of 36,000 years from the Flood to the reign of Alexander the Great.

their records are said to have been put into written form. If it was the basis for the calculation, it is either proof that the Jewish period of 1656 years is a late invention of the Bible compilers or an exceedingly strange coincidence. Another Jewish tradition gives 974 generations before Adam and 26 generations from Adam to Moses, making 1000 generations in all. (Shab. 88b. Hag. 13b, 14a).

Comparison of the divine Ages of the Gods with the accompanying table for reckoning earth time will show that the great Ages of the Gods are enormously enlarged counterparts of the seconds, minutes, hours, days, etc. of mundane time, the whole system constituting a series of cycles within cycles. For example: 72 years equal 25,920 days and 25,920 years is the time given for the equinoctial cycle. Three hundred sixty years equal 129,600 days or 4,320 months, both figures having important places in calculations of the equinoctial precession.

CIRCULAR MEASURE

60 seconds	=	1 minute
60 minutes	=	1 degree
30 degrees	=	1 sign
360 degrees	=	circumference or circle
1 Decan	=	10 days
1 Dodecan	=	5 days
72 "	=	360 days

MUNDANE TIME

Days	Hours	Minutes	Seconds
	1	60	3,600
	6	360	21,600
	12	720	43,200
1	24	1,440	86,400
3	72	4,320	259,200
30	720	43,200	2,592,200
50	1,200	72,000	4,320,000
60	1,440	86,400	5,184,000
360	8,640	518,400	31,104,000

YEARS OF 360 DAYS

Years	Months	Days
3	36	1,080
4	48	1,440
5	60	1,800
6	72	2,160
7	84	2,520*
12	144	4,320
18	216	6,480
24	288	8,640
30	360	10,800
36	432	12,960
40	480	14,400
60	720	21,600
70	840	25,200
72	864	25,920
100	1,200	36,000
120	1,440	43,200
144	1,728	51,800
180	2,160	64,800
360	4,320	129,600
600	7,200	216,000
1,200	14,400	432,000
1,800	21,600	648,000
2,160	25,920	777,600
3,600	43,200	1,296,000
6,000	72,000	2,160,000
7,200	86,400	2,592,000
12,000	144,000	4,320,000
21,600	259,200	7,776,000
36,000	432,000	12,960,000
43,200	518,400	15,552,000

*2520 is the smallest number that can be divided by every number from 1 to 9. 25,920, the number of years in a precessional cycle, can be divided by every number except 7.

NUMBER OF DAYS IN 27-DAY MONTH PERIODS

2 months	—	54 days
3 "	—	81 "
4 "	—	104 "
8 "	—	216 "
12 "	—	324 "
16 "	—	432 "
4 years	—	1,296 "
8 "	—	2,592 "
40 "	— 12,960 "
80 "	— 25,920 "

Another important version of the Ages of the Gods is given in the Indo-Persian system of Zoroaster and appears to be based on the widespread tradition that the world was made in 6 days or ages. It gives 6,000 years for creation of the world and another 6,000 for its duration, after which the world is to be destroyed and a new cycle begun. The period of creation consists of

1st	1000 years	—	Creation of the sky.
2nd	1000 "	—	"	"	"	water.
3rd	1000 "	—	"	"	"	earth.
4th	1000 "	—	"	"	"	planets.
5th	1000 "	—	"	"	"	animals.
6th	1000 "	—	"	"	"	man.

The first 3,000 years of the creative period constituted a spiritual age in which creatures were unthinking, unmoving, intangible. The second 3,000 years were the age of Gayomart, the primeval man and the primeval ox. The creative period began with the sun in the zodiac sign of Cancer and continued through Leo and Virgo.

The second 6,000 years covers the history of the human race, beginning with the creation of Mashya and Mashyoi, the first man and woman, the period being divided into 2 lesser periods of 3,000 years each. The advent of Zoroaster on earth comes 30 years before the end of the first 3,000 years and he is followed by 3 virgin-born saviors, each of whom rules for 1,000 years to the end of the world. This period opens with the sun in Libra and extends through Scorpio and Sagittarius, agreeing in this respect with the Babylonian legend that the end of the world will come when the sign of Capricorn is reached.

Like the 4 Ages of the Brahmans, the Zoroastrian 12,000 year period is divided into the Four Metals, or Four Ages of Gold, Silver, Steel and Iron.[3] After the first 3,000 years a conflict breaks out between Ahura Mazda, the Prince of Light, and Ahriman, the Prince of Darkness; and the struggle continues for 9,000 years. During the first 3,000 years the contest goes in favor of Ahura: in the second they are on equal terms, and in the final 3,000 years Ahriman is vanquished. The time preceding the coming of the 3 saviors is a period of deterioration marked by misery and impiety, but the closing period is described as an advance toward the glorious consummation.

In the last millenium, only those die who are smitten with weapons or reach old age. When 53 years of the millenium still remain, the sweetness and nutrition of milk and vegetables become so perfect that, on account of the freedom of men from desire for meat, they will stop eating it and their food will become milk and vegetables. When 3 years of the period remain people will even stop drinking milk and their food and drink will become vegetables and water. The milk of one cow will be enough for 1,000 men. At the end of the 12,000 years comes the dissolution and regeneration of the world under the savior Saoshyant.

The Aztecs of Mexico also divided creation into 4 ages. They believed that the present era was preceded by 4 ages or suns; the sun of the earth, sun of the fire, sun of the air, and sun of the water, each age being terminated by a terrible catastrophe. They looked forward with dread to the end of the present era. It is related by Lord Kingsborough (*Mexico,* vol. 6), that when the Spaniards arrived in Mexico the natives became panic stricken when they saw the commander riding a horse, because they had a tradition that the end of the world would be heralded by the appearance of a strange white animal. This tradition appears to coincide remarkably with the Brahman belief that the end of the world will be brought about by Kalki in the form of a white horse.

The manner in which the Persian dogma of the world's destruction and renewal passed to the western nations and became a pillar of Christian faith demonstrates the far reaching influence sometimes produced by ideas which, at

---

3—See APPENDIX: Zoroastrianism.

the time of their inception, appear to be but of minor or, at least, local importance.

Attention has already been called (p. 91) to the great changes in the Jewish religious structure which were brought about through enforced contact with Persians and Babylonians during the Exile. Under these influences Jewish thoughts turned, after the Exile, to the belief in a coming destruction and judgment of the world. The first reference to this dogma appears in a prophecy attributed to Isaiah (26:19,21), which dates, according to Cheyne, from about 334 B.C. From that time onward the coming end of the world became the dominant thought of almost every Post-Exilic prophet and apocalyptic writer.[4]

Daniel's Four Metals and Four Beasts seem to have been based upon the Oriental conception of the Four Ages of the Gods. II Esdras 14:11 divided the duration of the world into 12 parts, 10 of which had already passed.[5] Rabbi Kalina (Sanh. 97a) believed that the world will last six milleniums and be destroyed in the seventh: 2000 years are a period of chaos; 2000 years cover the reign of the Law, and 2000 years are to be ruled by the Messiah.

The *Assumption of Moses* stated the aeon to be 5,000 years. "A day of God is 1,000 years" said the *Book of Jubilees*.[6] *Apocryphal Barnabas*[7] prophesied that in 6,000 years all things would come to an end: "a day is as 1,000 years", said Barnabas.

Rabbi Akiba's *Alphabet of Letters* said the end of the world will come in 6,000 years, with a resurrection to follow.

The *Slavonic Book of Enoch*[8] said: "Let the days be after the fashion of 7,000", while the *Ethiopic Book of Enoch*[9] gave a day of judgment and destruction at the end of 10 periods or "weeks", 7 of which had passed. The 8th was to be an era of universal righteousness when the saints

---

4—"that day" *Zec.* 14:9, "the day of judgment" *Mal.* 4:3, "the great day" *Mal.* 4:5, "the day of vengeance" *Jer.* 46:10, "the day of the kings" *Dan.* 12:2, God's "day is 1000 years" *Lev.* Rab. 19, *Sanh.* 19, and *Psalm* 90:4.

5—"Then the Highest looked at his times . . . lo, they were at an end and his aeons were full. . . . now the earth will be refreshed and return. . . . and trust in the mercy and judgment of the creator". IV *Esdras* 11:44,46.

6—*Book of Jubilees*, Robt. H. Charles, Ch. 23:26, 27.

7—*Apocryphal Barnabas*, Ch. 13:4, 5.

8—*Slavonic Book of Enoch*, Morfil & Charles, Ch. 33; 1, 2.

9—*Ethiopic Book of Enoch*, Robt. H. Charles, Ch. 91, 93.

would reign. The 9th was to open with judgment and the former heaven and hell were to pass away and be succeeded by a new heaven which would be peopled by the righteous dead after their resurrection. Heaven and hell would be transformed and the mountain of God's throne would be set in the south.

That the end of the world was thought to be imminent at the beginning of the Christian era is, of course, known to everybody. Much of the early success of Christianity was due to the belief that Christ would soon return in a second divinity and would reign for 1000 years.[10] The New Testament presents Christ as frequently urging his followers to prepare for the coming day of judgment, and the authors of the Gospels often refer to "latter days", "last times", and the end of the world.[11]

Irenaeus believed that, as the work of creation lasted 6 days, the world would last 6,000 years and be followed by 1,000 years of rest, corresponding to the Sabbath after creation. St. Augustine believed that 5 periods had passed and the world was then passing through the 6th, with the end of all things to come in the 7th. Bede (d. 725), in his *Chronicles,* adopted the 7 ages and predicted that the last one, ending with the year 1000, would mark the end of the world.

About 800 B.C., Hesiod placed the Deluge in the second stage of the world and his own life in the fifth, or iron age. Juvenal said, about 100 years after Christ, that the iron age was about to end at that time. In the time of Augustus, Virgil wrote: "The last age of the world (the 7th millenium) is approaching and a new generation will arise out of the elevated heaven. Be thou chaste, Lucina, O be propitious to the coming child with whose advent the iron age will close".

The ancient books known as the *Sibylline Oracles* contained prophecies that the age of the world will be divided into 10 generations, after which a Savior will come. The 8 books are not in accord as to when the 10 generations of the world began; 7 of them make the first generation begin

---

10—II *Peter* 3:13; *Rev.* 20:2,7.

11—*Matt.* 23:36; 24:34; 28:20; *Mark* 13:30; 14:62; *Luke* 11:32; *John* 5:28; *Acts* 2:17; *I Thess.* 3:13; 4:15, 16, 17; *II Thess.* 1:9, 10; 2:2; *James* 5:8, 9; *I Peter* 1:5, 20; 4:7, 17; *II Peter* 3:8; *I John* 2:18, 28; *Rom.* 16:20; *I Cor.* 7:29; 10:11; *Phil.* 4:5; *Heb.* 9:26, 28; *I Tim.* 6:14; *Rev.* 20:2 to 7.

with the Flood, while only one of them makes it begin with Adam.

In the early Christian centuries, the Sibyls were highly venerated by the Roman Church, being quoted in the *Apostolic Constitution* and by many leaders of the Church. Michaelangelo was commissioned to portray the 8 Sibyls for posterity, and his great paintings still adorn the ceiling of the Sistine Chapel, although the failure of the predicted events to materialize in the passing centuries has caused the Oracles to become discredited. Long ago the Church ceased all reference to the Sibyls and many modern Romanists agree with the contention of Protestant scholars that they are forgeries.

Plato said the oracle in Delphi prophesied the birth of a son of Apollo who was to restore peace and justice to the earth. The prediction in the Sibyls of a coming Messiah may have been derived from the same prophecy.

Bernard, a hermit of Thuringia, and many preachers of the tenth century made allegorical interpretations of the Apocalypse upon which they predicted the coming of Anti-Christ and the end of the world.

According to an old Roman tradition, about 600 years after the founding of the city, the populace was seized with a great fear that the *saeculum* was drawing to a close. A similar state of mind prevailed in Europe as the year 1200 A.D. approached. Imminent realization was anticipated of the prophecy in the Gospel of John[12] that one would come to complete the mission of Christ, and a frantic desire to force the Mohammedans out of Jerusalem before the coming of the Savior was one of the motives which inspired the great Crusades of that time. The immediate coming of the Savior was predicted in the twelfth century by Joachim, Abbot of Curacio, in Calabria, a famous interpreter of prophecy. St. Bernard made similar predictions.

Mohammedans insist that the Gospels originally named Mohamed as the Paraclete who is to come, but that his name was expunged from the manuscripts, therefore, he is rightly the 10th or final Savior, the one who is to come to restore peace and justice to the world.

Various other teachers of religious doctrines were believed by their followers to be the Paraclete. For in-

12—*John* 14:16, 18, 26.

stance, Simon Magus, Montanus, Marcion, and Manes were so considered; and Christian leaders persecuted them for encouraging the belief that they were the Holy Ghost.

If the Ages of the Gods were of astrological origin, as is shown to be the case, it should be possible to prove that the periods given for the regeneration of the world were based upon astronomical cycles. It is time to see what evidence exists to support this conclusion.

The Oriental unit of 1200 years consisted of a day of 600 years and a night of equal length. Originally, however, these were astrological years of 360 days each, the 600 years consisting of 216,000 days (360 x 600 or 60 x 60 x 60) and forming a period which the Italian astronomer Cassini called the most perfect astronomical cycle known.

If the various ways of reckoning the ancient lunar year be compared with this solar period, it will be found that 600 solar years of 216,000 days are exactly, or almost, equal to 608, 610 or 666 lunar years, depending upon how the latter are calculated.

600 solar	yrs. of	360	days	= 216,000	days	(7200 lunar months).
*608 lunar	" "	355.264	"	= 216,000	"	
610	" " "	354	"	= 215,940	"	
610	" " "	354.1	"	= 216,001	"	
666	" " "	324	"	= 215,784	"	(7992 mos. of 27 days).
666	" 8 mos. "	324	"	= 216,000	"	(8000 " " 27 ").

*The sidereal month of 29.530589 days gives a true lunar year of 354.367068 days.

From these figures it will be seen that a very slight error in calculation would have given the ancient astrologer-priests a 608, 610 or 666-year cycle. The 608-year period was known to the Greeks, Romans, and Etruscans. It was mentioned by both Juvenal and Virgil as well as in the *Sibylline Oracles*. The Romans had cycles of 12 and 120 years, but do not seem to have had a clear knowledge of the 600-year cycles.

If a 365-day solar year is used as the basis for calculation, almost equally interesting results are obtained, viz:

600	solar	years of	365	days	= 219000	days.	
608	"	" "	360	"	= 218880	"	
650	lunar	" "	336	"	= 218400	"	(12 x 28 = 336)
676	"	" "	324	"	= 219024	"	(12 x 27 = 324)
618.6	"	" "	354	"	= 219000	"	
632	ecliptic	" "	346.5	"	= 218988	"	
633	"	" "	346	"	= 219018	"	

But the revolutions of the planets provide an even more remarkable demonstration. If we omit all fractions, as the ancients did, and reduce the revolutions of the planets to round numbers of days, not only will the cycles of the sun and moon be synchronized in periods of 216,000 days, or 600 years, but *all* the planets that were known to the ancient world will mark time together in this unique cycle.

Planets	Actual Days per Revolution	Days per Revolution in Round Nos.	Revolutions per cycle of 600 years	Total Number of Days
Mercury	88.969	90	2400	216000
Venus	224.7	225	960	216000
Earth	365.24	360	600	216000
Mars	686.979	686	315	216090
		675	320	216000
Jupiter	4332.5879 (12 yrs.)	4333	50	216650
		4320	50	216000
Saturn	10759.2010 (30 ")	10800	20	216000
Moon	29.53	27	8000	216000
		28	7714	215992
		29	7448	215992
		29.5	7322	215999
		30	7200	216000

Some of these planetary cycles were known to the Babylonians. As might be expected, the greatest variations from the correct figures occur with the planets Jupiter and Saturn because they complete their orbits but once in 12 and 30 years, respectively. The long periods of observation necessary to calculate the length of their revolutions produce greater errors. The several reckonings for the lunar periods give the most remarkable results for, regardless of the length of the month employed, they fit exactly, or nearly so, into the required period an even number of times.

If this very small toleration for error be allowed, it is easy to see how the ancient astronomers might well have reckoned that after the creator had sent the sun, moon, earth, and other planets spinning on their way, all of them would meet again in the heavens after 600 years, thus marking the end of one era and the beginning of another.

Having first calculated the periods in which the sun and moon mark time together, the next task of the astronomers was naturally that of estimating the periods in which the cycles of all the planets are harmonized, for a universal cycle, to be complete, must include all of the lesser cycles. If the minor events on earth were regulated by the conjunctions of the sun and moon, the more important events would logically coincide with conjunctions of several planets. The end of the Great Ages, bringing the destruction and renewal of the world, would come at a conjunction, or after a certain number of conjunctions, of *all* the planets.

It is generally conceded that the reckoning of zodiacal periods began with the entry of the sun into the sign of Taurus, in approximately 4800 B.C. If this date be accepted as a starting point, and an allowance be made for the coming of a Savior every 600 years, the beginning of the 9th Avatar or Messiac period would coincide with the time of Christ's birth and the 10th period would be marked by the birth of Mohammed. The 8th period would be marked by the rise, in the 6th century B.C., of Buddha in India, Confucius in China, and Zoroaster in Persia, all of whom were honored by their followers as Saviors. During the same period, King Cyrus was equally esteemed by the Jews for having freed them from captivity.

The numerous variations in the prophecies of later Jewish writers, however, and the lack of a fully developed system of Ages, make it clear that, although the Oriental belief in the regeneration of the world became widespread among the Jews, they never acquired a comprehensive knowledge of the astronomical cycles upon which the theory was based. This may be accounted for by the fact that the dogma of a future day of resurrection and judgment was not taken up seriously by the Jews until after the Exile, and by the further fact that the laws against "dividers of time" made the study of astronomy a tabooed subject for them, so that they had very little knowledge of that science. Although they found it expedient to adopt the Egyptian solar year for their civil calendar, for long periods the Jews preferred to reckon time by the reigns of their kings or leaders or from important local and national events, instead of reckoning by centuries, eras, and astronomical periods.

Traces of several systems of chronology may be found crossing each other in the Old Testament, all of which are of late origin, but none of which is employed consistently. The overlapping, contradictions, and general inconsistency in dates and periods, have made Biblical chronology extremely unreliable.[13]

The period of 4,000 years allowed by the Bible for the time from Creation to Christ has every appearance of being a symbolical figure rather than a historical one. Some writers have noted that it is equivalent to the Babylonian "world number" representing 100 generations of 40 years each or two-thirds of a 6,000 year period. The curious parallel between the time given by Babylonian annals and the Bible for the period from Creation to the Flood has already been pointed out.

Attempts have been made to fix accurately the dates of Biblical events by reference to the genealogical tables in Genesis, Chronicles, Matthew and Luke; by the peculiar reference to certain periods mentioned in the Book of Daniel and by various other means. For example: the author of Matthew (1:17) attempts to trace the generations from Abraham to Christ as follows: 14 generations from Christ to the Exile, 14 generations from the Exile to David, and 14 generations from David to Abraham. The enumeration is obviously incorrect and appears to be a conscious but clumsy attempt to make history conform to a definite plan, one supposition being that each generation was estimated to represent 71-1/3 years after the manner of the Hindu Manvantara periods, giving 1000 years for each 14 generations, or 4,000 years from Adam to Christ.

Daniel's cryptic remarks in regard to "the 1335 days," "2300 days," and "a time, times and half a time" were once thought by some writers to contain esoteric prophecies of the coming of Christ, but this theory has been discarded by modern writers. It is now known that the Book of Daniel, instead of having been written about 600 B.C. and prophesying events to come far in the future, was actually written about 165 B.C., and speaks symbolically of events then past and present.

Some knowledge of cycles is indicated, however, by the peculiar manner in which the Jews fixed the dates of important festivals. The adoption of solar time for the civil calendar and lunar time for the religious calendar made it

---

13—For the period from Adam to Abraham the Greek translation of the Pentateuch gives 1,500 years more than the Hebrew version. Originally the Samaritan Pentateuch commanded greater prestige than the Hebrew version, yet it gives an entirely different chronology.

desirable to evolve some method of reconciling the two systems. How this was done is explained in Leviticus 25:8 where Moses commanded the Israelites to observe ". . . 7 sabbaths of years unto thee, 7 times 7 . . ." The 50th year was celebrated as Jubilee year after which a new cycle began.

From the beginning of the first year to the end of the sixth month of the forty-ninth year is forty-eight years and six months. The first day of the seventh month was declared a Sabbath and the tenth day of Atonement. If calculated on the basis of 365 days for the year and 29.5 days for each lunar period, there is a total of 17,700 days or 600 lunations. This period is equal to 50 lunar years of 354 days each.

For the complete span of 49 solar years the true calculation is 17,896.7 days ($365.24 \times 49 = 17,896.7$). The true length of a lunar cycle is 29.53 days, therefore, the 17,896.7 day period is equal to 606+ lunations, or 50 lunar years plus 6 months 1.7 days ($606 \times 29.53 = 17895$).

CHAPTER XX

THE HOLY THREE

I<small>T HAS BEEN SHOWN</small> that the efforts of primitive peoples to explain the origin and workings of the universe produced a philosophy in which the world was envisaged as deriving from a bi-sexual creative power personified as a god or gods, of whom the human male and female were the pattern. The male power was believed to be the active force in the generation of life, the female power being merely the passive vehicle in which actual production took place. It was further assumed that, as the male organs of reproduction are of tripliform character, every act of creation has a three-fold aspect. This belief appears to have been the source of the custom of dividing the universe into three great departments, ruled by triads of gods.

In addition to the triads of principal deities there were numerous secondary and minor deities, sometimes forming triads and sometimes not, ruling over the wind, storm, lightning, fire, thunder, rain, etc., while local demons, or spirits, dwelt in rocks, trees, mountains, and streams. Each nation, tribe or cult had its own national, local, or tribal god. There were also household gods to whom family groups paid special devotion. In India and Babylonia, the gods and minor deities, or demons, were numbered in the thousands.

TRIADS OF GODS[1]

Arabian	Al-Lat	Al-Uzzah	Manah
Assyrian	Anu	Asher	Ea
Buddhist	Boodhash, the developer	Darmash, the developed	Sanghash, "hosts developed"
Chaldean	Anu	Bel	Ea
China	The One	The Second, from the First	Third, produced by the Second
Christian	Father	Holy Spirit	Son or Logos
Egypt	Tum	Shu	Tefnut
	Amon	Muth	Chans
	Kneph-Osiris	Pthah-Isis	Phre-Horus

1—From *Rivers of Life*, Maj. Gen. James G. R. Forlong, vol. 1, p. 467.

German, according to the Greeks	Perkunos	Pikolos	Pothrimpus
India-Vedic	Brahma	Vishnu	Siva
Greek	Om or On	Dionysius or Bacchus	Herakles
	Zeus	Poseidon	Pluto
Greek-Latin	Zeus-Jupiter	Neptune	Pluto-Hephaistos
Kaanite or ancient Phoenician	Yachaveh Baal-Spalisha	Ana Self triplicated	Ea Baal or Ba-El
Mexico	The Blessed	Holy Spirit	Their Offspring
Orpheus, 14th cent. B.C.	Aither-God	Phares, the Spirit	Kaos from both but imperfect
Phoenician	Belus (sun)	Urania (earth)	Adonis (love)
Plato	The Infinite	The Finite	A Compound of the Two
Pythagoras, 6th cent. B.C.	Monad	Duad	Triad
Samothracian	Almighty, the Fecundator	Holy Spirit Fecundiatrix	Kasmilus
Scandinavian	Odin	Thor	Friga
	Har	Jafner	Thrido
	Othin or Odin	Vile	Ve
Syria	Monimus	Azoz	Ares, Aries or Mars

The three supreme deities generally appeared as rulers of the three original elements out of which the universe was believed to be created. In some instances these were earth, water, and sky: in others they were sun, fire, and water, or water, fire, and sky. Before the oldest pages of history were written, the number three had already become the sacred number of the gods.

In the Babylonian system, the sky or region of the sun was the domain of Anu or Anna: the earth was ruled by Enlik and the subterranean waters, which were believed to flow around and under the earth, were governed by Enki. This great triad can be traced to the very beginning of recorded history, its names being engraved in an inscription dating from King Lugatzaggigi, one of the earliest Sumerian rulers of whose reign we have record. In later Babylonian history, the members of this triad were known as Anu, Bel

and Ea, but the chief actors in the historic period were
Shamash (sun), Sin (moon), and Ishtar (mother goddess).

The Brahman religion of India has endured as a continuous system longer than any other form of worship; and
its long accumulation of traditions and myths, the rise of
new gods and the gradual decline of others have made the
Brahman pantheon the most intricate and confused of all.
Both heaven and earth are divided into three parts, with
different gods ruling each sphere or aspect, assisted by hosts
of minor gods, spirits, demons, so numerous as to make the
casual reader despair of untangling the system's ramifica-
tions. Agni, the god of fire, appears under many forms and
titles and those under which Vishnu and Siva appear are
countless. In its most important aspects, however, Brahmanism maintains the triadic grouping of the gods and
as this grouping is the sole subject of the present inquiry,
we need not be concerned with other details of the system.

In the religious systems of some nations, the existence
of 3 great gods at the beginning of creation was explained
by representing the first god as having created the other 2
members of the holy triad. In other cases all 3 members
of the triad were represented as being but different forms
or manifestations of the same god. This idea is found not
only in some of the pagan cults; it is perpetuated in the
Christian doctrine of a Trinity in Unity: Father, Son, and
Holy Ghost, 3 persons in 1, 1 person is 3.

In Greece the images of Bacchus, Mercury, and Diana
were often portrayed with 3 heads or bodies representing
their 3-fold character. Lucina, guardian of birth; Diana,
guardian of health, and Hecate, guardian of death, are but
different forms of the same goddess. Figures of Hecate
were often placed at cross roads to keep away evil spirits,
the goddess being portrayed with 3 bodies placed back to
back so that she could see in 3 directions at once. Jupiter
was symbolized by a 3-fold thunder bolt; a 3-pronged trident
was the symbol of Neptune, and Pluto was represented by
the 3-headed Cerberus.

When the priests of Heliopolis, in Egypt, formulated
their theogony, they represented Tum as a form of the
sun god, and as having produced the 2 gods Shu and Tefnut.
The Japanese portrayed some of their gods with 3 heads
and the ancient Peruvians had a god named Tanga Tanga
whom they called 3 in one, 1 in 3. Plutarch relates that

Ahura Mazda, the supreme god of the Persians, "thrice multiplied himself". Mithra was the son of Ahura, yet he was Ahura himself. The Chinese Taoists worshiped a self-created trinity endowed with 3 abstract attributes which Lao-tse called I-He-Wei, a term almost identical in sound with the Hebrew Yahweh. When preceded by the title Adonai, Yahweh is pronounced YēHōWih.

In the Hindu system, Brahma created Vishnu and Siva, the second and third members of the Trimurti, or Trinity. Yet they are not 3 separate beings but are merely 3 different manifestations of the same deity.

United with Brahma (meaning prayer) is Vach or Saraswati, his heavenly consort and divine energy. Vishnu and Siva also have Saktis or divine energies, Siva being united with his consort in one body, that is, in androgynous form.

Brahma is at once the creator, preserver and destroyer, the self-created, self-existent great father and great mother blended in one person and is, therefore, the primeval androgyne who unites in himself the combined attributes of all 3. In another sense Brahma is the rising sun; Siva is the sun at noon, and Vishnu is the setting sun.

> "In these 3 persons, the same god is shown,
> Each in his place, each last in one land
> Of Brahma, Vishnu, Siva each may be,
> First, second, third among the blessed three".
>
> —MONIER WILLIAMS

Although he reigns theoretically over the 3 major divisions of earth, water, and atmosphere, Brahma more nearly represents abstract intelligence, impersonal, passive, unchanging. Being incapable of action himself, his thought is given form by his divine energy Vach (meaning speech or voice). Brahma's neutral character is not one to stir the imagination, consequently Hindu myths and scriptures assign to him a very minor role. The important figures in the Trinity are Vishnu and Siva, who, perhaps, originally represented the active, creative energy of elemental water and fire.

A god revealed his various powers by appearing in different forms, each of which was given an individual title and regarded as a distinct entity. For example, the words water, ice, vapor, steam, are titles denoting different things,

IN PRINCIPIO CREAVIT
COELVM ETTERRAM:

84. The Holy One in three-fold form creating the universe, as related by the Gospel of John. From a French miniature of the 16th century. (From MSS. of King Henry II, Bibl. Royale). At the bottom is the eagle of the evangelist in the center of the seven planets of the zodiac.

yet they are but varying forms of the same element. Thus, Agni, the Brahman god of fire, is worshiped as Surya, fire in the sun, Trita, as lightning in the sky, and Agni as fire on earth. Each manifestation is regarded as fire, yet Agni comprehends all 3 forms, hence he is called Tryambaka, or Three-Mothered. In another sense Agni is Varuna in the evening, Mitra in the morning, Savitr as he traverses the air and Indra as he illumines the sky in mid-day.

Similar reasoning prevailed among the Babylonians and Sumerians. To them the formally spoken word or the breath of any great god was a real divinity in itself. When they spoke of a god's "word", the term was not used in the modern sense but as the name of a tangible entity.

The *inem*, or word for a thing, was considered equivalent to the thing itself. The oath of even a priest or witness to an agreement, or a formally spoken promise, or threat, possessed magical and terrible power. From *inem*, Babylonian magicians coined the expression *inim-inim-ma*, which was spoken as an incantation accompanying their feats of magic.

> The Word which on high shaketh the heavens,
> The Word which beneath causes the earth to tremble.

Babylonian philosophy is thus described by Prof. Langdon[2]: "The Sumero-Babylonians invariably regarded water as the uncreated first principle and source of all things created. The creative form or principle resided in the primordial watery chaos. . . . Evidence adduced . . . for the beneficent activity of the god's word and breath induces the conjecture that the Sumerians employed the term *inim* (word) for cosmic creative form or reason. But, at any rate, we know that the term *mummu* was said to mean 'loud voice,' apparently because the roar of the thunder or rain god was adopted as a term for the indwelling wisdom of water.

"The reality of a thing consisted in its 'forms', i.e., the divine mental concept which is revealed to mankind by its name. All knowledge is revelation and the reality of things was not their tangibleness but the mental concept and things cannot exist until the god has this mental concept. Fundamentally, all things, material and immaterial, rest upon the mental activity of the water god (Ea) which is personified as mummu or cosmic reason."

Babylonian worshipers of spirits believed the voices of gods were heard in the sound of thunder, ocean waves, and water falls; in rustling leaves; in the creaking of swaying trees; in the faint sound of water dripping in deep caverns and in many other natural sounds. The friendly presence of a god's spirit or breath was felt in the caress of a gentle breeze, or gust, while high, turbulent winds indicated his anger.

According to the Book of Genesis, Abraham migrated from the Babylonian city of Ur to Canaan and founded the Jewish nation. The language and culture of the Jews re-

---

2—Hastings' *Encyclopedia of Religion and Ethics*, vol. 12, p. 751, Article: *Word*, by Stephen H. Langdon.

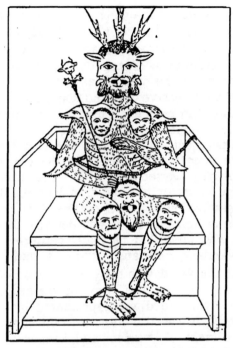

*85. The devil in three-in-one form.
From a French miniature of the
15th century; in BIBL. ROYALE.*

flected a Babylonian origin. Spiritism is in evidence
throughout Genesis, and both Abraham and Jacob are
shown to have had strange dreams and visions; to have
planted trees and set up pillars and heaps of stone as
dwelling places for their deity.

The expressions "Word of Wrath", "Word of God", and
"Spirit of God" were used by the Jews as personifications
of the divine essence in the same sense as that in which
the Babylonians employed them.[3] This is demonstrated in
Genesis 1:1 where the Word is the active agent which carries out the will of the creator: "God spake the Word and
the worlds were made."

How the Oriental conception of the Word as a creative
agent of the deity was adopted by western nations, how the
term increased in significance until it eventually became

3—He sendeth forth his commandments upon the earth. His word
runneth quickly. *Ps.* 147:15. Also see *Ps.* 33:4, 33:6, 33:9; *Isa.*
2:1; *Jer.* 23:29.

personified as the deity, is one of the little known chapters in the history of the origin of Christian dogma.

The desire of Christian propagators to strengthen the claim that the Scriptures contain divine revelations, unlike any other records in the world, has not been conducive to the pursuit of an objective investigation which would show the true relationship between Christian and pagan beliefs. Therefore, when Bible readers see the term "Word" used in the Old Testament to designate the creative power of God, and as a synonym for Christ in the Gospel of John, the term is usually passed by without the reader's having any knowledge of its origin and significance. But, as will be shown in the following brief outline, this peculiar concept was closely related to, if not derived directly from, beliefs which had prevailed for many centuries among the Hindus, Babylonians, Persians, Egyptians, and Jews.

In Persia, the Word was the great weapon of Zoroaster. In Greece, Mercury was the Word or messenger of Zeus; to the Romans, the Word was represented by the goddess Fama. In Egypt, it was the creative agent of the god Thot. As the embodiment of wisdom and keeper of the secret of the divine Word, Horus, the god of light, was portrayed with a finger to his lips, symbolizing secrecy or silence.

According to Maspero's[4] interpretation of their records, the Egyptians believed that the spoken word of the gods, on issuing from the mouth, thickened into tangible substance, endowed with creative power and energy.

4—Of the creative power of the Word in Egypt, Maspero says that Thot: "recited them (words) with that true intonation which renders them all powerful and everyone became, like himself, master of the universe . . . in fact, the articulate word and the voice were believed to be the most potent of creative forces, not remaining immaterial and issuing from the lips, but thickening, so to speak, into tangible substance; into bodies which were themselves animated by creative life and energy; into gods and goddesses who lived or who created; even Tumu had called forth by a very short phrase the gods who ordered all things; for his "Come unto me," uttered with a loud voice upon the day of creation had evoked the sun within the lotus. Thot had opened his lips and the voice which proceeded from him had become an entity: sound had solidified into matter and life from his mouth without bodily effort on his part and without spoken evocation. . . . Creation by the voice is almost as great a refinement of thought as the substitution of creation by the Word for creation by muscular effort. . . . At first it was believed the creator had made the world with a Word, then that he had made it by sound; but further conception of his having made it by thought does not seem to have occurred to the theologians." *The Dawn of Civilization*, Gaston Camille Chas. Maspero, 1894, pp. 145-147.

86. Ancient three-headed god found at Condat, France.

The Egyptian word for spirit is very similar to the word *rehk,* meaning spittle; and the Egyptian belief that the creator's spirit or breath became a definite entity on passing the lips, is probably the origin of the custom of priests to touch the finger tips to their tongues and anointing young children with spittle to open their eyes and ears to spiritual understanding. Jesus is said to have cured blindness by touching the eyes with spittle, and backward people all over the world have looked upon the practice as a form of baptism or spiritual awakening, similar to the Biblical practice of "laying on of hands".

By the seventh century B.C., the influence of Indian and Babylonian culture began to be felt in the West and, when Greek philosophers turned their attention to the nature of reason and the cosmic processes, their conclusions reflected the influence of Oriental philosophy. The universe was generally regarded by the Greeks as the product of a cosmic intelligence which formed and ruled all things. Their speculations were devoted principally to the form or manner in which this intelligence was manifested, whether reason or divine wisdom was imminent in the universal creative process or was an independent force speaking from without.

Thales adopted the Babylonian conception of water as the universal element and the source of cosmic intelligence. In the sixth century, Heraclitus discarded the Babylonian theory and adopted fire as the universal element, which he sometimes called the "hot breath". Heraclitus envisioned a ceaseless transformation of all things from fire or heat, then back again to fire. Finding "the Word" too restricted in meaning to express the operating principle of this cosmic law, or reason, he designated it by the word Logos which denotes both revelation and reason.

Anaxagoras formulated a theory of a supreme intellectual principle not identified with the world but independent of it, the regulating principle of the universe being the Logos, which he envisioned as the divine intelligence acting as intermediary between the creator and the world.

The Stoics also adopted a theory of an active principle pervading the world and determining its form. This operative principle they called both Logos and Creator. The Logos, they said, exists as thought as long as it is unuttered, but becomes the Word as soon as it is spoken. Like Heraclitus, the Stoics regarded fire as the primordial substance, the material principle of the divine power. Endowed with inherent productive activity, it is the "seminal reason" of the world which manifests itself in all phenomena of nature. The world is a living creature whose spirit goes through all things, the creator of forms though itself formless.

Greek thinking regarding the activity of cosmic intelligence in creation reached its greatest intellectual and imaginative heights in the philosophy of Plato. In Timaeus, a cosmological myth based largely upon Pythagorean geometry and astronomy combined with principles of physiology and medicine, Plato gave to Greek philosophy its first conception of a creator god. He visualized the material world as a living organism, created by Reason and Necessity, molded into spherical form after the likeness of an eternal pattern, being without beginning or end with reference to time, and composed of the four primary elements fire, air, water, and earth in order to provide the greatest degree of unity.

The world soul, Plato said, was formed by the creator out of the constituents Existence, Difference, and Being, compounded in the proportions of a musical harmony. The soul was placed in the center of the cosmic body and permeated it throughout, making the body also its exterior environment.

The world was girdled by the circles of the equator and ecliptic, the latter being split into the seven lesser circles of the planets and the two (equator and ecliptic) were animated in opposite movements, their principal motion being that which is most appropriate to mind and intelligence.

Then there were formed the various subordinate gods and the higher or immortal parts of the human soul, these coming direct from the hands of god himself. The formation of the human body and the lower, or mortal, elements of the human soul was effected by the activity of the created gods (i.e., the stars). This theory of god's creative activity being manifested in an "upper" and a "lower" sphere was later made an important feature of the Jewish Cabala.[5]

5—"God did not make the soul after the body, although we are speaking of them in this order. . . . He made the soul in origin and excellence prior to and older than the body to be its ruler and mistress.

"God made the soul out of the following elements and in this wise: God made the soul before the body out of the indivisible and the unchangeable and also out of that which is divisible and has to do with material bodies. He compounded a third and intermediate kind of essence, partaking of the nature of the Same and of the Other and this compound he placed accordingly in an amount between the indivisible, the divisible and the material.

"He took the three elements of the Same, the Other and the essence and mingled them into one form, compressing by force the reluctant and unsociable nature of the Other into the Same. This entire compound he divided lengthwise into two parts which he joined to one another at the center and bent them into a circular form, connecting them with themselves and each other at the point opposite to their original meeting point and comprehending them in a uniform revolution upon the same axis: one he made the outer circle and the other he made the inner circle.

"Now the motion of the outer circle he called the motion of the Same and the motion of the inner circle the motion of the Other or Diverse. The motion of the Same he carried around by the side of the right and the motion of the Diverse diagonally to the left and he gave dominion to the motion of the Same and the Like for the single and undivided: but the inner motion he divided into six places and made seven unequal circles, having their internals in ratios of two and three, three of each and bade the orbits proceed in a direction opposite to one another: and these (Sun, Mercury, Venus, Mars and Jupiter) to move with unequal swiftness about the three and about one another but in due proportions." *Timaeus*, by Plato, pp. 34-36.

318 SYMBOLS, SEX, AND THE STARS

Although there is a tremendous gulf between Plato's conception of creation and present day scientific thought on the subject, his cosmology exercised considerable influence on religious and philosophic thinking in his own and succeeding centuries. Even today, his fame endures as one of the greatest thinkers of all time. His theory may, therefore, be accepted as representative of the results which have been produced whenever men have resorted to intuition and imagination as a substitute for the methods of science.

In the first few years of the Christian era, Philo Judaeus, a Hellenized Jew, made an attempt to reconcile the pagan pantheistic theories with Jewish conceptions of God. He was a member of the Alexandrian school of philosophy and a student of the theories of Heraclitus, Plato, Pythagoras, the Stoics, and other Greek philosophers. He was probably also familiar with the Oriental philosophies then being taught in Alexandria.

Philo conceived the Logos to be not merely immanent in the cosmos: he gave it an independent existence as intermediary between God and the world. His theory was confused, contradictory, and sometimes unintelligible, yet its importance in the history of Christianity cannot be over-estimated, for it was principally from Philo that the early Christian fathers derived the concepts upon which to base their doctrine of a Trinity in Unity.

As visualized by Philo, God is unchangeable, passive, unthinking, eternal, incomprehensible. He did not create matter, but found a passive, primeval mass of it on hand at the time of creation. He can have no connection with evil, even to punish it. As matter is essentially evil, God can have no connection with the creation of man but must call upon the Word to aid him. In the conception of God as an abstract, passive being who functions through an intermediary, Philo's theory is strongly reminiscent of the Hindu conception of Brahma. The Word or Logos, then, is the active intelligent principle in creation and God is reduced to a mere name. Sometimes the words Wisdom and Spirit are used in the same sense as the Logos. Later, this conception of God loomed large in the theories of the Gnostics and Cabalists.

According to Philo, God begot the Word, yet by some hocus-pocus which he does not make clear, it was not begotten like angels or creatures and, because of this peculiar generation, Philo declared the Word or Logos to be the first-born Son of God, the prototypal man in whose image all other men are created. Again, he is the idea, or ideas, the whole mind of God giving out of himself in creation. He is both the high priest and Shekinah; the Glory of God as well as the intelligible world. Although, at one time, Philo speaks of the Logos as if it were a being distinct from God under the figure of a son, at another time the Logos seems to be merely a manifestation of the divine wisdom. As an orthodox Jew, however, Philo could not accept belief in any mortal formed in the likeness of God or even brought into comparison with him.

His distinction between God and his rational power, or Logos, in contact with the world was maintained in later developments of Hellenistic speculation by the Neo-Platonists, even to the extent of predicating 3 Gods; first, a supreme God; second, God or the Demiurge, or Logos, and third, God, or the world.

Philo's effort to fuse Greek wisdom and Jewish religion was naturally unacceptable to the Jews, but it was received enthusiastically by the early Christians, some of whom thought he was a Christian.

Although the Jews were not willing to accept the radical theories of Philo, their own theories had already developed far in the same direction. As their culture had advanced to such a point that they were no longer able to believe in an anthropomorphic God who had walked in the Garden of Eden and joined them in battle against their enemies, their conception of him had become less sharply defined. His form became blurred, ghostly, and abstract. As it did so, he receded into the distance until, finally, he was thought to reside in some vague region beyond the stars. His remoteness from the earth then made it difficult for his worshipers to believe that he heard their prayers or that he retained a warm, protective interest in them.

It was at this point that the Jews began to hope for a Messiah or intermediary to bridge the gulf between God and man. The Messiah was expected to not only intercede with God on behalf of man; he was to be the active agent who carried out activities which God himself was no longer able or willing to perform. Wherever the king or Messiah is mentioned in the Old Testament,[6] it was accepted as equivalent to the Word or Logos and the Jewish conception of the Messiah became closely analogous to the intermediaries of the gods of India, Persia, Babylon, and Egypt.

The title Messiah seems to be derived from *Mes* (Greek *mesos*, Latin *mezzo*), an old root meaning "middle", "from the middle", "out of"; hence "born of" or "son of". Meshken, meaning birthplace, combines *mes* (middle) and *ken*, a nest or womb.

In Egyptian usage, the sons of Ra, Thot, and Aah were designated Ra-mes, or Ra-meses, Thotmes and Aahmes. Mesopotamia denotes "in the middle of the rivers". From the ancient practice of commanding a person to place his hand under the thigh of his interrogator when swearing under oath, a witness was termed a *mesitis* or "middleman". When the Jews looked forward to the coming of a Messiah, they had in mind the Mess-iah, or Mess-Jah, that is, a middleman, interceder, or mediator with Jahveh.

After the Babylonian period, speculations regarding God's mediator increased tremendously, and practically every Jewish writer discussed his nature and the time of his coming. The continued failure of the Messiah to appear upon the earth caused the attributes of God to be adopted as pale substitutes for him and God was represented as functioning through them as his agents or emanations. The Wisdom, the Shekinah or Glory, and the Spirit of God were considered as intermediaries between God and man and even the Law could be regarded as an independent spiritual entity in much the same sense that the Word or Voice was believed by pagans to be the active creative agent of their gods.

In the Targumim,[7] the doctrines of the Word, the Angel and the Wisdom of God assume concrete form and emerge definitely as his intermediaries. Passages of the Bible which state that the Word appeared or acted are translated repeatedly by the commentary of Onkelos as "the Word of the Lord" appeared or acted. God is shielded by his intermediaries from any contact with man or from any active part in creation. Inasmuch as the Targum of Onkelos was held in the highest esteem by the Jews, we may be sure

---

6—See *Ps.* 45:11, *Ps.* 72:11, *Ps.* 2:12.

7—See Appendix: Talmud.

that his usage of words was approved by the best authorities of his time. In the Targum of Jonathan, also, "Word" is used in the same sense. In the Mishnah, the 10 passages in Genesis (Ch. 1), beginning with "our Lord said", are spoken of as the 10 ma amarot (words or speeches) by which the world was created.[8]

Wisdom, which dwelt with Ea in the depths of the sea, according to Babylonian mythology, became, in Jewish literature, the encompassing intelligence of God, the helper of the creator, the foundation of the world. Israel's God was believed to be ruler of the universe, and Wisdom was regarded as the cosmic power. It was God's master workman (Prov. 8:30); the first of his works (Prov. 8:23), and his designer. (Prov. 3:19; Ps. 104:24).

Under the influence of Greek philosophy, Wisdom became a divine agency of a personal character (Wisdom 7:22, 30), so that Philo termed it the daughter of God, "the mother of the creative Word".

According to the *Wisdom of Solomon*, a Jewish work written in Alexandria during the first century B.C., Wisdom is immanent in God, belonging to the divine essence, yet existing in a quasi-independent state side by side with him. Wisdom, the Logos and the Holy Spirit were closely identified as active agents in the creation of the world, selecting among the divine ideas those which were to be actualized in the created universe. Wisdom is the cosmic principle dwelling on the throne of glory next to God and knowing and designing all things (Wisdom 9:1; 4:10), being identical with the creative world (9:1), and the Holy Spirit (9:17). Ecclesiasticus, the Book of Enoch, Testimony of the Twelve Patriarchs and other works speak to the same effect.

8—It was not the Lord that appeared to Abram, but the Word of the Lord. It was the Word of the Lord that appeared to Adam and Jacob. The Word of the Lord created man in his image.
The Heavens were made, not by the Lord but by the Word of the Lord. (Deut. 33:37).
The *Jerusalem Targum* declares the Word created the earth.
Moses went up to meet the Word of the Lord. (*Ex.* 19:3). It was the Word of the Lord that spoke to Moses (*Ex.* 3:2), says Onkelos.
Where the Gentile version says "I heard thy voice in the garden" the *Targumim* say "I heard the voice of the Word in the garden".
The Spirit is spoken of as a person in the beginning of *Gen.* 2 and *Gen.* 6:3; in *Num.* 11:25,26; *Ps.* 33:6; *II Sam.* 13:23.
"And the Word of the Lord bless thee and the Word of the Lord said to them, be ye fruitful and multiply and replenish the earth". (*Gen.* 3:5,9) and so on.

The term Shekinah (dwelling) is used in the Talmud and Midrash in place of Word (Memra). Onkelos translates Elohim as Shekinah in Genesis 9:27 and elsewhere. The terms "presence" and "faces" of God are translated in the same way.[9] The Targumim psuedo-Jonathan and Jerusalem adopt a like system as in Psalms 21:8 and 89:47.

Maimonides, a celebrated Jewish theologian of the twelfth century, regarded the Shekinah of God as of the same character as the Memra (Word) and the Logos: to him the Shekinah was a distinct entity, and a light created to be an intermediary between God and the world. Nahmanides, an eminent Jewish theologian of the thirteenth century, considered the Shekinah to be the essence of God manifested in a distinct form.

When the Wisdom, Spirit, and other attributes of the Almighty came to be considered as distinct entities, culmination of the evolutionary process could not be far off: personification of the attributes was the only step which remained to be taken. Paul prepared the way for this step when he taught that Jesus was born a man and became God. When the author of I John followed Paul with the declaration that God, Jesus, and the Word (Spirit) were one and the same, it marked the final phase of a belief which had been developing among the Jews for several centuries.

Paul's writings show a thorough knowledge of the Alexandrian philosophy and the portrayal of Jesus which he gives in his Epistles is an effort to breathe life into Philo's conception of the Logos and the "second God".

As seen at this distance, Paul's message seems much more revolutionary than it appeared to the people of his day. The period was one of intense religious speculation and there was widespread belief that the end of one of the great ages of the world was approaching. It was expected that the coming of the long-looked for Avatar or Messiah would be followed by the destruction and regeneration of the world.

9—Presence: *Gen.* 3:8; 4:16; *Ex.* 33:14; *Lev.* 22:3; *I Chr.* 16:27,33; *II Chr.* 20:9; *Job* 1:12; 2:7; 23:15; *Psa.* 16:11; 17:2; 31:20; 51:11; 68:2,8; 95:2; 97:5; 114:7; 139:7; 140:13; *Isa.* 19:1; 63:9; 64:1,2,3; *Jer.* 4:26; 5:22; 52:3; *Ezek.* 38:20; *Jonah* 1:10; *Nah.* 1:5; *Zeph.* 1:7. Face: *Gen.* 4:14; 32:30; 33:10; *Ex.* 33:11,20,23; *Lev.* 17:10; 20:3,5; 20:6; 26:17; *Num.* 6:25; 14:14; *Deut.* 5:4; 31:17,18; 34:10; *Jud.* 6:22; *I Kings* 13:6; *I Chr.* 16:11; *Psa.* 27:8; 34:16; 88:14; 105:4; 119:135; *Isa.* 65:3; *Jer.* 33:5.

Both in the Jewish Scriptures and in pagan mythology there were numerous accounts of miraculous births and of men being wafted to heaven in life or after death. Faith healing and wonder-working were every day occurrences and no one doubted the ability of the holy men to raise the dead, drive out devils, cure people of fevers, epilepsy, and other diseases, restore sight to the blind, and perform many other miracles.

Many religious leaders claimed to be, or were believed by their followers to be, the Messiah, and to some of these men miracle-working was attributed. Simon Magus,[10] Apollonius, Bar Jesus[11], Theudas,[12] and a Jesus ben Pandira were condemned and some of them put to death because of their claim to possess supernatural power.

Paul began to teach of the crucifixion and resurrection of the Son of God at a time when the minds of the people were thoroughly prepared for extraordinary changes and a restless expectancy pervaded all Judea. There could hardly have been a more favorable moment for spreading new doctrines. Yet Paul admits that the Jews were indifferent or hostile to his work and he was forced to confine his proselytism solely to the Gentiles.[13]

By their rejection of Paul's teaching, the Jews compelled Christianity to change from a Jewish to a Gentile religion, thus altering the whole course of Western history. It is extremely important, therefore, that we know what Paul taught, upon what evidence his testimony was based and why the Jews rejected his teaching.

10—*Acts* 8:9,10.
11—*Ibid.* 13:6.
12—*Ibid.* 5:36.
13—*Ibid.* 18:6.

CHAPTER XXI

THE HOLY THREE

(Continued)

PAUL'S CONVERSION WAS NOT the result of long investigation or mediation; it struck him suddenly, like a thunder bolt. In the Acts of the Apostles, a book said to have been written by Luke, a companion of Paul, it is related that while on his way to Damascus an intense white light appeared before Paul, and he heard the voice of Jesus reproaching him and commanding that he proceed to the city where he would be given further instructions.[1]

For three days thereafter he remained blind and helpless, and he was not quite sure in later years whether he had seen Jesus or an apparition.[2] Throughout his epistles, Paul speaks of visions, of being in trances, of having bodily afflictions,[3] and if he suffered from epilepsy, as appears to be the case, his vision of Jesus was probably an hallucination during an epileptic coma.

Aside from the bare statement that Jesus was crucified and resurrected, Paul says very little to present him as more than a phantom or symbolic figure. Nowhere in his writings does Paul mention the time, place, or virgin birth of Jesus; his personal appearance is not described; his travels, teachings, and miracles are not mentioned nor does Paul give any details of the events which immediately preceded and followed the crucifixion. He had studied with the priest Gamaliel in Jerusalem and must have been in that city at the time Jesus is supposed to have been teaching and performing miracles there; yet Paul had no personal knowledge of him. Although, after his conversion, Paul made several visits to Jerusalem in order to gather all available information about Jesus, one reads his writings in vain for intimate details which would give a vivid picture of the Savior's life. His failure to mention the virgin birth, the miracles, the Sermon on the Mount, and other teachings of Jesus is especially inexplicable because they were the strongest testimony he could have presented to his listeners.

1—*Acts* 9:8,9; 22:11; 26:13.
2—"I knew a man in Christ above 14 years ago (whether in the body I cannot tell; whether out of the body I cannot tell.) *II Cor.* 12:2.
3—Visions, trances: *Gal.* 2:2; *I Cor.* 12:1,4; *Acts* 16:9, 18:9, 22:17, 23:11, 27:23; *Gal.* 4:13,14; *Acts* 10:10; *II Cor.* 12:7,10.

Nowhere does Paul acknowledge that his teachings are shared by or derived from the Apostles. When he speaks of Jesus as the first begotten Son of God who died to save all men, he speaks as if the fact were his own revelation. "Jesus was raised from the dead according to *my* gospel" says Paul (II Tim. 2:8) and, again, he mentions "that gospel which *I* preach". (Gal. 2:2). It is not the gospel of the Apostles but the gospel of Paul.

His ideas about morals and right living, to which he devotes much attention in his Epistles, are precisely the same ideas that the Essenes had been teaching for more than a century, and Paul does not even claim that they represent the views of Jesus. There existed at that time numerous small groups or sects such as the Essenes, who ate communal meals, held weekly prayer meetings and observed secret doctrines. Paul himself mentions having appeared before such groups[4] and he says nothing in his Epistles which precludes the possibility that the Christ whom he preaches was derived from the doctrines of one of these obscure groups.

When Paul stated (I Cor. 15:3) that "Christ died for our sins according to the Scriptures", he could not have referred to the Jewish Scriptures for they contained no such statement; he could not have referred to the Christian Gospels, for they were not written until many years afterward; but the Essenes did have Scriptures as well as Tracts and Gospels.

The mystery of the origin of Paul's doctrines deepens considerably when the attitude of the Jews toward Jesus is taken into consideration. Judged by the reaction of the public today to any unusual event, it seems fair to presume that if it were known that the Savior had been born in a manger at Bethlehem, runners would have carried the momentous news to every corner of Judea: rejoicing celebrants would soon have gathered in every town and village; the roads would have been filled with ecstatic Jews hastening to Bethlehem to stand in the presence of the Son of God and pay him honor. For this was no ordinary miracle of a virgin birth. Here men were witnessing the unique spectacle of the Almighty Father of the Universe sending his other self to earth.

4—*Acts* 16:13, 19:1,4; 20:7, 18:25.

If the infant Savior were sent to redeem the people of all nations, and not the Jews alone, the signs in the sky which heralded his coming should have been visible to the Gauls, Greeks, Romans, Egyptians, Hindus and Chinese, in fact to the people of every nation, tribe, and clan on earth so that they, too, might rejoice in his coming.

One should expect to read that from earliest infancy, Jesus was worshiped, shielded, protected, every incident in his life being observed and recorded with infinite care. But history gives no such picture. In pagan countries his birth was entirely unknown. Even Jewish records failed to mention his birth, and the Gospels support the conclusion that until he began his ministry at about the age of twenty-nine years, he lived in utmost obscurity and, apparently, in poverty. With the exception of a passage in Josephus' *Antiquities* (18:3 Sec. 3) which is obviously an interpolation, no Jewish historian of that period even mentions the name of Jesus. The failure of Philo Judaeus, the most reliable contemporary Jewish writer, to mention him is particularly significant. When Paul appeared before Porcius Festus and related how he had seen Christ in a vision, Festus had never heard of Christ and, probably knowing of Paul's affliction, thought he had been merely seeing visions in a trance.[5]

The absence of any reference to Jesus of Nazareth (or Bethlehem) in the Jewish records is accentuated by the readiness with which the rabbis recorded the life of another reputed Messiah, Jehoshua (Jesus) ben Pandira. According to the Talmud, Rabbi Joshua b. Perahyah[6] went

---

5—*Acts* 26:24.

6—Jehoshua, son of Perahyah, was a president of the Sanhedrin, being the fifth, reckoning from Ezra as the first. He was one of those who received and transmitted the oral law, as it was claimed, direct from Mount Sinai.

Perahyah began to teach about 154 B.C., therefore we may infer that he was born not later than 180-170 B.C., and that it was probably not later than 100 B.C. when he went to Egypt with his pupil, for it is said he went there to escape persecution. This doubtless refers to a civil war in which the Pharisees revolted against King Yannai, about 105 B.C. If we assume the age of the pupil Jehoshua ben Pandira to be 15 years, it would place his birth at about 120 B.C. Yannai reigned from 106 to 70 B.C. and was succeeded by his widow Salome, whom the Greeks called Alexandra. She reigned nine years. Traditions, especially of the first "*Toledoth Jehoshua*", say the queen of Yannai and the mother of John Hyrcanus, who must, therefore, have been Salome, showed favor to Jehoshua and his teaching and was a witness to his wonderful works. She tried to save him from his religious enemies because he was related to her, but that during her reign, he was put to death.

to Alexandria, Egypt, to escape the persecution of the Jewish king Yannai and took with him a pupil named Jesus. There is some confusion as to the surname of the pupil, certain passages referring to him as Jesus ben Pandira while others refer to him as Jesus ben Stada.

It is probable that while in Egypt this Pandira, or Stada, became a member of the sect of Therapeutae which was located near Alexandria, for it is said that while there he learned to perform miracles by magic, the formula for which he cut in his skin. (Shab. 104b). After his return from Egypt "he practiced magic and deceived and led astray Israel" (Bab. Sanh. 107b; Sotah 47a; Yer. Hag. 77d) and his disciples healed the sick "in the name of Jesus Pandira". (Yer. Shab. 14d Ab. Zarah 27b; Eccl. R. 1,8).

According to the Babylonian Gemara (the Mishna of tract Shabbath), this Jehoshua, or Jesus, was stoned to death and crucified by hanging on a tree in the city of Lud, or Lydda, on the eve of Passah, the day before Passover. The *Toledoth Yeshu,* written in the Middle Ages, states that Jesus was named after Perahyah, who was his mother's brother, and this is supported by Kirkisani who wrote a history of Jewish sects in 937 A.D.

Celsus mentions the story (in Origen's *Contra Celsum,* l.c. 1,32) and gives an authority. According to his version, Jesus' mother was seduced by a Roman soldier named Panthera. Two centuries later Epiphanius (*Haeres,* lxxviii, 7) gives the surname Panther to Jacob, an ancestor of Jesus; and gives his genealogy as Jacob, called Panther, Mary-Joseph, Cleopas, Jesus. John of Damascus (*De Orthod.,* Fide iv, sec. 15) gives the name Panther and Barpanther in the genealogy of Mary.

The garbled condition of the Talmudic records makes it impossible to determine the details with any degree of certainty, but they leave no doubt that there was a Jesus ben Pandira or Stada; that he was taken to Egypt; that he practiced magic and was crucified about one hundred years before the date given for the birth of the Biblical Jesus.

The failure of the Jews to mention Jesus of Nazareth cannot be accounted for by assuming that they erased his name from their records because they became disappointed with his teachings and considered him a false Messiah. They were as much opposed to the works of Pandira as they are reputed to have been to those of Jesus, yet they permitted Pandira's name to be mentioned several times in the Talmud. It must also be borne in mind that the supposed disappointment of the Jews did not come until near the end of Jesus' life when, as his historians assert, his life and work had become so widely known that knowledge of them could not have been suppressed. During his infancy and youth the Jews had no reason to suppress the story of his miraculous birth because they had no reason then to suspect that he was destined to disappoint them.

Upon turning to the Gospel writers for confirmation of Paul's testimony, it becomes apparent that the historicity of Jesus cannot be established by a calm, critical appraisal of the evidence presented, but must be accepted through faith alone.

As Christianity spread in the century following Paul's ministry, a great number of Gospels were written by anonymous authors who frequently signed the names of Apostles to their works in order to make them appear authoritative. The four Gospels which were finally selected by the church as authentic or inspired were claimed to be "according to" the Apostles Matthew, Mark, Luke, and John, thus implying that the events they describe were related to the authors by eye-witnesses.[7] The Gospels purport to quote many of the parables and discourses of Jesus word for word, including the comments and reactions of his listeners: they describe, in minute detail, a great number of acts and incidents in his life, some of which are of minor or even trivial interest.

Actually, however, the Gospels were written by Greek-speaking aliens and a reading of their testimony reveals an unfamiliarity with the history and geography of Palestine and an imperfect knowledge of Jewish laws and customs. While giving the impression that they were closely associated with Jesus by describing intimate details which could easily have been invented and could not be disproved, the authors seem to have avoided mention of many important details which could be verified from historical records. They are not clear as to the year in which Jesus was born or the year of his crucifixion: they give no information about his youth and early manhood or the length of his ministry: they

---

7—"Even as they delivered them unto us, which from the beginning were eyewitnesses, and ministers of the word." *Luke* 1:2.

do not know, or at least do not state, what became of his father, mother, brothers, and sisters and, in general, exhibit but a remote and sketchy knowledge of his life.

The Gospels are supposed to have been written while the incidents they describe were still fresh in the minds of the eyewitnesses, yet the Apostolic Fathers (Clement of Rome, Ignatius and Polycarp), who lived and wrote in the first half of the 2nd century, did not write anything which indicated that they had ever heard of the Gospels.

In the middle of the 2nd century Justin Martyr sought to prove the divinity of Jesus, but when he tried to refute the claims of pagan critics he could only state: "When we say also that the Word, which is the first birth of God, was produced without sexual union and that he, Jesus Christ, our teacher, was crucified, died, and rose again and ascended into heaven, we propound nothing different from what you believe regarding those whom you assume to be sons of Jupiter."[8]

In placing the Christian belief in Jesus on the same level as the pagan belief in Jupiter, Justin admitted, inferentially, that he had no more proof of the historicity of Jesus than the pagans had of their supreme god. If he had been familiar with the Gospels, this would have been the time for him to drive home his argument by calling upon the testimony of the Gospel writers to prove that the story of Jesus was history, whereas the story of Jupiter was merely mythology. But Justin made no mention of the Gospels or their authors.

Papias, a contemporary of Justin, is credited with having mentioned certain writings of Matthew and Mark, but there is no indication that the works referred to were the Gospels. The four Gospels were first definitely mentioned by Irenaeus, writing about 190 A.D., over one hundred fifty years after the alleged crucifixion.

In Matthew (23:25) Jesus criticizes the Jews for slaying Zacharias, the son of Barachias. This event took place in the temple in 69 A.D., therefore, the author of Matthew makes Jesus comment on an event which did not take place until about forty years after his death and twenty or thirty years after the Gospel of Matthew is supposed to have been written. Luke is supposed to have been a companion

---

8—*First Apology*, Chapter 21, Ante-Nicene Library, Justin Martyr.

of Paul. The Gospel bearing Luke's name is addressed to Theophilus and the only known person to whom this can refer is Theophilus, bishop of Antioch, who lived late in the second century, a hundred years after Paul's death.

The authors sought to record incomparably the greatest event since the world began. If they believed they were writing authentic history, they should not have deemed it necessary to magnify the importance of their story by embellishing it with fantastic and unbelievable incidents. Yet they wrote as if they were creating a mystery drama for propaganda purposes.

Knowing in advance that the pagans whom they wished to convert had traditions, which had been handed down for many centuries, of miraculous births, crucifixions and re-births among the gods, the authors of the Gospels must have realized that, in order to win the unbelievers, it would be necessary to convince them that the new savior had duplicated every miracle of the pagan gods and performed even greater ones. Accordingly, incident after incident would be invented or borrowed from ancient literature to furnish an imposing story. It is obvious that this was the method pursued. The result was a mixture of miracles and the moralistic teachings which were then very popular. Into this combination was blended practically every important incident that had been associated with the old world-wide myth of the sun god's birth and re-birth.

Conservative Biblical authorities place the writing of Mark's Gospel between 56 and 63 A.D. If the author of this Gospel had known of the virgin birth he surely would have mentioned it, but he says nothing about it, nor does the author of the Gospel of John which, it is claimed, was written between 78 and 97 A.D. The story first appears in the Gospel of Luke and, as related by him, Mary conceived her child before her marriage to Joseph who seems to have believed the child was his own. The Gospel of Matthew gives a somewhat different version. According to Matthew, Joseph knew the child did not belong to him, but was dissuaded from divorcing Mary by an angel who appeared to him in a dream and informed him that the child had been conceived by the Holy Ghost.

Luke's statement (2:15,17) that Jesus was attended at birth by shepherds is strongly reminiscent of a myth that the Persian god Mithra was born in a cave and was adored by shepherds. Matthew changes the shepherds to Wise Men (2:8) and adds the Star of Bethlehem. The anonymous shepherds eventually become three kings, whose names are not mentioned anywhere else in history. Matthew says that Mary and Joseph fled with the infant Jesus to Egypt to escape the wrath of King Herod; but Luke knows nothing of this and says that after the forty days of purification were over the father and mother of Jesus presented him at the temple in Jerusalem where Herod could easily have laid hands upon him.

The Gospel of Matthew begins with a genealogy of Jesus in order to prove that he was descended from David, the son of Jesse, thus fulfilling the Old Testament prophecy of Isaiah[9] that a branch of David would be born to redeem the world. Matthew's genealogy gives fourteen generations from Abraham to David, fourteen generations from David to the Exile, and fourteen generations from the Exile to Jesus, or forty-two generations in all; forty-two being a symbolic number for pain, hardship and regeneration.

Luke gives a wholly different genealogy of Jesus. He lists forty-two generations from Joseph to David. Not one name on Luke's list agrees with the corresponding name given by Matthew. From Jesus to Abraham, Luke gives fifty-six generations and from Jesus through Abraham and Adam to God a total of seventy-seven; all of these numbers being of high mystical significance.

The Gospel writers represent Jesus as being the very essence of gentleness and unbounded love, champion of the meek and lowly, yet picture him as refusing to recognize his own mother.[10] They quote him as declaring that he came to earth to send not peace but a sword. (Matt. 10:34). They have him saying in a parable, "But those mine enemies which would not that I reign over them, bring hither and slay before me" (Luke 19:27) and making other intem-

9—*Isaiah* 9:6, 11:1, 7:14. In order that this prophecy of a coming Messiah might not be misconstrued, however, Isaiah repeated at least ten times in Chapters 43 to 48 the warning that ". . . before me there was no God formed, neither shall there be after me". (43:10). "I, even I, am the Lord and beside me there is no savior". (43:11). "I am the Lord and there is none else". (45:6). "A just God and a savior, there is none beside me". (45:21,22). "For I am God and there is none else: I am God and there is none like me". (46:9). "I am the Lord; that is my name: and my glory will I not give to another". (42:8). "I am he; I am the first. I also am the last". (48:12).

10—Woman, what have I to do with thee? *John* 2:4.

perate statements which are contrary to the character of a patient lover of humanity who preached forgiveness and the return of good for evil.[11]

Jesus is made to prophesy that he would be followed by a Comforter,[12] for whom the world is still waiting. Again he is made to predict the coming end of the world, intimating that it would occur within the very lifetime of his listeners. How the Son of God could falsely forecast the end of the world is a question which has embarrassed theologians for nearly nineteen hundred years.

Matthew, Mark, and Luke seem to have formulated no clear idea as to whether Jesus was God or man. In certain passages he is quoted as saying that he and his father are one: in others he complains that his father has forsaken him. It is only in John's mind that the point is definitely decided. In the Gospel of John, Jesus becomes the incarnation of God from birth, in the form of man. The Word which Philo had envisioned as a "second God" becomes flesh by the birth of God's only begotten Son. "The Word was with God and the Word was God". (John 1:1). Almost the whole doctrine of the Logos is given in John's effort to relate the life of Jesus from the viewpoint of the Philonic theory.

In John's Epistle (I John 5:7) the long evolution of the Word and the Holy Spirit reach their culmination in John's announcement that "there are three that bear witness in heaven, the Father, the Word, and the Holy Spirit: and the three are one".[13] The belief in a sacred Trinity which, for many centuries, had been a prominent feature of Oriental religions, had at last become a part of Christian doctrine. The Word, which the ancient religions of India, Babylon, Greece, and Egypt had created as a mystic inter-

---

11—And the Lord said unto the servant, Go out into the highways and hedges, and compel *them* to come in, that my house may be filled. *Luke* 14:23.
  If any *man* come to me, and hate not his father, mother, and wife, and children and brethren, and sisters, yea, and his own life also, he cannot be my disciple. *Luke* 14:26.
  Suppose you that I am come to give peace on earth? I tell you, Nay; but rather division. *Luke* 12:51.

12—*John* 14:16,26.

13—The revised version of the Bible omits *I John* 5:7 as an interpolation. Many modern authorities believe this verse and the last twelve verses in the 28th chapter of *Matthew* were forged by the same writer in order to strengthen the doctrine of the Trinity and offset verses 10:5,6 and 15:24, which command that the word of Christ shall be preached to none but Jews.

mediary to carry out the work of their passive gods had, according to John, materialized in human form. John, however, could not have been quite sure of Jesus' oneness with God for in his Gospel (14:28) he makes Jesus say: "I go unto the Father; for my Father is greater than I".

The events narrated by John are irreconcilable with those of the other Gospels: either his work or that of the other writers must be false. Probably the principal reason why John's Gospel was accepted by the early Church Fathers as an inspired work was that he was the only Gospel writer who directly stated that the Father and Son were one. It was on the authority of John alone that the doctrine of the Trinity was established.

His stature as a historian is well revealed in the last verse in his book wherein he says, "There are also many other things which Jesus did the which, if they should be written every one, I suppose that even the world itself could not contain the books that should be written". Yet, the author is speaking of a man whose public career probably did not last more than one year.

It is now conceded by Biblical scholars that the last twelve verses of the Gospel of Mark, which tell of the resurrection and ascension of Jesus, were not written by Mark but were added by a later hand. Mark, therefore, said nothing of the resurrection. Matthew was the first to write that Christ rose from the dead. Luke gives the story in greater detail and, later, John devoted two full chapters to it. John speaks of nail holes in Jesus's hands and feet, but Luke (23:39) says Jesus was hanged.[14]

Matthew says that at the moment of Jesus's death on the cross, darkness obscured the sun, the earth heaved, saints came out of their graves[15] and walked the streets, yet nowhere on earth were these events noted except in Jerusalem. Even the Jews who are supposed to have seen them did not record them. Nor are the Gospel writers in agreement regarding details of the crucifixion, Christ's disappearance from the sepulchre, or as to the time and place he was last seen on earth before ascending to heaven.

14—Christ hath redeemed us from the curse of the law, being made a curse for us: for it is written, Cursed is every one that hangeth on a tree. *Gal* 3:13. "hanged on a tree." *Acts* 5:30; 10:39; 13:29.

15—*Matthew* 27:45,53. See also *Luke* 23:44,45.

When these many details are considered together, they fail in several respects to qualify as authentic history, as measured by modern standards. First: One of the primary requirements of history is that events described must appear to be reasonably probable. Evidence given to substantiate a claim should be in proportion to its degree of probability or improbability. Stories of events of an extraordinary or improbable character require extraordinary verification. If a modern writer were to state that he had seen an athlete jump 22 feet his statement would, in ordinary circumstances, appear reasonably credible because it is well known that such an accomplishment is a physical possibility. But, if the writer were to claim that the athlete had jumped 75 feet, critical readers would demand that the story be supported by a motion picture record and affidavits from many reliable witnesses because such a feat would be so extraordinary as to be outside of human experience.

Not only do the Gospel writers fail to offer appropriate evidence to substantiate their claims upon grounds of reasonable probability, but their numerous discrepancies, contradictions, and omissions, their readiness to accept as facts rumors and legends which they had heard at third and fourth hand; their obvious role as reformers, their desire to promote religious doctrines and their apparent willingness to even invent stories to promote these doctrines is proof that, instead of being objective historians, they were decidedly propagandists. Indeed, if any subject other than religion were involved, it is extremely doubtful whether any body of thoughtful men would take the writings of such men seriously.

The Gospel writers portray God as the kindly Heavenly Father who loves all of his earthly children. It is inconceivable, therefore, that he should visit the earth without making his teachings and his presence known to every nation and tribe in the world. Yet only a tiny minority of mankind were favored with a knowledge of Christ and his activities.[16] A God who could give all of his devotion

---

16—These twelve Jesus sent forth and commanded them, saying, Go not in the way of the Gentiles, and into any city of the Samaritans enter ye not. But go rather to the lost sheep of the house of Israel. *Matt.* 10:5,6.
But he answered and said, I am not sent but unto the lost sheep of the house of Israel. *Matt.* 15:24.

to the Jews and show no interest in the other peoples of the world would be unworthy of worship or even respect. This fact alone stamps the Jesus story as the creation of provincially-minded men who thought only in terms of their own little community and did not expect or intend that their messages would be disseminated throughout the world.

The Gospel writers, furthermore, revealed their lack of perspicacity when they represented Jesus as telling his listeners on numerous occasions that the end of the world was imminent, assuring them that it would come within their own lifetime. They made statements in this connection which the future would positively prove or disprove. By representing Jesus as trying to instill fear and anxiety into the minds of the ignorant and credulous with prophecies of a world-wide catastrophe which never materialized, they unwittingly portrayed him as a false prophet and cruel charlatan. If it be assumed, however, that these warnings originated in the minds of the Gospel writers, that they merely seized upon a widespread superstition that the world would soon come to an end and attributed their own false prophecies to Jesus in order to frighten people into an acceptance of the new religion, then they were unscrupulous writers who wrote with intent to deceive.

God is represented, on the one hand as the omnipotent and omniscient ruler of the universe and on the other as the author of history's greatest and most tragic failure, for his visit on earth utterly failed to redeem mankind. Men continued, after the reputed resurrection, to be as selfish, as lustful, and as cruel as before.

An all-powerful and all-knowing God could have transformed the hearts of men by the mere waving of his hand; at least, he could have devised an easier and more practical way to save humanity, and a far more successful one, than the long, painful method described by the Gospel writers. But that would have made the task too simple. Unless the object of their worship performed all kinds of marvelous and even ridiculous feats, how would people know that he was the true God? This is why the creators of ancient mythology always endeavored to excite the awe and wonderment of the people by inventing round-about ways and difficult tasks for their godly heroes, involving pain, hardships, persecutions, and supernatural performances. Such tragic and spectacular incidents characterize the religious literature of every age and country and constitute the tell-tale trade marks of the myth makers.

Having considered the testimony of the Gospel writers and the silence of the Jews regarding Jesus, it is clear why his contemporary, Paul, failed to report the miracles and teachings of Jesus which were reputedly well known to other men who wrote many years after Paul's death. Paul said nothing of these matters for the reason that he knew nothing of them. The Apostle to the Gentiles was ignorant of these things because in his day they had not yet been invented.

CHAPTER XXII

THE HOLY THREE

(Continued)

WITH THE PRONOUNCEMENT of the three-fold manifestation of God, the authors of the Gospels apparently thought the relation of the Word and Spirit to the Godhead was disposed of for all time and required no explanation. At least they did not explain the relationship, and perhaps did not realize just what it was.

Opponents of the doctrine, however, charged that, in its worship of the Father, Son, and Holy Ghost, Christianity was not essentially different in that respect from the pagan worship of triads of gods.

There being in the first centuries no central organization to define the limitations of belief, each church tried to refute the charges of tritheism and explain the Trinity in its own way. Consequently, differences and contradictions soon developed in the theories advanced by various leaders, which constantly involved the church in schisms and charges of heresy. Among the many questions which arose were these:

Was Christ a mere man endowed with divine wisdom and power?

Did the divine spirit abide in the man Jesus or was the incarnation a mere figure under which God was revealed to man?

Could Christ, being mortal, be of the same substance as God or was he inferior?

If his birth was contrary to nature, could he be a real man?

Did he possess both divine and human natures in one or was he wholly divine?

Was he capable of change, i.e., possessed of freedom of will and choice of good and evil or was he incapable of sin?

Was he co-existent with the Father from the beginning or was there a time when he did not exist?

The orthodox position of the church on such questions developed slowly out of hair-splitting discussions of numerous charges of heresy where a defendant's guilt or innocence was sometimes decided by the shades of meanings of a single word.

High-lighting this phase of early church history were the heresies of Sabellius, a presbyter of Libya, Paul of Samosata, the prelate of Antioch, and Arius, a presbyter of Baucalis, a suburb of Alexandria.

Sabellius was condemned for declaring that Christ and the Holy Ghost were mere characters by whom God is revealed to men. Paul of Samosata was condemned for asserting that Christ was a mere man in whom the divine Logos dwelt. Arius, a tall, ascetic man who had a sharp, brilliant mind, was the most difficult adversary. He contended that Christ had no existence before he was begotten. As God was the Father, he must have existed before the Son, and as the creator is superior to that which he creates, God is superior to his Son. Being a creature, Christ could not be of the same substance as God. As a creature, Christ had freedom of will and was kept sinless only by his own virtue.

Arius gained many supporters and the controversy over his theories still raged when the bishops finally assembled at Nicea in 325 A.D. to define Christian belief.

The bishops knew that the very existence of the church depended upon their decisions. They had to devise a formula which would heal the wounds produced by 200 years of strife; preserve the Trinity, and avoid the appearance of tritheism. No body of men ever sat down to solve a more insoluble problem. In such a situation their decisions were bound to be dictated by political considerations rather than by facts and logic.

F. J. Foakes-Jackson quotes the historian Socrates as saying: "What took place was a fight in the dark; no man knew whether he struck friend or foe". The author then adds: "A fear of heresy on the one hand and of innovation on the other made them waverers; yet it was by the vote of such as these that the matter had to be decided."[1]

It was evident that the only way to exclude Arius from the church was to pronounce Christ divine, yet wholly

---

1—*The History of the Christian Church*, F. J. Foakes-Jackson, p. 307.

mortal; of the same substance as the Father; existent, not merely from the moment of his human· birth as the man Jesus, but generated by God from the beginning. As a mortal, Christ was capable of sin but as a result of the Logos' taking the place of the higher soul, there could be in him only one nature.

That this formula was contradictory and impossible was realized from the beginning. It was only 50 years since Paul of Samosata had been condemned and driven from the church for declaring that both divine and mortal natures dwelt in Christ. Humiliating as it was for the church to reverse its own decision, it had to be done. Any other decision would have been equivalent to declaring that the Father and Son were not one God but two, and this the delegates dared not do. Some of the bishops failed to comprehend the actual meaning of the point at issue and approved the Creed with tongue in cheek.

The doctrine of a Tri-une God ruling the world was urged upon the council by Athanasius, Bishop of Alexandria, supported by bishops of the eastern churches who, doubtless, were aware of the age-old heathen belief in the triadic character of the gods and were, perhaps, shrewd enough to realize the advantages of such a doctrine in winning converts from the heathen cults. At any rate, the Holy Ghost was treated as an extraneous issue throughout the council meeting. Except for requiring a belief in the Holy Ghost, the council did nothing toward defining its relation to the Godhead, and it remained a useless appendage, serving no purpose other than to complete the Trinity. There being no personage to represent the third member of the Trinity, it became customary in later religious art to represent this member as a dove, the mystic symbol of the Holy Spirit.

As finally adopted at Constantinople, in 381 A.D., the Creed says:

> "(We believe) . . . in one Lord, Jesus Christ, the only begotten Son of God, begotten of the Father before all worlds, (God of God), Light of Light, Very God of God, begotten not made, being of one substance with the Father; by whom all things were made; who, for us men and for our salvation, came down from heaven and was incarnated by the Holy Ghost of the Virgin Mary," etc.

This affirmation should be re-read and given searching thought by every reader. No other religion in the world ever put forth such an astounding doctrine. From the works of the Gospel writers, particularly John, the bishops at Nicea formulated the doctrine that Jesus is not merely the Son of God, but that he is God, the two names referring to different manifestations of the same person.

Secondary details omitted, the Creed and the Gospels together affirm that God was grieved by the sinfulness of his children on earth and decided to come down from heaven to redeem them. For this purpose his Spirit entered the womb of Mary and, in due time, he was born in human form. After birth, he lived as a normal but obscure person for about thirty years. Then he began to teach and perform miracles and, finally, contrived to have himself crucified. (The crucifixion must have been part of his plan for the redemption of the world: being omniscient and omnipotent, he could have prevented it had he wished to do so).[2] After being dead for part of three days, he resurrected himself from the tomb and, after an uncertain period (the Gospel writers do not agree on this point), returned, still in human form, to his throne in heaven.

Converts to Christianity were required to accept these beliefs as sacred truths: persons who did not accept them were doomed to eternal torture in hell. For many centuries thousands of men and women who could not, in all conscience, subscribe to such incomprehensible dogmas suffered the agonies of a real hell on earth by persecution, exile, torture, or burning at the stake.

Almost from the moment of its adoption, the Nicean Creed became the subject of violent criticism by Arian partisans. Before the opposition was permanently put down in 381 A.D., Macedonius, the Patriarch of Constantinople, had been condemned for denying the divinity of the Holy Ghost, and the theory of the Two Substances in one person had been discarded by the church and again restored.

At the council of Chalcedon, in 451, it was declared that in the person of Christ are united two complete

---

2—No man taketh it (life) from me, but I lay it down of myself. I have power to lay it down, and I have power to take it again. *John* 10:18.

natures, divine and human. This was supplemented at the third council of Constantinople, in 680, by the statement that each of the natures contains a will, so that Christ possesses two wills. The western church adopted the decisions of Nicea, Chalcedon, and Constantinople, therefore the doctrines of the Trinity and the Two Substances of Christ were handed down as orthodox dogma for the churches of the East and the West.

The doctrine never ceased to be a cause of contention. Until two or three hundred years ago, it remained a prime source of debate in the church. Opinions of churchmen regarding the relationship of the members of the Trinity changed back and forth. Although churchmen held that God and Christ are one, the charges of heresy made against the theologian Abelard by St. Bernard, in the twelfth century, were based, in part, upon Abelard's declaration that Christ did not fear God.

From the beginning, a minor Christian element persisted which could not accept belief in a Holy Trinity which did not include a female member. The Ophites, an early sect, solved the problem by adopting the pagan concept of a Trinity consisting of Father, Mother, and Son. Hippolytus found in them an Assyrian dogma of a trinity of the soul. The Mandaeans, another Christian sect, regarded the Ruha (Holy Spirit) as the mother of the Messiah, a view which harmonizes with the Cabalistic theory that the Holy Spirit is feminine.

The influence of the ancient tradition may still be seen in the modern tendency of the Catholic Church to subordinate or replace the Holy Spirit by greatly magnifying the role of the Virgin Mother. In the last century, Cardinal Newman carried this tendency to its logical conclusion in his *Golden Manual* (Response V, p. 649) with the statement that "The God himself created her (Mary) in the Holy Ghost and poured her out among all his works."

Many volumes have been written in unsuccessful efforts to rationalize the Trinity and make it appear plausible. Realizing the hopelessness of trying to make it understandable, most present-day churchmen prefer to avoid controversy by simply contending that the composition of the

Trinity is an incomprehensible mystery of divine revelation.[3]

Stripped of its mystic pretensions, however, the doctrine is strictly a human invention, evolved painfully out of two hundred years of bitter and sometimes bloody dissension, and is incomprehensible only for the reason that an effort was made to write meanings into it which did not make sense, even to its authors. Early in the third century, Tertullian wrote what still stands as perhaps the most candid and the most inane apology for the Christian doctrine that has ever been made. Said he: "I reverence it because it is contemptible: I adore it because it is absurd: I believe it because it is impossible."

At this late day no religious body would dare amend or discard the doctrine, and it remains a lasting token of men's willingness to subscribe to beliefs which they can neither prove nor comprehend.

3—"Although the Christian Church soon came to look upon the Trinity as an incomprehensible mystery of revelation which reason may not probe, her theologians have not refrained, either in ancient or in modern times, from speculations upon the doctrine." *Enc. of Rel. & Ethics.*, v.12, p.460.
"We maintain it is a mystery not to be measured by human intelligence but necessary for human salvation." Pref. to *Synopsis of the Gospels in Greek* by Dr. A. Wright, p. vi.
"The conclusion is obvious that while we are taught by the Scriptures to believe in the three subjects in the Godhead who are described as persons, we are still unable to determine in what manner or in what sense these three have the divine nature so in common that there is only one God." McClintock & Strong's *Cyclopedia of Biblical, Theological and Ecclesiastical Literature*, vol.10, p.555.

CHAPTER XXIII

THE TRINITY IN JUDAISM

AN INQUIRY INTO the idea of a Trinity in Unity would not be complete without some further words about its relation to Judaism. In tracing the evolution of "the Word", it has been shown that as the anthropomorphic God receded into the distance, the Jews came to look upon the Word as a creative agent of the Almighty. This idea spread until Wisdom, Understanding, the Shekinah, the "presence" or "faces", in fact every power, attribute or aspect of God visible to man had become an entity, as if God were a many-armed being with each arm performing some specific part of his work. Nothing has been shown, however, which indicates that these powers were conceived as forming a Trinity or Triad. Among both Christians and Jews there is an assumption that the Trinity was peculiarly Christian in origin, wholly unrelated to old Jewish beliefs.

The fact that God had 3 principal titles—Yahwe, Elohim and El Shaddai; that Adam and Noah each had 3 sons; that 3 angels appeared before Abraham on the plains of Mamre; that Moses, Aaron, and Miriam formed a triad; these are considered to have been mere coincidences and to have no significance.

But the reader has probably observed that Oriental writers liked to draw analogies and to recite history in the form of parables. The mere facts of history were not considered as important as were the symbolic relationships which could be drawn from them. Both words and numbers were often used, especially by early writers, not in a strict, factual sense but in a way which made the event described conform to the writer's notions of its symbolic connotations. Religious rites, customs, and practices were not mere haphazard, spontaneous developments but were carefully planned to symbolize certain beliefs, many of which were known only to the priesthood.

An example of this may be seen in the placing of cherubim to the right and left of God's place on the mercy seat in the Holy of Holies. The Bible does not tell why this was done and Bible authorities can offer no definite explanation of it; but if God were envisioned as of 3-fold

character, it would not have been unreasonable for the
Israelites to have provided seats for the 3 members of the
Godhead. This seems to have been been the conclusion
reached by Philo for in one place he stated that although
God is one, this is not to be understood with respect to
number and in another place he declared the cherubim were
symbols of the 2 eternal powers of God. The same thought
appears repeatedly in the Targumim.

Again, all Jews were commanded to wear upon their
foreheads leather phylacteries or frontlets on which were
inscribed the 3-pronged letter Shin and no explanation
was given as to why this particular letter was adopted as
an emblem of Yahweh.[1]

Small square pieces of parchment were placed within
the phylacteries and on them were written 4 verses from
the Scriptures, the first of them being the fourth of Deuteronomy, chapter 6, in which the name of the Lord is
repeated 3 times—"Hear, O Israel, our Lord God is one
Lord." Every Jew was commanded to repeat this verse
at least twice daily. A similar repetition of the holy name
appears in the blessing of Israel given in Numbers 6:24,25,26
and in Isaiah 33:22 and 6:3.

A similar device was worn upon the left forearm. In
this case the leather strap on the device was wrapped
around the middle finger three times so as to form the
letter Shin; then the strap was wound around the forearm
seven times and tied with a knot which formed the letter
Yod or Jod, the emblem of Yahweh.

When giving the eternal blessing to the assembly, the
priest makes the sign of the Trinity, as Mohammedan and
Brahman priests do, by raising the right arm and extending the 3 middle fingers. In reciting the blessing, the priest
reads the verse from Numbers 6:24 3 times, speaking in
a different tone of voice with each reading.

That these customs were symbolic of certain Jewish
beliefs is obvious, but the Bible does not shed any light
upon what the beliefs were. Therefore, it is to the Cabala
and other esoteric works that we must go to learn something
about them.

1—And thou shalt bind them for a sign upon thine hand and they
shall be as frontlets between thine eyes.
And thou shalt write them upon the posts of thy house and on
thy gates. *Deut.* 6:8,9 and *Ex.* 13:9,16.

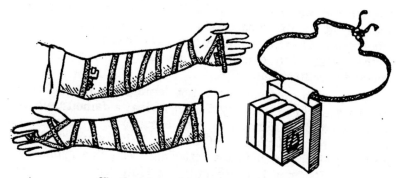

87. Jewish head and arm phylacteries.

Modern critics are generally inclined to belittle the Cabala as an example of the more extravagant form of Jewish speculations, which it is. Yet it must be conceded that its authors were learned men who had a deep knowledge of Jewish history and traditions, and in writing the Cabala they were only putting into organized form concepts which had been current for many centuries among those who were familiar with the higher, esoteric phases of Jewish mysticism.

The *Zohar* (book of the Cabala) speaks of Elohim as being 3-fold and proceeds to explain this dogma by a quotation from a Rabbi R. Jose, as follows: "Come and see the mystery in the word Elohim (Aleim)! There are 3 degrees and every degree is distinct by himself, yet notwithstanding, they are all one and bound together in one, nor can they be separated each from the other."

Again quoting from R. Jose (Exod. col. 75), the same authority gives the following explanation for the repetition of the Lord's name in Deuteronomy 6:4 and the change of voice when reading Numbers 6:24: "They must know that these 3, viz., *ieue Aleim ieue* (Jehovah Aleim Jehovah) are one *unum* and that is the secret which we learn in the mystery of the voice which is here: the voice is one *unum* but it contains 3 modes, viz., the fire, the air and the water. Now these 3 are one in the mystery of the voice and they are but one *unum,* so in this place, Jehovah our Lord Jehovah are one *unum*". According to this view the hidden, or secret, meaning of the 3 modes seems to have been that Jehovah was Lord of the 3 great divisions of the universe, fire, air and water which, as we have seen, was exactly the role played by the great gods of India, Babylonia, Greece and Egypt. Elsewhere the author says that the 3 branches of the letter Shin denote the heavenly fathers who are named in Deuteronomy 6:4.

That such opinions were not confined to the Cabalists may be seen in a work by Rabbi Akiba, a famous scholar of the second century who was considered a paragon of wisdom. In his *Alphabet of Letters* Akiba says: "Why is the letter aleph written as a letter and read as a syllable of 3 letters? Because it represents the Holy One who is one and the reading of his name is a 3-fold, as it is written: "Hear, O Israel, our Lord God is one Lord."

Rev. Father Calmet observed that Raymond Martin, Galatine and several other scholars of the Middle Ages undertook to show that the Chaldee paraphrase of the Pentateuch and the ancient rabbis made express mention of the Trinity and of the 3 persons. Calmet says: "We find indeed in their writings the word Shalishith, which signifies Trinity and Memar (Memra) which signifies the Word and Ruach Kakkadoshah, which signifies the Holy Spirit. We also find God the Father, God the Son, and God the Holy Spirit. Lastly the Tri-une, Three-in-One and One-in-Three and Jehovah to express the Father, the Memara-jah for the word of the Father and Shekinah for the Holy Ghost."[2]

Anastasius Kircher, a seventeenth century Jesuit scholar, wrote that on all of the Hebrew manuscripts which he had seen in the Vatican the 3 Jods were printed in a circle as a symbol of JVH.[3] Elsewhere he gives a quotation in which all the persons of the Trinity are named, thus: Pater Deus, Filius Deus, Spiritus Sanctus Deus, Trinus in Unitate et Unus in Trinitate;[4] God the Father, God the Son, God the Holy Spirit, Trinity in Unity and Unity in Trinity.

The Cabala designates God as En Soph or Infinity, consisting of 10 Sephiroth which are interpreted as "faces" and a great distinction is made between the first 3 and the last 7 Sephiroth. The first 3 are designated the Crown, Wisdom

---

2—*An Historical, Critical, Geographical, Chronological & Etymological Dictionary of the Bible*, 3 vols., 1732, by Rev. Father Dom Augustin Calmet, v.3, p.100.

3—*Oedipus Aegyptiacus*, 1662 by Anastasius Kircher, Tomi 2, p.114.

4—*Ibid*, Tomi 2, p. 246.

or Understanding and the Ruach, or Holy Spirit. This conception could not merely have been drawn from the authors' imagination for, as we have seen, Wisdom and the Holy Spirit were considered as agents of the divine essence in Post-Exilic times if not earlier. They are self-created personalities or modes of existence, yet they are all one and the name is one, the name Jehovah applying equally to the 3 Sephiroth. In other words God is manifested in 3 forms: Crown, Wisdom and Holy Spirit.

The author of the *Zohar* and the author of the *Book of Habbakir* declare that the 2nd Sephira proceeds from the 1st and that the 3rd proceeds from the 2nd. This is comparable to the Indian tradition which makes Vishnu proceed from Brahma, and Siva to issue from the forehead of Vishnu. Calabists designate the Holy Spirit as being feminine, and this belief is also sanctioned by very old tradition. St. Jerome observed that it was common among the Nazarenes.

The last 7 Sephiroth are called Middoth or measures, that is attributes and characters which are visible in the works of God, such as fear, justice, beauty, etc.

Rabbi Menachem, a noted Cabalist, declared it was the Shekinah that appeared to Adam after his sin and made clothes for him; that he appeared to Abram and Jacob and that it was he who spoke to Moses and gave the law to the people.

A Cabalist, Rabbi Joseph ben Gekatilia, quoted Isaiah (11:2) to the effect that the Messiah and Wisdom were the same. "The spirit of Wisdom shall rest upon him (the Messiah), the Spirit of Wisdom and Understanding." Isaiah 48:16 and 59:19,20,21 are given similar interpretations.

Another Cabalist, Ehat Rabbi Salomon Jarchi, declared upon the authority of Isaiah 11 that the Cochma (Wisdom) shall be in the middle of the Messiah and the Book of Enoch says: "The Messiah exists from the beginning; he sits on the throne of God and possesses universal dominion; all judgment is committed unto him". This is almost precisely the position taken by the bishops at the Council of Nicea in their struggle against Arianism, and it proves that the theories of the Cabalists were deeply rooted in Jewish tradition.

Turning from the opinions of Cabalists and others to the Bible itself for further light on the 3-fold nature of the

Godhead, brings us at once to one of the Book's great mysteries. Two of the principal titles of God (Elohim and Adonai), are plural words but in the translation of the Bible they have been used repeatedly in a singular sense.

In defense of the interpretation which has thus been placed upon the names, Bible authorities maintain that the authors of the text perhaps followed a custom which was widespread in ancient times of employing plural titles for deities to signify majesty and power. But in view of the great pains the Jews took to distinguish between Yahweh and the heathen gods, not only does this explanation appear superficial, but it creates the suspicion that an effort has been made to conceal something. Presently it will be shown that this suspicion is quite justified.

Genesis 11:7 now reads, "Go to, let *us* go down and there confound their language . . .", and in Genesis 3:22 God does not say of Adam, "behold the man has become like me", or even "like us". He says rather, *"as one of us"*. Here the language is direct, simple and clear; and there can be no question about the intended meaning. Had it been intended in the first part of these sentences to convey the idea that the words were spoken by God, in the first person singular, the construction of the entire sentence would have been different.

Again, in Genesis 49:25, appeal is made to what appear to be two distinct Gods: "By the God (Al) of thy father, who shall help thee, and by the Almighty (Shaddi), who shall bless thee with blessings". In this case the word Shaddi is translated "Almighty" whereas in Leviticus 17:7 and Deuteronomy 32:17 *i shdim* (the shaddim) is translated "devils".

Deuteronomy 32:17 reads: "They sacrificed unto devils (*Shdim* or Shaddim) not to God (Ale); to gods (Aleim) whom they knew not, to new gods (Aleim) that came newly up. . . .'" Here "Ale'" means God, singular: Aleim refers to gods plural and the word Shaddim is translated "devils".

When Aaron speaks of a golden image of the Egyptian bull Apis which the Israelites had made during the absence of Moses, there can be no question of his using the word Aleim in a plural sense: "These be thy gods (Aleim) O

Israel, which brought thee out of the land of Egypt" (Exodus 32:4).

In Exodus 2:23 the word Aleim is preceded by *e* meaning "the" and the sentence should read, "Their cry came up to *the gods*". In Exodus 6:7, 15:3, 40:32, 35:5 and elsewhere the singular rendering is given, but in Exodus 18:11 and Deuteronomy 10:17 and 12:30, 31 *e aleim* is translated "gods".

In Genesis 35:7 the plural Aleim is joined with a plural verb and should read: "And (Jacob) called the place El Beth-el *because the gods there appeared to him*". Joshua 24:19 should read, "You cannot serve the Lord, for he is the Holy Gods."

Many similar examples of mistranslation appear, not only in the Pentateuch, but in Job 35:10; Psalm 119:1; II Samuel 7:23, Isaiah 49:24, 54:5 and elsewhere.[5] The term *ieue aleim* (Jehovah Gods) is always translated incorrectly, "Lord God," and efforts are made to have it appear that Lord and God are synonymous terms. In passages where Aleim is used as a name for Jehovah it denotes one God, but when used as a name for heathen gods it is translated as a plurality of gods. Wherever it was the intention to denote one God the title Aleim or Elohim might have been used in its singular form, Eloah, but this was seldom done.

Had the rabbis understood that Aleim was to be read as a singular word, they would have interpreted "I saw gods" (I Samuel 28:13) as referring to one person but they did not do so. Their own Talmudists have concluded that this passage referred to two persons, namely, Moses and Samuel.[6]

Further evidence that the rabbis were well aware that Aleim referred to Gods, plural, is given elsewhere in their own records. In commenting upon the Greek translation of the Pentateuch, which was made at the request of Ptolemy Philadelphus, the Talmudists state that in parts of the text Aleim was translated into Greek as a singular noun, because to have made it plural would have given the

5—See *The Judgment of the Ancient Jewish Church Against the Unitarians,* Peter Allix, Oxford, 1821.

6—*Midrash Sam. Rabbatha,* cap. 27: Tanchuma fol. 63, col. 2.

Egyptian king the impression that the Jews worshiped more than one God. Had they not known that Aleim should be read in a plural sense, they would not have deemed it necessary to explain why it had, in some instances, been rendered in the singular.

Names or titles were, for Jews, as they were for the Babylonians, not mere appellations, but were revealing of the things themselves. They sought to make sure that a name or title truly indicated the character of the person or thing to which it applied, and a change of character or status was accompanied by a change of name. This was particularly true of important figures.

When the names of Abram, Sarai, and Jacob were changed to Abraham, Sarah and Israel, the change indicated an alteration in their status or character. The change from the name Hebrew, to Israelite, and then to Jew marked important changes in Jewish religious concepts. Accordingly, when the Holy One appeared to Moses and announced that henceforth he was to be known only as Jahveh (Exodus 6:3), it marked the end of an old and the beginning of a new concept.

Observe how the incident is described in Exodus. Four hundred thirty years are supposed to have elapsed since the Jews had arrived in Egypt, and during that time they had drifted away from the worship of Jahveh and no longer remembered him. When Jahveh told Moses to announce his return, Moses asked whose name he should give as the source of his information, and Jahveh answered Moses in the manner of a modern sales manager giving a "pep" talk to subordinates. ". . . say unto the people of Israel that Ahih (I AM), hath sent you." (Exodus 3:14).[7]

"Tell your people I am the God of your fathers, Abraham, Isaac, and Jacob," says Jahveh, "And I appeared unto Abraham, unto Isaac, and unto Jacob, by the name of God Almighty, but by my name Jahveh (Jehovah) was

---

7—Ahi is a title which the Egyptians gave to their god Horus, and Jahveh's designation of himself as I AM or I AM THAT I AM, is a title which the Persians gave to their god Ahura Mazda. "My name is Ahmi, I AM, . . . and my twentieth name is Ahmi Yad Ahmi Mazdeo, I AM THAT I AM." *Avesta* xvii, 4, 6. "The ineffable name of the Parsees, *Soham Asmi* translates I AM THAT I AM." *Sacred Books of the Hindus*, Part 1, Vol. 1, p.8 Introduction.

I not known to them". (Exodus 6:3). Tell your people I am the Lord, says Jahveh, "And I will take you to me for a people and I will be to you a God". (Exodus 6:7). Speaking as one who had long been absent, he says: "Tell your people I have surely visited you and seen that which is done to you in Egypt". (Exodus 3:16). No reason is given for abolishing the old names Elohim and Al Shaddai, but these and subsequent passages of Exodus reveal the new conception of God as being quite unlike that of the old God of Abraham, Isaac, and Jacob, and really amounting to the beginning of a new religion.

Biblical chronology places the date of this incident at about 1500 B.C. According to Prof. Stephen H. Langdon,[8] however, in the earliest written records of Samaria, the name was written Yaw or Yah, not Jahveh, and among Samaritan exiles in Assyria the name invariably appeared in this form in proper names. As late as the sixth or fifth century, B.C., a Jewish colony in Elephantine, in southern Egypt, wrote in Aramaic and pronounced the name of their principal god Yaw, whom they associated with the Canaanitish mother goddess Astarte or Anat, as Astarte-Yaw or Anat-Yaw. The name Yahweh or Jahveh did not exist. The name Elohim, in its singular form, Eloah, is equivalent to and apparently is derived from the south Arabic deity Il or Ilah, or from the north Arabic deity Allilah or Allah, who became the supreme god of the Mohammedans.

In the text quoted above, Jahveh appears to be anxious that his name should be known to every Jew, but, subsequently, a mysterious and very important change took place. To seek to know his nature or to understand the mysteries of his work, was sinful. Even his proper name became a profound secret, and to pronounce it was a gross sacrilege. When those who knew the holy word referred to Jahveh, they called him Adonai, meaning "My Lords". Leviticus 24:16 clearly implied that to utter the holy name was punishable even by death, and as late as 130 A.D. an Abba Saul denied eternal blessings to any one who pronounced the sacred word with the actual consonants. Whereas the feeling of the Jews toward the old Jahveh was one of nearness and warmth, it was now succeeded by a feeling of remoteness, impersonality, and austerity.

8—*Myths of all Races*, vol. 5, p. 42.

The nearest approach to an admission that the old names Jahveh, Elohim and Al Shaddai were titles of different deities rather than alternate titles of the same God, is contained in the statement of Isaiah (26:13): "O Lord our God, others beside thee have had dominion over us."

That there were many things relating to the worship of Jahveh which were carefully withheld from the common people is confirmed by Jewish traditions that, in addition to the written Laws and records, there were certain others which were deemed too profound for popular understanding. These sacred Laws and records, it is said, were committed by Moses to Aaron and the priesthood and by them handed down orally only to the learned from generation to generation.

Another tradition credits the Chaldean priest-scribe Ezra with rewriting the Books of Moses after the original Books had been destroyed by Nebuchadnezzar's army in the attack on Jerusalem in 586 B.C. This tradition was certainly known to the author of the Fourth Book of Ezra, or Esdras, for in that work Ezra laments that because of the destruction of the holy city, "thy law is burned, therefore no man knoweth the things that are done of them, or the works that shall be done". (Ch. 14, v.21).

As the re-writing of the holy records is described in IV Ezra, Jahveh responds to Ezra's grief and gives him a cupful of wonderful water which strengthens his memory and enables his heart to utter understanding and wisdom. Jahveh then commands him to procure many tablets and five scribes, and to tell people to stay away for forty days. Ezra does this and although it is nearly a hundred and fifty years since the records were destroyed, Ezra miraculously reproduces them by dictation from "memory"; and within the prescribed time, ninety-four books are written, twenty-four of which compose the Jewish canon, and are to be published. But Jahveh commands that the remaining seventy books be kept secret, saying: "These words shalt thou declare, not hide thee . . . then shalt thou declare some things openly unto the perfect and some things shalt thou speak secretly unto the wise . . . the first that thou hast written, publish openly that the worthy and unworthy may read it, but keep the seventy last that thou mayest tell them only to such as be wise among the people. For in them is the spring of understanding, the

fountain of wisdom and the stream of knowledge".[9]
(Chap. 14:6, 26, 45).

In refutation of Ezra it may be pointed out that this work contains references to events which did not occur until the first century A.D. Its real author certainly could not have been the Biblical Ezra. It is obvious that Ezra could not have re-written more than a small portion of the Scriptures because they are composed of many styles of writing and give, in many instances, contradictory accounts of the same events, which would not have been the case had the entire work come from the hands of one man.

IV Ezra does indicate, however, that even in the first century, there was a tradition that the Scriptures had been destroyed, and that part of them contained certain doctrines, and perhaps described secret rites and practices, which the priests did not dare make known to the common people. The destruction of the records seems to be confirmed also, by II Chronicles 36:18,19, II Kings, Chap. 25, and Jeremiah, Chap. 52 where it is stated that Nebuchadnezzar's army took all the holy treasures and other things of value from the temple, then burned it to the ground. The spoil was taken to Babylon. It is not stated that the records were saved at that time and, so far as is known, every vestige of them was destroyed. Aside from these uncertain references, the existence and whereabouts of the Scriptures is not mentioned from the beginning of the Exile until Ezra turned up with them in Jerusalem.

According to Nehemiah (Chapter 8), Ezra took the Books from Babylon to Jerusalem and there read them to the people in 444 B.C., and gained popular acceptance for them in exactly the same manner that Josiah had secured acceptance of the Book of Deuteronomy two hundred years earlier. How Ezra obtained possession of the Books is not disclosed.

9—The secret things belong unto the Lord our God, but those things which are revealed belong to us and to our children forever that we may do all the words of the law. *Deut.* 29:29.
Search not the things that are too wonderful for thee. And seek not that which is hid from thee ... thou hast no business with the secret things.
—Ben Sira.
The learned may penetrate into the significance of all Oriental mysteries, but the vulgar can only see the exterior symbol. It is allowed by all who have knowledge of the Scriptures that everything is conceived enigmatically. *Letter of Origin to Celsus.*

It will probably never be possible to determine definitely when or by whom the existing version of the Pentateuch was written, nor will it be possible to ascertain to what extent it differs from the original records that were destroyed in the burning of Jerusalem. No inscriptions or documents from Pre-Exilic times, written with the square Hebrew letters now in use, have ever been discovered. Furthermore, the forms of writing employed before the Exile do not appear on any known records of the Post-Exilic period. In fact, Origen, St. Jerome, and other authorities have definitely attributed the invention of the square letters to Ezra. It is clear, therefore, that all existing manuscripts were put into their present form after the Exile.

The evidence indicates beyond doubt that during and after the period of the Exile, a staff of priestly writers in Babylon was engaged in compiling all of the known Jewish myths, folklore, history, psalms, proverbs, etc. These writers included, in addition to this material, many beliefs and myths which they had derived from the Persians and Babylonians. In order to revive the national spirit among the captive Jews, they gave the combined material a heightened background which aggrandized the Jewish people, and made them appear superior to all their neighbors in culture and religion.

The priestly scribes probably deleted the crudest portions of the record and made such other alterations as would make the work acceptable to the people of their day. Old beliefs or customs which conspicuously revealed a similarity to the pagan cults were minimized or glossed over, and whatever information the records contained regarding the plural titles and the three-fold nature of Jahveh, was eliminated.

Since the finding in the last century of ancient Babylonian tablets containing myths of the Creation and the Deluge, it has become certain that the Biblical accounts of these events were taken from Babylonian sources. None of the early patriarchs or prophets make any references to the stories of Creation, the Fall of Adam and Eve, or the Flood. It is, therefore, altogether unlikely that these stories found their way into the Scriptures before the sixth or fifth centuries B.C.

The remainder of Genesis is strongly colored by Babylonian customs and spiritism, and appears to be symbolic mythology rather than history. The name of Abram seems to be a reversal of the Hindu name Bram-a. Abram's wife is Sara: Brahma's wife is Saraswati. Brama committed incest with his sister, Vach: Abram represented Sara as his sister. Milka, the sister of Sara equates with Milka-tu, an epithet of Ishtar. These parallels are too close to warrant their being dismissed as mere coincidences.

Now that it is known that many of the Laws of Moses were adapted from the Laws of Hammurabi and that many important details in the birth, life and acts of the supposed great law-giver of the Jews may be found in myths about King Sargon of Babylonia, and the Greek god Bacchus, there is no longer any doubt about the mythical character of the Moses legends. Although there may have been a Jewish leader who bore the name of Moses, the accounts of his birth, of his miracles in Egypt, of the forty years of wandering in the desert, and of his receipt of the divine commands from God on Mount Sinai, seem to have been invented for the purpose of making it appear that the beliefs and statutes which the priests gave to the people were not of their own making, but were handed down directly to Moses by Jahveh himself.

After the first editors had made such revisions, additions, and deletions as they deemed expedient, later redactors and compilers continued to do likewise until long after the time when the Pentateuch was translated into Greek, about 280 B.C. Thus the Books of Joshua, Samuel, Judges, Kings, Chronicles, and the Books of the Prophets refer to events which did not occur until years, even centuries, after the time in which they are supposed to have been written.[10] Where several existing manuscripts refer to the same subject, they frequently differ from one another, particularly in figures and proper names.

After the beginning of Christianity the task of "improving" the Scriptures was taken up by Christian editors and translators. Innumerable obscene words were eliminated or mistranslated so that, in many cases, the original meaning of the text was completely altered.

Nor did the Books of the New Testament escape the hands of the revisionists. Zealous churchmen inserted

---

10—See *The Old Testament in the Jewish Church*, William Robertson Smith.

verses and even entire sections into the New Testament writings in order to make it appear that dogmas mentioned in the forgeries were authorized by the Gospel writers.[11] By the sixteenth century there were in existence hundreds of conflicting texts of the New Testament. Books which were at one time considered inspired were later declared spurious. Both the Catholic and Protestant Churches have recently prepared new editions of the Bible in which the discrepancies are increased between the letter and spirit of the Hebrew and Greek manuscripts and the English translations.

11—"Victor Tumunensis, an African Bishop who flourished about the sixth century and who wrote a chronicle ending at the year 566 said, 'When Messala was consul (that is the year 506 A.D.) at Constantinople, by order of the Emperor Anastasius, the Holy Gospels, being written by illiterate evangelists, are censored and corrected.'" *Credibility of Gospel History*, Nathaniel Lardner, Ch. civ, London, 1815. Further changes are said to have been made by Lanfranc, head of the monks of St. Maur, about 1050 A.D. and by Nicholas, Cardinal and librarian of the Roman Church. "Lanfranc, a benedictine monk, Archbishop of Canterbury, having found the Scriptures much corrupted by copyists, applied himself to correct them as also the writings of the fathers, agreeable to the orthodox faith *secundum fidem orthodoxam*". From Cleland's *Life of Lanfranc*.

THE END

APPENDIX I

CABALA

THE TERM CABALA (Hebrew Kabbalah), meaning "to receive" or "traditional lore", sometimes called "Secret Wisdom", is applied to certain traditional doctrines constituting a system of religious philosophy or theosophy which has played an important part in theological literature ever since the Middle Ages.

The Cabala is claimed by Jews to be an exposition of the oral law which Jewish tradition maintains was revealed to Moses on Mount Sinai and committed to Aaron and other priests and great prophets and finally recorded in the Mishna. The Cabala was reputedly transmitted along with the Law and Talmud and contains a deeper or more initiated style of instruction that was revealed only to the wise. Other traditions credit the origin of the Cabala to Adam, Abraham, Moses or Ezra. In comparatively recent times it has been used to denote a peculiar mystic method of interpreting the Old Testament.

That many sacred books contained secret lore and were kept hidden by the wise is clearly indicated by IV Esdras 14,15,16, where pseudo-Ezra is told to publish 24 books of the canon openly that the worthy and unworthy alike may read them, but to keep the other 70 books hidden in order to "tell them only to such as be wise", for in them are the fountain of wisdom.

On the philosophical side, the Cabala attempted, by a system of allegorical interpretation, to rationalize the Scriptures and bring them into harmony with universal reason.

It was seen that an all-wise, all-perfect Creator must be perfect in all of his works; that the creation of an imperfect world by a perfect Creator was inconceivable. It was also obvious that inequalities and imperfections did exist, and that the hand of fate seemed at times to strike at random, as though men were like trees in a forest, some to be cut down early or blighted and under-nourished, while others thrived. Some people, through no fault of their own, seemed to suffer undeserved poverty, pain, disease and oppression; some were born physically or mentally deformed, while others, without particular virtues or abilities, were blessed with lives of health, comfort, wealth and pleasure.

The aim of the Cabalists was to formulate a conception of God and his works which would philosophize away the conflict between theological dogmas and the realities of life. How this was accomplished constitutes, with the exception of the Talmud and the sacred books of India, perhaps the greatest feat of verbal acrobatics ever performed. The meanings of words were tortured and distorted to make black mean white, and white mean black. By virtue of the Cabalistic philosophy, God becomes deserving of praise for all that is good and is absolved of responsibility for anything that is bad. He does everything, yet he does nothing; is everywhere and nowhere; is everything and nothing.

God is above everything, even above being and thinking, possessing neither will, intention, desire, thought, language or action, since these attributes which belong to man have limits, whereas God is boundless in every way because he is perfect. His infinite nature implies absolute unity and immutability; there is nothing without him; he is therefore called En-Soph, *without end, boundless,* and can neither be comprehended by the intellect nor described by words for there is nothing which can grasp and depict him to us. In this incomprehensibility or boundlessness, God or En-Soph is in a certain sense non-existent, since so far as our minds are concerned that which is incomprehensible does not exist. Hence, without making himself comprehensible his existence could never have been known. He had therefore to become active and creative in order that his existence might become perceptible.

But the will to create implies limits and the circumscribed and imperfect nature of this world precluded the possibility of taking it as the direct action of him who can neither will, nor produce anything but what is like himself, boundless and perfect. Yet the beautiful design and order displayed in the world plainly indicates intelligent and active will and cannot be regarded as the offspring of chance, therefore the En-Soph must be viewed as the Creator of the world in an *indirect manner* through the medium of 10 "Sephiroth" or *intelligences* which emanated from the En-Soph.

From his infinite fullness of light the En-Soph sent forth at first one spiritual substance or intelligence; this intelligence, which existed in the En-Soph from all eternity, and which became a reality by a mere act, contained the other 9 intelligences or Sephiroth. Great stress is laid upon the fact that the 1st Sephira was not created, but was simply an emanation, and the difference between creation and emanation is thus defined: in the former a diminution of strength takes place, while in the latter strength remains intact.

From the first Sephira emanated the second, from the second the third, from the third the fourth and so on; one proceeding from the other to the number 10. These Sephiroh form among themselves, and with the En-Soph, a strict unity, and individually represent different aspects of one and the same Being, as the flame and spark that proceed from the fire and that appear different things to the eye, form only different manifestations of the same fire. Differing thus from each other simply as different colors of the same light, all the 10 emanations alike partake of the En-Soph. These are boundless and yet constitute the first finite things; so that they are both finite and infinite. They are infinite and perfect like the En-Soph when he imparts his influence to them, and finite and imperfect when that fullness is withdrawn. The finite side of the emanation of the Sephiroth is absolutely necessary, for thereby the incomprehensible En-Soph makes his existence known to the human intellect, which can grasp only that which has measure, limit and relation. From their finite side the Sephiroth may even be called bodily, and this renders it possible for the En-Soph, who is immanent in them, to assume bodily form.

The 10 Sephiroth, of which every one has its own name, are divided into 3 groups of 3 Sephiroth, each respectively operating upon 3 worlds, that is, the world of intellect, the world of souls, and the world of matter. The first operates in the intellectual world, and consists of

Sephira 1, denominated the Crown or the Inscrutable Height;
"   2, Creative Wisdom;
"   3, Conceivable Intellect.

The result of the combination of the latter two (as "father and mother"), is likewise represented as knowledge, i.e., concrete thought, the realm of mind.

The second group exercises its power upon the moral world and consists of:

Sephira 4, called Infinite Grace (also Greatness);
" 5, Divine Justice or Judicial Power;
" 6, Beauty, and is the connecting link between 4 and 5.

The third group exercises its power upon the material world and consists of:

Sephira 7, called Firmness;
" 8, called Splendor;
" 9, Primary Foundation, and is the connecting link between the two opposite, numbers 7 and 8.

Sephira 10 is called Kingdom and denotes Providence or the revealed Deity (Shekinah) which dwells in the midst of the Jewish people, going with them and protecting them in their wanderings and captivities.

In order to make the description more intelligible, the 10 Sephiroth are arranged in a diagram, called by Cabalists, the primeval man, or Adam Kadmon. (Plate 88).

These Sephiroth, or God through them, created the lower and visible world, of which everything has its prototype in the upper world. "The world is like a gigantic tree full of branches and leaves, the root of which is the spiritual world of the Sephiroth; or it is like a firmly united chain the last link of which is attached to the upper world; or like an immense sea, which is being constantly filled by a spring everlastingly gushing forth its streams."

The Sephiroth, through the divine power immanent in them, uphold the world which they have created and transmit to it the divine mercies by means of 22 channels. This transmission of the divine mercies can be accelerated by prayer, sacrifices, and religious observances; and the Jewish people, by virtue of the revelation and the 613 commandments given to them, have especially been ordained to obtain these blessings for the whole world. Hence the great mystery of the Jewish ritual; hence the profound secrets contained in every word and syllable of the formulary of prayers; and hence the declaration that "the pious constitute the foundation of the world."

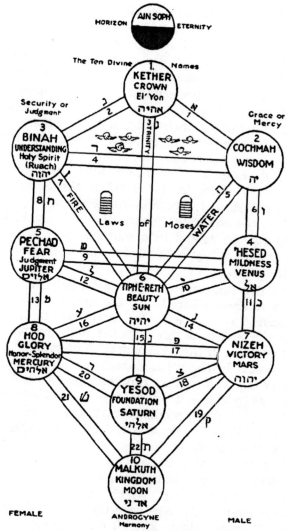

88. *The primeval man, or Adam Kadmon, of the Cabalists. The ten Sephiroth are connected by 22 canals corresponding to the 22 letters of the Hebrew alphabet. Sephiroth Nos. 1, 2, 3 constitute the upper world, the World of Emanation, called the "Boundless"; Nos. 4, 5, 6, the World of Creation, and 7, 8, 9 the World of Formation.*

Not only does the En-Soph reveal himself through the Sephiroth, but he also becomes incarnate in Sephira 4, Abraham; 5 *Power* in Isaac; 6 *Beauty* in Jacob; 7 *Firmness* in Moses; 8 *Splendor* in Aaron; 9 *Foundation* in Joseph; 10 *Kingdom* of David. They constitute the chariot throne.

All human souls are pre-existent in the world of the Sephiroth and are without exception destined to inhabit human bodies and pursue their courses upon earth for a certain period of probation. If, notwithstanding its union with the body, the soul resists all earthly trammels and remains pure, it ascends after death into the spiritual Kingdom and has a share in the world of the Sephiroth. But if, on the contrary, it becomes contaminated by that which is earthly, the soul must inhabit the body again and again till it is able to ascend in a purified state, through repeated trial (restricted by Nahmanides and later Cabalists to 3 transmigrations).

The apparently undeserved sufferings which the pious have sometimes to endure here below are simply deigned to purify their souls. Hence God's justice is not to be impugned when the righteous are afflicted and the wicked prosper. This doctrine of the transmigration of souls is supported by an appeal to the injunctions in the Bible that a man must marry the widow of his brother if he died without issue, inasmuch as by this is designed, say the Cabalists, that the soul of the departed one might be born again and finish its earthly course. Very few souls enter into the world, because many of the old souls that have already inhabited the bodies have to re-enter those who are born, in consequence of their previous bodily existence. This retards the great redemption of Israel, which cannot take place till all the pre-existent souls have been upon earth, because the soul of the Messiah which, like all other souls, has its pre-existence in the world of the spirits of the Sephiroth, is to be the last one born *at the end of days;* which doctrine is supported by an appeal to the Talmud.

In olden times secret philosophical science and magic went hand in hand. The principle of the mystic interpretation of the Scriptures is universal. We find it in Philo, in the New Testament, in the writings of the fathers, in the Talmud and the *Zohar;* and the more it departs from the spirit of the sacred text the more the latter had to be brought to its support by distortion of its meaning. For such operation there are 20 known rules except the exigencies of the case and the subjective mass of the senses. In the meantime the Jews had already, by the arbitrary character of their alphabet, arrived at all manner of subtleties of which we have isolated examples in their earliest writings, but which practice is especially established in post-Zoharic times. From this rose the following species of Cabalistic transformation:

1st Gematria:

The art of discovering the hidden sense of the text by means of the numerical equivalents of the letter. It is called Gematria also when Biblical numbers, for instance, dimensions of buildings, are expressed in letters and words made of them.

2nd, the "Figurative" Cabala Notarikon:

Consists of framing with each letter of a word several new ones, e.g., from the first word of Genesis, (these can thus be framed). We thus learn the correct scientific nature of the universe besides the proper meaning of the text. Again it consists in taking the first letter of several words to form a new word, e.g. Deut. 13:12.

3rd, Temurrah (Permutation):

The anagram, of two kinds. The simple one is a mere transposition of the letters of a word, e.g., we thus learn that the angel in Exodus 13:23 was the angel Michael. The more ingenious kind is that by which, according to certain established rules, each letter of the alphabet carries the significance of another; as Aleph that of Tau, both that of Ayin, then again the letter may read forward and backward (which constitutes the alphabet of Athbash) or the first letter with that of the twelfth, the second with the thirteenth and the reverse (making the alphabet called Albam), the more multifarious these trifles the easier it is to arrive in every given case at a result and the less wit or thought is required.

Origin

The only books which can be said to embody the principles of the Cabala are two that became the acknowledged texts of the system in the latter part of the Middle Ages.

The older of these is the *Sephir Yezirah*, "the book of the creation," a short treatise of obscure meaning which is founded on the Pythagorean idea of the creative numbers and letters.

The other book is the *Sephir haz-Zorah*, "book of light," which was first printed at Cremona and at Mantua in 1560. Jewish tradition ascribes it to Simeon ben Jochai, a Galilean rabbi of the second century A.D., but modern commentators are inclined to credit the work to a Spanish Jew named Moses of Leon, in the thirteenth century. Whatever its origin, it is composed of material of a far earlier date, and appears to be a syncretism of Jewish, Essene, Gnostic, Platonic, Pythagorean, Zoroastrian, and Babylonian ideas, and was probably completed by the eighth century. The assumption that the Cabala is a product of the thirteenth century does not take cognizance of the wide use of letters and numbers in a symbolic and esoteric sense throughout the East from very early times. Use of the Tetragrammaton for JHVH is a familiar instance. In fact the Talmud makes mention of a secret doctrine imparted to only a few carefully selected persons and even applies to it certain names signifying speculative cosmology and theosophy. The *Book of Jubilees* written during the reign of King John Hyrcanus contains much Cabalistic lore, and the Mishnah (Hag. i,1), recognized that cosmology and theosophy were esoteric studies and prescribed that care should be taken "not to expound the chapter on creation before more than one hearer, nor that of the heavenly bodies to any but a man of wisdom and profound understanding."

Exodus 15:26 is an incantation mentioned in the Mishna, and Exodus 14:19,21 is of great magical importance. Each verse consists of 72 letters, and one of the mysterious names of God consists of 72 letters, and these 3 verses are believed to represent the ineffable name blended, transposed and manipulated to form 72 groups of names of 3 letters, one letter for each of the 3 verses. Again, Numbers 23:22,23, if read backward, form a palindrome, and Psalm 67 is written in the form of an amulet of the 7-branched candlestick in a peculiar manner with the initial and final letters combined to form mystic names.

The chief elements of the Cabala are contained in the Apocalyptic writings of the Essene sect of the second and first century B.C. According to the historian, Josephus, such mystic writings were in the possession of the Essenes who jealously guarded them against disclosure. This was verified at an earlier period by Philo Judaeus, himself a Cabalist, who asserted that the writings were of great antiquity. Similar opinions of these Essenean writings have been expressed by Rabbi Adolf Jellinek and other modern scholars.

The dual system of good and evil powers which is found in the Cabala goes back to the Zoroastrians, and ultimately to Chaldea. The conception of a Cabalistic tree in which the right side represents light and life and the left side the source of darkness and impurity was known to the Gnostics. The theory of Kelippot (scalings of impurity) which are prominent in the medieval Cabala are found in the old Babylonian incantations. K. Kessler, in describing the beliefs of the Mandaeans, a Gnostic sect existing in Persia and Mesopotamia, south of Bagdad, asserted that the Cabala is derived from the old Babylonian worship of Marduk (Article: Mandaeans, *New Schaff-Herzog Enc. of Rel. Knowledge*, v.13, p.146). Lenormant (*Chaldean Magic*, pp. 29-43), was of the opinion that belief in the magic power of the letters of the Tetragrammaton JHVH and other names of the deity, originated in Chaldea.

APPENDIX II

ESSENES AND THERAPEUTAE

Wᴵᴛʜ ᴛʜᴇ ɢʀᴀᴅᴜᴀʟ decline and disintegration of the old pagan religions toward the end of the pre-Christian era, popular interest became focused upon the newer ideas which were slowly developing in Greece, Asia Minor and Egypt (especially in Alexandria). The spread of Greek influence to the East following the victories of Alexander the Great, had also brought a corresponding spread of Oriental ideas to the West. It was a period of great religious confusion in which a new, popular religion had not yet risen to take the place of the old worn out beliefs, and new cults and schools of philosophy were mushrooming up in which the speculations of Plato, Pythagoras, and other Greek philosophers were mixed with varying degrees of Oriental mysticism.

The Essenes, Eclectics or Ecclesiastes were a product of the religious ferment which boiled throughout the eastern Mediterranean during this period. They were a sect of Jewish ascetics which seems to have developed from a group of zealous religionists called Hasidaeans (Hebrew: *Chasidim,* meaning pious). They gathered in numerous small colonies along the shore of the Dead Sea and scattered throughout Asia Minor from early in the second century B.C., to about 70 A.D., and consisted of about four thousand members.

The Essenes practiced complete communism, with common ownership of property, living in communal groups and eating communal meals. They had churches, monasteries, bishops, ministers, monks, friars, deacons, who were closely organized under a strict religious government. Membership was by initiation after a two-year novitiate, with members consisting of four classes who observed caste distinctions very much like the Brahman Hindus. The four classes kept aloof from each other and for a member of one class to have contact with a member of a lower grade constituted defilement.

They had all the moral virtues of the Zoroastrians, and their tenets seem to have been derived from the same source, but unlike the older sect, the Essenes lived within

366

their own groups, practiced celibacy and shunned many of the metaphysical theories of the Parsees. While they believed in eternal existence of the soul, the Essenes did not, however, believe in the resurrection of the body.

The sect observed the Sabbath and all important religious holidays, wore only fine linen, opposed slavery and animal sacrifice, refused to take an oath but were held in high esteem because of their unswerving integrity. They abhorred the use of oil, abstained from meat, practiced baptism, took daily baths, and, in a sense, worshiped the sun. They were abstemious, modest, humble, helpful, devoted to almsgiving, healing, practicing medicine, and giving other forms of assistance without compensation or publicity. One of their activities was, as they believed, the casting out of evil spirits.

The Essenes wrote and distributed tracts, and revered certain ancient esoteric works, which were said to be derived from their apostolic founders, the secrets of which books they would not divulge, even under torture. Their scriptures were believed to possess a hidden meaning, which they expounded in allegories. They also held the Books of Moses in extreme reverence, and any disparagement of them was considered highly blasphemous.

The headquarters of the Therapeutae was located at Lake Mareotis, near Alexandria in Egypt. They had numerous colonies in Africa and their doctrines were so similar to those of the Essenes that both sects were generally considered the same. The Therapeutae, however, were a purely Egyptian sect and differed from the Essenes in that their members lived in separate huts, or cells, were vegetarians, led a less active and more meditative life, and included nuns or elderly virgins in their membership. Moreover, the Essenes and Therapeutae were so similar to the early Christians that they were generally believed to be of the same sect.

John the Baptist corresponds fully to the description of an Essene, and if he was not a member of the sect, he was at least strongly influenced by it. Mark is said by Eusebius to have been sent to Egypt to teach and establish churches, and there is no reason to doubt that while there he had contacts with the Therapeutae and learned their doctrines.

St. Paul, a Pharisee who professed to be familiar
with all the ancient religions, knew the Essenes, and in
a small country like Palestine it is doubtful if any of
the Apostles could have avoided knowing them. Paul
bitterly opposed the Essenes in the three epistles to the
Colossians, Ephesians, and Timothy, but like them, he
practiced healing and exorcism, urged his followers not
to take oaths, and preached continence, temperance, truthfulness and other virtues identically as the Essenes taught
them. Like the Essenes also and other early cults, Paul
looked upon religion as a mystery, and refused to permit
outsiders to partake of certain parts of the religious services.
Further, he favored the allegorical exposition of the Scriptures as did the Essenes, because "the letter killeth, but
the spirit giveth life". (II Cor. 3:6). "Which things are
an allegory." (Gal. 4:24).

Other passages in the Epistles suggest the possibility
that not only may the first Christians have modelled their
teachings after those of the Essenes, but that they may
have absorbed many of the Essene churches. If so, the
fact would account for certain passages in the Epistles
and the Acts which have puzzled Biblical scholars. For
instance, the Epistles and The Acts are supposed to have
been written a considerable time prior to the four Gospels
and before the Apostles had suffered martyrdom; they
speak of Paul's work while the church was still in an
early stage of development, when it consisted of only a
few widely scattered groups. The Christian churches existed as individual cells with important differences in their
doctrines until Irenaeus initiated the work of bringing them
all together in the Catholic Church at the end of the second
century. Yet Paul refers to the branches of the church
with its saints, its martyrs, its bishops, and deacons as
if it were a long established institution. (Acts 15:22, Rom.
12:13, I Cor. 1:2 and 8:4, Eph. 1:15, Col. 2:28). Matthew
18:15,16,17 speaks of the authority of the church to settle
disagreements as if it were an old, fully organized, and
authoritative body; and when Matthew 6:3,4 urges the
giving of alms and assistance without praise or publicity
the speaker cannot be distinguished from an Essene.

Before the work of the Apostles was completed and
before any of the Gospels were written, Paul spoke of
the gospel "which ye have heard and which was preached

to every creature which is under heaven" (I Col. 1:23), thus indicating that he was preaching things with which his listeners had long been familiar. Again he speaks of the death and resurrection of Christ "according to the Scriptures" at a time probably more than fifty years before the earliest Gospel of the New Testament was written. (I Cor. 15:4).

In Ephesians 1:15, he addresses his readers as though he were a stranger who had only recently heard of them, but in Acts 20:18 he addresses the leaders of the church, declaring "I have been with you at all seasons". This is paralleled by Luke's admission that his Gospel covered events that had been recorded by many earlier writers. (Luke 1:1,4).

Acts 12:4 is most extraordinary. It relates that Herod cast Peter into prison intending after Easter to bring him forth to the people. There was no Easter celebration among the Jews, the word Easter had not yet come into use among the Christians, and Paul's mention of an Easter festival remains a deep mystery.

That the doctrines of the Apostles had been taught previously by the Therapeutae is argued in the zeal with which a certain educated Jew named Apollos, who lived at Alexandria before any of the Apostles had preached the Gospel in that city, went to Ephesus and taught of the Lord in the synagogue, although knowing only the things of John the Baptist. Afterward Aquilla and Priscilla took Apollos in hand and explained to him the way of the Lord more perfectly. (Acts 18:24-28).

The most complete description of the Therapeutae is given by Philo Judaeus, a semi-Christian Jew, member of a family of priests and brother of the Jewish magistrate of Alexandria. Nearly all of Philo's writings have been lost, but Eusebius, the fourth century church historian, quotes from them at length and gives it as Philo's opinion that the Therapeutae were Christians. Not only does Eusebius accept this opinion of Philo, he declares: "These facts appear to have been stated by a man who has paid attention to those that have expounded the sacred writings. But it is highly probable that the ancient commentaries which he says they have are the very Gospels and writings of the Apostles and probably some Expositions of the ancient Prophets such as are contained in the Epistle of the Hebrews and many others of St. Paul's Epistles". (Euseb., *Eccl. History*, Bk., Ch. 17, quoted by Rev. C. F. Cruse).

Most modern writers, while recognizing the strong influence of the Essenes and Therapeutae on the form of the Christian organization, its teachings and practices, nevertheless fail to find a direct connection between the different groups, and incline to the view that both Josephus and Philo were mistaken in assuming that Essenes, Therapeutae, and Christians were all one body. Eusebius is thought to have depended too much on the sole opinion of Philo.

Inasmuch as the Essenes and Therapeutae and all their works disappeared during the Jewish War in the first century A.D., the extent to which Christianity was influenced by the earlier cults must remain one of the unknown factors in its early development. But that Eusebius was not alone in thinking that the roots of Christianity went far into the past may be seen in the writings of numerous other figures in the early church who held similar opinions.[1]

1—Said Lactantius an orthodox Christian: "If there had not been any one to collect the truth that was scattered and diffused among the various sects of philosophers and divines into one and to reduce it into a system, there would indeed be no difference between him and a Christian." Admission 10.

From a letter of Origen to Celsus: "That the Christian religion contained nothing but what Christians held in common with heathens—nothing that was new or truly great." Bellamy's Translation, Ch. 4.

St. Augustine declared his religion "was before in the world." Admission 12.

"There could be found no other difference between paganism and popish worship before images but only this that names and titles are changed." Blount's *Philostratus*, pp. 113-114 quoting Ludovicus Vivus, a learned Catholic.

APPENDIX III

MITHRAISM

ON BEING TAKEN to Babylon by the Persians, the cult of Zoroaster encountered the philosophical theologizing of the Babylonian priests who identified Mithra with the sun god Shamash. To the cult they added elements of astrology which later came to have a large part in the ritual. The cult was then carried to Armenia and Asia Minor, where it came into contact with other mystery cults then popular, the chief of which was that of Cybele. Between 250 and 100 B.C., its ritual and doctrine probably took the form which it afterward retained.

The cult was probably taken to Rome by soldiers returning from Asia Minor and by visiting merchants about 70 B.C., and became widespread among Rome's slaves, civil servants, and soldiers, who carried it to Africa, Europe, and even to Scotland. Popular among the common people, the new religion also claimed followers among senators and other high officials. Nero, Aurelian, and Emperor Julian were adherents. Diocletian, Galerius, and Licinius dedicated a temple to Mithra in 307 A.D.

In the western form of the cult, Mithra was no longer the chief Yazata of Ormuzd but became the head of an independent religion. He was the guardian of truth, fidelity and justice; lord of the countryside, strong, sleepless, and possessing full knowledge; his piercing eyes saw all things, therefore he was witness of oaths and good faith, chastising liars but protecting those who kept faith.

The births of Mithra and Christ were celebrated on the same day, the births being honored in each case as having taken place in a cave. In both Christianity and Mithraism the central figure was a Mediator who was one of a Trinity: in both, there was a sacrifice for the benefit of humanity, and the purifying power of blood from the sacrifice was of basic importance. Both Christians and Mithraists regarded Sunday as sacred.

Regeneration, or second birth, was a fundamental tenet in both faiths. In both faiths, also, the conception of the relation of the worshipers to each other was the same: they were brothers and both had sacraments, among which were included baptism and a communal bread and the cup. Both had mysteries from which the lower orders of initiates were excluded; ascetic ideals were common to both. Both religions taught the doctrine of immortality, heaven and hell, the resurrection from the dead, judgment after death, the final conflagration by which the world is to be consumed, and the ultimate conquest of evil. "We may say that if Christianity had been arrested in its growth by some mortal malady, the world would have been Mithraic. . . . It needed to destroy it the terrible blows struck at it by the Christian empire." (*Marcus Aurelius*, p. 432, London, n.d.).

The worshipers formed small mithreum, like modern lodges, the groups of members generally not exceeding 100, and often organized as burial associations in order to achieve legal status. Brotherhood, loyalty, and equality were stressed. Lustrations and libations were frequent. Women were not admitted to membership.

There were seven degrees of initiation in which the neophyte assumed the names of raven, griffin, soldier, lion, Persian, courier of the sun, and father. On certain occasions they donned a costume symbolic of the bird or animal imitated and simulated its actions, as was the custom in other mysteries of the period. Those who passed the grade of lion were "participants" because to them was administered the sacrament of bread and water commemorative of Mithra's banquet at the end of his labors. This participation was supposed to impart immortality.

The guardian bishop went through a ceremony of espousing the church in accordance with the old mystery in which was recited the formula "Hail to thee, new spouse, Hail new light." His mitre was called a crown or tiara and it corresponded to the headdress of Mithra. The Mithraic priests wore red military boots, said to be emblematical of the spiritual warfare in which they were engaged. This may have more than an incidental relation to the custom in the Roman Catholic Church of placing red military boots on the feet of the deceased popes when they are prepared for the funeral ceremony.

The four elements, fire, water, earth and air were deified and worshiped, and the sun, moon and planets were held in high reverence. Each day of the week was believed to be controlled by a different planet and with each a metal was associated, while the signs of the zodiac, which took creation under control, marked the devotions of the month. Kronos (unending time) figured as the lion-headed human figure with four wings, sexless and passionless, his legs and body in the embrace (sometimes 6-fold) of a serpent receiving the motion of the sun in the ecliptic.

In many of the monuments of Mithra there are two torch bearers, which are to be interpreted as the double incarnations of Mithra with himself, forming a triple Mithra. One of these with torch erect symbolized the growing sun and life: Mithra himself in the center was the sun at noon and the figure of life; the other torch bearer, with torch turned downward, was the declining sun and death.

Mithra was pictured as born of a rock and sculptures represents him issuing from a rock with knife and torch in his hands. It was then his task to demonstrate his invincible strength and his first trial was with the sun, whom he conquered, then adorned with the rayed crown and made his faithful ally. His next labor was with a bull and this became the central point of the Mithraic myth, the portrayal of which furnished the set piece in Mithraic art.

The bull was caught and mastered after a severe struggle and dragged by Mithra to his cave, whence it escaped, and Mithra was commanded to pursue and sacrifice it, which he reluctantly did. From its body then sprang all kinds of useful herbs, and from its blood the grape which furnished the wine of the mysteries; from its spinal marrow came wheat, while its soul became Silvanus, guardian of herds who is also a leading figure in the mysteries. The bull was, therefore, a source of life and for this reason took its place in the Mithraic ceremony.

Meanwhile, the first human pair had been created and were under Mithra's protection. This protection was necessary because Ahriman was assailing humanity with drought, flood, conflagration, pestilence and other calamities, and therefore had to be overcome. The ending of Mithra's labors was the occasion of a celebration and last supper after which Mithra retired to heaven, whence he still protects the worshipers. But the battle between Ahura Mazda and Ahriman continues so far as humanity is concerned. Life is warfare and to win, the faithful must ever obey Mithra's commandments.

Shortly after Constantine made Christianity the religion of the Roman state, the Christians demanded the suppression of the Mithraic cult, and before long no one dared to look at the rising or setting sun and farmers and sailors were afraid to observe the stars. At times the persecution of the cult was bloody and the remains prove that the priests were sometimes slain and their corpses buried in the mithreum in order to desecrate the site.

APPENDIX IV

TALMUD

THE TALMUD IS the work which embodies the canonical
and civil law of the Jews. It consists of the Mishna (oral
repetition), a systematic collection of religious decisions
developing the laws of the Old Testament, and the Gemara,
(supplement), containing a mass of opinions, comments, and
illustrations, legal and otherwise.

The Mishna forms the foundation of the Gemara and is
divided into six *sedarim*, or orders, containing a number
of tracts, or *massektoth*. Further material relative to the
Mishna is preserved in the Tosephta (Aramaic, "addition"
or "appendix"), and the Midrash. Together with the Targumim they represent the orthodox rabbinical literature
connecting the Old Testament with medieval Judaism.

Midrash means to search, investigate, explain, and,
primarily, the study or exposition of the Scriptures. It
attempts to go beyond the mere literal sense; to penetrate
into the spirit of the Scriptures and to examine the text
from all sides in order to formulate interpretations which
are not immediately obvious. The text is interspersed with
maxims, ethical sayings of illustrious men, parables,
legends, biographical sketches of Biblical persons, philosophical discussions, poetical allegories, symbolical interpretations, etc. Legal prescriptions form the Halakoth;
and free interpretations compose the Hagadoth. The first
are the rules of conduct which must be observed; the
others are merely considered to be "what is said" by the
sages.

Beginning as a supplement to, or interpretation of, the
Mosaic Law, the Mishna developed into such a voluminous
mass of contradictory opinions and hair-splitting legalism
that a second supplement became necessary to explain the
first. "This task was carried out by the Amoraim, or
Gemarical doctors, whose *very singular* illustrations, opinions, and doctrines were subsequently to form the Gemara,
i.e., the Palestinian and Babylonian: a body of men charged
with being the most learned and elaborate triflers that ever
brought discredit upon the republic of letters. . . . With

unexampled assiduity did they seek after or invent obscurities and ambiguities, which continually furnished pretexts for new expositions and illustrations, the art of clouding texts in themselves clear having proved ever less difficult than that of elucidating passages the words or the sense of which might be really involved in obscurity."[1]

The Talmud fills more than sixty volumes and represents the labor of several hundred rabbins over a period of about five centuries. The work is divided into two great recensions, consisting of a Babylonian Talmud, written in eastern Aramaic dialect and a Palestinian Talmud, written in western Aramaic. The western version never became as popular as the eastern, and now survives in a very incomplete form.

Eventually, many of the rabbins became awed by the immensity of the product of their labors, and considered the Mishna and Gemara more important than the Mosaic Law. "The 'written law,'" they said, "is like water, the Mishna is like wine, and the Gemara is like spiced wine". But modern authorities are inclined to take a more critical view of these writings. McClintock and Strong,[2] for instance, describe the Babylonian Talmud as being "composed in a dialect neither Chaldaic nor Hebrew, but a barbarous commixture of both of these and of other dialects, jumbled together in defiance of all the rules of composition or of grammar, it affords a *second* specimen of a Babylonian *confusion of languages*. . . . Abounding, moreover, in fantastic trifles and rabbinical reveries, it must appear almost incredible that any sane man could exhibit such acumen and such ardor in the invention of those unintelligible comments, in those nice scrupulosities, and those ludicrous chimeras which the rabbins have solemnly published to the world."

In their efforts to further define the Mosaic Law dealing with relations between men and women, the framing of opinions pertaining to sexual functions, particularly those of women, became an obsession with the Talmudists. Entire sections of the Mishna and Gemara were devoted to the sexual peculiarities of women, much of the text being so

1—*Cyclopedia of Biblical, Theological and Ecclesiastical Literature,* McClintock and Strong, vol.10, p.168.

2—*Cyclopedia of Biblical, Theological and Ecclesiastical Literature,* McClintock and Strong, vol.10, p.168.

obscene that it is considered too shocking for English-speaking readers, and consequently, quotations from it are given only in Latin.

Nothing that occurs in human life seems to have been too unimportant for consideration by the dictators (Amoraim), the opinionists (Seburaim), and the sublime doctors (Geonim), and every fact or idea, however trivial, which came to their attention became the subject of a learned opinion or decree in which facts were mixed with errors in almost every department in science, natural history, chronology, genealogy, logic and morals.

The learned rabbins wrote lengthy treatises specifying the proper time and manner for giving blessings, offering prayers, and paying tithes; for planting and harvesting crops; for the cultivation of fruit trees, the correct performance of social and household duties, etc., including such details as how and when to place a cover on a stew-pot, how to weave, sew, cook, wash, tie and un-tie knots, fold garments and make beds, clean pillows, strain wine, light lamps, pick up crumbs from the table, and thousands of other activities equally trivial.

It is improbable that the average Jew ever observed more than a small portion of the opinions and legal prescriptions handed down by the learned doctors, because to become even slightly familiar with all of them would have required years of study. Even so, the lives of the people were metaphorically fenced in by countless regulations and taboos which conditioned and regimented their acts and thoughts from birth to death.

Targum

After the Exile it became the practice to read the Law in public with the addition of an oral paraphrase in the Babylonian dialect. The paraphrase was called Targum, meaning translation or interpretation, and was designed to meet the needs of the unlearned who had ceased to understand the Hebrew of the Old Testament. There are three Targumim of the Pentateuch, the oldest of which was highly esteemed in the Babylonian divinity schools and, later, in Palestine. Its authorship has been attributed to a teacher named Onkelos and it is called the Babylonian Targum or the Targum of Onkelos.

Much of the Jerusalem Targum consists of fragments or remnants which are not contemporary, and many passages contain several versions of the same verses, while certain sections are designated additions. Consequently, it is frequently called the Fragmentary Targum. Many of the fragments consist of single words, or portions of verses, fused together. They probably were originally comments written without system or completeness by copyists on the margin of the Onkelos Targum.

A second Jerusalem Targum, also called the Jonathan, or pseudo-Jonathan Targum, dates from about the seventh century A. D., and attempts to correct and supplement the Targum of Onkelos. In his translation from the Hebrew, Jonathan is careful to avoid anthropomorphisms and to give the complete sense by very simple metaphors, although his method is not as thorough as that of Onkelos. Jonathan also attempts to gloss over or modify all Old Testament passages which seem derogatory to the ancestors of Israel, and to amplify everything which redounds to their credit.

Other Targumim exist for the Psalms, Proverbs, and the Books of the Prophets, Job, and Chronicles, but they are almost entirely imitations of earlier works.

APPENDIX V

ZOROASTRIANISM

THE HISTORICITY OF Zoroaster was long in doubt but eminent authorities are now inclined to the view that he was an historical character, born between 660 and 630 B.C. in Bactria (Iran) or in Azerbaijan west of the Caspian Sea.

The religion which Zoroaster formulated was derived largely from beliefs of the Brahmans which had long been creeping westward from India. The teachings of Zoroaster are found in the Zend-Avesta, which are written in one of the seven branches of the Indo-European family of languages closely resembling Sanscrit. The language in which the principal translations and commentaries were originally written is Pahlavi, the language of medieval Persia. The alphabet is Semitic, and the vocabulary of the documents is in Aramaic and Perisan.

As enunciated by Zoroaster, Ahura Mazda (Ormuzd in the shortened form), "the god of light", is the creator, omniscient, holy, beneficent, eternal in the full sense; bestower of health and responsible for happiness; bestower of all that is pure and good. He is opposed by his brother Angra Mainyu (or Ahriman), "hostile spirit", the Prince of Darkness, who represents ignorance, death, and all that is evil in the world. In the conflict between the two brothers, the old mythical struggle between Light and Darkness develops into an ethical religion and becomes a struggle between Good and Evil.

Man is considered of 5-fold character: (1) spirit or angelology; (2) knowing power; (3) conscience; (4) soul, perhaps moral choice, and (5) *fravashi*, which seems to be the post mortem personality.

In his creative work, Mazda gave man a free will, and, therefore, holds him fully responsible for his deeds, in contradistinction to his status in the older religions in which every act was assumed to be determined by a god. There is no pardon for sin apart from the fact that a convert is relieved of the consequences of sins committed prior to his conversion, when he was ignorant of the religion. Yet man is not left wholly alone in his efforts to achieve goodness, for guardian angels assist him in overcoming temptation and in avoiding the pitfalls set by the demons. By a true confession of faith, by word and deed, he may impair the work of Ahriman (Satan), and establish a claim to reward from Mazda. Sacred virginity is considered irreligious; self-mortification is regarded as sinful; and later writings seem to be directed against Christian asceticism. Inhibitions of sexual intercourse, where they exist, rest in the main upon considerations of healthful propriety.

Mazda created six Amesha Spentas (Amphaspands), "immortal beneficents" as servants to assist him in the guidance of the world in his conflict with Ahriman. These are personifications of virtues or abstract qualities, their names signifying "Good Thought", "Best Righteousness", "Desired Kingdom", "Holy Harmony", "Saving Health", and "Immortality". The first three are male and the second three female. To offset the Amphaspands, Ahriman creates devas, archdemons or evil spirits.

Beside the Amesha Spentas there are a number of other characters which receive special honor. Notable are the Yazatas, angels, abstractions or personifications of natural elements, bodies or qualities. They are assigned to the protection of elements in the world such as animals, metals, fire, earth, water, vegetation.

The greatest of the Yazatas is the "thrice born" Mithra, "the eye of Mazda", the knower of truth, witness to oaths and contracts, judge of the dead, the god that gives victory to armies and is the next in importance to Mazda himself. As Mediator and Benefactor, he is associated with the light and warmth of the sun and was probably originally a solar god.

Other figures among the Yazatas are Sraosha, "abundance", Rashnu Razista, "genius of truth", Gosurvan (Gos, Drvaspa), as the cow or bull, the abstract representation of the animal kingdom; Kavaem Hvareno, "kingdom majesty", or "royal glory"; Ashi Vanguhi, "piety, wealth, health and intellectual vigor", and Arstat, "truthfulness". Animals are given particular consideration and it is sinful to kill them.

Next to Mithra among the Yazatas is Atar, or fire, the purest of the elements. He is the messenger of Mazda, the holiest spirit, and stringent regulations are drawn against his defilement in material form. Fire is considered a representation of the divine essence of earth and the priests are fire priests. It is the essence of life burning in the bodies of men and animals, in the stems of plants, in air and paradise itself, but, as with Agni in India, the conception varies from material to spiritual and from personal to impersonal. From the cult associated with this element, the Zoroastrians were erroneously called "fire worshipers".

Of special significance is the doctrine of Saoshyant, usually rendered "savior" who is to come, having been foreshadowed by virgin born prophets in the line of Zoroaster. He is to end the battle with evil, preside over the resurrection and accomplish the regeneration of the world.

After death, the soul remains near the body for three days in pain or joy, its experience depending upon the individual's actions during life. On the fourth day at dawn it takes up its journey to its final home, being cheered on its way by delightful experiences; and is met by a beautiful maiden, the personification of its good deeds done in life, and is guided to the Chinvat Bridge, where Mithra, Sraosha, and Rashnu weigh its good and bad deeds in the scales of judgment. These experiences of the soul clearly foreshadow the Christian doctrine of a Day of Judgment.

Then the soul passes to the bridge of angels. Being finally received by Vohu Monah, the soul passes before Mazda and the Amphaspands to take up its permanent abode with the righteous. But the wicked soul is met by an ill-favored hag, and, after judgment, is dragged to the depths of darkness. There is, however, a place called Hamestagan, the abiding place of souls whose good and evil deeds balance. These souls and the evil they have committed abide in their places until the last day, when the human denizens of hell, having been purified, join with the Hamestagan and are placed in the new heaven. Conversion and final happiness are, therefore, the goal ultimately reached, and hell is not eternal torture or retribution.

On the day of final judgment Saoshyant completes the last victory over evil, and enters upon a reign of 57 years. At the expiration of that period, man will have become spiritualized, requiring neither food or drink. A star will fall from the heavens and its heat will melt the terrestrial metals, and the molten mass thus formed will course over the earth, bringing about the purification of man and render the earth a mountainless plain. Then will take place the resurrection: all the souls will gather and the wicked shall suffer three days in hell. Souls will pass through the molten flood, which, to the good, will be a pleasant experience and to the evil, extremely painful. Then will begin the one, undivided kingdom of Mazda in heaven and earth.

In addition to the triad of Mazda, Mithra, and Ahriman, the Mazdean religion contains one other member who has no essential function in the plan but was possibly adapted because of the Oriental custom of including a virgin goddess in the religious pattern. She is Anahita, or Ardvi Sura Anahita, "the spirit of waters", "the high, powerful, immaculate being", the heavenly spring and source of all terrestrial waters, located on the summit of a mythical mountain in the region of the stars and the habitation of many holy heroes before and after the prophet. Having power to fertilize the earth, she uses this power beneficently for the good of animals and mankind and is the genius of marriageable girls and parturient women. Her cult came to have a widespread independent vogue in Armenia and Asia Minor, where she became confused with the great mother goddess. The Greeks identified her with Athene and Aphrodite.

Much attention was also given to the stars, and the "star Yazatas" were of great importance, these being the fixed stars, not the planets, which were regarded as creations of Ahriman.

The Zoroastrians, driven out of Persia by the Mohammedans in 641 A.D., eventually settled in Bombay, where they are known as Parsees. At the present time there are perhaps 8000 members of this sect in Persia while in Bombay the Parsees number approximately 100,000. Many of them are wealthy merchants.

Among the features of Zoroastrianism which were later to become parts of Christian religious thought were the soul, free will, heaven and hell, angels and devils, confession, baptism, rosaries, purgatory, a mediator, a virgin born savior, catechisms, a day of resurrection, and final judgment.

INDEX

Equinox, precession of, 271, 286, 287, 295.

Erech, 30, 67, 68, 71.

Ereshkigal, 37, 38.

Eridu, 30, 31.

Erigos, Dionysius, 118.

Esdras II, 299.

Essenes, 217, 325.

Estimation of the Height (of God), 111.

Ethiopic Book of Enoch, 299.

Eunuchs, 44, 45, 217.

Eve, 170, 186, 187, 250, 251.

Evil eye, 158, 166, 194, 222.

Evil spirit of Jahveh, 85.

Evil spirits, destroying, 235.

Exile in Babylon, 87, 89, 299, 354.

Exodus, Book of, 79, 82, 169, 170.

Exodus from Egypt, 80.

Eye, All-Seeing, 158, 159.

Ezekiel, Prophet, 18, 81, 87, 126, 131, 135, 167, 214, 215, 221, 236.

Ezra, 81, 92, 352, 353.

Ezra, Book IV, 352, 353.

F

"Faces" of God, 221, 322, 343, 346.

Faith healers, 91, 103, 323.

Fall of Man, 71, 72, 88, 186.

Fascinus, 227.

Fascinator, 227.

Fate, Goddess of, 34, 118.

Fateaux, 224.

Faunus, 182.

Feast of Assumption of Virgin Mary, 48.

Female characteristics, 129.

Female generative organs, 129, 132, 133, 168, 192, 193, 208, 226, 232.

Female symbol, basic, 142.

Feet, 152.

Fertility gods and worship, 90, 114, 118, 128, 144, 146, 174, 182, 196, 210, 212, 214, 215, 216, 218, 225, 226, 228, 233, 234, 235, 236.

Festival of Floralia, 226.

Festival of Hanukkah, 123.

Festival of Hilaria, 49.

Festival of La Fete des Pinnes, 224.

Festival of Liberalia, 226.

Festival of Lights, 122, 123.

Festival of May, 226.

Festival of Passage of the Virgin, 48.

Festivals, solar, 49, 51, 120, 122, 210.

Festival of Weeping Women, 39.

Fete Dieu, 225.

Fetich (see Images and Idols).

Fevers, driving out, 19, 91, 102.

Fig and fig tree, 188.

Fire, destruction of the world by, 290.

Fire as the primordial element, 316.

Firmament, 65, 67, 98.

First fruits of the womb, 235.

Fish, 174, 176, 256, 259, 288.

Fish, eating on Friday, 174.

Fish-eyes, 174.

Fish gods, 56, 58, 196, 288.

Fissures in the earth, 129, 206.

Fixed stars, 275.

Fleur de lys, 164, 188.

Flood (see Deluge).

Foakes-Jackson, F. J., 338.

Foretellers, 76, 77, 81, 82.

Foretelling events by planets and stars, 267, 279, 280, 281, 284, 285, 290.

Forty, number of pain and hardship, 18.

Four Beasts of Daniel, 299.

Four Metals, 298, 299.

Frazer, Sir James, 19, 22, 42, 234.

Freemasonry, 132, 134, 144, 157, 158, 258.

Free will, 88, 89.

Friday, woman's day, 174, 176.

Frog-headed goddess, Heqet, 193.

Frog swallows the sun, 54.

Future life, 50, 91.

Fylfot, 152.

G

Games of the Circus, 273.

Gardens, 75, 81, 82, 181, 214, 215.

Gardens of Adonis, 43.

Garden of Eden, 214.

Garden of Paradise, 71, 72, 184, 186.

Gateways, 198, 202.

Gaza, 61.

Gematria, 247.

Genealogy, Biblical, 305.

Genealogy of Jesus, 331.

Lightning Source UK Ltd.
Milton Keynes UK
18 October 2010

161504UK00001B/65/P

9 781585 093359